S0-BJN-838

GOD'S RULE AND KINGDOM

GOD'S RULE AND KINGDOM

RUDOLF SCHNACKENBURG

BURNS & OATES

HERDER AND HERDER

HERDER AND HERDER NEW YORK
232 Madison Avenue, New York, N. Y. 10016

BURNS & OATES LIMITED
25 Ashley Place, London S. W. 1

Original edition "Gottes Herrschaft und Reich",
Herder, Freiburg, 4th ed. 1965. Translated by John Murray.

1st edition 1963
2nd impression 1963
2nd enlarged edition 1968

Nihil Obstat: Andreas J. Moore L. C. L., Censor deputatus.
Imprimatur: Georgius L. Craven, Epus. Sebastopolis, Vic. Cap.
Westmonasterii, die 22a Maii 1963

The Nihil Obstat and Imprimatur are a declaration that a book
or pamphlet is considered to be free from doctrinal or moral error.
It is not implied that those who have granted the Nihil Obstat and Imprimatur
agree with the contents, opinions or statements expressed.

Library of Congress Catalog Card Number: 63-12766

Printed in West Germany by Herder

CONTENTS

III
GOD'S REIGN AND KINGDOM IN EARLY CHRISTIAN TEACHING

ABBREVIATIONS

B.J.R.L.	*The Bulletin of the John Rylands Library* (Manchester, 1903 ff.)
B.Z.	*Biblische Zeitschrift* (Freiburg i. Br., 1909–29; Paderborn 1931–39; 1957 ff.)
D.A.C.L.	*Dictionnaire d'archéologie chrétienne et de liturgie* (Paris, 1924 ff.)
Ev.Th.	*Evangelische Theologie* (Munich, 1934 ff.)
Exp.T.	The Expository Times (Edingburgh, 1898 ff.)
G.C.S.	*Die griechischen christlichen Schriftsteller der ersten drei Jahrhunderte* (Leipzig, 1897 ff.)
Harv.Th.R.	The Harvard Theological Review (Cambridge, Mass., 1908 ff.)
J.B.L.	*Journal of Biblical Literature*, published by the Society of Biblical Literature and Exegesis (Boston, 1881 ff.)
J.Th.St.	*The Journal of Theological Studies* (London, 1899 ff.)
L.Th.K.	*Lexikon für Theologie und Kirche* (Freiburg–Basel–Wien, 1957 ff.)
Mü.Th.Z.	*Münchener Theologische Zeitschrift* (Munich, 1950 ff.)
N.T.St.	*New Testament Studies* (Cambridge–Washington, 1954 ff.)
R.A.C.	*Reallexikon für Antike und Christentum* (Stuttgart, 1941 ff.)
R.B.	*Revue Biblique* (Paris, 1892 ff.; new series since 1904)
R.G.G.	*Die Religion in Geschichte und Gegenwart* (3rd ed., Tübingen, 1956 ff.)

R.H.Ph.R.	*Revue d'histoire et de philosophie religieuse* (Strasbourg, 1921 ff.)
R.Q.S.	*Römische Quartalschrift für christliche Altertumskunde und für Kirchengeschichte* (Freiburg i. Br., 1887 ff.)
Schol.	*Scholastik* (Freiburg i. Br., 1926 ff.)
St. Th.	*Studia Theologica, cura ordinum theologicorum Scandinavicorum edita* (Lund, 1948 ff.)
Th.L.Z.	*Theologische Literaturzeitung* (Leipzig, 1878 ff.)
Th.Q.	Theologische Quartalschrift (Tübingen, 1819 ff.; Stuttgart, 1946 ff.)
Th.W.B.	*Theologisches Wörterbuch zum Neuen Testament* (Stuttgart, 1933 ff.)
Th.Z.	*Theologische Zeitschrift* (Basel, 1945 ff.)
Tr.Th.Z.	*Trierer Theologische Zeitschrift* [till 1944: *Pastor Bonus*] (Trier, 1888 ff.)
V.T.	*Vetus Testamentum* (Leiden, 1951)
Z.A.W.	*Zeitschrift für die alttestamentliche Wissenschaft* (Berlin, 1881 ff.)
Z.N.W.	*Zeitschrift für die neutestamentliche Wissenschaft und die Kunde der älteren Kirche* (Giessen, 1900 ff.; Berlin, 1934 ff.)
Z.Th.K.	*Zeitschrift für Theologie und Kirche* (Tübigen,1891 ff.)

FOREWORD

THE PURPOSE of this study is to trace the notion of God's kingship from the Old Testament to the early Christian period and to pay special attention to its changing forms and expanded usage. Variously expressed as is this notion in the Old Testament and in late Judaism, it is our task to show its point of contact with Jesus' gospel of God's reign, to compare this with the interpretations current at the time, and to bring out its special and distinctive notes. But even the eschatological and final gospel of Jesus enters yet another stage of its preaching after Easter. In the early Church Jesus was regarded as raised to the right hand of God and established as the "Lord" who, in a special manner, exercises God's royal power until his Parousia inaugurates God's perfect kingdom. Only when we consider the history of salvation and revelation in some such way as this, can we, in my opinion, give a satisfactory answer to the oft-repeated questions: how the notion of God's reign, so central to the gospel of Jesus, could be eclipsed in the early Church by other ideas and doctrines; in what relation "kingdom of God" stands to "Church"; how we are to interpret Christ's rule over the Church and the world?

FOREWORD

This study in Biblical theology, to which frequent requests have prompted me, is primarily intended to serve a theological purpose. It is often said that Catholics are not sufficiently clear or united about the basic theme in the preaching of Jesus. This may be due simply to the want of a sound theological terminology, but there are also more fundamental differences of view. It is with this situation in mind that the exegete wishes to make his contribution and to try to uncover the original meaning of what Jesus said and of the preaching of the early Church. Even the New Testament does not provide us with clearly differentiated notions, and we could scarcely expect it to do so when we reflect upon the historical development of revelation. But it is firmly and vividly rooted in these ideas and also contains valuable suggestions for a better terminology.

This study is an attempt to distinguish between God's present reign and future kingdom, God's reign and Christ's lordship or dominion, Christ's rule over the world and over the Church, and so to elucidate with greater clarity the relation of "kingdom of God" to "Church". It is an attempt, springing from love of the Church, to obtain a deeper understanding of her character, her salvific function in the process from the first to the second advent, and thus also her pathway on earth. I am very conscious of the difficulties involved which derive from the texts themselves and wish this study to be accepted merely as a basis for discussion and for further theological encounter.

May this work stimulate the love of the Bible and Biblical theology and give some slight joy to Professor Dr. Dr. h. c. Josef Schmid to whom it is reverently dedicated in gratitude for his sterling assistance and friendship.

The Author

I

The Kingship of God in the Old Testament and in Later Judaism

THE OLD TESTAMENT

1. God's Kingship over Israel and the World

The idea of God's royal sovereignty has its roots deep in the Old Testament. The Jewish scholar, M. Buber, considers that "the realization of God's all-embracing reign is the Alpha and Omega of Israel";[1] but this opinion is naturally disputed by other scholars. In their view this notion of the kingship of Yahweh is not an original element in the religion of Israel which had other ways in which to express its attachment to Yahweh and the subordination of all life to him, in particular the ideas of covenant and election.[2]

God's royal titles and the liturgical honour paid to him as *melekh* (king) cannot be proved conclusively to be anterior to the era of the historical kingdom. Yahweh was addressed as king in the poetic exuberance of religious hymns rather than from any principle of belief.[3] The earliest source we come across is the ancient canticle of the sea, sung by Moses and the children of Israel after their crossing of the Red Sea and the destruction of

[1] *Königtum Gottes,* LXIV.

[2] A. Alt, *Gedanken über das Königtum Jahwes,* p. 345.

[3] G. v. Rad in *Th.W.B.* I, pp. 568, 29–47; also *Theologie des A.T.* I pp. 330 seq.

the Egyptians. This runs as follows: "Who is like to thee, among the strong, O Lord? Who is like to thee, glorious in holiness? Terrible and worthy of all praise, doing wonders! Thou stretchest forth thy hand: and the earth swallowed them. In thy mercy thou hast been a leader to the people which thou hast redeemed: and in thy strength thou hast carried them to thy holy habitation . . . . The Lord shall reign for ever and ever" (Exod. 15:11-13, 18). The intervening verses speak of the fear and terror of the peoples of Canaan and naturally presuppose the conquest of the Holy Land. But this canticle was subsequently revised and adapted for liturgical purposes with the result that it is difficult, if not impossible, to establish the original text. If, however, we study its contents, we are struck by one idea which must have inspired Israel during the years of wandering: Yahweh is the guide of his people who leads and strengthens its hosts, a provident and protecting Lord. Whether the predicate of royalty was actually employed is of less significance. The notion itself which is genuinely Semitic, is at least a prelude to or primitive form of the kingship of Yahweh.[4] This is confirmed by the prophet Balaam who was compelled to call down a blessing upon Israel in the plains of Moab and to prophesy its victory: "There is no idol in Jacob, neither is there an image-God to be seen in Israel. The Lord his God is with him: and the sound of the victory of the king in him. God hath brought him out of Egypt, whose strength is like to the rhinoceros" (Num. 23:21 seq.). The powerful ruler of his people who humbles his enemies and against whom no other people can stand (Num. 24:8) – this is one sturdy root of the kingship of Yahweh, as Israel conceived it and rejoiced in it, even if the full tones of

[4] See also H. Groß, *Weltherrschaft,* p. 22; and O. Eissfeldt in *Z.A.W.* 46 (1928), pp. 82–8, 104.

jubilation were not yet present. Deuteronomy puts a further emphasis on these historical memories from the time of the exodus from Egypt: "Beware lest . . . thy heart be lifted up and thou remember not the Lord thy God, who brought thee out of Egypt, out of the house of bondage: who was thy leader in the great and terrible wilderness, full of fiery serpents and scorpions, and in dry and waterless places . . ." (8:14 seq.). Or in Moses' blessing: "He hath loved the people: all the saints are in his hand. And they that approach to his feet, shall receive of his doctrine" (33:3). The union of the people is praised as the royal act of God. "He shall be king with the most right: the princes of the people being assembled with the tribes of Israel" (33:5). The memory of and reference to this time of grace provides a recurring theme in the mouths of the prophets (Mich. 6:4; Jer. 2:6 seq.; Isa. 63:11–14) and in religious worship (Ps. 77:12–21; 78:3–29).

These texts show us that Israel experienced Yahweh's kingship in the historical action of its God. This is no "kingdom" and no "sphere of dominion" but a kingly leadership and reign which develops from Yahweh's absolute power and shows itself in the guidance of Israel. This original meaning, namely that Yahweh as king actively "rules", must be kept in mind through the whole growth of the *basileia* theme. God's kingship in the Bible is characterized not by latent authority but by the exercise of power, not by an office but a function; it is not a title but a deed. Israel was conscious that Yahweh was its king, king of the chosen people of the covenant. It is questionable whether the covenant on Sinai was conceived, at any rate originally, within the framework of this notion of kingship, whether, in other words, Israel was consciously making a kingly covenant with its God (M. Buber). Yahweh's words to Israel, "You shall be to me a priestly kingdom (= of priests) and a holy nation" (Exod. 19:6)[5] express their obligation of holiness; it is not a 'theopolitical' idea. In God's eyes Israel is no political instrument for a projected world dominion but a people that shall observe his law in the sight of all other peoples undertake a "priestly service" for the world (H. Groß). In return, God promises his blessing, takes it beneath his protection and assists it in its struggles but God is scarcely regarded as a political leader and king. The religious covenant works itself out in the people's political life without itself assuming political character. God provides Israel with its leaders who govern and guide it in his name. They may be so deeply saturated with the sense of God's supremacy that Gideon, the Judge, can declare: "I will not rule over you, neither shall my son rule you: but the Lord shall rule over you" (Judges 8:23) and the prophet Samuel becomes angry at the people's desire for an earthly monarch (1 Kings 8:7; 10:19; 12:12).[6]

On the other hand the idea of temporal dominion can be reconciled with the kingship of Yahweh. The kingdom of David soon becomes aware that it was instituted by God and established by God's favour for ever (2 Kings 7:12–16). The prophet Nathan announces in God's name to David: "Thy house shall be faithful, and thy kingdom for ever before thy face; and thy throne shall be firm for ever" (7:16). Yahweh accepts the king on Sion as his son (2 Kings 7:14; Ps. 2:7; 89:27 seq.). For the author of Paralipomenon the throne in Jerusalem becomes the "throne of the kingdom of the Lord over Israel" (1 Par. 28:5; 29:23; 2 Par. 9:8).

This divine favour conferred upon the royal house of David

[5] See on this point J. Bauer, "Könige und Priester, ein heiliges Volk' (Exod. 19:6) in *B.Z. NF* 2 (1958), pp. 283–6.

[6] In the account of 1 Kings critical examination distinguishes between two rival statements (cf. the remark in 9:17, approving of kingship and

is far removed, however, from the divinization of the monarch found in Egypt and Babylonia. The so-called "Myth and Ritual School"[7] insists that the idea of a divine kingship prevailed in Israel as throughout the whole East and that the great prophets of the eighth century B.C. were the first to remove from the religious conceptions everything that was not compatible with strict monotheism. This idea establishes a liturgical and mystical system in which the king played a decisive rôle. At the beginning of each year the renewal of life both of the world and the people was celebrated. The king represented the people and at the same time the deity who went through a liturgical and symbolic process of death and resurrection. This God-king thus performed for the whole people a function that was of vital significance and was expressed year by year in the New Year liturgy. Such ideas find a certain support in the Egyptian cult of fertility and the kingly ideology of Babylonia and they have been further encouraged by texts discovered at Ras Shamra, the ancient Ugarit of Syria, which contain chants that reflect the cult of a dying and resurrected deity, though it must be confessed that these chants are difficult of interpretation. And so the circle seems complete, since a similar cult system has been

referring it back to God's will). The extracts quoted in the text reflect later notions about kingship; v. Rad, *Theologie*, p. 327.

[7] Founded by S. H. Hooke, Collected volumes: *Myth and Ritual* (London, 1933) and *The Labyrinth* (London, 1935). Other works: *The Origins of Early Semitic Ritual* (London 1938); *Myth, Ritual and Kingship* (Oxford 1958).

Works of the so-called Uppsala School include: I. Engnell, *Studies in Divine Kingship in the Ancient Near East* (Uppsala 1943); H. Riesenfeld, *Jésus transfiguré* (Lund 1947); A. Bentzen, *Messias, Moses redivivus, Menschensohn* (Zurich 1948); H. Ringgren, "König und Messias" in *Z.A.W.* 64 (1952), pp. 120–47; G. Widengren, *Sakrales Königtum im Alten Testament und im Judentum* (Stuttgart 1955); also A. R. Johnson, *Sacral Kingship in Ancient Israel* (Cardiff 1955).

proved to have existed on ancient Canaanite soil, bordering immediately on Israel.

But leaving aside the historical problem whether these texts do point to a uniform myth in the ancient East, it has certainly not been shown that Israel came under the influence of such ideas. On the contrary, everything suggests that, as with the story of creation, so also in ritual and worship Israel excluded and secured itself against these myths. This line of research, undertaken particularly in Sweden by the Uppsala school, soon awakened criticism and has been assailed with formidable objections. In a study on the origin and character of the Israelite kingship M. Noth comes to the conclusion that there was no such ideology of kingship in Israel, that its kingship was due to human action in a given historical situation and that the Jerusalem kingship – to say nothing of kingship in Israel and Judah – never included any note of divinity.[8] H. J. Kraus endorses the conclusions of other scholars that we have no proof of any annual festival of "Yahweh's ascent to his throne", at which the king could have enacted his part as a deity. His view is that there may have been a "royal festival of Sion", arising not from any mythical notions but from an historical event: namely, the choice of Sion and the dynasty of David, manifested externally in the translation of the ark of the covenant to Sion, represented by a procession in the liturgy for this annual feast.[9]

For criticism of this school, H. H. Schrey, "Die alttestamentliche Forschung der sog. Uppsala-Schule" in *Th.Z.* (Basle) 7 (1951), pp. 321–41; J. de Fraine, *L'aspect religieux de la royauté israélite* (Rome 1954); also the works of O. Eissfeldt (footnote 4), M. Noth (footnote 8) and H. J. Kraus (footnote 9).

[8] M. Noth in *Ges. Studien zum A.T.*, pp. 211 and 225; also E. Fascher in *Numen* 4 (1957), pp. 88–99; S. Mowinckel, *He that cometh,* pp. 21–95.

[9] *Königsherrschaft Gottes,* pp. 50–90.

Actually, the ark of the covenant was looked upon as God's throne. This notion goes back to the years of wandering (Num. 10:35 seq.) and it survived when first the shrine at Silo (1 Kings 4:4) and later the temple of Solomon (3 Kings 8:6 seq.; 4 Kings 19:14 seq.) gave shelter to the ark. They could thus envisage God's "dwelling" with his people in the holy tabernacle (Exod. 25:8; 40:34–38; Num. 14:10) as a kind of royal residence. It was from the "tabernacle of the covenant" that lay outside the camp[10] that the Lord gave his instructions to Moses (Exod 33:7–11). When David transferred the ark of the covenant to Jerusalem (2 Kings 6:15), Sion became the setting for the shrine and for the royal palace in which the house of David reigned in God's name. When Solomon's temple was constructed, God finally took possession of a "house" on Sion in which his "Name" should dwell; his true "dwelling" is of course in heaven (consecration prayer of Solomon, 3 Kings 8:27–30).

The "throne of Yahweh" in the Holy of Holies within the temple recalls other texts referring to God's heavenly throne and court. This is so peculiar and early a concept that we must regard it as an important and independent root of the many-branched concept of the *basileia*. In his great vision of his call to the prophetic office Isaias beholds the Lord "upon a throne high and elevated". Seraphim move unceasingly around him and chant: "Holy, holy, holy, the Lord God of hosts *(Yahweh Sebaoth)*; all the earth is full of his glory." That is for him a vision of a king. "I have seen with my eyes the king, the Lord of hosts" (Isa. 6:3, 5). Even if the prophet describes the heavenly

[10] For the problems associated with the tradition of the "sacred tent" or tabernacle see P. Heinisch, *Das Buch Exodus* (Bonn 1934), pp. 236 seq.; F. Nötscher, *Biblische Altertumskunde* (Bonn 1940), pp. 270–9; for the significance of the ark, W. Eichrodt, *Theologie des A.T.* I, pp. 59 seq.

sanctuary in terms of the earthly temple of Solomon, the expression *"Yahweh Sebaoth"* and the presence of the celestial beings suggest older conceptions.[11] It should be observed that the Seraphim are praising his glory that fills the entire earth. A broad cosmic vision opens before us; from heaven the Lord permeates all dimensions of creation. Whatever be the ultimate source of this concept of God's heavenly throne and court, it reveals in the Old Testament a further aspect of God's kingship: his dominion encompassing the whole world from the moment of its creation. The prophet Micheas, son of Jemla, has a vision very similar to that of Isaias when he goes before Achab and bluntly prophesies Israel's defeat in the Lord's name (3 Kings 23:19). The heavenly court also appears in the prologue to the book of Job (1:6; 2:1) and in its poetic description of creation (38:7). When God manifests himself in the majesty of thunder, as described in Psalm 28, the "sons of heaven" pay homage to the Lord and the psalm concludes with the following words: "The Lord is enthroned above the flood, the Lord shall be seated as king for ever." But from his sacred hall, from his throne in heaven, his eyes also scrutinize the children of men (Ps. 11:4). The prophets declare that Yahweh descends from his heavenly abode to intervene in wrath and punishment and also to protect and save (Mich. 1:2 seq.; Isa. 31:4: cf. Amos 4:13). The cosmic kingship of God is exalted in Psalm 102:19, in these words: "The Lord hath prepared his throne in heaven: and his kingdom shall rule over all." Ezechiel's splendid vision of God's "moving throne" (Ezech. 1) is rich in symbolic references to the universal and yet wholly transcendent kingship of God.[12]

[11] A. Alt, op. cit., p. 351: "From all this there emerges a connection which goes further back than Isaias between the kingship of Yahweh, his title of *Yahweh Sebaoth* and the ark as his representation."

[12] W. Eichrodt, *Theologie des A.T.* II (Leipzig 1935), pp. 102 seq.

In these canticles and prophecies we seem to detect notes that differ from the delight in kingship which Israel offers to the Lord of its covenant in thanksgiving for deliverance and victory. But with the passage of time they have been blended into one rich harmony. The creator and ruler of the universe, enthroned within his heavenly court, is the same God who has set up his throne among his people in an earthly shrine. The "correspondences" in the visions of the prophets and especially their preaching lend substance to this belief (Isa. 6; Ezech. 1). The heavenly Lord of all is the same God who once led their fathers out of Egypt and through the desert. Psalm 144 is a unique hymn of praise of God's all-embracing royal dominion in the world and throughout man's history: "Thy kingdom is a kingdom of all ages; and thy domination endureth throughout all generations" (v. 13). It is only these fuller notes that are heard in Paralipomenon: "Thine, O Lord, is magnificence and power and glory and victory: and to thee is praise. For all that is in heaven and in earth is thine. Thine is the kingdom, O Lord, and thou art above all princes" (David's prayer, 1 Par. 29:11). Yet this splendid king draws near to the man that devoutly prays: "But thou, O God, art my king from the very beginning who hast fulfilled deeds of salvation upon earth" (Ps. 73:12) and he is addressed familiarly as "my king and my God" (Ps. 5:2; 43:5; 67:25; 83:4; 144:1). The notion of a purely transcendent kingship of Yahweh, limited to the heavenly realm, was quite foreign to Israel. When subsequently in Judaism the "dwelling place" of God was removed further and further from this earth and set in the highest heaven in order to stress its supremacy and transcendence,[13] heaven was not designated

[13] G. Westphal, *Jahwes Wohnstätten nach den Anschauungen der alten Hebräer* (Gießen 1908), pp. 214–73; G. v. Rad in *Th.W.B.* IV, pp. 503–7; H. Traub, ibid. pp. 511 seq.; H. Bietenhard, *Die himmlische Welt*

as God's kingdom.[14] In Hebrew thought God's sublime sovereignty always directs both the world and history. Jesus himself preserves this heritage. There is one passage in the Sermon on the Mount in which he expresses this far-ranging vision of cosmic kingship: "But I say to you not to swear at all: neither by heaven, for it is the throne of God; nor by the earth for it is his footstool; nor by Jerusalem for it is the city of the great king" (Matt. 5:34 seq.).

It is only logical that Yahweh rules also over the other peoples. As he led Israel out of Egypt, so also he proved himself in concrete historical fact the Lord of Philistines and Syrians, as Amos indicated (Amos 9:7). This follows inevitably from the absolute monotheism proclaimed by the prophets: "Who shall not fear thee, O king of nations, for thine is the glory? Among all the wise men of the nations and in all their kingdoms there is none like unto thee" (Jer. 10:7). The heathen gods are only images, fashioned by the hand of man: "but the Lord is the true God; he is the living God and the everlasting king. At his wrath the earth shall tremble, and the nations shall not be able to abide his threatening" (Jer. 10:10). Jeremias bases Yahweh's exclusive dominion explicitly upon his status as creator: "The gods that have not made heaven and earth, let them perish from the earth and from among those places that are under heaven. He made the earth by his power, prepared the world by his wisdom, and stretched out the heavens by his knowledge" (vv. 11–2).

im Urchristentum und Spätjudentum (Tübingen 1951), esp. pp. 53–6; F. J. Schierse, *Verheißung und Heilsvollendung, Zur theologischen Grundfrage des Hebräerbriefes* (Munich 1955), pp. 13–19.

[14] This occurs only in the book of Wisdom which is strongly influenced by Hellenistic ideas. There is a reference to Jacob's vision in Bethel in the sentence: "She (Wisdom) showed him the kingdom of God (βασιλείαν Θεοῦ) and gave him the knowledge of holy things" (10:10).

The religious man who senses God's dominion in nature is convinced that Yahweh rules also over the peoples of the world: "For the kingdom is the Lord's; and he shall have dominion over the nations" (Ps. 21:29). Nor is it the living alone who feel his mighty arm; the dead too pay him homage. "All they that sleep in the earth fall before him; whoever descendeth to dust shall bow the knee" (Ps. 21:30). It is true that God's reign has not yet been fully proclaimed among the gentiles, but this remains an inspiring hope for the final era of salvation (see below, section 3).

Although the idea of God's kingship may have various roots, these had grown together in the peak period of the Old Testament religion and formed a unified pattern. God rules over creation, over Israel and the nations, in varying degrees and in different ways. Full royal honours are his due but his power is not acknowledged everywhere or in equal degree. The rise and fall of history is a mirror which shows how individuals and peoples stand in relation to God's kingship. God may employ heathen monarchs such as Cyrus to realize his designs but he is always the Lord holding the reins by which he administers the world and directs the history of salvation (Isa. 44:24–28; 45:1–6). Its own destiny and the power of foreign kings and kingdoms compelled Israel to reflect continually on God's kingship. And all the time new branches were springing from the root stem of ancient beliefs.

2. The Kingship of God in Liturgy

Before we study the most vigorous offshoot of the *basileia* theme, namely the expectation of God's eschatological reign, it will be worth our while to examine the liturgical praise of the kingship of God. The so-called "throne ascent" psalms have long been the subject of lively discussion among scholars.[15] The psalms in question, if we restrict their number to those generally accepted, are 46, 92, 95 to 98. They contain the paean: "God is (or 'has become') king" (Ps. 92:1; 95:10; 96:1; 98:1), which many scholars would like to interpret as a liturgical salute to God ascending his throne. In other psalms Yahweh's assumption of kingly power is extolled with rapture, as in 46: 6–9: "God is ascended with jubilee: and the Lord with the sound of trumpet. Sing praises to our God; sing praises to our king. For God is the king of all the earth: sing ye wisely. God shall reign over the nations: God sitteth on his holy throne."[16] "For the Lord is a great God, and a great king above all gods" (94:3). "With long trumpets and the sound of cornet make a joyful sound before the Lord our king . . . in the presence of the Lord, because he cometh to judge the earth. He shall judge the world with justice, and the people with equity" (97:6–9).

It is debated whether the exclamation "Yahweh Malakh" should be rendered as "Yahweh is king" or "Yahweh became king".[17] Grammatically, both should be possible. In the latter

[15] We cannot deal here with the rapidly growing literature on this subject and therefore refer the reader to the account by A. R. Johnson in *The Old Testament and Modern Study,* edited by H. H. Rowley (Oxford 1951), pp. 189–97; also Groß, *Weltherrschaft,* pp. 36–44.

[16] The author notes that verse 9 can be understood in the present tense. The German original makes it past: the English Douay makes it future, as above. The Knox version uses the present: "God reigns over the heathen; God sits enthroned in holiness." The present, as the author observes, is found in the version of F. Nötscher (*Echter-Bibel,* Würzburg, 1947): "König ist Gott über die Heiden. Gott sitzet auf seinem heiligen Thron." (God is king over the heathen. God sits upon his holy throne).

[17] H. J. Kraus tried to establish "Yahweh became king" as the definitive

case, the choir seems to be giving a vivid representation of God's actual ascent to his throne, as though they were celebrating a present event. From this we might have an easy transition to a liturgical festival, the exaltation of the throne of Yahweh. Psalm 46 in particular lends support to this view, and this argument was used by S. Mowinckel in his *Psalmenstudien* II (Oslo, 1922) to postulate a special feast for Yahweh's throne ascent; the proposal is still keenly discussed (see footnote 15). The Myth and Ritual school adopted this thesis to prove the existence of a uniform myth in the ancient East (see above section 1). In his latest work S. Mowinckel dissociated himself from these wide-ranging and generalizing conclusions[18] but he continues to postulate the actual liturgical setting and tries to account for the emergence of an eschatological hope through these liturgical ideas we have been considering. From them, in his opinion, Deutero-Isaias was able to develop the expectation of the eschatological kingship of Yahweh.[19]

Other scholars detect a relation between the great prophet of future salvation and these psalms, but of an opposite kind. H. Gunkel, for instance, acknowledged the existence of the festival and associated these chants with it but he saw the origin of the festival in the prophetic spirit which, influenced by the experience of Babylon, directed its gaze towards the future and anticipated in liturgy God's eschatological kingship.[20] In

translation (op. cit., pp. 3–8); for the opposite opinion, see Groß, *Weltherrschaft,* pp. 41 seq.

[18] *He that Cometh.* The notion of divine kingship in Egypt and Babylonia has at times other assumptions and expresses itself differently (pp. 27–51). We are not certain that the king at Ugarit represented God in the liturgical drama (pp. 52–5) and it is impossible to construct a universal "liturgical scheme" (p. 27). [19] Op. cit., pp. 138 seq.

[20] *Einleitung in die Psalmen* (Göttingen 1933), pp. 115 seq.

Gunkel's view, Psalm 46 commemorates "in the spirit of lyrical prophecy the Last Days when Yahweh himself occupies the world throne and becomes king over the entire earth".[21]

It is more likely, however, that these psalms with their announcement that Yahweh is coming to judge the peoples presuppose the preaching of the prophets and, so far as their notion of an eschatological kingship is in question, of Deutero-Isaias in particular.[22] H. J. Kraus who supports the hypothesis of a royal festival of Sion would prefer not to associate these psalms with the ancient festival for this very reason. As their liturgical setting he proposes a "royal procession" taking place at New Year, even in the second temple. This in his view represents "Yahweh's return to Sion as announced by Deutero-Isaias" (52:7–10) and celebrates Yahweh's coronation as the king of his people who concludes a pact with Israel and the whole created world. "A new realm is inaugurated. The final stage of history has begun."[23] This hypothesis cannot, strictly speaking, be proved.[24] But the contents of these chants, with their reference to the divine kingship suggest that they had some liturgical setting.

It is scarcely possible to doubt that these full-throated hymns of praise had liturgy as their background. If we examine their contents, we find them glorifying God's abiding sovereignty

[21] *Die Psalmen übersetzt und erklärt* (Göttingen 1926), p. 201.

[22] See also R. de Vaux's review of Mowinckel's work in *R. P.* 65 (1958), p. 104.

[23] Op. cit., p. 122.

[24] See Groß's criticism in *Weltherrschaft,* pp. 40–3. His conclusion is the following: "This royal salute (to Yahweh as king) would have been a basic and formative idea in all Hebrew feasts as in the entire life of the people, so that there is no need to regard it as a liturgical welcome in any particular festival" (p. 43).

over earth and heaven but also the wonders he wrought in the history of Israel and his power over all nations. We establish relations with creation and history, with the beginning and the end of things – and this last because the peoples will one day submit wholly to God's rule and resign themselves to God's judgment. We seem to hear echoes of old hymns of creation in Psalm 92: "He hath established the world which shall not be moved. Thy throne is prepared from of old; thou art from eternity there. The floods have lifted up, O Lord; the floods have lifted up their voice. The floods have lifted up their waves with the noise of many waters. Wonderful are the surges of the sea: wonderful is the Lord on high!" Equally cosmic is the description in Psalm 96 which rises *crescendo* to the declaration: "For thou art the most high Lord over all the earth; thou art exalted exceedingly above all gods" (v. 9). Yet we are conscious as well of the glance towards Israel's history, in which God realized his wonders.

"He hath subdued the people under us: and the nations under our feet. He hath chosen for us his inheritance, the beauty of Jacob which he hath loved" (46:4–5). "Sing ye to the Lord a new canticle, because he hath done wonderful things . . . He hath remembered his mercy and his truth towards the house of Israel" (97:1, 3). "Moses and Aaron among his priests, and Samuel among them that call upon his name. They called upon the Lord and he heard them" (98:6). Both creation and history are indicated in Psalm 94, although possibly this may not be one of the "throne ascent" psalms, yet it is important for an understanding of the liturgy. After describing God's supremacy over all deities and over creation (vv. 3–5), the psalmist continues: "Come, let us adore and bow down, and bow before the Lord that made us. For he is the Lord our God, and we are the people of his pasture and the sheep of his pasture. Today you must listen to his voice" (vv. 6–7). Experience of the past, the obduracy of their fathers in the wilderness, God's warnings and punishments (vv. 8–11) stand as a vivid threat to Israel and become "today", as the liturgical hymn re-echoes, a passionate appeal to hearken to God's voice. The eschatological note is not sounded in this psalm; it may have been given in the content of the liturgy which accompanied it. But in other chants it breaks forcibly through. "Say ye among the gentiles: the Lord hath become king. For he hath corrected the world that it may not be moved. He holds just judgment on the peoples" (95:10). The whole of creation has its share in this event. "The fields and all things in them shall be joyful. Then shall all the trees of the woods rejoice before the face of the Lord because he cometh to judge the earth. He shall judge the world with justice and the people with his truth" (95:12 seq.). Psalm 97 has a similar strain: "Let the sea be moved and the fullness thereof; the world and they that dwell therein. The rivers shall clap their hands; the mountains shall rejoice together in the presence of the Lord, because he cometh to judge the earth" (vv. 7–9). But God's kingship over the peoples shows itself not only as a judgment but also as a blessing if they acknowledge his dominion: "The princes of the people are gathered together with the God of Abraham; the strong ones of the earth belong to God who is exalted exceedingly" (Ps. 47:10).

Liturgical thought thus associates God's dominion over creation from the beginning, his control over history and his eschatological kingship. In this is revealed both the unique character of the religious belief of Israel and a fundamental element in its worship. The ideas of this people are so interwoven with historical events that any purely mythical interpretation of its hymns of creation is quite inadequate. The Lord enthroned above the waters is the same Lord who made his covenant with their fathers and brought about Israel's victories and defeats, its advance and its humiliation. Israel's feasts are no recurring festivals of natural phenomena, dramatized into myths, but new and vital encounters with the God who made it his chosen people. Israel's worship would appear to be its own reflection upon itself and its God. Only so can we explain how its great hope was awakened in a period of national impotence, the hope that one day God would powerfully restore his kingship over Israel and utterly subject the foreign nations that were now oppressing his chosen people. However we account for the rise in Israel of this eschatological hope of salvation, it received a strong impetus from the solemn festivals and liturgical hymns then chanted.

The psalms we have been dealing with make this abundantly clear since they reveal a type of cult known as "liturgical representation", in this case of God's kingship. In recalling God's saving acts in former ages and his warnings and promises, they "re-present", that is "make present once again", God's historical encounter with the people and establish his kingship anew. At the same time they summon the future from a remote distance and realize in liturgical anticipation the fulfilment of God's reign. This mighty joy in the kingship of God is no mere self-intoxication with visions of the future, it embraces both present certitude and liturgical fulfilment. In this sense, we might almost speak of a "liturgical" kingship of God. If all creation is to unite its voice in praise, if elements from Paradise mingle with the eschatological pattern, if the oldest memories and the boldest prophecies meet in one and the same hymn, then worship has become a middle point between first beginning and last end, between salvation in past and future, and has a reality all its own.

Whether we understand the royal salute to Yahweh as

proclaiming a kingship that has always endured or as the liturgical exaltation of a king, it has in either case a particular actuality, which is expressed in the "today" of Psalm 94 (cf. Heb. 3:7–4:13 for a Christian interpretation). "The real significance of solemn religious worship as an encounter between God and people is realized in this, that the old historical tradition of salvation, embracing creation, election and the covenant made on Sinai, is here renewed as a present, sacred event . . . and God manifests himself to his people in power and saving grace."[25]

There are other psalms that call for consideration from this point of view and reveal or at least suggest liturgical usage. Psalm 23 describes a most lifelike scene obviously taken from a procession of the ark of Yahweh to the temple. When it reaches the door, they chant: "Lift up, o gates, your heads: be lifted up, o eternal gates. The king of glory will enter in." From the gates issues the challenge: "Who is this king of glory?" – to meet the answer: "The Lord who is strong and mighty, the Lord mighty in battle." This ritual dialogue is repeated till the "password" (Gunkel) is given: "The Lord of hosts *(Yahweh Sebaoth)*, he is the king of glory" (vv. 7–10). God enters into the sanctuary as king upon the ark of the covenant: a motif from very ancient liturgy. What is remarkable is that this fragment is pieced together in this psalm with other fragments, first, with a praise of the creator and lord of the world (vv. 1–2), and then with a "Torah-liturgy" (Gunkel), which inquires into the moral character of the man who wishes to enter the temple (vv. 3–6). Possibly this juxtaposition hints at a different ritual usage of the psalm at a later date. We need not further inquire about the concrete circumstances but once again we can recognize the liturgical thought which associates past events (entry of the

[25] A. Weiser, *Die Psalmen* II (Göttingen 1950), pp. 413 seq.

ark into the temple) with present ritual (entry of pilgrims) and sees the whole process in the light of the thought of God's glory in the temple, a glory that in itself fills the entire world but reveals itself in a special manner in the temple. Processions must frequently have taken place. Psalm 131: 8–10, 14, envisages the entry with the ark, once again represented in ritual drama. Psalm 67:25 seq. also describes a procession: "They have seen thy goings, O God, the goings of my God and king into his sanctuary. Princes went before, with singers, in the midst of young damsels playing on timbrels. In the churches bless ye God the Lord, from the fountains of Israel." Then follows the prayer: "Command thy strength, O God: confirm what thou hast wrought in us, from thy temple in Jerusalem."

Here too God is experienced as Lord and king, actually present, and the fragment forms part of a psalm that depicts God's immense power in scenes of war and events in nature, and presents his sway both in creation and in history. All these currents meet in the psalmist and produce in him the one single conviction that Yahweh still raises his strong protective arm over Jerusalem and his people. The Sion psalms too belong to this perspective. "With the joy of the whole earth is mount Sion founded, on the sides of the North, the city of the great king: in her houses shall God be known, when he shall protect her" (Ps. 47:3 seq.). Psalms 83, 86 and 121 are further instances. Even the royal psalms that refer to the earthly king on Sion become in the final resort a praise of God's kingship since the scion of David is only the vicegerent of the eternal king and Lord of the covenant with Israel (see especially Ps. 2, 19, 20, 44, 71 and 131).

We cannot pursue this theme further. The extracts already given must suffice to demonstrate that the idea of God's kingship penetrated the entire length and breadth of Israel's worship and at the same time received from it a powerful impulse and in fact reached in it its highest expression. Furthermore, the liturgical praise of Yahweh as king was a particular expression of God's kingship – his omnipotence in the present, rising from the roots of the past and from the hope in a final achievement and fulfilment in the future.

3. The Eschatological Kingship of Yahweh

"The fundamental idea in the future hope (of Israel) is always the kingly rule of Yahweh, his victorious advent as king and his reckoning with his enemies. Yahweh's victory is followed by the manifestation of the kingship. He appears as king and takes possession of his realm."[26] The original roots of Israel's hope of salvation are shrouded in mystery. Attempts have been made to derive them from mythical elements, from liturgical cult, from foreign influences (in particular, that of the Parsees) but also from the historical experience of the Jewish people and finally from its belief in God. We need not enter into this complicated problem. What we are looking for are the fundamental ideas on which Jesus could graft his teaching.

Yet one thing is certain. Throughout the severe catastrophes

[26] Mowinckel, *He that Cometh,* p. 143; see also Eichrodt, *Theologie* I, pp. 326 seq. Mowinckel's view expressed in his *Psalmenstudien* was very soon adopted by A. Freiherr von Gall, βασιλεία τοῦ Θεοῦ, pp. 20 seq. though he rejects the notion of a Jewish hope of salvation prior to the exile. He discovers a close connection between this hope for a kingdom of God and the transformation of the pre-exilic religion of Israel into the post-exilic Jewish religion of the Law (pp. 197 seq.). In his view, all the prophecies concerning the kingship of God belong to the period after the Babylonian captivity and, when they are found in pre-exilic prophets, they are to be treated as subsequent interpolations (pp. 290 seq.).

which swept over Israel, the annihilation of the kingdoms of Israel and Judah, the Babylonian captivity and the arduous reconstruction in the Persian period which brought no national independence, the current of Messianic ideas and eschatological hope gathered in strength, caught up and carried the whole of subsequent Judaism and was stronger than ever in the lifetime of Jesus. The smaller the chances of development from their own resources, the further the prospect of a prosperous national kingdom receded (the rule of the Hasmoneans proved a serious disillusionment), so much the more did they set their hopes on God's promises and his victory, and they desired all the more intensely God's kingdom of glory at the end of time. In this outline we must of necessity limit ourselves to the essential feature of this picture of the future in Old Testament prophecy and distinguish whatever variants make themselves reasonably clear.

The prophets do not often speak of the kingship of God; they employ other images and concepts. This may reveal their critical attitude towards the worldly kingship of their time. In their eyes the kings of Israel and Judah were mostly caricatures of kingship and their government was not a suitable form in which to express the eschatological reign of God. But it has been well observed that the preaching of the prophets presupposes the idea of the kingship of Yahweh, both when it speaks of disasters and of the promise of salvation, and that the picture with its sharp contrast of black and white has this as its common ground.[27] Because Israel was disloyal to the God of its covenant yet still remained Yahweh's "first begotten son" (Exod. 4:22; Osee 11:1; Jer. 31:9, 20), the prophets foretold severe temporal punishments for the people but nevertheless

[27] L. Dürr, *Ursprung und Ausbau der israelitisch-jüdischen Heilandserwartung* (Berlin 1925), pp. 40 seq.

opened before them the vision of an ultimate salvation in the future. Since Yahweh's kingship over Israel was established for ever, he would one day overthrow her foreign oppressors and judge them so that his blessed rule over Israel will manifest itself anew and more gloriously, indeed in its full grandeur. The prophecies of woe and weal merely present the "two sides of one coin" (L. Dürr). Similarly, judgment and salvation on the "day of Yahweh" are only another expression for the advent of God's future reign.

The judgment of the people, whether envisaged as a judgment in time or increasingly as a judgment at the close of time fills many pages of the prophetic books and does not require to be developed here. It leaves traces in the "throne ascent" psalms. Jeremias' description of God's great assize contains, it is true, world-embracing features. All peoples will drink of the cup of God's wrath (Jer. 25:15 seq.). After the kings that border on Israel the prophet will give it to all the kings to drink, "near and far, one after the other, and to all the rich ones of the world who dwell upon earth" (v. 26). "The Lord shall roar from on high and his voice shall issue from his holy habitation . . . . The noise is come even to the ends of the earth, for the Lord enters into judgment with the peoples, and delivers the wicked to the sword" (vv. 30 seq.). Ezechiel's account of the onslaught of Gog and his armies from the North assumes cosmic dimensions. When Gog advances into the territory of Israel, God's anger flashes forth and the whole earth is caught up in his wrath (Ezech. 38:18–23). He annihilates the godless army of the peoples (39:1–7). "I will set my glory among the nations, and all nations shall see my judgment" (39:21). Equally cosmic is the horizon in the "Isaias Apocalypse" (Isa. 24–27). Chapter 24 describes the depopulation of the earth, the curse that is consuming it, and then God's frightening and earthshaking judgment and his final victory over all created powers, even those that guide the stars in the heavens. "The Lord shall punish the host of heaven on high and the kings of the earth beneath . . . for the Lord of hosts shall reign in mount Sion and in Jerusalem" (Isa. 24:21–3). In Daniel's visions, especially in chapters 2 and 7, the kingdoms of the world are supplanted by the everlasting kingdom of God, but his general description, with its symbolic allusions, its heavenly visions and apocalyptic details has a different character. Here we are on the threshold of later Judaism (see below, section 6).

More significant for our purpose is the prophecy of the glory of God's future kingdom, its condition of bliss after judgment has completed its purification. There is no dearth of passages which use the distressed and troubled relation of Israel to its God as a stepping-stone to the thought of God's kingship and to proclaim the restoration of Israel to its ancient status as God's chosen people.

Of course it is difficult to give a definite date to such oracles. When comforting utterances of this kind are found in earlier prophets, critics question whether they are not in fact subsequent additions. Yet there is no reason to be basically sceptical about a pre-exilic prophecy of salvation. Isaias, greatest of all the prophets, has not a little to say about future salvation and the Saviour, and in a genuinely prophetic vein. There is considerable doubt about the dating of many passages in the minor prophets, as regards both contents and style, and this is easily understood when we recall the way in which they were passed round and then ultimately collected. Commentaries should be consulted for problems raised by particular passages.

The ancient notion of the kingship of Yahweh revives in the prophecy of Micheas when he depicts the scattered community of God under the images of shepherd and flock: "I will put them together as a flock in a fold, as the sheep in the midst of the sheepcotes . . . and the king shall pass before them, the Lord at the head of them" (2:12 seq.). Jerusalem will be the focal point of God's new reign over his people. "And I will make her that halted, a remnant, and her that hath been afflicted, a mighty nation. And the Lord will reign over them in mount Sion, from now on and for ever" (4:7), runs another prophecy. The return will be like a second exodus: "Guide thy people with thy rod, the flock of thy inheritance . . . . As in the days of thy coming out of the land of Egypt I will show him wonders" (7:14 seq.). The image of Yahweh as good shepherd is linked in Jeremias 23:1–4 and Ezechiel 34 with the complaints against the former human shepherds of Israel. Ezechiel's great shepherd chapter 34, draws the ideal portrait of the divine shepherd, as it is developed in the era of humiliation. "I will feed my sheep and I will cause them to lie down, saith the Lord God. I will seek that which was lost, and that which was driven away I will bring again. And I will bind up that which was broken and strengthen that which was weak: and that which is fat and strong I will preserve, and I will feed them in judgment" (vv. 15 seq.). The prophet then announces that Yahweh will exercise his pastoral care for Israel through his appointed shepherd, his "servant David" (vv. 23 seq.). Here another Messianic hope can be felt and it merges into the ideas that precede it (see also Jer. 23:5 seq.).

One special consequence of God's eschatological kingship is that the gentiles will stream towards Sion. The pilgrimage of the nations to the mountain of God is an ancient theme that is found both in Micheas (4:1–4) and Isaias (2:2–4). Whatever older notions may be discovered in this mountain of God,[28] Hebrew prophecy uses them all in the service of the future

[28] H. Greßmann, *Der Messias,* pp. 164—70; in criticism, Dürr, op. cit., pp. 94–105; Groß, *Weltherrschaft,* p. 59; also H. Wildenberger, *Die Völkerwallfahrt zum Zion, Jes.* II, I–5: *V. T.* 7 (1957), pp. 62–81.

glory of Yahweh. Sion is then to be the "highest peak" of the world, upon which Yahweh will set up his throne as monarch of the whole world. From this he rules the nations and teaches them his ways. Implicit in this is a note of universal salvation which was of the greatest significance for the teaching of Jesus (cf. Matt. 8:11 seq.). Side by side with the judgment passed upon the godless there is salvation for those of good will who are ready to be converted. They will be subject to God's beneficent rule, even if Israel is to retain its privileged status. Freely they stream towards Jerusalem, where God manifests his glory – a theme that continues to be active down to the time of the New Testament itself (Jer. 16:19; Isa. 56:7; 60; 66:19–21; Zach. 2:14 seq.; 8:20–22; 14:16 and other passages).[29] This universal kingship of God involves the realization of his holy and sanctifying will, a new moral order. The Law (Torah) proceeds from Sion, and Yahweh's word from Jerusalem (Isa. 2:3). As a result, peace is achieved among the peoples (2:4; cf. 9:6; also Zach. 9:9 seq. – as the achievement of the Messias who is prince of peace).[30]

The whole of creation, and not merely the gentile peoples, will have their share in the eschatological kingdom of God's peace. The beasts of prey lay aside their savage nature (Isa. 9:6–9); God concludes a covenant with "the beasts of the field, the birds of the air and the creeping things of the earth" (Osee 2:18). Nature is wholly and wondrously transformed, the serenity of Paradise is renewed (Isa. 35:1–10). At this point an idea can be detected that is to play a leading rôle in all eschatology. The last things will be like the first things, the beginning returns in the end.[31]

[29] J. Jeremias, *Jesu Verheißung,* pp. 48 seq.

[30] For further details see H. Groß, *Weltfrieden,* pp. 96–103.

[31] Much attention has been paid to this notion, especially since the publication of H. Gunkel's book, *Schöpfung und Chaos in Urzeit und*

It should not surprise us that the fertility of the earth, an abundance of corn, wine and oil – those blessings that represented good fortune to the oriental mind (Gen. 27:28; 49:11) – should be introduced to ornament the picture of the future kingdom of God. "But how could or should the happiness of that day have been better described in harmony with the general oriental outlook by which the Bible was influenced than in terms of these ancient oriental ideals?"[32] The prophets are very far removed from any materialist and this-worldly vision of the future kingdom of God.

These various themes, conversion of the peoples, assembly on the mount of God, and complete happiness, are brought together in the glorious picture of the divine banquet in the Apocalypse of Isaias (25:6–8). The dominant idea is the communion with God which Israel and all the peoples will find there and that will be their true happiness and delight (v. 9). As his own banquet parables indicate, Jesus did not reject this splendid picture of communion at God's table, the assembly of the redeemed in God and, as a consequence, the serene blessedness of every individual.

Deutero-Isaias on the other hand interprets the idea of God's kingship in a new and unique way and in so doing, becomes its particular prophet. He too is familiar with the theme of the new exodus which is not a hasty flight, as was the original exodus from Egypt; it develops peacefully beneath the full protection of God (Isa. 52:11 seq.). "The Lord will go before you; the God of Israel will gather you together."[33]

The dominant picture is of God advancing through the

Endzeit (1895; 1921, 2nd edit. dealing with Gen. 1 and Apoc. 12); more recently Groß, *Weltfrieden,* pp. 64–8, 78–93.

[32] Dürr, op. cit., p. 101.

[33] The idea of a "new exodus" is found frequently: Osee 2:16 seq.;

wilderness along a broad and even royal highway (40:3 seq.). His arrival becomes a royal manifestation (40:5). Jerusalem will speak to the cities of Judah as an ambassador of joy: "Behold your God. Behold the Lord God shall come with strength" (40:9 seq.). He will again be seen as shepherd (40:11) but a shepherd wholly garbed in kingly raiment (43:15; 44:6). Yet the divine sovereign does not come to repay and judge but to redeem his people. The full title of this picture of God drawn by Isaias is: "Yahweh, king of Israel and its redeemer, the Lord of hosts" (44:6). Yahweh's return to Sion is preceded by a message of joy (LXX: Εὐαγγελιζόμενος): "He preacheth peace, He sheweth forth good, He preacheth salvation. He saith to Sion, thy God shall reign" (52:7) — a passage with which the teaching of Jesus is directly linked and which is made the starting point of his gospel.[34] This factor introduces a new era in the history of salvation, the true and final period of redemption. Men are to intone a new hymn to God, a hymn of praise from the ends of the world (42:10). "Remember not former things: and look not on things of old. Behold, I do new things" (43:18 seq.). In unison with the prophet's high esteem of his God and creator (40:12–31; 42:5; 44:6–20; 45:12–18) the whole of creation is to unite in one paean for the salvation of Israel (42, 10; 49:13). The parched land is freshened (43:19), all flesh beholds God's salvation (40:5). The nations glorify God (45:14–17); the temple is made a house of prayer for all the peoples (56:7).

Isa. 11:16; Jer. 31:2–6; Ezech. 20:33–38. On this matter consult J. Bright, *Kingdom of God,* pp. 142 seq.; J. Bonsirven, *Règne de Dieu,* p. 15.

[34] Compare Mark 1:14 seq. with Isa. 52:7 in LXX; Matt. 11:5; Luke 4:18 with Isa. 61:1 in LXX. The verb εὐαγγελίζεσθαι is found in Isa. 40:9 and 60:6; the noun εὐαγγέλιον is first found in this sense in the New Testament: see also G. Friedrich in *Th.W.B.* II, pp. 706 seq.; 715 seq.; 724–6.

This prophetic vision contains all the fundamental elements that are crystallized to form the *basileia* concept of Jesus: the glad tidings of the dawn of God's kingly reign, its orientation towards eschatological salvation, a completely new era, in which God reigns to the delight of the redeemed; but also its universal scope which does not exclude the gentiles, the glad honour given to God by all and their free subjection to his holy will. This is a wholly pure, wholly religious notion of the kingdom of God, that is not toned down or thinned out in mere images. It is God's eschatological reign that is to have absolute sway over mankind and creation.

But one idea is completely lacking in Deutero-Isaias, that of an earthly vicegerent of God's kingship. "He proclaims Yahweh's royal rule in all its consequences for the new Jerusalem but to the complete exclusion of the house of David — a divine sovereignty such as was recognized in the period before the monarchy in the union of the twelve tribes."[35] Instead, the "Servant of God" occupies a decisive place, and however this was originally to be interpreted, Jesus adopted it as applying to himself. Yet despite this close relation between Jesus and the Deutero-Isaian prophecy — the most significant of all in the light of the Jewish religious heritage — his teaching could not be fully grasped without reference also to other sources.

The expectation of an ideal ruler from the house of David is all the more strongly stressed by other prophets. The ancient promise is never forgotten that "thy house shall be faithful, and thy kingdom for ever before thy face; thy throne shall be firm for ever" (2 Kings 7:16). An old oracle declares that "in that day I will raise up the tabernacle of David that is fallen, and I will close up the breaches of the walls thereof and repair what

[35] H. J. Kraus, op. cit., p. 104.

was fallen" (Amos 9:11 seq.).[36] The wonder child foretold by Isaias sits upon David's throne. He will strengthen and defend the kingdom in right and righteousness (Isa. 9:6); he is a shoot from the root of Jesse (11:1). Of this ruler Micheas writes that he derives from very ancient times and that he will be mighty until the end of the world (Mich. 5:1 seq.). Jeremias promises that God will raise up in the future a "just branch" to David: "A king shall reign, and shall be wise, and shall exercise judgment and justice on earth" (23:5). David seems to be re-incarnated in Ezechiel's shepherd (34:23 seq.) and king (37:24) whom God designates: "David, my servant, shall be their prince for ever" (37:25). In his Messianic kingdom God's new and abiding covenant is fulfilled and God establishes his sanctuary for ever in the midst of Israel. "My tabernacle shall be with them; and I will be their God, and they shall be my people" (37:27). This expectation of the king and kingdom of David became the main motive of Messianic hope in later Judaism but its form varies according as this ideal ruler is envisaged as Prince of peace or God's warrior and his kingdom as a realization of God's holiness and justice or as a political restoration of Israel.[37] At the close of the Old Testament the purely religious notion of the Messias-king is dominant, as expressed by the prophet Zacharias: "Rejoice greatly, daughter of Sion, exult for ever, daughter of Jerusalem! Behold thy king will come to thee, the just one and saviour . . .

[36] The passage is generally regarded by the critics as a post-exilic prophecy, see Greßmann, *Messias,* pp. 233 seq., Mowinckel, *He that Cometh,* pp. 18 seq.; this opinion is now rejected by F. Nötscher (in the *Echter Bible*) and by J. Klausner, *The Messianic Idea in Israel* (New York 1955), pp. 42 seq.

[37] This "militant" and "warrior" character of the Messias is very ancient, see Eichrodt, *Theologie* I, pp. 320 seq. For the prophecy about David, see also G. F. Moore, *Judaism* II, pp. 324 seq.

He shall speak peace to the gentiles: and his power shall be from sea to sea, and from the rivers even to the end of the earth" (Zach. 9:9 seq.). Yet this picture does not remain undisturbed. There were other ideas and trends which filled the period "between the two testaments". To understand the situation in which Jesus had to proclaim his gospel of the eschatological kingship, we must examine later Judaism in greater detail.

LATER JUDAISM

4. THE EXPECTATION OF THE MESSIANIC KINGDOM OF ISRAEL

STATEMENTS about the kingly reign of God are not as frequent in late Jewish writers as might have been expected from the evidence in the gospels. Yet it would be wrong to look merely for the actual expression "reign of God" in the widespread apocryphal and rabbinical literature and the writings of Jewish Hellenism and of the sects. The notion pervades the rich and highly differentiated Jewish eschatology and itself assumes various forms.[1] We have no intention of classifying the manifold concepts of God's reign and kingdom but in the interests of this enquiry we do require to stress certain typical views.

The old "national" eschatology represents the thoughts and sentiments of the broad mass of the Jewish people in the two centuries prior to Christ and in the time of Jesus and the early Church. The idea that predominated, the usual and ordinary idea, was that God would send the Messias-king, the "son of David", and through him restore the kingdom of Israel, with the ancient glory of the re-united tribes, liberated from foreign

[1] Bousset-Greßmann, *Religion des Judentums,* pp. 213–22; Moore, *Judaism* II, pp. 371–6; Bonsirven, *Judaïsme* I, pp. 435–57; Volz, *Eschatologie* pp. 368–81.

occupation and poverty but at the same time restored to a true service of God and a holy fulfilment of the Law.

In spite of much misunderstanding it should be emphasized that this expectation did not lose its religious character and that men were not thinking merely of political liberation. Zachary's hymn of praise, the *Benedictus,* may well give us the best impression of what a devout Jew had in mind (and not merely the group of solitaries): "delivery from our enemies and from the hands of those that hate us" in order then "to serve God in holiness and justice all the days of our life" (Luke 1:71, 75). On this point the Zealots were at one with the rest of the people. They differed in imagining, because of their intense longing for an exclusive kingship of God in Israel, that they should employ weapons and armed insurrection against the foreign oppressors of God's people.

It should further be noted that this "national" eschatology had itself developed from an earlier stage in the prophets to a subsequent stage in later Judaism. In the former view, God himself was to establish his kingship and have it administered in his name by the Messias; in the latter, the Messias was frequently regarded as "God's victorious instrument for the establishment of the kingdom".[2]

Evidence for this expectation of the Messianic kingdom of Israel is best provided by the gospels which take for granted the general Jewish background though they do not describe it. They serve as valuable sources for the popular views. The two sons of Zebedee reveal hopes of an earthly triumph in their request for the first places (Mark 10:37 par.). So does Simon Peter when he attempts to deter Jesus from the way of suffering

[2] Mowinckel, op. cit., p. 313. He suggests that the "warlike spirit of the house of the Maccabees" provided the turning point in this change of view; cf. also Billerbeck IV, 858–80.

(Mark 8:32 par.). The same outlook is shown repeatedly by the disciples in Luke's account (Luke 19:11; 22:38; Acts 1:6), by the Galileans after the multiplication of bread (John 6:15), the crowds at the entry into Jerusalem, even though the expression "the future kingdom of our father David" is exceptional and striking (Mark 11:10), by the thief crucified with him (Luke 23:42 in the reading, "when thou comest with thy royal power") and by the disciples at Emmaus (Luke 24:21). This blending of national with religious hopes which Jesus had to disappoint, is best illustrated from the *Psalms of Solomon* that derive from Pharisee circles of the first century B.C. According to *Psalms of Solomon* 17:23–51, the son of David will crush the foreign oppressors, cleanse Jerusalem from heathens, gather together and rule the ancient people of God that it may live justly and holily. Foreign settlers will be expelled from Israel but gentiles come from far and wide to behold God's glory in Jerusalem, and over them too the Messias reigns as their just king, appointed by God. God thus sets up his rule on earth through the Messias and through his anointed, the scion of David, exercises his rule over Israel and the heathens associated with Israel. It concludes with the sentence, "The Lord himself is our king for ever and ever". Thus the old dream of a kingdom of David is fulfilled in which the Lord's Anointed is God's vicegerent upon earth. His rule is pictured as a religious rule, bringing peace and blessing to Israel and the gentiles through a true following of the divine law.

The notion of Israel's revival and dominion under its God and king runs through the expressions of Jewish belief, however diversely they may portray the Messianic blessings. Valuable evidence for the popular hopes is found in ancient Jewish prayers which, though in part of later date, do not reflect merely the atmosphere after the great national catastrophes, the Jewish war and the rebellion of Bar-Kochba. We read in the older Palestinian version of the Prayer of the Eighteen Benedictions (*Shemoneh 'Esre*): "Bring back our judges as in former days, and our counsellors as in the beginning: be king over us, thou alone" (Eleventh petition). For this, it will be necessary to defeat the godless Roman dominion. "Root out this government of scoundrels and hasten to destroy them in our days" (Twelfth petition). We discover in the *Qaddish* (the prayer of blessing for divine worship): "May he establish his royal rule, may his redemption develop and bring forth his Messias and save the people in your lifetime and in your days in the life of the whole house of Israel, speedily and in the near future."

This prayer for the destruction of Rome's godless rule recurs in the *Musaph* petition for the New Year and it continues: "Thou, Yahweh, our God, reign as king, with speed, over all thy works in Jerusalem, thy city, and on the mount of Sion, the dwelling place of thy glory." Finally, the '*Alenu* prayer, attributed to Rab (d. 247) gives voice to the hope that Yahweh will rule as everlasting king over all inhabitants of the globe.[3] The consuming desire for the Messias, the wish for the destruction of a godless rule but at the same time the religious and moral character of the Messianic kingdom are equally marked in these expressions of religious sentiment and life.

The *Book of Jubilees* (probably 2nd century B.C.) makes no mention of the Messias but it illustrates Israel's hope of an eschatological covenant of salvation with God. "Then I build up my sanctuary in your midst and abide with you; I will be your God and you my people in truth and justice" (1:17

[3] For the texts see Billerbeck 1, 178; the complete text of the '*Alenu* prayer with the accompanying *malkhiyyoth,* in P. Fiebig, *Rosh ha-shana: Mischnah,* 2:8 (Gießen, 1914), pp. 49–53. Also Dalman, *Worte Jesu* I, pp. 311–14; Bonsirven, *Judaïsme* I, pp. 446 seq.

seq.). Mount Sion will be the centre of God's universal reign. "The Lord will manifest himself to every eye, and all will know that I am Israel's God, the Father of all children of Jacob and king on mount Sion for eternity. Then Sion and Jerusalem will be holy" (1:28; see also 23:26–31). We seem already to detect the "our Father, our king" of later Jewish prayers. Israel's primacy is maintained in the Henoch literature which places a sharper emphasis on the moral opposition between the elect and just and the godless and sinners. In the great vision of the shepherds of the nations it is the Israelites faithful to the Law, whom God glorifies after persecution and oppression. "Then I saw how all remaining sheep and all other beasts on earth and all the birds of heaven bowed low and paid honour to those sheep (the Jews true to the Law) and prayed to them and attended to their word" (*Ethiopic Hen.* 90:30). The *Testaments of the Twelve Patriarchs,* in which it is often difficult to separate what is genuinely Jewish from subsequent Christian recension,[4] contain a number of passages referring to the appearance of God himself[5] and in *T. Dan.* 5:13 we learn: "No longer does Jerusalem remain desolate, no longer is Israel a captive. The Lord is there within . . . and Israel's Holy One is its king."

This must be the Jewish original. We can trace a Christian adaptation wherever the manifestation of God's kingship is referred unmistakably to Jesus Christ as in the continuation of the sentence quoted above, "in humiliation and poverty; whoever trusts in him, will be truly a king in heaven". This

[4] See M. de Jonge, *The Testaments of the Twelve Patriarchs* (Assen 1953), for the quoted passages, especially pp. 90–2.

[5] *T. Sim.* 6:5; *T. Lev.* 4:4; 5:2; *T. Jud.* 22:2; 23:5; *T. Zab.* 9:8; *T. Napht.* 8:3; see, on this subject, R. Eppel, *Le piétisme juif dans les Testaments des douze Patriarches* (Paris, 1930), pp. 96 seq.

Christian adaptation is interesting for the *basileia* theme in early Christianity (2nd century), for example, the concept of heaven as a *basileia,* which occurs only late in the New Testament and as a marginal notion (see below, section 24). Other passages refer to God's kingship over Israel in historical terms belonging to the past; for instance, *T. Jos.* 19:12: "My kingship is destroyed among you like a hut in a vineyard that disappears after the harvest" or *T. Benj.* 9:1: "The kingdom of the Lord will be no longer among you; He taketh it away immediately." This clearly recalls Matt. 21:43. It would appear that these Christian circles had accepted Jewish ideas of an historically immanent manifestation of God's kingship that are inconsistent with a strictly supernatural view. In their opinion, the kingship of God was already manifest in Jesus Christ: *T. Jud.* 24:5: "Then rises up the sceptre of my royal dominion; a flower emerges from your root." God's kingdom is taken away from Israel and is thrown open principally to the gentiles: "From it arises for the gentiles a sceptre of justice, to judge and rescue all who call upon the Lord" (ibid. v. 6).

In the Jewish parts of the *Sibylline Books* images and ideas are mingled in rich profusion, among them the eschatological kingship of God and the glory of the new Jerusalem: "Then appears the great kingdom of the eternal king among men. A holy monarch comes and rules the entire world through all the ages. But when is that day to arrive and the judgment of the everlasting God, the mighty king?" (*Sib.* III, 47–56). All must offer sacrifice to the great king (ibid. III, 808). With these are blended apocalyptic pictures. The Messias descends from heaven with a sceptre given him by God, exercises justice and destroys the seats of the men who practised evil (ibid V, 414–19). But "the city which God chose he made splendid, more splendid than the stars, sun and moon, he adorned it with ornaments and fashioned there a temple . . . ." (ibid. V, 420 seq.). All who are true and just can now contemplate God's glory and proclaim his fame; violence and sin vanish. This is the final era of holy men, when God, architect of the great temple, completes it (V, 426–433). This evidence comes from Jewish Hellenism (Egypt) even if the Jewish origin of book five has been called in question.[6] A similar hope is that of the ancient Tobias far from his homeland. The Israelites "will return home from the lands of banishment and rebuild Jerusalem in glory. God's house will arise as a magnificent mansion for all eternity as the prophets in their turn have foretold" (Tob. 14:5). Thoughts of revenge are not harboured by this devout and gentle Jew; instead he looks forward to the conversion of the gentiles. "Many gentile nations come hither to honour the name of God, the Lord, they bring presents in their hands and gifts for the king of heaven. Whole tribes rejoice in thee" (13:13; cf. 14:6).

These ancient hopes are sustained in the two great Jewish apocalypses of the first century A. D. which offer comfort for the catastrophe of Jerusalem despite their markedly apocalyptic character and the differences of eschatology. The *Syriac Apocalypse of Baruch* includes the vision of Israel's restoration and ennoblement. The Messias summons all the peoples, spares the lives of some of them and slays others. Those that did not know Israel and did not oppress her, remain alive but in submission to Israel (72:2–6). The *Fourth Book of Esdras* also acknowledges the Messias of David who accuses the nations of their deeds of wickedness (12:32). In another part of the work, that of the vision of the Son of man who announces redemption for all creation (13:26), we are again told of the Saviour that "he

[6] H. C. O. Lanchester: R. H. Charles, *Apocrypha* II, pp. 373 seq. The translation given here takes notice also of A. Kurfess, *Sibyllinische Weissagungen* (Tusculum-Bücherei) 1951.

ascends to the summit of mount Sion. Then Sion comes again and is revealed to all men, completely re-established" (13:35 seq.). However these extracts may vary, the ancient national hope runs through them like an underground river, flowing continuously onwards.

We should naturally expect to discover it in learned Jewish writings but here the high esteem for the Torah and its formal piety, closely associated with it, have coloured and transformed the *basileia* theme in a particular way. Yet the old national heritage is preserved and fused with the theology of the Torah. To begin with, we should observe how the idea of the kingship of God is systematically emphasized. The old Aramaic versions, the Targums, which both comment upon and clarify the Hebrew text, speak readily of the kingship of God and notably in the abstract of God's "kingship" *(malkhutha)*.

The Targum quotes Mich. 4:7, "Yahweh will reign as king" with the comment, "The royal kingship of God will be made manifest".[7] This makes it evident that the term "God's kingship" (or if the divine name be avoided "the kingship of heaven") does not describe a kingdom but indicates the exercise of God's kingly power. God's kingship will be "manifested" eschatologically, that is God will then be fully proclaimed in his dominion over Israel and the world. Late Judaism was fond of these abstractions in place of the concrete verb. The expression "God's reign" became at this period a technical term. Passages which dealt with God's kingship were called by the rabbis *malkhiyyoth*.

The rabbis demanded that the kingship of God should be an object of unceasing praise. "A blessing which does not invoke

[7] Dalman, *Worte Jesu* I, p. 83 with further examples; cf. also Billerbeck I, 179.

God's kingship is no real blessing."[8] It was laid down by the Mischnah that at the New Year's feast men should pronounce no less than ten *malkhiyyoth* sentences (in honour of the kingship of God).[9]

If we study the contents of this literature which stresses more definitely the concept of a kingship of God, unfading and ceaselessly exerting its influence, we find that it also emphasizes the hope of a reign of God established over Israel, quite in accord with the old national eschatology. The Targums apply many scriptural passages to the Messias; they see in them a reference to the Messias who is to come with divine power, overthrow foreign rule and set up the kingdom of Israel.[10] The rabbis expect the full realization of God's kingship over Israel to be achieved with the Messianic era. This is how R. Jose, the Galilean (c. A.D. 110) understands the Imperfect tense in Exod. 15:18, which signifies "Yahweh is king" as a Future and adds the following comment: "If the Israelites by the sea had said, Yahweh has become king for ever (perfect), then no nation and tongue could have had power over them: what they said was, Yahweh will be king for ever and ever, namely in the future."[11] Therefore, Israel does not yet enjoy God's unrestricted reign but this hope remains for the future. R. Elieser ben Hyrcanus (c. A.D. 90) deals with the "When" and "How" at the stage of the deepest humiliation under the Roman yoke: "When will this name (that of Rome) be rooted out? When the worship of idols is uprooted with its worshippers, and when God is alone in the world and his reign is for ever, in that hour

[8] *B. Ber.* 12 a (Goldschmidt. Smaller Edition, I, p. 50).
[9] *Rosh ha-shana* IV, 6 a (Fiebig, p. 103).
[10] In fuller detail, in v. Gall op. cit., pp. 397–400; also Mowinckel, op. cit., pp. 282 seq.
[11] *Mekh. Exod.* 15:18: consult Billerbeck I, 179.

will Yahweh sally forth and fight with these pagans . . . . Then will Yahweh be king over the entire earth."[12] Israel's triumph is more vigorously expressed in the Midrash to Psalm 99. For the verse of the psalm, "Yahweh has entered upon his kingdom, the peoples are shaken" R. Jehuda (ben Simon, 320) proposes this explanation in the name of R. Shemuel (ben Nachman, c. 260): "As long as the Israelites are in exile, God's reign is not fully achieved, and the peoples of the world remain undisturbed. But once Israel is redeemed, God's reign is complete and the peoples of the world tremble." The Targum on Abd. 21 has this sentence: "Deliverers will ascend mount Sion, to judge the great city of Esau (Rome); the rule of Yahweh will manifest itself over all dwellers on earth, and Yahweh's kingly reign will endure for ever."[13]

If to conclude we examine the particular sects, the Qumran texts are of particular interest. They rarely have the expression "royal reign" *(malkhuth)* of God but the idea is none the less present. We read in the "war roll" (IQM. VI, 6): "But to the God of Israel will belong the kingship, and he will give strength to the saints among his people"; and in another passage (IQM. XIX, 5–8): "Sion, rejoice exceedingly and exult, all cities of Judah . . . . The possessions of the peoples and their kings will serve thee, and they will bow before thee . . . . Daughters of my people, speak with joyous voice, adorn yourselves with radiance . . . . Israel will be an everlasting kingdom."[14] In the so-called appendix to the rules for the sect a blessing for the high priest

[12] *Mekh. Exod.* 17:14; consult Billerbeck, ibid.

[13] Also quoted by Billerbeck, 1. c.

[14] The translation of these passages from the "war roll" (IQM) are taken from H. Bardtke in *Th.L.Z.* 80 (1955), pp. 401–20. The dots indicate gaps in the text, and the square brackets attempted emendations by Bardtke.

includes these words: "May the Lord present to thee everlasting peace and the kingdom *(malkhuth)*" . . . unfortunately the text breaks off at this point.[15]

Yet in these texts the notion of God's reign is treated differently. A familiar theme is praise of the sovereign power governing and pervading all creation, especially in the hymns of praise *(Hodayoth)*. According to IQH. XIII the works of creation announce God's honour through his "rule". There is also another term, *memshala,* which is employed synonymously. We are surprised to find a further and by no means infrequent manner of speaking of God's angels and saints in heaven as in his "reign", with the consequence that heaven appears to be God's particular dominion. This is made clear from the parallelism in IQM. XII, 1 seq.: "For an assembly of saints is [for thee] in heaven and hosts of angels in thy holy rule *(z'bul)*... and the elect of the holy people thou hast set among [the heroes and the number] of the names of the entire host are with thee in the place of thy holiness and . . . in thy glorious rule *(z'bul)*."

But *memshala* and *malkhuth* seem to have the same significance. A few lines subsequently, we read (IQM. XII, 7): "But thou, O God, art [honoured] in the glory of thy royal rule *(malkhuth)* and the community of thy saints is in our midst for everlasting aid". In a further passage (IQM. I, 14 seq.) we read: "And in the seventh lot God's mighty hand casts down [the army of Belial] beneath all the angels of his kingdom *(memshala)* and all men [of his choice]." Heaven is therefore not an exclusive "kingdom" of God but a special realm where God's kingship is acknowledged. For the rest, the host of heaven fights together with the elect on earth and gives these a share in heavenly glory. Finally,

[15] *IQS b III, 5:* consult D. Barthélemy - J. T. Milik, *Qumran Cave* I (Oxford, 1955), p. 123.

in the Qumran texts God's rule over heaven, creation and (on his eschatological triumph) over the world of men is one whole. An all-embracing note of praise is found in IQH. X, 8: "Thou art the prince of the angels, and the king of all in glory; thou art the lord of every spirit and the ruler over all creatures."

More important than the vocabulary is the theological notion behind this conception of the "warfare between the sons of darkness and the sons of light". It is difficult to interpret the details provided in a purely symbolic sense and they must therefore be looked upon as indications of holy war. The date of this roll is disputed but its origin must be sought in a very early period, close to that of the Maccabees.[16] The work preserves the martial spirit of that epoch and expresses men's belief that they must have recourse to arms for God's kingship and its victory, assured of God's assistance and that of his angelic hosts.

If this view be accepted of the earlier period of the Qumran community or other related groups, the later Zealots who were contemporaries of Jesus and the Jewish War appear in another light.[17] These are no mere champions of political

[16] L. Rost in *Th.L.Z.* 80 (1955), pp. 205–8; the same in *Ev.Th.* 18 (1958), p. 108; a different dating, namely during the Roman period, in Y. Yadin, *The Scroll of the War* (Jerusalem 1955) (critical comment by F. Nötscher in *B. Z.* 1957, p. 153); also J. T. Milik, *Dix ans de découvertes dans le désert de Juda* (Paris 1957), pp. 109 seq., who sees in IQM an "Essenism with Zealot characteristics" and contemporary with Jesus (pp. 58–62). Whether the document be early or late, it shows indisputable traces of Zealot ideas. J. Carmignac, *La Règle de la Guerre . . .* (Paris 1958), XIII, attributes the work to the "Teacher of Justice" at the end of the second century, B.C.

[17] See W. R. Farmer, *Maccabees, Zealots and Josephus* (New York, 1956), who claims that the Zealots also held the position which we have been discussing.

freedom, no fanatical nationalists and wild rebels with no mercy for fellow—Jews holding contrary opinions. They were fighting for the kingship of God and the theocratic kingdom of Israel in the old spirit of the Maccabees. Judas the Galilean was therefore not a "sophist" who established "his own sect" that "had nothing to do with the others", as Flavius Josephus says,[18] but a man who entertained the ancient ideal common to all Jews faithful to the Law and who thought he could put it into practice in a way that the Pharisees repudiated, namely through open and armed revolt against Roman rule. It is probable that for some time the Qumran community had more peaceful intentions but the fact, proved by the archaeological remains discovered at Khirbet Qumran[19] that it must have taken an active part in the Jewish war shows that there was "a living continuity between the Maccabean era and that of the Zealots", Jewish nationalism "underwent no essential change between the period of the Maccabees and that of the Zealots".[20]

A glance at this evidence from varying sources reveals variants upon the common Jewish theme, the inheritance from the history and religion of Israel, and the universal hope; the memory of God's covenant with Israel and God's kingship established over Israel and the nostalgic turning towards the realm in which this kingship will manifest itself in its full radiance. There is a widespread expectation of the scion of David as Messias-king and of Jerusalem as the centre of his kingdom but also as the mount of God, to which the peoples will come in pilgrimage. From time to time the figure of the Saving Lord recedes into the background. At one moment God's rule is described more fully in terms of its moral and religious

[18] *Bell. Jud.* II, 118 (Niese VI, p. 176).
[19] R. de Vaux in *R.B.* 61 (1954) pp. 232–4 and *R.B.* 63 (1956), p. 567.
[20] Farmer, op. cit., pp. 169 and 171 (the main thesis of his book).

influence, at another moment less completely so. The manner of its advent is again variously foretold. In one passage it "appears" through God's exclusive intervention, as in the ancient prophecy; in another, it is established through the power of his Anointed; in yet others, the sons of Israel must arm themselves for the Holy War but they may reckon upon the assistance of the heavenly hosts. The longing for the Messianic kingdom of Israel continues to be felt among the people.[21] In time of need and struggle it grows and rises to an urgent, passionate appeal: Hasten, hasten, even in these our days shall God's reign be manifest!

5. The Rabbinical Teaching about the Reign of God, its Present Concealment and Future Manifestation

The Pharisees who were learned in the Scriptures had a more profound theological concept of God's kingly dominion. This comprehensive notion was based upon God's universal control of the world, as it was established through his creative act. God is the Lord of heaven and earth. The *'Alenu* prayer, which crystallizes and hands on the rabbinic concept of this kingship and was attributed[22] to the great scholar, Rab (more properly Abba Arikha, founder of the school at Sura on the Euphrates, d. about A.D. 247), begins as follows: "It is our duty to praise the lord of all, to magnify the creator of the world." In contrast to the heathens who worship what is null and vain, "we bow

[21] Bousset-Greßmann, *Religion des Judentums,* p. 233: "The specifically nationalist hope for a powerful earthly monarch always survived" among the broad masses of the people.

[22] The text is found in P. Fiebig, *Rosh ha-shana,* 49–51. It has been slightly altered in translation.

before, and adore, and thank the king of all kings, the Holy One; praise to him who has stretched out the heaven and established the earth: his glorious throne is in heaven above, and the abode of his power is in the height of heights".

These are the same familiar melodies which we discovered in Old Testament canticles and psalms and also in later Jewish writings. But what is the relation of this everlasting kingship of Yahweh over the whole creation, never abandoned or to be abandoned, his dominion fully acknowledged in heaven and extolled by the angels, to his kingship over men, over Israel and the peoples? This point had been particularly studied by the rabbis and their religion of the Law, which interpreted the Torah as Yahweh's special gift to Israel and at the same time the great responsibility imposed on it, was subordinated to this concept of the kingship. It is evident that God's claim to sovereignty is not yet recognized by the peoples. This is the particular prerogative of Israel on earth and it is realized through a faithful and unswerving monotheism and a zealous and continuous fulfilment of the Law even in its slightest details. The '*Alenu* prayer continues: "He is our God; there is no other. Our king is truth, there is nothing apart from him . . ." However, in their moral and religious efforts, the worshippers of the one true God also hope that Yahweh's kingship will one day show itself before the whole world, in the sight of all the peoples. The entire second part of this prayer is devoted to this hope: "Therefore, Yahweh, our God, we hope soon to see thee hasten in the garment of thy power, to banish idols from the earth; then shall those who deny thee be outrooted; to order the world through the rule *(malkhuth)* of the Almighty, and all children of man shall call upon thy name . . ."

This provides the theological framework for Israel's place among the nations. But Israel's history becomes one long object-lesson in the consequences of the kingship of God among men. The calling of the patriarchs, the election of God's people, the conclusion of the covenant on Sinai, Israel's own relation, so rich in variety and intensity, to the God of its covenant, all these are now subsumed under the idea of God's sovereign rule. A kind of redemptive theology of God's kingship starts to grow; Israel's thoughts about the glories and disasters of its history adjust themselves to this submission of Israel to its one monarch.[23] The generation of the Flood had thrown aside the commandments and the yoke of God (*Slav. Hen.* 34:1) and God's rule was effective only in heaven; but "Abraham made him king over heaven and earth."[24] The Midrash interpreted the 'then' of Exod. 15:1 in the sense that for the first time since the canticle of the sea, God's throne was established on earth (Ps. 92:2).[25] In Egypt and on Sinai Israel accepted God's kingship and bound itself in concluding the covenant to observe his commandments. In *Mekh. Exod.* 20:2 it is stated in greater detail that because of his benefits conferred on the people in the wilderness God had acquired a special claim to rule the Israelites as king. Their solemn assent expressed their unanimous readiness to welcome God's dominion with joy.[26] In these and similar explanations these scriptural experts readily turned to parallels with earthly monarchy. Before his rule over Israel Yahweh is a king who "abides"; then he has a throne upon which he "sits"; a monarch only issues his edicts after his subjects have acknowledged his rule. Solomon sat on Yahweh's

[23] For what follows, see Billerbeck I, 172–8.
[24] *Siphre Deut.* 32:10, 313; Billerbeck I, 173; Bonsirven, *Textes rabbiniques,* No. 355.
[25] *Ex rabba* 23:1: Billerbeck I, 173; S. M. Lehrman, *Midrash Rabbah* (ed. H. Freedman and M. Simon), *Exodus* (London, 1951), p. 279.
[26] Billerbeck I, 274; Bonsirven No. 132.

throne at a period of earthly theocracy. This was in retrospect idealized till it appears as a genuine reign over the world. "As God's throne rules from one end of the earth to the other, so also the throne of Solomon rules throughout the world."[27] But when the Israelites sinned, "the dominion was taken from them and given to the peoples of the world .... Tomorrow, as soon as the Israelites do penance, he takes it back from these peoples and restores it to Israel."[28]

It is surprising to discover many voices that recognize the godless "government of the earth", for instance Rab Shela (c. 220): "Praised be the God of mercy who hath given a government on earth that is like the government of heaven."[29] These moderate rabbis sought an accommodation with worldly power but God's overriding authority is never forgotten. The shepherds who misused their power, went beyond the commission allotted to them and slew more sheep than God had enjoined, will have to render an account to God and be punished (*Ethiop. Hen.* 90:22 seq.). Other commentators regard Israel's subjection to foreign conquerors as an intolerable disaster. R. Jochanan ben Sakkai condemns Israelites who desire to remain permanently enslaved. "He casts away the yoke of God's rule and takes upon himself the yoke of flesh and blood."[30] God's command is that "the Israelites are to be my servants, but not servants for other servants".[31]

God's royal rule remains for the time being partially concealed.

[27] *Midrash* H. L. I, I; Billerbeck I, 175; M. Simon, *Midrash Rabbah, Song of Songs* (London, 1951), p. 14.
[28] *Midrash Est.* I, 2; Billerbeck I, 175; M. Simon, *Midrash Rabbah, Esther* (London, 1951), p. 29.
[29] *Ber.* 58 a; Billerbeck I, 176; Goldschmidt I, p. 259.
[30] *P. Qid.* I, 2 (59 d); Billerbeck I, 176; Bonsirven No. 1557.
[31] *P. Qid.* 22, b: Billerbeck I, 176; Goldschmidt VI, p. 580.

It is no accident that his yearning for the eschatological kingship includes the statement that it will "appear", will "manifest itself". We can scarcely argue that it is pre-existent in heaven. "What exists and has always existed is God as ruler. The new element which time will bring is the manifestation of his rule."[32] Even though in their view the kingship of God is wholly supernatural, not affected by man and though his eschatological reign is to be realized exclusively through his will, the rabbis still consider they have something to contribute to the reign of God in the present by means of their active devotion to the Law; they can prepare the way for its recognition. This challenge of the kingship of God is strongly emphasized in the rabbinical tradition, as is seen from the expression "to take upon oneself the yoke of the heavenly rule (or kingdom)", an expression which gradually hardened into a fixed formula. We read towards the conclusion of the '*Alenu* prayer: "(All dwellers upon the earth) shall bow before thee, Yahweh, our God, and fall down in thy sight, and pay tribute to thy name's honour; they shall all take upon themselves the yoke of thy rule, and thou wilt rule over them for ever and ever." This stage has not yet been reached. But at least the Jew who serves God and observes the Law assumes "the yoke of the heavenly rule". In practice, this signifies the profession of monotheism and the Torah. R. Jehoshua ben Qarcha (c. A.D. 150) put the question: "Why (in the *Shema*) does the extract 'Hear, O Israel' (Deut. 6:4–9) precede the passage 'When you shall hear' (Deut.11:13 to 21)? In order that a man may first accept the yoke of God's rule (kingdom) and afterwards the yoke of the commandments."[33] God's rule and the Torah are therefore very intimately con-

[32] Dalman, *Worte Jesu* I, p. 83.

[33] *Ber.* II, 2 b; Billerbeck I, 177; O. Holtzmann, *Berakot* (Gießen, 1912), p. 49.

nected. "If the Israelites pay attention to the words of the Torah, given to them, then no nation and no (earthly) sovereignty can win power over them. And what does the Torah tell them? "Take upon yourselves the yoke of God's rule."[34] The proselyte who professes monotheism with all its practical implications (observation of the Torah) "takes on himself God's rule".[35] And since this resolution is expressed by every Jew in the *Shema,* the formula of belief and prayer to be recited twice each day, morning and evening, the phrase "to take upon oneself the rule of God" means formally the recitation of the *Shema.*[36] But behind the formula stands a deep moral earnestness as may be seen from the moving account of the martyr death of R. Akiba. They tore his flesh with combs of iron but he "took upon himself the rule (kingdom) of God," that is, he recited the *Shema.* When his pupils said to him, "Master, it is enough", he answered, "My whole life I have paid attention to this verse, 'Love Yahweh . . . with thy whole soul' (Deut. 6:5), even if he takes the soul, that is life, away. I wondered when I would have an opportunity of putting this verse into practice. Now that this opportunity has come, shall I not make use of it?"[37] Behind this is the theological conviction that God's reign becomes realized effectively whenever a man submits himself in obedience to the one God.

God's royal rule does not, however, remain wholly hidden in this world era. One passage enumerates four "reflections" of it: in Egypt, at the promulgation of the commandments, in the

[34] *Siphre Deut.* 32:29, § 323: Billerbeck I, 176 seq. (with a critique of the text); Bonsirven No. 362.
[35] See passages in Billerbeck I, 176.
[36] Billerbeck I, 177 seq.
[37] *Ber.* 61 b: Billerbeck I, 177; Goldschmidt I, p. 278: somewhat differently in *P. Ber.* IX, 5 (14 b); Bonsirven No. 467.

days of Gog and Magog, and in the period of the Messias.[38] Two of these belong already to the past, two are still awaited. This suggests that the reign of God manifests itself in a rhythm immanent in history. By "the days of the Messias" is meant the transient kingdom of the Messias which belongs to "this aeon" according to the new eschatology then developing.[39] The statements of individual rabbis on this point cannot be fully harmonized.

Wherever the national hope of the Messias-king, the Son of David, became very prominent, the purely supernatural character of the rule of God was endangered. Many rabbis, for example, considered they could hasten the days of the Messias and, as a consequence, of liberation, speed up their advent, through penance, observation of the commandments, study of the Torah and works of charity.[40] They were not speaking in that context of the eschatological kingdom of God but they awaited this after the Messianic era. The religion of the Law with its energy and drive is very noticeable here: men would like actively to intervene in the course of history which God is directing.

A point much discussed among the rabbis was whether redemption would come at a fixed historical point purely from God's mercy or only under the condition that Israel did penance.[41] In one passage Isaias, the teacher of Israel, is introduced as a

[38] *Siphre Deut.* 33:2, § 343; Billerbeck III, 833; Bonsirven No. 372; cf. Volz, *Eschatologie,* p. 167.

[39] Moore, *Judaism* II, pp. 375 seq.; Billerbeck IV, 816–21 with the proofs added. Billerbeck shows that the notion of a "future aeon" is very uncertain (threefold sense, 820); see further J. W. Bailey, *J.B.L.* 53 (1934), pp. 170–87.

[40] Billerbeck I, 599–601.

[41] Billerbeck I, 162–5.

speaker: "The morning comes for the just, and the night for the godless; the morning for Israel and the night for the peoples of the world. They inquired, When? And he replied. When you will, he will."[42] According to R. Elieser ben Hyrcanus and Rab, the redemption of the Israelites is made to depend upon penance or on penance and good works.[43] Penance had a very important function ascribed to it. To the Jewish mind, however, penance was not originally regarded as an "achievement" but as an appeal to divine mercy, but in the long run the rabbis could not avoid treating it as a meritorious work.[44] Many passages suggest that it has the power to hasten the Messianic redemption.[45] R. Levi (c. 300) declared: "If only the Israelites did one day's penance, they would be redeemed immediately, and the Son of David would come at once."[46] The same scholar speaks similarly about the observance of the Sabbath: "If the Israelites observed one Sabbath as it should be observed, the Son of David would come immediately."[47] This power of hastening redemption was also attributed to the study of the Torah and to works of charity. To be sure, the rabbis hold that God is sovereignly free in his dispositions but can he not look upon the human efforts of Israel as part of his plans? R. Jochanan (d. 279) expresses himself as follows: "God spoke to the Israelites: Since I have appointed for the end (that is, for the days of the Messias) a definite time when he is to come, whether you do penance or not, so he will come at the appointed

[42] *P. Ta'an.* I (64 a); Billerbeck I, 164.
[43] *Sanh.* 97 b; Billerbeck I, 600; Goldschmidt IX, p. 68.
[44] E. Sjöberg, *Gott und die Sünder im palästinischen Judentum* (Stuttgart-Berlin, 1938), pp. 144–53; 154–69.
[45] *Yoma* 86 b; Billerbeck I, 599; Goldschmidt III, p. 255.
[46] *Midrash H. L.* 5, 2 and *Pesiq* 163 b; Billerbeck I, 599.
[47] *P. Ta'an* I (64 a); Billerbeck I, 600.

hour. But if you do penance, if only for a single day, then I will permit him to come exceptionally, before the appointed time"; see Ps. 95:7, "Today when you hear his voice."[48] These passages reveal the theological problems which rose from the very principles of the religion of the Law.

The rabbinic concept of this heavenly reign has both its nobility and its limitations. The former consists in the purely ethical and religious demands it makes on men, and in the fact that its eschatological manifestation is conceived as purely religious, "one of the few, if not the only strictly religious concept in later Judaism".[49] In principle, therefore, earthly national and political hopes were excluded. In point of fact, the national longing for the Messias from the family of David runs parallel with it, and wishful dreams of a worldly kind are associated with it. There is always the danger of putting too much weight on the human factor, of too great an emphasis upon and pride in the human effort. The perfect rule of God will reveal itself at the end of time, in other words, will be inaugurated solely through the divine will. But men imagine they can hasten on the "days of the Messias". The religion of the Law, in its severity and exigence, lays down the conditions which God's reign imposes on men. But nowhere do we read that this shows itself as grace and salvation for the wretched and for sinners. And so its demands, as laid down by the Torah, can become an oppressive yoke (Matt. 23:4; 11:28–30).

[48] *Ex rabba* 25:12; Billerbeck I, 600; Lehrman, *Midrash Rabbah, Exodus,* p. 315.
[49] K. G. Kuhn in *Th.W.B.* I, p. 753, 8 seq.

6. The Apocalyptic Expectation of the Universal and Cosmic Reign of God

One notion of the kingship of God diverging considerably from those we have been considering and found only partially and indistinctly in them becomes prominent in apocalyptic literature. The national hope was directed largely towards an earthly Messianic kingdom, in which according to many passages a leading part is to be played by the Messias from the house of David. This happy future of Israel was characterized by peace and relief from suffering, the fertility of the land and abundance of children, length of life and also by justice and holiness, piety and religious devotion even among the heathens who come as pilgrims to Jerusalem. But they were not envisaging a completely different world, an earth transformed in a heavenly sense, a transfigured universe. The picture of a transfigured eschatological world grew out of an apocalyptic mentality.[50] The reign of God in its turn was involved in this movement in the history of ideas. Although several trends of thought meet in the apocalyptic writings and the ancient national hope is to some degree accepted, especially in the *Syriac Baruch* and the *Fourth Book of Esdras*, we are right in considering the apocalyptic concept of God's kingship as a special type of its own.

The many-sided Jewish hope of redemption can be reduced to these two fundamental forms: the national and Messianic, and the cosmic and eschatological. These two currents originally independent gradually intermingled without ever achieving

[50] Volz, *Eschatologie*, pp. 4–10; H. H. Rowley, *The Relevance of Apocalyptic* (2nd edition, London, 1947), pp. 11–50 (Lit.); S. B. Frost, *Old Testament Apocalyptic, its Origin and Growth* (London, 1952); J. Bloch, *On the Apocalyptic in Judaism* (Philadelphia, 1952).

complete harmony. At the commencement of the Christian era the two great apocalypses, the *Apocalypse of Baruch* and the *Fourth Book of Esdras,* and contemporary rabbis made a distinction between these various strands of tradition; the "days of the Messias" belonging to the present aeon were given a position in the time sequence; they were followed by the mighty final happenings, Resurrection and Judgment, when the future aeon began.[51] We are not here concerned with the difficult evolution of Jewish eschatology which was never systematically worked out. Our purpose is to recognize the particular notes of this cosmic apocalyptic concept of the reign of God, to let them speak for themselves and to study the particular ideas of the apocalyptic writers.

The Book of Daniel may fairly be taken as the original pattern for apocalypses and it already portrays the heavenly and cosmic character of the eschatological kingdom of God. Chapter two applies Nabuchodonosor's dream of the column with its different metals to the four world empires which succeed one another but are eventually destroyed. "In the days of those kingdoms the God of heaven will set up a kingdom that shall never be destroyed. And his kingdom shall not be delivered up to another people. And it shall break in pieces and shall consume all these kingdoms and itself shall stand for ever" (2:44). God himself intervenes and destroys the world empires as is shown by the stone "cut out of the mountain without hands" which shatters the column.

The heavenly origin and character of God's eschatological reign emerges even more clearly in the vision of the four beasts and the "one who is like the Son of man" in chapter 7. After the

[51] Moore, *Judaism* II, pp. 323 seq.; 374 seq.; Billerbeck IV, 808 seq.; Mowinckel op. cit., pp. 274–8.

judgment passed on the beasts at the heavenly assize (vv. 9–12) there appeared "one like the Son of man", and with the clouds of heaven – the whole scene takes place in the heavens – and "(God) gave him power and glory and a kingdom; all peoples, tribes and tongues shall serve him. His power is an everlasting power that shall not be taken away, and his kingdom one that will not be destroyed" (v. 14). The vision does not inform us where and how this dominion is to be exercised but the "interpretation" adds that full authority over all kingdoms under heaven will be entrusted to the "people of the saints of the Most High" (v. 27). There can be scarcely any doubt that Daniel is envisaging the people of Israel at the end of time but still attached to its national hope, as also in the later visions of the seventy weeks of years (9:20–27) and in chapters 10 to 12. But no description is offered of the Messianic kingdom. Sufficient that it is the perfect and universal dominion of God, to which the wise and the just awake (12:3). However we interpret the "Son of man", he is in no sense an earthly saviour who wages war in God's name and exercises justice. He is a heavenly and pre-existent being.

These traits are even more marked in the so-called *Book of Parables of Henoch* (*Ethiopic Henoch,* 37–71). The community of the just becomes "visible" (38:1); (earthly) kings and rulers will then be annihilated and delivered into the hands of the just and saintly (38:5). God's "chosen one" sits upon the throne of glory and no man can number the dwelling places of the elect. "Then I allow my chosen one to dwell among them, and I transform heaven to an everlasting blessing and light. And I transfigure the earth to blessedness. Then I permit my chosen ones to abide there but sinners and evil-doers must not walk upon it" (45:3–5). Both heaven and earth are transformed by God's own operation; the elect dwell there and rule with the Saviour who is called now "chosen one" and now "Son of man".[52] "The chosen one sits in those days upon my throne and from his mouth stream forth all the secrets of wisdom and counsel; for the Lord of the spirits gives this to him and glorifies him. In those days the mountains leap like rams, the hills frisk like lambs, fed with milk, the countenances of the angels in heaven are bright with joy" (51:3 seq.). Eschatological joy fills heaven and earth; there is a new world after the resurrection of the dead (51:1); the just and elect dwell, it is true, upon earth but on a new and transfigured earth. "The just then are in the sun's radiance and the elect in the light of everlasting life" (58:3). "The Lord of spirits dwells above them and they eat with the Son of man . . ." (62:14). This glorification of the blessed occurs after the resurrection. "The just and elect rise from the earth and cease to cast down their gaze. They will be garmented with the robes of glory and these are the robes of life from the Lord of spirits" (62:15 seq.). This is a vision and portrayal of the full and imperishable glory of the world to come (58:3; 62:16). It is realized only by the just and the elect. There is no mention of Israel. The purely religious note appears in the judgment passed upon the kings and rulers of the earth. Those who merely sought power and built upon it must now recognize and confess before the Lord of spirits that their guilt lay in their contempt of his sovereignty and in their sins (63:7–10). Now they praise and glorify him: "Praised is the Lord of spirits, the Lord of kings, the Lord of the mighty, the Lord of rulers, the Lord of glory and the Lord of wisdom, before whom all mysteries remain

[52] 46:24; 48:2; 62:7, 9, 14; 63:11; 69:26 seq.; 70:1; 71:14, 17. Cf. v. Gall, op. cit., pp. 420 seq.; R. Otto, *Reich Gottes,* pp. 132–70; E. Sjöberg, *Der Menschensohn im äth. Henochbuch* (Lit); T. W. Manson, "The Son of Man in Daniel, Enoch and the Gospels" in *B.J.R.L* 32 (1950), pp. 171–93; Mowinckel, op. cit., pp. 353–6; 358–450 passim.

open. May thy power endure from generation to generation, and thy glory from eternity unto eternity . . ." (63:2 seq.).

These apocalypses place the strongest possible emphasis on God's sovereign action and his final intervention without any co-operation on man's part. In the *Assumption of Moses* 10:1 God's kingship "appears" above all creatures and, in 10:7, "the All Highest, the eternal God, rises alone" (that is, without assistants or instruments) and "advances openly" to punish the heathen and to destroy all their idols. The *Ethiopic Henoch* (1:3) describes God's assumption of power at his own decision in the following words: "The holy and mighty one will come forth from his dwelling, the eternal God will tread the earth on mount Sinai and appear from heaven in the strength of his power." He "comes" with myriads of "holy ones" (angels) to pass judgment upon all and to annihilate all the godless (v. 9). In another part of the *Book of Henoch* that is predominantly ethical and admonitory in character (cc 91–105) sinners and the godless, the wealthy and the violent are continually threatened with this sudden and unexpected judgment (94:6–11; 97:2–5; 99:9; 102:1). The just are to pray that judgment may come. "Only pray, pray for the judgment, and it will be realized: for God will visit all your suffering upon the rulers and their agents who have exploited you" (104:3). The Sibyl also thinks of God as bringing a swift judgment: "Judgment will come upon you from the mighty God, and all will perish at the hand of the Immortal One" (*Sib.* III, 670 seq.). According to the *Sibylline Oracles* (V, 348) God assumes the direction of things (ἡγεμονεύσῃ). This is an exclusively divine action as on the morning of creation. "Through myself alone and no other were (the works of creation) fashioned: so too will the end arrive through myself alone and through no other" (4 *Esdras* 6:6). The great vision of the eagle in the *Fourth Book of Esdras* (chapter 11) allots a rôle in the final drama to the Messias (the lion) but it is not the decisive rôle. He accuses the godless power of the world and its representatives of their sins and brings them before God's judgment "but the one who 'sets its bounds' to the last kingdom of the world, banishes the eagle, that is its last head and holds judgment, is God himself" (11:39, 44 seq. – somewhat differently in the interpretation given in 12:31–34). God's glory is made visible (*Syr. Bar.* 21:23, 25): and this alone signifies the end of the worldly powers, terror in heaven and on earth (*Eth. Hen.* 102:3; 4 *Esdras* 8:51) judgment (4 *Esdras* 7:87) and blessedness (*Eth. Hen.* 25:3; 4 *Esdras* 8:51 seq.).

As regards the place in which salvation is to be realized the data vary and remain often indefinite. But in contrast to the national eschatology which focuses on Palestine and the earthly Jerusalem, there is a marked tendency as we have already noted in the *Parables of Henoch,* to introduce a new and purified earth, a transfigured cosmos, the heavenly Jerusalem and paradise as the abode of the elect and the blessed. The *Assumption of Moses* declares that Israel will rise aloft, that God will elevate her and set her in the starry firmament, and from above she will look down upon the hell of her enemies (*Ass. Mos.* 10:8–10). In the *Slavonic Henoch (The Secrets of Henoch)* where the individual eschatology is more fully developed, Henoch on his journey through heaven beholds the dwelling place of the just in the third heaven "in the midst of paradise, in a place beautiful beyond all description" (8:1 – Vaillant, chap V, p. 9). The same visionary describes the end of time in a completely unearthly manner. Seasons and time disappear; there is "one aeon only", and in this great aeon the just are gathered together and become immortal. They have no more weariness, sickness, anxiety or need but only "great light". They will occupy a great rampart that cannot be destroyed (against the region of the wicked?) and a bright paradise that cannot pass away. Then all perishable things vanish and all that remains will be everlasting life (65:6–10 – Vaillant chap. XVII, p. 63). Even though the influence of Hellenistic thought here is unmistakable[53] this transference to the heavenly regions is striking enough. Favourite images to represent salvation are light, life, glory, all the attributes which express a transformed condition. The account in the *Syriac Apocalypse of Baruch* (51) is particularly detailed. The faces of the just are transformed till they shine in the radiance of their beauty; they thus become able to receive the immortal world they have been promised (v. 3). Their abode is in the heights of that world, they are like angels and stars. They change into all possible forms, as they wish, from beauty to loveliness, from light to the splendour of glory (v. 10). We find similar imagery in the *Book of Parables (Ethiopic Henoch)*. The Book of Wisdom employs the simile of a crown: "Accordingly they will receive the royal crown of glory and the diadem of beauty from the Lord's hand" (5:16). Theirs is also the dignity of rulers: "They shine forth at the final judgment and are like sparks that blaze in fields of stubble. They will judge peoples, rule over nations and the Lord will be eternally their king" (3:7 seq.).

The concept of God's rule in which the faithful have their share is thus maintained but at the same time spiritualized and raised above the temporal level. But it is worth noting that in passages like these which place more emphasis on the happiness of the individual and treat his ethical behaviour as the one standard of salvation, the idea of membership of the people of Israel increasingly recedes. The company of the redeemed con-

[53] Charles, *Apocrypha* II, p. 426; A. Vaillant, *Le livre des secrets d'Hénoch* (Paris 1952), chap. XII seq.

sists of the just and elect who have stood firm in the severe trials of the final era of testing. "As gold in the furnace he hath proved them, and as a victim of a holocaust he hath received them" (Wisd. 3:6). Experience among his own people and in the Diaspora may have contributed to this. Men came to recognize sinners and godless in their own community, with whom the faithful observers of the Law were frequently contrasted (for example, the Pharisees, the Qumran community),[54] and they discovered godfearing heathens in the Diaspora. And so the lines of demarcation in the eschatological company of the saved are altered. Even if many apocalypses distinguish merely between the just and sinners, the door to salvation which it must be confessed the majority of the rabbis never closed to them,[55] is opened more easily for good and devout pagans.

As regards the salvation of all Israelites, the prevalent opinion of the rabbis was that only the just had a part in the future aeon and that sinners could reckon on divine mercy only through repentance.[56] Yet the conviction kept recurring that the whole of Israel would indeed be saved because of the signs of divine grace and the privileges (descent from Abraham, circumcision, possession of the Torah, merits of the fathers etc.) (cf. also *Rom.* 9-11; *Sanh.* X, 1a.). In excluding these privileges and demand-

[54] *Eth. Hen.* 94–102; also *Book of Parables,* 38:1, 3; 41:2; 45:25 seq. and others; *Ass. Mos.* 7:3 seq.; *Abr.* 31:6–10 and elsewhere. For rabbinical notions: *Abot* III (K. Marti and G. Beer, *Abot*, Gießen 1927, pp. 76 seq.); *Sanh.* 10, 1 (S. Krauss, *Sanhedrin-Makkot*, Gießen 1933, pp. 266–72).
[55] Cf. the debate between R. Elieser ben Hyrcanus and R. Jehoshua ben Chananya in *Tos. Sanh.* 13, 2 (Billerbeck IV, 1180; Bonsirven No. 1930). R. Elieser ben Hyrcanus would allow the heathens no share at all in the world to come. R. Jehoshua recognized that there were also just men among the heathens who would have a share in it. In the opinion of Moore, *Judaism* II, p. 386, the latter was the prevailing view.
[56] Sjöberg, *Gott und die Sünder,* pp. 109–44.

ing purely moral standards the writers of apocalypses seem to have advanced a considerable step further.[57] The apostacy and guilt of many of their correligionaries frequently raised an imperative question: who then will be saved? (4 *Esdras* 7:10 seq., 46 seq.). The problem of the destiny of well-disposed pagans was not often explicitly introduced and, when it did emerge, it was usually answered in the sense of the pilgrimage of the nations to Sion (*Eth. Hen.* 10:21; 90:30–3; *Sib.* III, 710–23; V, 420–33; *Syr. Bar.* 68:5). In the assessment of good works, however, each individual is examined and judged without regard to person (4 *Esdras* 1:33; *Syr. Bar.* 51; *Sib.* IV, 40–6; *Slav. Hen.* 65:6 seq.). There were also many rabbinic voices which assured pagans of the divine mercy for their works of charity.[58]

The moral basis of the apocalypses inevitably tended towards belief in the universal salvation of all who were good. Men of goodwill draw more closely to one another in this permanently wicked world. We read in the *Syriac Apocalypse of Baruch*: "This world came into existence for your sake (that of the good); for your sake too the world to come will appear" (15:7). But the "Son of man" – after the pattern of the Servant of God in Deutero-Isaias (Isa. 42:6; 49:6) – becomes also in Henoch's pictures the "light of the pagans"; "He will be a staff for the just on which they may lean and not fall; He will be a light for the peoples and the hope of the oppressed" (*Eth. Hen.* 48:4).

[57] Sjöberg, op. cit., pp. 224–50. Commenting on apocalyptic literature the author observes that "the accompanying notion that all Israelites would have a share in the future era is not present" (p. 224, note 1).

[58] R. Jochanan ben Sakkai, with many others who influenced him, declared: "As sacrifice provides atonement for Israelites, so the activity of good works brings atonement to the peoples of the world" (*Baba bathra* 10 b; Goldschmidt VIII, p. 40). Further examples in Volz, *Eschatologie*, p. 283; Moore, *Judaism* I, p. 279.

This apocalyptic writing seems, therefore, to have reached a lofty and pure conception of God's eschatological reign. Yet this picture, purified and widened though it be, is marred by a number of typical "apocalyptic" features. Their warm longing for redemption and the consciousness that they were living in the Last Age[59] tempted them to seek an insight into the mysteries of God. If God has determined when the end shall come, and the time is fulfilled,[60] they think they can reckon the advent of this final stage and recognize the signs that precede it. Accordingly, they divide the history of the world into periods, on the lines of the four world empires (Dan. 2:37–45, ibid. 7; 4 *Esdras* 11 seq.; *Syr. Bar.* 36–40; in rabbinical theology also, *Siphre Deut.* 32: 11; *Mekh. Exod.* 20:18) or according to weeks of years and jubilees, seven times seven, as the *Book of Jubilees* does; or after the seventy shepherds of the peoples (*Eth. Hen.* 89 seq.), or after ten (*Apocalypse of Weeks,* in *Ethiopic Henoch* 93; 91:12, 17; *Sib.* IV, 47 seq.) or in some cases twelve epochs (4 *Esdras* 14:11 seq.; *Syr. Bar.* 53 seq.; *Abr.* 29:2). They inquire how much of the course of world history has elapsed and then work out the conclusion. On this point as on others Daniel with his seventy weeks of years is the spiritual father of the writers of apocalypses. The final week of years is halved and it appears that only three and a half years are left.[61] According to 4 *Esdras* 14:11 seq., nine and a

[59] *Esdras* 4:38–43; 8:61; 14:10–12; *Syr.Bar.* 23:7; 82:2 and others.
[60] Tob. 14:5 *Dam.* IV, 8, 10; frequently in the Qumran texts, for example, IQS IV, 18, 25; IQpHab VII, 2, 13. One finds the parallel notion that a fixed number of (just) men must be attained, *Syr. Bar.* 23:5; 4 *Esdras* 4:36; also IQH 1:18 seq.
[61] Dan. 9:24–27. Similarly, in 12:11 a concrete number is given: 1290 days – a little more than three and a half years – will pass after the daily sacrifice is suppressed and the "abomination of desolation" is set up; in 12:12 the man is lauded who holds out and reaches 1335 days, that is 45 days longer.

half of the twelve periods are struck off, only two and a half are still outstanding. The meaning remains obscure and is reserved for the authors of "secret books". At times it is applied to actual occurrences and to the march of events (4 *Esdras* 12:11 seq.).

In addition to these divisions and assessments of time portents play an important rôle. "When thou shalt see that a portion of these signs has now occurred, then mayst thou know that this is the time when the All-highest will visit the world which he has made. As soon as earthquakes occur and the peoples are confused and the masses fight among themselves and rulers fall and princes are bewildered, then shalt thou observe that the All-highest hath proclaimed this from the earliest days. Then, as the beginning of all things in the world is made clear and the end revealed, so also are the times of the All-highest; their beginnings are manifested through wonders and power, and their end through deeds and signs" (4 *Esdras* 9:1-6).[62] This extract shows that men were looking for definite events in this last period of frightful affliction (Dan. 12:1), among them a final general onslaught of the evil forces of the world against Jerusalem (*Eth. Hen.* 56; 4 *Esdras* 13; *Sib.* III, 663 seq.) - a further development of the ancient prophecy of Gog (Ezech. 38 seq.) which was frequently commented upon by the rabbis.[63] The *Book of Jubilees* which is not explicitly apocalyptic describes all generations which "from now on will arise until the great day of judgment" in the following terms: "Plague follows on plague, wound on wound, sadness upon sadness, evil report after evil report, sickness after sickness and other sore punishments, one after the other, sickness,

[62] The latter portion of this passage is textually uncertain. The translation follows B. Violet, *Die Apokalypsen des Esdra und des Baruch in deutscher Gestalt* (G.C.S 32) (Leipzig 1924), pp. 123 seq.

[63] Greßmann, *Der Messias,* pp. 118–34; Billerbeck III, 831–40; Volz, *Eschatologie,* pp. 150–2; K. C. Kuhn in *Th.W.B.* I, pp. 790–2.

upheaval, snow, frost, ice, fever, cold, stiffness, hardship, death, sword, captivity and every kind of pest and suffering" (*Jub.* 23:13). "All this comes upon the evil generation which is sinning on earth" (v. 14). This ancient pattern is applied in the apocalypses to the final period of affliction, and amplified.

The *Syriac Apocalypse of Baruch* enlarges it to twelve stages of affliction, which end by mingling with, extending and intensifying one another, "so that the dwellers upon earth do not observe that it is the end of time". The *Apocalypse of Abraham,* clearly modelling itself on the plagues of Egypt, records ten plagues which God is preparing for the pagan world, when the twelfth and final hour is struck on earth: the tenth plague brings thunder, voices and a destructive earthquake (chapter 30). The *Sibylline Oracles* III, 528–44, speak finally of a blazing fire which God will send on earth and from which only a third of mankind will escape with their lives. Hand in hand with this runs an increasing deterioration of mankind which (*Sib.* IV, 152–61) we are told, makes it clear that God, in the fury of his wrath, will annihilate mankind through a mighty conflagration. The course of nature is altered, the strangest situations are to be seen. Injustice and folly prevail (4 *Esdras* 5:1–12). The whole of creation is shaken (*Syr. Bar.* 32:1), the order of the stars is disturbed (*Eth. Hen.* 80:4–7), a baleful comet appears (*Sib.* III, 334 seq.). Swords are observed in the night sky, a cloud of dust falls from the heavens, there is a rain of blood, and stones begin to speak (*Sib.* III, 796 seq.). All these elements: this dwelling on fantastic and fearsome pictures, this conscious stirring of anxiety and fear, the descent into a mood of complete defeatism, the boast of a special apocalyptic gnosis (4 *Esdras* 14; *Syr. Bar.* 86 seq.; *Sib.* passim), this concealment from the people and revelation to the *illuminati* "in whom flow the spring of insight, the source of wisdom and the stream of knowledge" (4 *Esdras*

14:47), the pride of the elect and their scorn for the *massa damnata,* their very spirit of revenge and their perverted joy in the annihilation of the wicked: all these are dark shadows on an otherwise bright picture of the fulfilment of the world and a blemish in the apocalyptic authors who composed them. However noble their conception of the kingship of God, it betrays a human pettiness and narrowness that are quite unbecoming in the "elect". Their apocalyptic excess of fervour and the way in which they calculate and reckon the advent of God's reign do serious damage to the genuine vision of transformation found in many places in their literature.

II

The Reign of God in the Preaching of Jesus

GENERAL CHARACTERISTICS OF THE REIGN AND KINGDOM OF GOD AS PROCLAIMED BY JESUS

7. The Eschatological Character of the Reign of God

The evangelist Mark sums up the initial proclamation of Jesus in these words: "The time is accomplished and the kingdom (reign) of God is at hand. Repent and believe the gospel" (Mark 1:15). Before we examine the content of these sentences, we must ask ourselves whether the evangelist is here putting his finger on the central point in Jesus' redemptive teaching. Were these tidings that the reign of God was close at hand what caught men's attention and brought him such crowds to listen to him? The strong and vivid impression which the words of Jesus made on his Jewish contemporaries were connected not with this proclamation (κηρύσσειν) but rather with his teaching (διδάσκειν). "And they were astonished at his doctrine, for he was teaching them as one having power and not as the Scribes" (Mark 1:22). The teaching of Jesus was of course much wider than what immediately concerned the kingship of God. We never hear that Jesus explained this concept to them; he takes it for granted and makes a "proclamation" about it. A review of all that we possess of the preaching of Jesus shows that it includes a great deal not directly concerned with the reign of God. The *Formgeschichte* (Form Criticism) school distinguishes different categories in the words of our Lord, for example, proverbs, prophetic sayings, juridical decisions, personal statements and parables.[1] In his teaching of which we possess abundant testimony, especially in the synagogues, Jesus adopted the external habits of teachers of the Law (Luke 4:18 seq.). He proposed interpretations of scripture, decided legal questions, gave advice on religious life and employed picturesque images and similes as did teachers trained in the orthodox rabbinical schools. The special character in the teaching of Jesus is found perhaps in questions put by enquirers like the rich man, "What shall I do to gain eternal life?" (Mark 10:17) or about the great commandment (Mark 12:28 par.) or in the flattering compliment of an adversary, "Thou teachest the way of God in truth" (Mark 12:14 par). "The entire teaching of Jesus is directed to the ordering of man's life towards God and towards the neighbour."[2] Yet it is evident that the teaching of Jesus is not unrelated to his announcement that the reign of God is at hand and that it receives from this its coherent basis, its significance and its urgency.[3]

Because Jesus received the task of delivering a special eschatological announcement from God, his teaching goes outside any ordinary framework. His explanation of scripture, his exposition of God's will, all he says of God and God's attitude, his appeal to sinners as well as to the just and devout, his radical demands on every man in the sight of God: all this bears the marks and characteristics of his eschatological proclamation. On closer examination even the Sermon on the Mount is seen to fit completely into this pattern. Jesus does not lay down "principles of wisdom", detached from their historical setting, he

[1] So Bultmann, *Geschichte der synopt. Tradition*, pp. 73–222.

[2] K. H. Rengstorf in *Th.W.B.* II, p. 143, 1 seq.

[3] See here and in the following pages Schnackenburg, *Sittliche Botschaft*, 1st part.

gives no general rules of life and provides no doctrine of religion for its own sake. Everything is subordinated to the proclamation of the *basileia* and related to the mystery of his own person. The "teaching" is naturally connected with the "proclamation" (compare Mark 1:21 seq. with 1:38 seq.; 6:12 with 6:30) but is at its service. Jesus was not a teacher in the sense of the Scribes. He belonged rather to the prophets though he surpassed them in the absolute certainty of his speech, his fullness of divine authority, the harmony of his words and actions, in short, in his eschatological mission. He consequently never put himself among the teachers of the Torah and never trained his disciples to be rabbis. He called them to a special kind of discipleship.

Therefore, in spite of or rather because of Jesus' teaching we are led to the gospel of the reign of God as the focus of his preaching. To this both the width and the weight of tradition bear witness. To judge merely by external data, the expression reign or kingdom of God (βασιλεία τοῦ Θεοῦ) occurs about a hundred times in the synoptic gospels. In the remaining books of the New Testament the references are only one quarter of this total, even if we include kindred terms, for example, kingship of Christ.[4] The idea becomes less pronounced in the preaching of the early Church yet it is faithfully recorded as part of the preaching of Jesus: it is an echo of the manner in which Jesus spoke.

A short comment must be added on the use of the actual terms. In place of "kingdom of God" (βασιλεία τοῦ Θεοῦ) Matthew and only Matthew usually employs "kingdom of heaven" (βασιλεία τῶν οὐρανῶν) thirty-four times as opposed to

[4] Of these references seven are in the Acts, clearly a reminiscence of Luke; four in Paul in what even then was the rather formal expression "inherit the kingdom of God"; for the rest, consult the third part of this work.

three (19:24 is textually uncertain). This phrase is nothing more than a circumlocution for the divine name and is in line with rabbinical usage.[5] One may doubt whether Jesus himself spoke of "kingdom of God" or "of heaven". He had no hesitation in speaking of God directly but generally conformed to the prevalent custom of referring to God by implication (through the passive or in the third person plural etc.). Mark and Luke might have employed the expression "kingdom of God" deliberately to avoid misunderstandings among their Hellenistic readers, as the Septuagint[6] did but in Mark 11:30 seq. and Luke 15:7, 18, 21, they had no such problem. Since they remain faithful to this way of speaking, it was probably Matthew, who made frequent use of his rabbinical knowledge, who altered the expression for his Jewish Christian readers, but with the article, as he did with the term "righteousness" (δικαιοσύνη). The use of βασιλεία without the article is also peculiar to him except for one or two passages in Luke: Luke 12:32 (where it is immediately preceded by "your Father"); 22:29 (without article; it signifies "reign"); Acts 20:25 (with additions in manuscripts). Matthew's changes of terms are seen in phrases like "word of the *basileia*" (13:19), "sons of the *basileia*" (18:12; 13:38), "gospel of the *basileia*" (4:23; 9:35; 24:14). For the *basileia* of Jesus or of the Son of man see below, section 14.

But how could the reign or kingdom of God as proclaimed by Jesus provide a novel, extraordinary and exciting gospel? Because of the announcement that God's eschatological kingship was very close! It is abundantly clear from the first part of this book that

[5] In rabbinical literature מַלְכוּת שָׁמַיִם (that is, "reign of heaven") was a technical term (without an article). The Targums on the other hand use the form "reign of Yahweh", "his reign"; see K. G. Kuhn in *Th.W. B.* I, 570, pp. 1–26.

[6] So Dalman, *Worte Jesu* I, p. 77.

Jesus could take for granted among contemporary Jews the general belief that God would eventually enter upon his royal reign. How he wanted this kingship of God to be understood, in contrast to the many opinions then current, would have to be gathered from the rest of his teaching; it might be left, so to say, to further discourses and treatment. What attracted immediate attention from every class of society was the announcement that the time is accomplished and the reign of God is near at hand.

Our study of late Jewish opinion has established that the Jews spoke of God's kingship not only in an eschatological sense but that they retained also the ancient notion of his ever-present rule over Israel and the peoples as well as over heaven and earth and that all these ideas were preserved and intermingled also in rabbinical theology and Jewish-Hellenistic circles (cf. already Tobias 13–14) and popular devotion (liturgical prayers) and that they came to a head in the eschatological kingship of God. What was the position of Jesus here? It must be insisted emphatically that the idea of God's reign in his mouth referred always to God's eschatological kingship, though he was familiar with the notion of God's continuous government of the universe and took it for granted. But when he refers to the "reign of God" he is not dealing with this. His ordinary usage of this term applies to God's eschatological kingship and the texts should not be explained or toned down in a non-eschatological sense.

Only on one occasion do we detect a marginal echo of God's perpetual rule in creation, when he forbids swearing: "But I say to you, not to swear at all, neither by heaven for it is the throne of God, nor by the earth, for it is his footstool" (Matt. 5:34 seq.). With this Jesus soon associates the thought that God's kingship reveals itself or will reveal itself in a particular manner over Jerusalem. He continues: "nor by Jerusalem for it is the city of the great king."[7] This merely indicates how deeply Jesus is saturated with the piety of the psalms and how he draws upon it. Notions about God's kingly administration are taken as self-evident, even in his hymn of praise: "I thank thee Father, Lord of heaven . . ." (Matt. 11:25 and Luke 10:21) but this is not the content of the special gospel of the *basileia* proclaimed by Jesus.

As announced by Jesus, the reign of God is not an awareness of God's sovereign power over the universe or of God's kingship over Israel, long established and still enduring, though both these concepts are presupposed. It is the announcement of God's kingship in its full realization, fully active, eschatologically irrevocable.

We speak of the gospel of Jesus as "eschatological" not only because it contains an eschatological concept (that was true of the prophets and of later Judaism generally) but because it bears the mark of an eschatological event. The kingly rule of God has drawn nigh. Subsequently, in chapters two and three, we shall examine how exactly Jesus understood this "nearness", whether as the nearness, intensified by prophecy, of something still uncertain in the future or as something actually close or even present, so that the kingship of God is fully there in his operations or as something present and future at one and the same time. For the moment we must take notice of a number of facts and passages which leave no doubt at all about the eschatological character of the gospel of Jesus:

1. John's appeal for repentance and baptism is only to be

[7] J. Jeremias lays stress on this point, *Jesu Verheißung*, p. 60. He instances the description of God as the "great king" which is found four times in the Old Testament and in all four passages represents God as the Lord of the world, to whose kingly domain all the peoples belong. Accord-

explained from a Messianic and eschatological standpoint. His prophetic warnings focus on a judgment of God in the immediate future and they announced a "stronger man" who would follow him (Matt. 3:7–10 and Luke 3:7–9). But, however his relation to John be envisaged, Jesus acknowledged the person and efforts of the great Baptist, confirmed them as God's appeal to his contemporaries and, in spite of notable divergencies (see below section 8) associated himself with John's preaching.[8]

2. The Jews of the time were in the grip of a Messianic excitement and an intense eschatological expectancy. When Jesus with his apostles approached Jerusalem, they imagined that God's reign would be manifested "on the spot" (Luke 19:11). Flavius Josephus speaks continually of popular pretenders whose Messianic promises found a ready ear among the people.[9] The Qumran community shows us a contemporary group of Jews living in a sensitive atmosphere of eschatological expectancy and in a state of serious legal, liturgical and moral preparation for the time of "God's visitation". This concentration on eschatology was quite common at that period among the Jews. The expectancy varied only in kind but the gospel of the reign of God preached by Jesus stands out as unique and incomparable.

3. Jesus associates the rule, reign or kingdom of God with verbs in which the temporal significance is fundamental. He teaches men to pray for its "coming" (Matt. 6:10 = Luke 11:2), assures his hearers that through his expulsion of devils it has already "come upon them" (Matt. 12:28 = Luke 11:20)

ingly, Matt. 5:35 is to be taken in an eschatological sense. The world of the nations will one day be brought under God's rule from Sion.

[8] Matt. 11:7–15 = Luke 7:24–30; Mark 11:30–32 par.; Matt 21:31 seq.

[9] *Ant.* XX, 97 (Theudas); *Ant.* XX, 167–70; cf. *Bell.* II, 261 seq. (concerning the Egyptian and other "deceivers").

and promises that some of those listening to him will experience its "advent with power" (Mark 9:1). These passages from Mark 1:15 and Mark 13:28 seq. speak of its "closeness". Jesus is asked when it is to come; he replies that it is "among you" (ἐντὸς ὑμῶν Luke 17:20 seq.). In the upper room Jesus speaks of its future "arrival" (Luke 22:18: somewhat differently in Mark 14:25 and Matt. 26:29).

4. Jesus emphasizes the importance of the present moment (Luke 12:54–56) and relates it to eschatological events (Luke 17:26–30 = Matt. 24:37–39; Mark 13:28 par.; 13:33–37 par.). The summons to conversion, the "crisis" similes, the words of threat and judgment (Luke 10:13–15 = Matt. 11:20–24; Luke 13:1–5; 19:41–44), the warning to watch and be ready (Luke 12:35–40; Matt. 25:1–13) belong to his proclamation of the *basileia* and reveal its urgency.

5. The radical moral demands made by Jesus that form part of the most unchallengeable tradition are based primarily on eschatological motives: entry into the kingdom of God, a share in the divine banquet, reign with God etc.[10] The early Church tended to interpret eschatological sayings in a general ethical sense[11] except where Jesus had brought them out in high relief. This indicates that the insistent eschatological note belongs to the teaching of Jesus himself.

6. Those who listened to Jesus, disciples as well as the crowd and their leaders, recognized that the gospel of Jesus compelled them at least to enquire into the Messianic significance of his words and actions, though naturally these did not correspond with their own Messianic ideas. The *basileia* proclamation must

[10] Schnackenburg, *Sittliche Botschaft,* pp. 96–100.

[11] Compare Matt. 7: 13 with Luke 13:24; Matt. 5:25 seq. with Luke 12:58 seq.; Matt. 7:24–27 = Luke 6:47–49. J. Jeremias, *Gleichnisse Jesu,* pp. 32–7.

have increased their interest in this matter and added to their perplexity.

We must not, therefore, exclude the urgent temporal note from the teaching of Jesus, whatever the difficulties in its interpretation. The eschatological character of the divine rule he was proclaiming assumes a special form we must now examine. It is exclusively the "seed and deed of God" (R. Otto). In itself, this note is already present in the late Jewish concept, the rabbinic concept of *malkhuth shamayim,* but with Jesus it appears in its full clarity. Men can pray for this to come (Matt. 6:10), implore God both day and night (Luke 18:7), strive and struggle to enter into it (Luke 13:24 cf. Matt. 7:13); men are to look for it (Luke 12:31 = Matt. 6:33); men can prepare themselves for it, hold themselves in readiness (Matt. 24:44; 25:10, 13; Luke 12:35–37) but with their own resources they can do absolutely nothing to bring it into existence or to hasten it or on the other hand to delay or hinder it. The seed grows of itself (Mark 4:26–29) and so the kingdom of God comes from divine power and grace.[12]

This supernatural and grace-given character of the *basileia* is discernible in expressions such as that God "gives" it (Luke 12:32) or "disposes" it (Luke 22:29 seq.). To certain individuals it is attached by Jesus as a "promise" (εἶναι with genitive) (Matt. 5:3, 10; cf. Luke 6:20; Mark 10:14 par.), as admission or exclusion, reclining at table (Matt. 8:11 = Luke 13:29; cf. Matt. 22:10 seq.) and also eating of bread (Luke 14:15), drinking of the fruit of the vine (Luke 22:18; Matt. 14:25). All these images portray the *basileia* as a saving benefit in the future, of which God alone can dispose. The reign of God is an event that is to occur for men, a good offered to them, a privilege

[12] For an interpretation of the parable see below in § 13.

that is also a challenge. It is never something of which they can dispose or that they can compel and insist upon.

The difficult and disputed passage about taking the *basileia* "by violence" (Matt. 11:12 seq. = Luke 16:16) should not therefore be interpreted in this way. And there can be no question of an effective, as distinct from an attempted, hindering of the reign of God from the days of John the Baptist or of a well-intentioned hastening of it by means of penitential practices and moral heroism.[13] Furthermore, certain turns of phrase which have become current are not found on the lips of Jesus: "to build up the kingdom of God", "to work at it", "to assist in its construction" etc.

In general the Jews also remained conscious of this supernatural character of the reign of God though there were times when they risked obscuring it (see sections 5 and 6). His pure concept of God made it impossible for Jesus to put pressure on him, lay down prescriptions for him, attribute to him human ways of thinking or to penetrate into his mysteries. For him, therefore, God's reign is a strictly eschatological and wholly supernatural concept.

8. The Saving Character of God's Reign

The purpose of both the word and work of Jesus is to announce and offer God's salvation to men. In the preaching of the prophets warnings and words of comfort are found side by side. They warn and reprimand God's people because of their idolatry, indifference and moral turpitude and at the same time sound a call to conversion. In later Judaism the awareness of sin

[13] A fuller discussion of this logion is found in § 12 below.

becomes stronger, prayers of penance multiply, men petition earnestly for God's mercy.[14] A mood of melancholy descends upon devout people without of course stifling their hope. But for all that, the apocalyptic literature is a flight into a realm of visions and dreams, a flight away from a steady faith, because men were calling for portents and calculating when the hour would come; they wanted, so to speak, to take a peep at the cards in God's hands. The clamour for divine vengeance upon the godless and sinners, on persecutors and oppressors is at least as emphatic as the yearning appeal for salvation and future glory. This is only too evident even in the austere members of the Qumran community.[15]

From Jesus we hear nothing about vengeance. One outstanding feature of his preaching is that salvation is proclaimed also and indeed especially for sinners.[16] In his eyes the reign of God is in the first place the realization of God's redeeming will, the fulfilment of the prophecies of Deutero-Isaias. Whether Jesus employed the term "gospel" (εὐαγγέλιον) or not,[17] the content

[14] Bousset-Greßmann, *Religion des Judentums,* pp. 382 seq.; Moore, *Judaism* I, pp. 507-19; E. K. Dietrich, *Die Umkehr (Bekehrung und Buße) im Alten Testament und im Judentum* . . . (Stuttgart, 1936); E. Sjöberg, *Gott und die Sünder,* pp. 125–69.

[15] *Damascus Document,* VII, 9: "All who despise these commandments will be judged and annihilated when God visits the earth to take vengeance upon the wicked": also VIII, 1 seq.; IQS IX, 23: "day of revenge"; I QH II, 24: " . . .that thou mayest glorify thyself through the judgment of evildoers"; IV, 26 seq.: " . . . to root out in judgment all who transgress (the commandment) of thy mouth . . ."; I QM VIII, 5: "in God's battle to destroy the enemy and annihilate him for ever . . ."; also I QH III, 27 seq.; I QM XI, 14, 16; XII, 5; XIV, 5 seq.; XIX, 2 and elsewhere.

[16] Mark 2:16 seq. par.; Luke 7:34 = Matt. 11:19; Luke 15:7, 10, 24, 32; 18:10–14; 19:7; Matt. 21:31.

[17] See G. Friedrich in *Th.W.B.* II, pp. 724–6. A positive answer is

of his preaching is a message of salvation, joy and peace on the lines of Isa. 52:7. The scandal aroused by his association with publicans and prostitutes (Mark 2:15–17 par.; Luke 7:34, 36–50; 19:7) clearly shows how unexpected and unwonted this attitude appeared to his Jewish contemporaries. He had to justify the divine love for sinners which shone forth in his actions in face of the just and devout, and this he did in more than one parable (Luke 15; Matt. 20:1–15) and saying (Mark 2:17 par.; Matt. 21:31; Luke 14:11; 18:14 among others).

Of course, the summons to penance is part of the teaching of Jesus and his warnings of judgment and woes are connected with it.[18] But in the first place he brings out the divine mercy, and to all without exception. The parable of the unmerciful servant (Matt. 18:23–35) describes how the master forgives his indebted servant a very large sum of money out of pure bounty and naturally expects this servant to pardon a slight debt owing from a fellow servant. God's goodness comes first, unparalleled in generosity and forgiveness. His wrath and judgment enter into force only when the grace received has been despised. The tax official, Zacchaeus, experiences a visitation of grace which becomes the basis of and occasion for a generous deed of grateful love (Luke 19:1–10). With Jesus, weal and woe are more than the warnings they are with the prophets. His preaching is not merely an appeal for conversion as was that of the great Baptist from the Jordan. He proclaims salvation as something already present and operative though not yet fully and perfectly realized. He assured many persons that their sins were immediately forgiven and his jealous enemies understood

provided on the other hand by J. A. E. van Dodewaard, *"Jésus s'est-il servi lui-même du mot 'évangile'?" Bib.* 35 (1954), pp. 160–73.

[18] Matt. 11:20–24= Luke 10:13–15; Matt. 12:41 seq. = Luke 11:31 seq.; 13:1–5,6–9.

that he was laying claim to divine power (Mark 2:1–12 par.).[19] This revealed God's mercy and salvific will to men and showed that the prophecies were fulfilled. His miracles of healing and the expulsion of devils were also intended as signs of the era of salvation (Matt. 11:2–6 = Luke 7:22 seq.). All that Jesus announced and achieved is one long evidence of God's saving purpose and of that alone. It is likely that his initial discourse at Nazareth was deliberately broken off with the reference to the "year of the Lord" and that no mention was made of its sequel in Isa. 61:2 and of a "day of vengeance of our God" (Luke 4:18 seq.). These are the "words of grace" which astonished his own people and at which they took umbrage (4:22).[20] Jesus' call to repentance has a meaning other than that of the prophets. He calls for a response to the divine offer of salvation, a reaction to God's saving activity that has already been inaugurated (Mark 1:15).

The statements of Jesus, which externally do not differ from the prophets' gospel of repentance (Luke 13:1–5, 6–9; 10:13–15 among others) must be interpreted in the sense that punishment and judgment refer to such as reject his offer of salvation from an inner hardening of mind and heart. This is made explicit

[19] Even if the two pericopes of the healing of the lame man (Mark 2:1–12 par.) and the woman penitent (Luke 7:36–50) may be suspect in their formal composition, it cannot be disputed that Jesus pardoned sins on earth: see the passages already cited, in which he appears as Saviour from sin, and also John 5:14; 7:53 to 8:11; finally the handing on of full authority, Matt. 16:19; 18:18; 20:23. A. Oepke in *St. Th.* 2 (1948), p. 162, writes: "If the full authority to forgive sins is taken away, then Jesus is made one prophet among others; he becomes a counterpart of the Baptist, though properly speaking there is no place for a second forerunner. In this case the whole gospel portrait of Jesus would be one immense falsification of history."

[20] J. Jeremias, *Jesu Verheißung*, pp. 37–9.

to the disciples prior to their mission, Luke 10:8–12 (Mark 6:11; Matt. 10:7 seq., 14 seq.). Only when men refuse to believe and reject their gospel of salvation are they to shake the dust from their feet as a sign and testimony (against them at the judgment) that they have parted from God's messengers and forfeited salvation.[21] It is God's great offer of grace at the last hour. Anyone who in this critical moment refuses to hear God's voice behaves like the obdurate generation of Noe (Luke 17:27 = Matt. 24:37–39) or the infatuated inhabitants of Sodom (Luke 18:28 seq.; cf. Luke 10:12 = Matt. 10:15).

It could also be said that the present is the hour of salvation because the gospel is proclaimed and divine mercy draws near to men through the actions of Jesus. But Jesus announces salvation and judgment for the near future according to the attitude which men here and now adopt to his gospel. Jesus, therefore, laments over Jerusalem: "If thou also hadst known, and that in this thy day, the things that are to thy peace . . ." (Luke 19:42). Jesus is conscious of himself, wholly and exclusively, as the bearer of salvation and his innermost desire is the salvation of all men. Yet he has the obligation, imposed on him by God, of making men understand the seriousness of their personal decision by which they decide their future destiny.

Judged from this point of view, there are important differences of emphasis and content from the preaching of John the Baptist. The preacher of penance by the Jordan began with the threat of judgment, insisted upon conversion and fruits of repentance before promising to penitents of goodwill a delivery from the future Messianic judgment (Matt. 3:7–12). Even his

[21] Percy, *Botschaft Jesu,* p. 115: "The kingdom of God is proclaimed by Jesus as a saving grace for all who will receive it. In other words, the God of Jesus demands everything because he has himself first given everything."

baptism cannot be accepted as an eschatological grace, whatever significance John may have attached to it. It remains a means by which men could escape from the wrath of future judgment but it does not communicate salvation. It is a sign of membership of the redeemed won through penance, at once a guarantee that sins are forgiven on condition of penance (εἰς ἄφεσιν ἁμαρτιῶν Mark 1:4) and a strengthening of the will to do penance (εἰς μετάνοιαν Matt. 3:11)[22] it is a preparation for the future, not yet an eschatological reality. Although the Messianic promise of salvation is by no means absent from the Baptist's preaching (Matt. 3:12) the great precursor did not know that God's intention is first to offer grace and salvation and then at some future date to separate and judge. His gaze is directed towards the last things: the intervening "year of the Lord" was hidden from him prior to the coming of Jesus (note his question asked from prison, Matt. 11:2 seq. par). He thus continues the line of prophets even if he does surpass them as God's immediate herald before the era of salvation (Matt. 11:9 seq.), as the man who fulfilled the prophecy of the Precursor (Mal. 3:23 seq.-Elias!), and he may thus be regarded as a living sign of the dawn of salvation (Matt. 11:14; 17:12 par.; also Mark 1:2 seq.).[23] But he retains that characteristic note of Old Testament prophecy of concentrating on the eschatological and this prevents him from seeing the period in between.

[22] C. H. Kraeling, *John the Baptist* (New York-London 1951), pp. 117 seq., interprets the voluntary immersion in water as a symbolic rite to express the readiness to accept the divine judgment. Yet the notion of a fire of judgment is not sufficiently clear for John. The Baptist must rather have stressed the idea of purification as it was then accepted in baptismal sects. See J. Steinmann, *S. Jean-Baptiste et la spiritualité du désert* (Paris, 1955), pp. 62–71 (with references to the Qumran texts).

[23] J. M. Robinson, *Das Geschichtsverständnis des Markusevangeliums* (Zürich, 1956), pp. 15–20.

It is, therefore, doubtful whether he clad his message in the same words as Jesus, "Do penance, for the kingdom (reign) of heaven is at hand" (Matt. 3:2; cf. 4:17). This parallel between the gospel of John and Jesus which is found only in Matthew reveals the tendency to approximate John and Jesus very closely and bring them into complete harmony. The formula too is Matthew's.[24] If, in spite of the silence of the other evangelists, John did speak formally about the reign of God, he must have envisaged it in its double Old Testament function of judgment and salvation but not in its present characteristic as grace.

The direct revelation of God's love for sinners as a mark of his eschatological reign, the grace bestowed upon all who accept the salvific gospel of Jesus and are converted, God's delight in forgiveness and the generous outpouring of his saving graces: all this is an original and unique feature of Jesus' gospel of the *basileia*. But there is another facet of his thought and another element in his preaching that distinguishes him from representatives of later Judaism. For him the whole content of salvation was found in the reign of God; all hope of salvation reaches its fulfilment here. The rabbis preferred to talk of a "share in the future aeon"[25] or of a final Paradise (Gan Eden).[26] The preference shown by Jesus for "reign (kingdom) of God" is no mere wish to have a term of his own. The deeper reason is to be sought in his living personal relation to God and his knowledge of God's plan of salvation. Where God comes to

[24] J. Schmid, *Ev. nach Mt.* 56, on "kingdom of heaven", p. 51.

[25] Dalman, *Worte Jesu,* p. 110 and Billerbeck I, 181 think that where Jesus spoke of "entry into the kingdom of God", the rabbis would have preferred the phrase, "share in the future aeon".

[26] See the material in Billerbeck IV, 1144–65, particularly concerning the "meal" in Gan Eden (1158 seq.), also IV, 1208 (under 4) and 1212 (under 11).

reign, man's purest religious aspiration is fulfilled, and particularly the aspiration of those who groan beneath suffering, poverty and persecution in this world in spite of their true service. The beatitudes in the Sermon on the Mount that mirror so clearly the spirit of Jesus towards the poor, the oppressed, the despised and downtrodden, culminate in the assurance that it is to them in a special measure that the future reign of God belongs. In Matthew's version, the *basileia*-promise in the first and last beatitude provides a framework for all the other texts which describe eschatological bliss under various images: "comfort" for those who mourn, "food" for the hungry, God's "mercy", the vision of God and divine sonship – these are all eschatological promises fulfilled in the reign of God. In the guarantee to the poor in spirit that they will "possess the land" (Matt. 5:5) there is a direct echo of the "entry into God's kingdom".[27] In the great picture of judgment (Matt. 25:31–46) the Son of man addresses the "blessed of the Father" as follows: "Possess you the kingdom prepared for you from the foundation of the world" (v. 34). Synonymous expressions occur in other passages: "enter into life" (Mark 9:43, 45 cf. 47), "receive life everlasting" (Mark 10:17 = Luke 18:18; a slight variant in Matt. 19:16 seq.; further Luke 10:25). The "hundredfold reward" to be received by those who abandon everything for his sake consists in eternal life (Mark 10:30 par.); but this is identical with a share in the future reign of God (cf. also Matt. 7:13 seq. = Luke 13:24; Matt. 12:34). The final companionship at table with Jesus and his disciples takes place in his "kingdom" (Luke 22:30; cf. 14:15) and in the same passage Matthew speaks of the "new creation" (Matt. 19:28). The pictures of the divine banquet with the Old Testament patriarchs (Matt. 8:11 = Luke 13:28 seq.), of the

[27] H. Windisch in *Z.N.W.* 27 (1928), pp. 167 and 179.

future reception or wedding feast (Luke 14:16–24; Matt. 22:1–10, 11–14), of the servants' joyful meal with their lord (Matt. 25: 14–30; cf. Luke 12:35–38) all refer exclusively to the coming reign of God.[28] The central and dominant idea remains always the reign of God. The same is true of his warnings of punishment. He does make use of traditional images[29] like that of Hell fire[30] but its use in connection with the eschatological meal shows that the real punishment is exclusion from the kingdom of God (Luke 13:28 = Matt. 8:12; Matt. 22:13; 25:30; cf. 24:51).

This insistence on the reign of God as the principal concept of salvation must be regarded as an original contribution of Jesus. In rabbinical thought salvation is "the consequence of the reign of God but not the reign itself".[31] With Jesus it is made the very marrow of salvation and it gives his gospel a great unity and concentration. He proclaims God's salvific will and redeeming mercy as a present reality in his concept of the royal reign of God and he makes it the ultimate motive for longing for salvation: a share in the fully developed and imperishable reign of God which brings the fullness of beatitude to the redeemed.

[28] J. Theissing, *Lehre Jesu von der ewigen Seligkeit,* pp. 71–81.

[29] A comparison of the synoptic gospels leaves it highly doubtful whether Jesus ever spoke of the "future aeon" (Matt. 12:32; Mark 10:30 = Luke 18:30; Luke 20:35). See also J. Schmid, *Das Evangelium nach Markus* (3rd edition, Regensburg 1954), on 10:30 (pp. 197 seq.); F. J. Schierse, article on "Aeon" in *L. Th. K.* I 2nd edition 1957, p. 681.

[30] Matt. 5:25 seq.; 18:9 = Mark 9:43, 45, 47; Luke 12:5 = Matt. 10:28; Matt. 13:42, 50.

[31] Billerbeck, 1, 181.

9. The Purely Religious and Universal Character of the Reign of God

The salvation proclaimed and promised by Jesus in this reign and kingdom of God is purely religious in character. Jesus entirely excluded the national and the politico-religious elements from his *basileia* concept and, in so doing, repudiated the widespread Jewish hope of a splendid Messianic kingdom of Israel. The gospels clearly reflect the hard struggle Jesus had with these deeply rooted prejudices. Zealots and their admirers paid careful attention to the work of Jesus and made several attempts to enlist the "prophet from Galilee" and great wonder-worker in their cause. After he had multiplied the loaves, a handful of men conspired to proclaim him as Messianic king but he was aware of their intentions and withdrew into the mountains "himself alone" (John 6:15). It is no accident that these men were Galileans because Galilee was the home (Judas the Galilean A. D. 6) and fruitful ground of the Zealots' movement. Probably this politico-Messianic enthusiasm of these Galileans who had witnessed the multiplication of the loaves was also the cause for the incident recorded in Luke 13:1: the butchery of Galilean Passover pilgrims by Roman soldiery when they were slaying their sacrificial animals in the temple.[32] The reaction of Jesus to this report is characteristic. The lesson he draws is purely religious: "Unless you do penance, you shall all likewise perish" (Luke 13:3). Whether and to what extent the crowds accompanying Jesus on his entry into Jerusalem (again, according to John 12:12 clearly Galilean pilgrims) intended their welcome as a Messianic and political demonstration is

[32] For greater detail see J. Blinzler, *Die Niedermetzelung von Galiläern durch Pilatus, N.T.* 2 (1957), pp. 24–49.

disputed; but that it did arouse such hopes can scarcely be doubted from the acclamations (even if variously recorded), especially in Mark 11:10, "Blessed be the kingdom of our father David that cometh". But in himself Jesus desires to be merely the prince of peace (Zach. 9:9). It was impossible to eradicate this tragic misunderstanding even from the inner group of the apostles. Simon Peter's rejection of the Passion foretold by Jesus (Mark 8:32 seq. par.), the request of the two sons of Zebedee for the first official places in his kingdom (Mark 10:37 par.), the display of the two swords in the Upper Room (Luke 22:38), Peter's onslaught when Jesus was arrested (Mark 14:17 par.) are indubitable evidence. Luke 19:11; 24:21; Acts 1:6 throw light on the mentality both in the closer and wider circle of his disciples. We need not look for hidden allusions to the Zealots everywhere and to their activities which Jesus repudiated,[33] but he was frequently forced to distinguish his position from this current notion of the Messias, very fundamentally in his struggle with Satan shortly after his baptism in the Jordan (temptation, Matt. 4:1–11; Luke 4:1-13), and then repeatedly when dealing with men who appeared to have no other concept of the Messias. This must have been the chief reason why he concealed his Messianic dignity. This basic misconception of the purely religious nature of the Messias (Servant of God) led to his estrangement from the masses and was perpetuated in the official indictment posted on the cross.

But this fundamental attitude of Jesus also emerges in his portrayal of the *basileia*. We have already emphasized the noble and pure

[33] O. Cullmann, *Der Staat im Neuen Testament* (Tübingen 1956), also adduces the following passages: Matt. 5:39; Matt. 11:12 = Luke 16:16; Matt. 7:15 (with a question mark); John 10:8, 18; Luke 23:28–30, (14 seq.) (33 seq.)

strains in late Jewish conceptions of the eschatological reign of God but these never rose to the purity and clearly religious character of Christ's preaching of it. With his own exalted conception of God he effectively banished all shadows and human additions from the picture of the future. He made use, it is true, of many traditional images but in contrast with the apocalypses, they were not imaginative fantasies and they "make no claim to be understood as actual descriptions of God's kingdom";[34] they are part of a symbolic religious language such as man must always employ to denote eternal things, heavenly reality and the wholly different nature of fulfilment. The banquet images, for example, are not meant to depict the delights of table and paradise, they represent the blessed and perfect association of God and the community of the redeemed with one another. Jesus is to drink wine "anew" with his disciples in the future kingdom (Mark 14:25 = Matt. 26:29) and even if this qualification had not been added, it would have been evident that he was referring to the eschatological "new creation" (see Matt. 19:28 though here the Greek term παλιγγενεσία means "rebirth"), a wholly different and transfigured world.[35] Late Judaism also referred to "new creation" without having clear and definite ideas how it would be realized. Not infrequently the future era of salvation, at least the "days of the Messias" were given the features of an earthly paradise. Unparalleled fertility, abundance of wine and oil, the rich blessing of children were to prevail on the earth which would be liberated from plagues, sufferings and corrup-

[34] J. Schmid. *Ev. nach Mk.*, p. 35.

[35] Dalman, *Worte Jesu* 1, pp. 145 seq.; Volz, *Eschatologie*, pp. 338–40. The expression is now attested in the Qumran documents, for example (in an eschatological sense) I QS IV, 25; I QH XIII, 11 seq.; cf XI, 13 seq. For the whole question consult E. Sjöberg, "Neuschöpfung in den Toten-Meer-Rollen" in *St. Th.* 9 (1955), pp. 131–6.

tion *(Ethiopic Henoch* 10; *Syr. Bar.* 29, etc.).[36] The un-earthly and un-worldly notion that Jesus entertained of this eschatological fulfilment is indicated in his reply to the Sadducees about the resurrection: "When they shall rise again from the dead, they shall neither marry nor be married but are as the angels in heaven" (Mark 12:24 seq.).

It was generally assumed that at the resurrection the dead would rise again with their former bodies because this secured the identity of the risen with the former earthly body.[37] In *Syr. Bar.* 50 seq. there is a detailed description "The earth restores the dead that had been entrusted to its keeping, and nothing in their appearance is changed" (50:2). "As the earth receives them, so it gives them back." The judgment then follows, (50:4), and only after it comes glorification (51). The schools of Shammai and Hillel differed on the question whether a man's development in the world to come happened as it did in a mother's womb.[38] To begin with, the dead rise with their former bodily infirmities; after the judgment God will remedy these.[39] Jesus does not admit this kind of speculation about the risen body. God's power fashions something entirely new, a body that is free from earthly needs and characteristics ("like the angels"). Paul also reveals to the Corinthians an eschatological "mystery". Not all will fall asleep but all will be "transformed" (1 Cor. 15:51). The immediate transformation of the living and the

[36] For greater detail, see Volz, *Eschatologie,* pp. 386–90.

[37] Moore, *Judaism* II, pp. 380–5; Volz, *Eschatologie,* pp. 250 seq.; Bonsirven, *Judaïsme* I, pp. 482–5.

[38] *Gn rabba* 14, 5 cf. Billerbeck IV, 815 seq.; H. Freedman, *Genesis Rabbah,* pp. 113 seq.

[39] *Gn rabba* 95, 1 cf. Freedman, pp. 880 seq. According to a statement in *Keth.* III b (Billerbeck IV, 1194; Goldschmidt V, 362) they will rise even with their own clothes.

dead Christians into the heavenly condition of "glory" (δόξα, see vv. 42–44) is the epitome of New Testament revelation.[40]

Jesus remained aloof from any apocalyptical calculation of the end, the point in time when the reign of God would manifest itself. "The kingdom (reign) of God cometh not with observation" (Luke 17:20). Consequently the "portents" in his eschatological discourse (Mark 13 par.) give no hard and fast dates, no clear signs for the advent of the final period, for "of that day or hour no man knoweth, neither the angels in heaven nor the Son — but the Father" (Mark 13:32). For Jesus the future kingdom of God is a reality subject only to God himself and over which God has sovereign control (see also Mark 10:40 par.); it is wholly beyond the range of human curiosity and speculation.

On account of its purely religious character, the gospel of God's reign preached by Jesus is directed to all mankind. This remains true in spite of his consciousness that he was sent to "the lost sheep of the house of Israel" (Matt. 10:6; cf. 15:24). But this indisputable statement sets no limit to his universal salvific will. It indicates the way ordained by God in which salvation is to be brought to them, namely through the ancient people chosen by God to whom Jesus was sent. But the expression may be understood as a widening of particularist Jewish opinion. Jesus turns to the whole of Israel, not to privileged groups and observers of the Law, the pure elite. The sheep of God's flock have been lost, they are scattered and leaderless (Jer. 50:6; Ezech. 34:5; Isa. 53:6; Mark 6:34). Jesus summons them all, the just and sinners, those who fulfil the Law and the "country folk" (the *am-ha-are* cf. John 7:49), even despised

[40] J. Jeremias, "Flesh and Blood cannot inherit the Kingdom of God" in *N.T.St.* 2 (1955–56), pp. 151–9.

groups like publicans and prostitutes. The notion of a "holy remnant" that he is to gather together from Israel is foreign to his mind.

This notion that can be traced back to 3 Kings 19:18 and was developed by the prophet Isaias (Isa. 6:13; 10:21; 11:11; 28:5 seq.) and maintained by the later prophets (Soph. 2:7, 9; 3:12 seq.; Jer. 23:3; 31:7; Zach. 13:8 seq.) was adopted in later Judaism by special groups who looked upon themselves as the holy stock of the chosen people that had grown unfaithful, for instance by the Pharisees with their Levitical purity and attachment to the Law (they had originally accepted this voluntarily and then gradually imposed it as a general obligation), by many baptist sects and by the Essenes.[41] The idea can be traced in the Damascus and Qumran communities which had affinities with the Essenes. In *Dam.* I, 4 seq. we find for example: "He left behind a remnant in Israel and never gave this over to destruction. He permitted the stock of a plant to burgeon from Israel and Aaron and to possess his land and to develop his soil": similarly, II, seq. The austere devotees of Qumran looked upon themselves as "the men of God's plan, who had preserved his covenant in the midst of evil, to make atonement for the land" and held themselves in readiness one day to take over "the whole community of Israel" and to direct it "in obedience against the ordinances of the priests, the sons of Sadoc and the men of his covenant".[42] If Jesus in fact did not win over the whole of Israel but only a "small flock" (Luke 12:32), this was

[41] J. Jeremias, "Der Gedanke des 'Heiligen Restes' im Spätjudentum und in der Verkündigung Jesu" in *Z.N.W.* 42 (1949), pp. 184–94.

[42] Appendix to the discipline roll (I QS a), I, 1–3, in Barthélemy-Milik, *Qumran Cave,* I, 109 and 111; cf. also L. Rost in *Th. L. Z.* 82 (1957), pp. 669 seq.: "When the era of salvation arrives, this group is not dissolved but becomes rather the centre of the new community. The people of

an historical development that in no way affected the universal character of his gospel.

Jesus leaves the separation of good from bad to the final judgment (Matt. 13:24–30, 47–50; 25:31–46) and he tolerates disappointment and disloyalty even in his intimate circle of apostles (Mark 14:27, 30 par.; Luke 22:31 seq.). He forms no esoteric group of saints but a community in faith of those to be saved, which lives upon the divine mercy. In this respect John the Baptist had been a genuine precursor in his desire to stir all Israel to repentance. The gospel of Jesus accordingly ran up against the opposition of the exclusive Pharisaic classes and his announcement of salvation for sinners must have had an even more unwelcome sound than the warnings and threatened judgment of the Baptist.

From the beginning Jesus opened the doors of God's kingdom to all peoples. The apparent contradiction that he confined his preaching to Israel and during his lifetime forbade his disciples to go to the Samaritans and heathen (Matt. 10:6) is resolved in the full synthesis of his doctrine. His promise to the gentile peoples is contained in these words: "Many shall come from the East and the West and shall sit down with Abraham and Isaac and Jacob in the kingdom of heaven. But the children of the kingdom shall be cast out into the exterior darkness. There shall be weeping and gnashing of teeth" (Matt. 8:11 seq.; Luke 13:28 seq.).

This presupposes that the patriarchs (and prophets, according to Luke) have risen and that the judgment has taken place (v. 12). The (unbelieving and obdurate) Jews, the first heirs of God's kingdom (the "sons of the kingdom") are cast into Gehenna and now behold (cf. Luke) the crowds of heathens (πολλοί) at the

Israel, the community, as the priesthood sees them, is joined to them, not vice versa" (p. 670). See also on the subject of a "holy remant" I QH VI, 8, 15; VII, 19; VIII, 6-11.

eschatological banquet (Isa. 25:6 seq.), at table with the Jewish patriarchs.[43]

This was a statement unprecedented for the Jews. John the Baptist had also attacked the view that exempted the children of Abraham from the wrath of judgment (Matt. 3:9 = Luke 3:8). But Jesus excludes the first and natural heirs in so far as they do not accept his gospel and refuse to repent and he opens for the heathen the door to the eschatological festal hall. That inevitably touched the Jews at a very sensitive spot—it is a sharp word of Jesus which throws a revealing light on his character and cannot have been a subsequent addition by the early Church with its missionary work among the gentiles because it is well substantiated (Q) and its Semitic touches prove it to be genuine. The simile of the nations' pilgrimage to Sion probably underlies the logion of the "city on the mountain", which cannot be hidden (Matt. 5:14).[44] But Matt. 8:11 seq. suggests that other banquet parables pointed to a share for the heathens so that Luke's clear reference to them (Luke 14:22 seq.) strikes no dissonant note.

The same concept is found in the great picture of the judgment (Matt. 25:31–46). All peoples will be assembled before the judgment seat of the Son of man. The separation follows not according to membership of the chosen people of Israel but because of their love for the poor and needy whom the judge acknowledges as his "least brethren". Among the new heirs of the kingdom are also, but not exclusively, heathens who never knew the Son of man during their lifetime (v. 39). [45] In other

[43] J. Jeremias, *Jesu Verheißung,* pp. 47 seq.
[44] So G. v. Rad, "Die Stadt auf dem Berge" in *Ev.Th.* 8 (1948–1949), pp. 439–47, and in this connection also J. Jeremias, *Jesu Verheißung,* p. 57.
[45] This passage that has been hotly disputed is dealt with more fully in section 14 below.

passages Jesus declared that at the judgment heathens would put to shame hard-hearted Israelites. The inhabitants of Nineveh and the queen of Saba will then rise again at the judgment with "this generation" (the unbelieving Jewish contemporaries of Jesus) and, as witnesses, condemn them (Matt. 12:41 seq. = Luke 11:31 seq.). Similarly, Jesus introduces the heathen citizens of Tyre and Sidon, and even of Sodom, who would long ago have done penance in sackcloth and ashes had they witnessed miracles like those of Jesus in Corozain, Bethsaida and Capharnaum (Matt. 11:21–24 = Luke 10:13). This might be pedagogically rhetorical, but it does show clearly that Jesus had no prejudices against the heathen. In Luke 4:24–27 we again see him reminding his own people at Nazareth who repudiated him that during the great famine Elias was sent to the widow of Sarepta and that Eliseus healed the Syrian Naaman, not lepers in Israel. In what may be partly the evangelist's own sentence, Matt. 21:43, which is not in the parallel passages in Mark or Luke, a thought of Jesus' is expressed. "The kingdom of God shall be taken from you and shall be given to a nation yielding the fruits thereof"; evidently for Jesus what is decisive for salvation is not membership of Israel but the fulfilment of the demand for conversion. Moreover, the parable of the vineyard (Mark 12:1–9 par.) with its striking image of the vineyard (Isa. 5), is clearly aimed at Israel and its leaders. The cursing of the fig-tree (Mark 11:13 seq., 20 seq.; cf. Matt. 21:18–20) can scarcely be understood in any other way.[46]

We need not consider here how salvation is finally to reach the gentiles. God's gracious mercy which associates them with

[46] Cf. finally C. H. Bird in *J.Th.St.* 4 (1953), pp. 177–9, who refers in the first place to Os. 9:10, 16 seq. (LXX) but also to Jer. 17:7 seq.; Ezech. 47:12 (in connection with the cleansing of the temple); J. W. Doeve, "Purification du Temple et dessèchement du figuier" in

the ancient people of the covenant and the mission calling upon them to make their decision are not mutually exclusive. It was right for Jesus to acknowledge Israel's prerogative and to have declined during his public life a mission to the gentiles. But the proclamation and offer of salvation to the gentiles must be traced back to a commission of the Risen Lord (Matt. 28:18–20). In the passages quoted Jesus sees the eschatological fulfilment of the old prophecies that the gentiles will come to adore and glorify God. But in them he places the emphasis on a serious acceptance of moral standards and a width of outlook of which there was evidence in later Judaism but which became fully developed only in the preaching of Jesus.

10. The Challenge of the Reign of God

The announcement that the reign of God is at hand swells to a mighty appeal to men to subject themselves to God alone. A survey of the full range of the discourses and sayings of Jesus in the synoptic gospels shows how this urgent note is in the forefront of his teaching. The divine sovereignty manifested in the actions of Jesus compels men to make their decision. The critical situation created by its presence and power in the words and deeds of Jesus, with the assurance of fulfilment in the future, necessarily involves an imperative, at once curt and comprehensive as in Mark. 1:15, "Be converted and believe the gospel" or metaphorically in the passages about entering into the kingdom of God. The Sermon on the Mount develops and illustrates the radical moral demands that God's kingly rule makes on men

N.T.St. I (1954/1955), pp. 297–308 explains the cursing by reference to Jer. 7:20: it signifies that the cursing of the city and the people had already begun.

and sums them up with the simplicity of genius in the great commandment of love of God and the neighbour. We cannot deal with this in detail[47] but merely remark how it illuminates the ethical character of God's reign and the demands it makes here and now.

In his basic demand for conversion (μετάνοια) Jesus reveals himself as a powerful advocate of God in the prophetic manner even if conversion, as we have seen (section 8), has a different place in his teaching from that of the prophets and John the Baptist. But his approach to the people and their rulers is just as forceful, as for instance when he allows only a brief respite to the barren fig-tree (Luke 13:6–9) or when, with the cursing of the fig-tree, he blends prophecy and parable as he not infrequently does.[48] He adopts the prophetic manner in calling for "penance in sackcloth and ashes" (Matt. 11:21 par.) and he recalls the ancient customs of mourning and penitence[49] without intending to describe the nature of the conversion he is demanding (cf. on the other hand, Matt. 6:16–18). His own concept is better illustrated in the parables of the prodigal son (Luke 15:11–32), the Pharisee and publican (Luke 18:10–14), the stories of the great sinner (Luke 7:36–50) and the customs official Zachaeus (Luke 19:1–10) and in sayings like those in Luke 18:14; Matt. 18:3 seq.; Mark 10:15 par. It is a profound change of heart, a rediscovery of God, an unreserved self-abandonment to his mercy, a grateful recommencement. The

[47] Further reference may be made to my book, *Die sittliche Botschaft des Neuen Testaments;* see also J. Bonsirven, *Règne du Dieu,* pp. 80–151.

[48] G. Stählin, "Die Gleichnishandlungen Jesu" in *Kosmos und Ekklesia,* Festschrift für W. Stählin (Kassel 1953), pp. 9–22; J. Jeremias, *Gleichnisse Jesu,* pp. 192 seq.

[49] Jos. 7:6; Judith 9:1; Esther 4:3; Isa. 58:5; Jer. 6:26; Ezech. 27:30; Dan. 9:3; Jonas 3:5 seq.; Job 2:8.

sinner is overwhelmed by divine love and will now love and serve God alone. He liberates himself from servitude to Mammon (Matt. 6:24), to sensuality (Luke 7:50; John 8:11) and from hatred and hardness of heart against his neighbour (Matt. 6:12; cf. 18:23–35). Such a conversion which Jesus demands from every man because he knows the guilt of all in the sight of God, even and indeed particularly of the self-righteous (Luke 18:10–14; cf. the woes in Matt. 23), is the indispensable precondition for a share in God's future kingdom. God has so great a joy in the repentent sinner (Luke 15:7, 10, 24) because his offer of salvation has found thankful acceptance. Those who were lost, even notorious sinners and prostitutes (Matt. 21:31) are now won for the kingdom, and God's rule of grace in the present epoch has reached its goal. The preaching of conversion becomes fully intelligible only when a man is convinced that God's eschatological reign is operative in the words and deeds of Jesus and that it has the active power to bring about salvation now.

The essential dependence of this call to conversion on the rule of God is confirmed by the intrinsic condition it imposes of belief in the good tidings. In the teaching of Jesus conversion and belief are two sides of the same basic attitude. Only the convert can believe that the time of salvation is already there and God's full reign is at the door. Belief, in its turn, is a conversion since it includes a recognition of guilt before God and the need for salvation and also the readiness to fulfil God's will in the radical form in which Jesus presents it. This closely-knit union of conversion and belief is well expressed in the two similes of the grumbling children (Matt. 11:16–19 = Luke 7:31 seq.) and the dissimilar sons (Matt. 21:28–31). Both are clearly directed towards the devout Pharisees whose reaction to the teaching of John the Baptist and to that of Jesus was one of superiority and stiffness. The simile of the children at play betrays the hateful criticism they levelled against John, the austere preacher of penance and against Jesus, the joyful prophet of salvation. The absence of a spirit of conversion prevents belief although they had to acknowledge in the actions of Jesus that "God is justified in his works" (Matt. 11:19).[50] A want of belief that "the hour is at hand" leads to a neglect of God's will. This is brought out in the parable of the two sons. All these zealots proclaim their loyalty to God's commandment and yet at the decisive moment they are disobedient. Sinners who till now defied God's will begin to reflect because they believed the Baptist's preaching (Matt. 21:32) and they now accept Jesus' gospel of salvation; they have become God's obedient sons and gain an entry into the kingdom.

Acceptance of the gospel of Jesus bridges the paradox that the yoke of Jesus is bearable and his burden light (Matt. 11:30) and that, nevertheless, God's radical demands, proclaimed by Jesus, have to be fulfilled. The Saviour's summons and the Sermon on the Mount can be harmonized only by the man who accepts Jesus as the saving mediator. He is conscious of being surrounded and sustained by divine love and can summon up his courage to force his way "through the narrow gate" (Luke 13:24). Perhaps the obscure reference to "taking heaven by violence" (Matt. 11:12; see Luke 16:16) refers to those champions of God, men of goodwill, who have never been lacking since the days of John the Baptist.

The new ethical attitude, which Jesus calls for, the "more abundant justice" (Matt. 5:20), "perfection" after the pattern of the heavenly Father (Matt. 5:48) can be understood only in

[50] For a translation and interpretation, see J. Jeremias, *Gleichnisse Jesu*, p. 141.

connection with his *basileia* gospel. When Matthew portrays Jesus in the Sermon on the Mount as the new lawgiver replacing Moses and surpassing him in his absolute proclamation of the divine will, he also announces his fundamental commandment for all who look for the kingdom of God. This is not a law which, "in itself", should always have been followed but a new lawgiving, at this moment in the history of salvation, through the mouth of the final and fully authorized legate of God, the Messias, and it is proclaimed in view of the promised kingdom of God. This is evident from the Beatitudes at the beginning (Matt. 5:3–10) as from the concluding picture which has an eschatological meaning (Matt. 7:24–7). Between these extremes we find repeatedly sayings about "entry" or "admission" (5:20; 7:13, 21, 22 seq.), characteristic of Jesus and employed only by him, and which formulate a share in the perfect reign of God as the urgent goal of all moral endeavour. The counsel of indifference to the world and of confidence in the heavenly Father is illuminated by the concluding sentence: "Seek ye first the kingdom of God and his justice, and all these things will be added (by God) to you" (Matt. 6:25–33). Finally, the prayer which Jesus taught them shows what is the ultimate issue: that God's reign may come, his holy will prevail on earth and all opposition to God's dominion be overcome (6:9–13).

To look upon the otherworldly, uncompromising commandments of the Sermon on the Mount as a programme of secular renovation is basically to misunderstand them. Jesus is not concerned with a social revolution or with a progressive advance towards some earthly realm of peace but with a transformation of man himself, in order that he may have a share in the future kingdom of God. It would, of course, be also a misunderstanding to regard the morality he is calling for merely as the ideal order of this future world, as the unrealized and unrealizable harmony of God's kingdom. In that case, no imperative would be necessary since God's law is inscribed in the hearts of men (Jer. 31:33; 32:40) and his spirit directs them (Ezech. 36:26 seq.). On the contrary, the demands of Jesus refer to conduct in the world of here and now, they are directed to the heirs of the future kingdom, and summon them to high purity of mind and determined action. And, to conclude, it would be also false to interpret this morality as affecting merely the brief period before the end, as a peculiar law in view of future catastrophe, as an interim ethics. The intention of Jesus is not to release his disciples from the world and their surroundings but from a worldly way of thought and life (Mark 10:42–44 par.). For the heir to the kingdom God's holy will, without distortion or abridgement, is the one and only guiding star. Jesus is not asking how it may be realized practically in the circumstances of the world. But both Jesus and the early Church were convinced that it should be, and with God's assistance could be, so realized.

The claims of Jesus, taken thus together, receive a positive significance. He has summed them up pointedly in the great commandment, that a man must love God with his whole heart and whole soul and all his strength and his neighbour as himself (Mark 12:29–31 par.). And so love of God receives for its sphere of action the love of our human brethren, indeed of all men who are in need and want assistance, without regard for origin or condition, race and nation (Luke 10:30–37) and the standard of this love of the neighbour is the unlimited character of love of self. This shows that Jesus was in no sense Utopian but a sober judge of reality with a profound knowledge of the human heart. He points out to all men practical ways in which to fulfil God's will (Matt. 25:34–45). What he condemned was the half measure. Man cannot serve God and Mammon, he cannot attach his heart at once to heavenly and earthly treasures (Matt.

6:19–21). Possibly the intervening picture of "light in thee", at least as Matthew understands it, (Matt. 6:22 seq.; cf. Luke 11:34 seq.) is to be taken in the same sense. God's light in us, his companionship and nearness, tolerates no shadows.[51]

In yet another way Jesus reduces to concrete practice God's absolute claim on the man who is to have a share in his kingdom. He calls him to a personal discipleship. This personal attachment is a new and unparalleled element in the claims of Jesus. The rabbinical school, like the rabbinical method of study, provided merely an external framework within which Jesus could develop his own doctrines.[52] The term "following" originally denoted an external attachment to a rabbi with the intention of becoming his "disciple". The following of Jesus also signifies adopting his habit of life and living in close company with him. But other demands are linked with this, which soon become the kernel of the statements on this subject.[53] The early Church was right in attributing these sayings about personal association with Jesus to all believers as is evident from the later use of the title "disciple".[54] In consequence, it is not always easy to know whether

[51] E. Sjöberg, "Das Licht in dir. Zur Deutung von Mt. 6:22 seq. par." in *St. Th.* 5 (1951), pp. 89–105; Jeremias offers another interpretation in *Gleichnisse Jesu,* p. 141: the phrase refers to the interior blindness and obduracy of his enemies.

[52] On the unique character of this discipleship cf. A. Schlatter, *Die Geschichte des Christus* (2nd edition, Stuttgart 1923), pp. 312–32; K. H. Rengstorff in *Th. W. B.* IV, pp. 448–54; Schnackenburg, *Sittliche Botschaft,* pp. 23 seq.: K. H. Schelke, *Jüngerschaft und Apostelamt* (Freiburg im Breisgau 1957).

[53] Luke 9:57–60 = Matt. 8:19–22; Luke 9:61 seq.; Mark 10:21 par.; Mark 9:38 = Luke 9:49; for Mark 8:34–38 par., consult the text of this page.

[54] Especially in the language of Acts 6:21 and in John's gospel; Rengstorf in *Th. W. B.* IV, pp 462 seq.

a sentence of Jesus is asking for a particular sacrifice from one man (for example the rich man, Mark 10:21 seq.) or is directed to all men. Jesus did not demand from everyone the abandonment of home and family, profession and property, as he did from the twelve apostles (Mark 10:28 seq. par.). Yet his words against riches have a very sharp ring (Mark 10:24 seq.) and he makes absolute demands upon each disciple (Luke 14:33). On the other hand, one should not say that Jesus "regarded the possession of riches as incompatible with a share in God's kingdom"[55] but rather that he called for a renunciation of earthly goods when these became an obstacle to entry into the kingdom (cf. the members of the body that give scandal, Mark 9:43–47 par.). He takes under his wing the men who have made themselves eunuchs "for the sake of the kingdom of God" (Matt. 19:12)[56] that is, live celibacy but he does not make this a law for all heirs to the kingdom.

These statements about "following" indicate the total demands of God on man and apply them practically to an attachment to Jesus. This is the impression given by the collection of aphorisms in Mark 8:34–38. They are directed to all his disciples, at a period when the masses no longer "followed" him and when it had become dangerous to profess belief in him. However the well-authenticated word "carry the cross"[57] be interpreted,[58] it

[55] Percy, *Botschaft Jesu,* pp. 93 and 105; an opposite view is given by M. Dibelius, *Jesus* (Sammlung Göschen 1130) (2nd edition, Berlin 1949), pp. 100 seq.; G. Bornkamm, *Jesus von Nazareth,* pp. 136 seq.

[56] On this passage consult J. Blinzler, Εἰσὶν εὐνοῦχοι *Z. N. W.* 48 (1957), pp. 254–70.

[57] Mark 8:34 = Matt. 16:24 = Luke 9:23; in addition, probably in an earlier setting, Matt. 10:38 = Luke 14:27; John 12:26 too probably refers to the same statement.

[58] According to E. Dinkler, "Jesu Wort vom Kreuztragen" in *Ntl. Studien für R. Bultmann* (Berlin 1954), pp. 111–29, the passage is referred

exacted the complete surrender of will from the followers of Jesus ("deny oneself") and the endurance of insult and contempt. The next passage, Mark 8:35, of which there exist variant readings[59] calls for readiness to sacrifice earthly life to gain eternal life. The disciple must be prepared for separation from his family and to be estranged from his closest relatives (Luke 12:52 seq. = Matt. 10:35 seq.) when the following of his Lord is in question. "For Jesus' sake" comes to be identified with "for the sake of the kingdom of God".[60] Moral endeavour is here given motives which could spring only from the *basileia* proclamation of Jesus.

In his ethical teaching Jesus is distinguished from the Pharisee experts on many points. He could not adopt their way of speaking of "taking on oneself the rule (kingdom) of God", in spite of the lofty meaning they attached to it. It was too closely linked with the yoke of their commandments and human prescriptions. For him the reign of God was revealing its presence differently, as grace and salvation. But he emphasized as they did,

to the *"Taw"*, the special sign of Yahweh according to Ezech. 9: 4 seq., by which a person devoted himself unreservedly to God's service; after the death of Jesus it was referred to the cross in a Christian sense. Consult further R. Koolmeister, *Selbstverleugnung, Kreuzaufnahme und Nachfolge. Eine historische Studie über Matt.* 16:28 in *Charisteria J. Köpp octogenario oblata* (Holmiae 1954), pp. 64–94 (especially the variety of interpretation of the passage!).

[59] Mark 8:35 = Matt. 16:25 = Luke 9:24: in addition, Matt. 10:39 = Luke 17:33; finally, John 12:25.

[60] "For Jesus' sake" ("for my sake", "for my name's sake"), Mark 8:35 par.; Matt. 10:39 (wanting in the parallel passage in Luke); Mark 13:9 par.; Matt. 5:11 = Luke 6:22. In one and the same logion we find Matt. 19:29 "for my name's sake"; Mark 10:29, "for my sake" and "for the gospel's sake"; Luke 18:29, "for the sake of the kingdom of God"; cf. also Matt. 19:12 "for the sake of the kingdom of heaven".

and not less seriously and consistently, the demands that God's eschatological kingdom makes on mankind.[61] From that standpoint there was much that linked him with and also much that divided him from his Jewish contemporaries.

In this analysis of the reign of God proclaimed by Jesus we could not avoid introducing certain features that are directly attached to Jesus himself. We shall deal with this problem later but it has been impossible to escape it since the person of Jesus is inseparable from his teaching. This emerges from the programmatic sentence with which we began, Mark 1:15. Its main significance is that the time is fulfilled and the reign of God near. But what is the ground for this? How comes it that this gospel is promulgated? Only because a special messenger of God, the eschatological ambassador, is raising his voice. Here lies the deepest mystery in that unique and incomparable picture of the *basileia* depicted so vividly in the preaching of Jesus.

[61] For "radicalism" in Qumran and with Jesus see H. Braun, *Spätjüdisch-häretischer und früchchristlicher Radikalismus* II (Tübingen 1957). For a criticism, K. Schubert in *B. Z. N. F.* 3 (1959), pp. 123 seq.

THE PRESENCE OF THE ESCHATOLOGICAL REIGN OF GOD IN THE WORKS OF JESUS

11. The Salvific Work of Jesus as a Sign of God's Reign

The central problem in the gospel preached by Jesus concerns the relation between the reign of God that he is proclaiming and his own person and activity. We must insist that he employs this concept in a single and purely eschatological sense. But does he envisage the eschatological kingship of God as still future or as a present force and reality or are both notions included at the same time? Many scholars believe that Jesus applies only one time category and they interpret the texts accordingly. Others, the majority, recognize different shades of meaning and level in his statements and attempt to harmonize them in one system; they alter emphasis and nuance in interpreting individual passages and from these build up their overall picture. It is not our purpose to examine and discuss these various opinions. We shall be content to mention a number of typical approaches in order to bring the problem into sharper focus. This makes us somewhat schematic, but we only want to distinguish trends of thought without forcing the individual views into categories. We trust that this procedure will be excused.

The main trends of interpretation are as follows:

i. Future eschatology:

Jesus did not proclaim the reign of God as immediate and in no sense as actually realized. He announced it for the near future, either during his active life on earth or shortly after his death (J. Weiß, A. Schweitzer, M. Werner, E. Grässer).

ii. Realized Eschatology (the opposite view):
The reign of God is already realized in Jesus and his operations; the future adds nothing essentially new. All the passages which refer to the near future are to be understood as present fulfilment (C. H. Dodd).

iii. Eschatology being realized:
The hour of fulfilment has arrived since the Saviour is there; but the consummation is not yet complete (J. Jeremias, *Gleichnisse Jesu,* p. 194).

iv. Eschatological polarity:
Jesus announces the reign of God as near (for the generation then alive) as a manifestation to be made to men but which in his person already affects the present, wins power through his actions and is perceptible as something sure of realization in the future.

v. Dialectical interpretations:
Both series of statements, concerning the reign as present and as future are equally justified. The dialectic of "already there" and "not yet there" is deliberately employed and provides two perspectives for one and the same reign of God.

vi. Interpretation in terms of Church history:
The reign of God has come in the person and action of Jesus and is now permanently present but it continues to develop both interiorly and exteriorly, as seen in the history of the Church, until its final consummation in the future. (Older Catholic interpretation).

vii. Interpretation in terms of the gradual unfolding of the history of salvation:

The final (eschatological) period has a beginning and an end. The reign of God has arrived with Jesus but only as initial salvation which still awaits its fulfilment. The intervening or penultimate period (O. Cullmann) is the real period of salvation, the era of the Church and its activity in the service of the perfect reign that is to come. But the reign of God is not to be identified with the Church or be realized in the earthly and historical sphere; it operates only in the Church and with the Church into this sphere. (More recent Catholic interpretation.)

Of these views, the first two have to take violent liberties with the texts and their interpretations, as will be shown later, are one-sided. No. vi which has had considerable vogue does not do full justice to the markedly supernatural and eschatological character of God's reign and is being increasingly abandoned by Catholic scholars. The other conceptions all recognize a certain polarity in the texts, they distribute the emphasis variously and select different categories for their interpretations. "Dialectic" does not appear the proper vehicle for biblical thought. The right method is suggested by the Old Testament relation between promise and fulfilment, fulfilment and consummation. Consequently, the notion of an historical development of salvation, in a comprehensive sense, must be accepted as fundamental. Yet the concrete application, the relation of the reign of God to the Church, provides many difficulties. The whole question is complicated by long-standing theological positions and made even more thorny by several much-debated texts. It depends to a large extent on interpretations of the *basileia* parables which all theologians have used to confirm their views. To find the full harmony of all these passages will always remain a matter for theological decision.

Our treatment may be more profitable if we examine this

eschatological problem of Christ's message in another context, which has today a greater urgency than ever. What significance did Jesus attribute to his own person and action in regard to the advent of the reign of God? Is he merely the prophet who proclaims it? Or has it already come with him? And if so, how? This includes several special questions: How is the activity of Jesus related to the coming of the Son of man? What is the significance of the interim period which historically is that of the Church? For its progress our study depends upon the answers to these questions so that it is only towards its conclusion (chapter four) that we can deal with the relation of the reign of God to the community of the redeemed in Jesus (the Church). We cannot omit the question whether the "mystery of God's reign" (Mark 4:11) is to be identified with the mystery of the person of Jesus. If this question is not faced or if it is deliberately suppressed, it becomes impossible or pointless to treat of the reign of God. When Jesus announces this reign, it is his own announcement, and that of no one else.

11. The Salvific Work of Jesus as a Sign of God's Reign

There is unmistakable evidence that Jesus associated his gospel of the reign of God with his own person. Not a few of his sayings refer to the significance of the hour of his advent and action. It transcends the coming of earlier prophets (Luke 16:16 a) and was rather the object of their aspirations (Matt. 13:17 = Luke 10:24). The gospel of Jesus stands high above the penitential preaching of Jonah and the wisdom of Solomon (Matt. 12:41 seq. = Luke 11:31 seq.). In the antitheses of the Sermon on the Mount Jesus places himself beside and above Moses, though he never impugns Moses' authority as the lawgiver acting on God's behalf.[1] This is clear from the new answer about divorce (Mark 10:1–9 par.). Consequently, Jesus is claiming an authority which is unique and, however it be interpreted[2], breaks through the limits of the prophetic category.

The Messianic claim of Jesus is still disputed even today. Men grant that his advent necessarily aroused Messianic hopes but not that he was conscious of himself as Messias. The Messianic element in him is contained in his preaching and activity but for himself he claimed no Messianic title.[3] But, if this were so, how could we give a positive explanation to his statements? How could we do justice to his summons to follow him and his demand that men shall attach themselves to him? The sentence of Luke 14:26, "If any man come to me and hate not his father and mother and wife and children and brethren and sisters, yea and his own life also, cannot be my disciple" is properly understood by Matthew as meaning, "He that loveth father or mother more than me is not worthy of me" (10:37). We have here a unique claim, not a summons to political association with the Messias to fight for freedom but an invitation to a

[1] Matt. 5:21–48; see on this point Schnackenburg, *Sittliche Botschaft,* pp. 36 seq.; 45 seq.

[2] E. Käsemann in *Z. Th. K.* 51 (1954), p. 145: "The only category which does justice to his claim is that which his disciples attributed to him, namely the Messias: this is totally independent of the further question whether he himself employed or claimed it." Ph. Vielhauer goes further in *Festschrift für G. Dehn,* p. 78: "The category of Messias does not do justice to this claim . . .". Jesus understood himself to be "God's final word to men. But he refused to express this claim in terms of a self-portrait drawn from the rich repertoire of Jewish eschatology." But is not this a purely modern approach? Was he not obliged to make himself understood by his Jewish contemporaries?

[3] So G. Bornkamm, *Jesus von Nazareth,* pp. 155–63; Ph. Vielhauer, (see previous footnote).

religious following, directed to the person who gave it and with definite religious objectives. Further, it is not merely an individual following but a corporate movement, the movement towards a community, the Messianic community of salvation (see below, section 17).

Jesus did claim to be the Messias. The claim was sufficiently concealed to avoid misunderstanding, but it was evident enough for those who could understand.[4] He claimed to be the Messias with a purely religious mission that was revealed in his preaching and salvific actions, and at the core of this was the near approach of the reign of God. This blend of preaching and action shows that his central proclamation cannot be dissociated from his person. Even could we imagine him to have done this, to have dissociated his gospel and teaching from his person and communicated this gospel merely as a prophet of God, this would be quite impossible in view of his actions and the manner in which he spoke of them. By his own testimony these are the fulfilment of the prophetic promises for the era of salvation. His answer to John the Baptist who from his prison had asked whether he was "he who is to come" is fundamental: "Go and relate to John what you have heard and seen: the blind see, the lame walk, the lepers are cleansed, the deaf hear, the dead rise again, the poor have the gospel preached to them" (Matt. 11:4 seq. = Luke 7:22 seq.). This passage from the Matthew-Luke tradition contains a clear allusion to several passages from

[4] E. Sjöberg, *Der verborgene Menschensohn,* especially p. 230: "His Messianic character was concealed; it was a mystery that could not be known immediately and that he did not make known through special instruction and proclamation. But he did not wish it to remain unrecognized. His words and actions called for reflection on the part of those who saw and heard them. His Messianic character was implicit in them. Anyone who could see and hear could discover this."

Isaias which here are assembled and combined. In the unabridged text of the Old Testament their meaning is even more obvious. In Isa. 29:18 seq. we read: "In that day the deaf shall hear the words of the book: and out of darkness and obscurity the eyes of the blind shall see. The oppressed *('anâwîm)* and the poor *('ebhyônîm)* experience joy in the Lord; the poorest of men rejoice in the Holy One of Israel." Verse 19 contains the very expressions which we suppose as the background of the early Beatitudes (Matt. 5:3, 5). The cure of the deaf is not only liberation from a bodily defect but also an opening of the ears for the words of salvation. In Isa. 35:5 seq. also, which again refers to the healing of blind and deaf, lame and dumb, the major emphasis rests upon the saving joy and happiness given by God. This thought emerges into the full light in Isa. 61:1 seq., "to preach to the poor the gospel of salvation". Jesus introduced this passage in his initial discourse at Nazareth (Luke 4:18 seq.), gave it a Messianic interpretation and declared that it was fulfilled. "This day is fulfilled this scripture in your ears." Jesus reveals what he wishes to be and to be considered, not through any public Messianic utterance but through his understanding of the scriptures which he applies to his own advent: namely, as the Saviour and Redeemer who brings God's grace and mercy, God's salvation and joy to those who accept his message, and this means the humble and the poor, those bowed beneath burdens and beneath guilt.

This testimony of Jesus to himself makes it obvious how closely his miracles and preaching are related. The point of the cures is to prove what he is proclaiming, the all-embracing salvific will of God; they are signs of the eschatological salvation which has come with Jesus. It is already there, in so far as the blind actually see, the deaf hear, the lame walk, the lepers are cleansed. It is not yet completely there, in so far as all sicknesses are not yet healed and the whole accursed earth not yet transfigured. It is precisely this salvation, perceptible already though not yet fulfilled, that is dawning with the reign of God manifested in these cures and wonders.[5] In this sense his preaching itself is one of the signs of the saving era. The gospel of divine mercy and forgiveness is announced to the poor. In itself, it stands beside and beneath the miracles; it is itself the miracle of God's mighty saving word. Jesus not only speaks of divine forgiveness which will be granted with the abandonment of divine punishment in the "acceptable year of the Lord" (Luke 4:19) to all who genuinely repent. He actually imparts this forgiveness to the men he meets (Mark 2:5, 10, 15–7 etc.). Here salvation is realized. The reign of God begins, in this specific sense; the miracles might be called the "kingdom of God in action".[6]

Could Jesus have accomplished this in complete detachment from his own person, merely as the mouthpiece of God among men? His concealed claim to be the Messias, in this purely religious sense, provides all too clear an answer. The early Church tradition, found in the evangelists, may have brought this out more forcibly; it certainly did not invent or distort it.

This is true, to begin with, of the initial discourse at Nazareth, already referred to (Luke 4:16–29). This was explicitly put back by the third evangelist to the beginning of the public life, as may be seen by comparison with the Nazareth extract in Mark 6:1–6 (compare Matt. 13:53–58). It bears traces of literary composition[7] but it was pieced together from frag-

[5] L. de Grandmaison, *Jésus Christ. Sa personne, son message, ses preuves* II (Paris 1929), pp. 330–68; A. Richardson, *The Miracle-Stories of the Gospels* (London 1941), *passim* but especially pp. 38–50.

[6] Grandmaison, op. cit., II, p. 366.

[7] J. Schmid, *Ev. nach Lk,* pp. 110 seq.

ments that were genuine.[8] The referring of Isa. 61:1seq. to the person and work of Jesus is in full accord with the answer Jesus made to John the Baptist. Subsequently, Jesus boldly attacks the belief of Israel that it is the one and only elect (vv. 25-7), with a deliberation and severity which reveal the true historical Jesus. Further, his words in which he speaks of his coming or mission[9] cannot be categorically dismissed as though they were inventions of the early Church and as though the Church blended the myth of a heavenly messenger and revealer with her portrait of Jesus.[10] A study of the content of these statements reveals ideas that were unique and characteristic of Jesus and assertions which the early Church could scarcely have invented (Mark 1:38, Luke 12:49 seq., 51-3). The fourth gospel has gone further with its kerygmatic formulation. With the synoptics, the markedly pictorial expressions and the Semitic turns of phrase offer further proofs that the tradition is a genuine one.

Like the gospel, the miracles are signs of the Messianic era and they too derive from the great grace of the presence of Jesus. This is evident from the greeting of Jesus to his disciples, Luke 10:23 = Matt. 13:16: "Blessed are the (Matthew: your) eyes that see what they see (Matthew: because they see, and your ears because they hear). For (Matthew: truly) I say to you, many prophets and kings (Matthew: and just men) have desired to see the things that you see and have not seen them, and to hear the things that you hear and have not heard them." The priority accorded to the apostles over prophets and kings (and just men) of the Old Covenant can only consist in their actual experience of the

[8] J. Jeremias, *Jesu Verheißung,* pp. 43 seq., with footnote 174.

[9] Mark 1:38; 2:17 par. (cf. Luke 19:10); 9:37 par.; 10:45 par.; Matt. 5:17; 15:24; Luke 12:49 seq.; Luke 12:51–53 = Matt. 10:34–6; Luke 7:33 seq. = Matt. 11:18 seq.

[10] R. Bultmann, *Geschichte der synoptischen Tradition,* pp. 164–8.

era of salvation and precisely in the preaching and operation of Jesus.

These two evangelists introduce this passage on different occasions and the occasion affects the meaning. Luke places it at the close of his account of the mission of the seventy disciples. Wherever they arrive, they are to announce that the kingdom of God is at hand (10:9, cf. 11). On their return they joyfully report that demons were subject to them in the name of Jesus (v. 17). Then follows a prayer of praise from Jesus and then this passage. What connects them is the thought of salvation present in the word they proclaimed and the expulsion of devils, that points to the nearness of the reign of God. Matthew puts the extract in the chapter that has seven parables of the "kingdom of heaven", more explicitly in contrast with men who are blind, who see and do not see, hear and do not hear and understand (13:13). His interpretation does not differ, however, from Luke's. The original meaning which both evangelists found in their common source cannot have been missed, for the content scarcely permits any other explanation. By linking it with Jesus' prayer of thanksgiving Luke is pointing out what God "had hidden from the wise and prudent . . . and revealed to little ones" (ταῦτα 10:21); this is the nearness of God's kingdom to be perceived in the words and action of Jesus. Matthew comments significantly on another passage. To the disciples it is given to understand "the mysteries of the kingdom of heaven" (13:11, cf. Mark 4:11). The circle is completed. All three passages refer, at least in the mind of the evangelists, to the same reality, hidden and at the same time revealed to those who believe – the fact that eschatological salvation is present in the acts of Jesus and that the reign of God, in one sense, has already come.

Sufficient has been said to show that Jesus' preaching of the reign of God and his cures are not independent but come to form one unity and together they confirm the eschatological reality manifested in him. Further, an ancient logion directly relates his actions to the advent of the kingdom. It refers to the driving out of devils. "If I by the finger of God (Matthew: through the Holy Ghost) cast out devils, doubtless the kingdom (reign) of God is come upon you" (Luke 11:20 = Matt. 12:28). In this sentence the authority of which is beyond dispute the following points should be noted: 1. The verb φθάνειν in the aorist cannot be understood except as "has actually come";[11] any attempt to tone down this note of fulfilment is unjustified. 2. The presence of the reign of God is recognizable by the driving out of demons. The conditional clause that posits an actual fact gives at once knowledge of the fact and the proof (note ἄρα). 3. The expulsion of demons is a fact, seen as a manifestation of power with effective results. Accordingly, the reign of God is seen as an effective power (not as a "kingdom", as an institution, nor as a purely interior reality). 4. This actual realization of the reign of God is brought about by Jesus; the rôle is uniquely his. Divine power or the Holy Spirit is entrusted to him to break the power of the demons.

No objection can be raised from the Jewish exorcists mentioned in the previous verse. This verse belongs to a different context, namely the negative argument that this success of Jesus could not be attributed to the power of Beelzebub. How Jesus looked upon the character and success of Jewish exorcists is not discussed. However much they may have expelled demons, it was in no sense for him a sign of the reign of God.[12]

[11] Dalman, *Worte Jesu* I, p. 88, infers an Aramaic *meta'* and compares with Dan. 4:21 "to come upon someone" so that he can no longer escape. For fuller discussion of the passage cf. W. G. Kümmel, *Verheißung und Erfüllung,* pp. 99–101; R. Morgenthaler, *Kommendes Reich,* pp. 36–45.
[12] A different view is registered by B. Noack, *Satanas und Soteria* (Copenhagen 1948), pp. 71 seq.

We may conclude from this passage that Jesus is conscious that the fullness of divine power has been given him and that in consequence God's eschatological reign is breaking through in his actions. This is not yet the cosmic manifestation of God's kingship but it is more than a hint or promise, and it is not the same as a purely interior or entirely concealed presence. The *basileia* is essentially a revelation of divine power, even though it is not yet the complete manifestation of his glory.

The casting out of devils is equally significant in Mark's gospel which does not contain this passage. In Mark the proclamation of the gospel is very closely linked with the expulsion of evil spirits (1:27, 39). The apostles receive a similar power and exercise it during their mission (6:12 seq.). The evangelist pays the greatest attention to the actual manner of expulsion (1:23–27; 3:11; 5:1–20; 7:24–30; 9:14–29). Its significance is brought home in the important passage 3:22–30. The accusation of his enemies that he is possessed by Beelzebub or that he casts out devils because of an alliance with the prince of devils (v. 22) gives Jesus the opportunity, not only of rejecting their suspicion as empty and meaningless but also of positively stating the meaning of his action. The passing simile of the stronger man who breaks into the strong man's house is intended to show that Jesus is now breaking the hold of Satan (v. 27). This is illustrated in Mark's concrete accounts of the expulsions. The devils resist him, at times with words of adjuration, at times employing his name to gain a magical influence over him,[13] but they have to yield to his majestic word of command. "And so the curtain rose on the final Messianic conflict and eschatological victory, but in place of a battle of spirits men saw only a special kind of casting out of devils."[14] God's reign which is coming into

[13] O. Bauernfeind, *Die Worte der Dämonen im Markusevangelium* (Stuttgart 1927), pp. 6–28. [14] O. Bauernfeind, op. cit., p. 90.

effect in Jesus' acts, forces back the power of Satan. That is the meaning of these exorcisms.

Finally, from Luke's particular tradition we have a passage in which Jesus describes Satan's downfall: "I saw Satan like lightning falling from heaven" (Luke 10:18). This single sentence gives no details about the time, occasion and circumstances of this "vision" but there is little doubt that it is connected with the casting out of devils. In Mark 3:23-26 also, Satan is regarded as the ruler of the devils whom he has gathered together as in a realm. The meaning of Luke 10:18 is identical with that of Mark 3:27. Satan's power is broken through the actions of Jesus. The fall like lightning from heaven is an image of the sudden, irresistible deprival of power in the same way in which Isaias (14:12–16) describes the fall of the king of Babel.[15] God himself may actually appear as the attacker but in reality Jesus is conscious of being not only an onlooker but the instrument of God.[16] Luke puts this passage in a context where the expulsion of devils by the disciples also is included as a proof of Satan's defeat (Luke 10:17).

Accordingly, we have in a threefold tradition ("Q", Mark and Luke's own particular source), the same idea that the casting out of devils demonstrates in a special manner the breaking of Satan's might and the dawn of God's reign. In the parables of growth we can sense a first and hidden presence of God's reign

[15] Neither the late Jewish teaching about the fall of the angels according to Gen. 6:1–4 nor the corresponding eschatological hope (cf. Apoc. 12:8 seq.; also *Ass. Mos.* 10:1; *Jub.* 23:29; *T. Sim.* 6:6; *T. Jud.* 25:3) are decisive about the time factor in this vision of Jesus. Though these notions may have affected the picture, the thought of Jesus is simply that Satan is now losing his power. J. Schmid interprets the passage correctly.
[16] T. W. Manson, *Sayings of Jesus,* p. 258 and R. Otto, *Reich Gottes,* pp. 75 seq., over-emphasize the action of God.

in the advent and activity of Jesus. These we shall examine later because of certain difficulties of interpretation (section 13). What has been said hitherto is sufficient for us to accept God's reign as actually present. What we must now bring into clearer focus is how Jesus himself regarded this presence of the eschatological kingship of God.

Our judgment of these "presence" passages must fall between two definite outside limits. It would be insufficient to regard the preaching, miracles and expulsion of devils on the part of Jesus as mere portents of the divine reign to come.[17] They are on the contrary indications of its presence. But it would be, on the other hand, too much to look upon this present and active reign of God as fully realized or as institutional. It still points like a sign to the fully realized kingdom of the future and at once guarantees and calls for it. The first of these two limits presents Jesus basically as a prophet, the second as realizing the final kingdom in the present, but neither of these does proper justice to his preaching and the testimony he bears to himself. But it is more difficult to give a positive note to this presence. Remembering various formulae, we may suggest that the reign of God present in Jesus and his actions is provisional, in that it precedes the future reign and is not complete or finally closed. It could also be termed a concealed reign but only relatively, that is, in comparison with the future revelation of glory, because it is manifested in the words and miracles of Jesus. We should avoid saying it is present in weakness since that is contrary to the nature of the divine rule. Jesus desired to manifest God's mighty and at the same time perceptible plan of eschatological salvation. He

[17] So among others J. Weiss, *Predigt Jesu vom Reiche Gottes,* p. 70; W. Michaelis, *Täufer, Jesus, Urgemeinde,* pp. 73 seq.; M. Dibelius, *Jesus,* p. 69; R. H. Fuller, *Mission and Achievement of Jesus,* pp. 35–43; E. Grässer, *Problem der Parusieverzögerung,* pp. 4–8.

himself teaches and acts with divine power (ἐξουσία). He performs "deeds of power" (δυνάμεις); in him divine forces are at work (Mark 6:14). Paul expresses it correctly when he declares that God's reign consists (where it is realized) "not in word but in power" (1 Cor. 4:20).

We may accordingly describe the presence of the *basileia* as dynamic but in a completely real sense: God's reign is actually in operation. We must avoid misunderstandings, as though it were only "potential" or "virtual" in contradistinction to "real" and "substantial". Philosophical distinctions like these are out of place. The biblical term "dynamic" puts the emphasis on the divine action already operative in Jesus as an effective production of salvation which, however, will be completed only in the future in terms of judgment and realized salvation. But we must also avoid thinking of this present reign of God as a tangible form or fixed establishment. If we remain faithful to the historical mode of thought of the Bible which moves in the categories of promise and fulfilment, our best way of understanding this presence of the reign of God, preached by Jesus, is as the Messianic era of partial but not complete fulfilment of grace or as the beginning of the eschatological era of salvation, moving always towards its higher level and culmination. And this much debated question of the presence and future of God's reign introduces the further question of the meaning of the eschatological gospel of Jesus.[18]

It is equally difficult to describe the precise relation of Jesus to the coming of the reign of God. If we again set limits, then the expression "Jesus establishes the reign of God" goes beyond the language of the evangelists. The opposite limit is given in the pertinent sentence of R. Otto: "It is not Jesus who 'brings'

[18] Kümmel, *Verheißung und Erfüllung,* pp. 133–47.

the kingdom – this notion is foreign to him – but the kingdom that brings Jesus."[19] This interpretation in its turn cannot be substantiated by any of the sayings of Jesus (certainly not by Luke 10:19, to which Otto appeals). What Jesus is proclaiming is that the reign of God is at hand; it has even (through his driving out of devils) already come. In all this the rôle of Jesus is not passive. His person has its significance for the advent of God's reign in the present. His coming coincides with the provisional advent of the *basileia*. He announces it but it can be announced only through his advent and actions. To try to establish premises and consequence here is beside the point. Both belong to God's salvific will which has associated the mission of Jesus with his eschatological kingship. God uses him to make his rule effective in the present for the salvation of men who are willing to be converted. His purpose is to confront men with a final decision and with complete assurance to proclaim his future kingship that will be openly manifested and which will bring with it the separation of the judgment and afterwards blessing and happiness for all the elect and saved.

12. Disputed Passages

On the basis of these earlier inquiries we can now tackle a number of disputed passages which are not easy to interpret with any certainty.

One of the most difficult is the so-called "violence" sentence in Matt. 11:12 = Luke 16:16. In Matthew it reads as follows: "From the days of John the Baptist until now the kingdom of heaven comes with violence (or perhaps 'suffereth violence')

[19] Otto, *Reich Gottes,* p. 75.

and the violent bear it away" (v. 13). "For all the prophets and the law prophesied until John." Luke 16:16 on the other hand runs thus: "The law and the prophets were until John. From that time the kingdom of God is preached, and every one useth violence towards it." The temporal clauses "from the days of John the Baptist until now" (or correspondingly "from that time") introduce a time-conditioned statement about the rule or kingdom of God that is important in assessing its mode of presence. But the exact meaning of the passage is obscure and disputed because of the way in which it has been handed down, the significance of the term βιάζεσθαι and the imagery employed.

Scholars are more or less agreed about the value of the form in Matthew and Luke. The expression "law and the prophets" as in Luke 16:16a is correct and Matthew had to alter it to suit his context. But βιάζεσθαι in Matt. 11:12 is in a more difficult, yet better constructed, form because of the parallelism between its two parts. Luke 16:16b contains an interpretation. Now what is the meaning of βιάζεσθαι? It can be taken in the middle voice in the sense of "make a forcible path for oneself"[20] or as "force one's way in violently" (so clearly Luke 16:16b); it may also be understood as passive, that is "be seized by violence". The meaning in Matt. 11:12 depends upon the way in which we understand the sequence of the two parts, the relation between βιάζεσθαι and βιασταί. Is the second portion intended to explain the first (synonymous parallelism) or does it make a new assertion (synthetic parallelism)? Many exegetes accept the first view and interpret the second part in a bad sense, to wit, that since the days of John attempts have been made to do violence to the kingdom of God, in other words violent men tried to rob men

[20] See Bauer, *Wörterbuch,* p. 279, 2 c; G. Schrenk in *Th.W.B.* I, p. 609, note 3.

of it.[21] In favour of this is the fact that βιάζεσθαι is more usually used for hostile action especially in connection with ἁρπάζειν.[22] But if this is so, then the second part adds nothing new and, further, one would not expect to find the *basileia* as object so that "from men" has to be added silently.[23] Linguistically, the sentence could be applied to men of goodwill, hungry for salvation, if βιάζεσθαι and ἁρπάζειν be taken in a strong and hyperbolical sense: men who believe the gospel and harness all their energies seek the kingdom of God and nothing else since the days of John the Baptist (ἀπό in an inclusive sense) and his preaching but only fully after the summons and appeal of Jesus (cf. Luke 13:24 = Matt. 7:14; Matt. 13:44, 45 seq.; Mark 10:28–30 par.; Luke 12:31 = Matt. 6:33 par.).[24] The first portion would then refer not to their violence ("the *basileia* is taken by storm") but to the power within God's rule itself ("it forces its way in").[25]

[21] Consult the different views in Bauer, *Wörterbuch,* p. 279, 1 a; in addition, Kümmel, *Verheißung und Erfüllung,* pp. 114–17; J. Kraeling, *John the Baptist,* pp. 156 seq. (his view is followed by A. N. Wilder, *Eschatology and Ethics,* p. 149 and J. A. T. Robinson, *Jesus and His Coming,* p. 41); O. Cullmann, *Der Staat im Neuen Testament* (Tübingen, 1956), p. 14; K. Staab, *Das Ev. nach Matthäus* (Würzburg, 1951); G. Bornkamm, *Jesus von Nazareth,* p. 46, 50. The Aramaic basis is dealt with in Dalman, *Worte Jesu* 1, pp. 113–16; M. Black, *An Aramaic Approach to the Gospels and the Acts* (2nd edition, Oxford, 1954), p. 84; 262 seq., note 3; in particular, D. Daube, *The New Testament and Rabbinic Judaism* (London, 1956), pp. 285–94 (this shows the various possible interpretations and at the same time the difficulty of deciding between them).

[22] G. Schrenk in *Th.W.B.* I, p. 609, note 7.

[23] W. Foerster in *Th.W.B.* I, p. 472, 14 seq.; E. Percy, *Botschaft Jesu,* p. 193.

[24] So several scholars: see Bauer, *Wörterbuch,* p. 279, 2; also J. Schniewind (German New Testament) and J. Schmid, l. c.; Percy, *Botschaft Jesu,* pp. 191–7.

[25] M. Black in *Exp.T.* 63 (1952), p. 290.

We would then have not a repetition of the same idea but a meaningful union of two statements, belonging to the proclamation of the reign of God: God's rule makes its way with great force and keen enthusiasts lay hold on it, that is, want to share in it (Matt. 19:12: there are men who have made themselves eunuchs for its sake). Jesus means that God's eschatological act has unloosed a storm for the man who hungers and thirsts for salvation. It is thus a cry of joy which recognizes that the period of waiting and hope (the era of the "Law and the prophets") came to an end with John the Baptist (Luke 16:16a). If this interpretation is accepted, Luke did not misunderstand the passage but intensified the note of joy. Every man strives to force his way into God's kingdom. This interpretation is definitely preferable. In either case the royal rule of God in this passage is a present, dynamic reality whether it be considered as "treated violently", that is, the violent attempt to take it away from men (present *de conatu*) or, more probably, that it forces its way in with power and makes it possible for the violent to lay hold upon it for their salvation. And the somewhat ambiguous addition "since the days of John" (is this inclusive or exclusive?) fixes a starting point for this process and leaves no doubt that since then the rule of God presses forward and manifests its power "until now". And so the passage fits in with the statement of Jesus that God's reign is at hand with himself but it is not yet perfect and does not yet show itself in its glory.

John the Baptist, therefore, provides a turning point. He stands on the frontier between prophetic prediction and eschatological fulfilment. But there is another passage that seems to indicate that personally the Baptist belongs only to the old order: "I say to you that amongst those that are born of women there is no one greater (no greater has arisen) than John the Baptist. But he that is the lesser in the reign (kingdom) of God (or of the heavens) is greater than he" (Luke 7:28 = Matt. 11:11).

The second part of this is frequently suspect as an early Church addition for apologetical reasons, to avoid putting too great an emphasis upon the Baptist as could have been suggested by the first (and genuine) part. But its secure status in tradition ("Q") and the pregnant parallel between the two portions favour its original character. The expression "in the reign (kingdom) of God" is surprising. It is absurd to think of John as excluded from the future *basileia;* but if we regard the reign or kingdom of God as actually beginning with Jesus it is considered as an established institution. O. Cullmann adopts the suggestion of F. Dibelius which has the authority of many of the Fathers[26] and interprets the text as meaning that "the lesser (Jesus) is greater in the kingdom of heaven than he (John)". The sentence comes from a period when Jesus was still working "in the shadow of the Baptist".[27] But this explanation runs into serious difficulties. The relation of the words is unnatural, Jesus' description of himself as the "lesser" is exceptional and there are no proofs of any period when Jesus "worked in the shadow of the greater, John" (see John 3:22–30, a passage which suggests the contrary).

The passage may be understood more easily if we concentrate on the parallel antithesis. There exist other Jewish instances of the use of the striking phrase "born of woman" to denote the region of earth as distinct from the heavenly and divine.[28] Here it would mean that as a man on earth John (in

[26] *Z.N.W.* II (1910), pp. 190–2. Dibelius finds this interpretation in Tertullian, Chrysostom, Hilary and (as the opinion of many), in Jerome (p. 192, note 1).
[27] O. Cullmann, *Christologie,* p. 31.
[28] Billerbeck 1, 597 seq.

his unexampled moral grandeur) is the greatest. But the reign of God belongs to another order of things, to be inaugurated by God's grace. Anyone who is permitted to enter this, is placed above all that is earthly. This would be understood as the divine reign of the future; there would be no question of John's exclusion since the first part refers to him in his earthly life. The second part would express the high value of the reign and kingdom as in the exclamation, "Blessed is he that shall eat bread in the kingdom of God (in God's reign)" (Luke 14:15). It may also reflect certain views about precedence in the kingdom of God (Matt. 18:1, "Who is the greatest in the kingdom of heaven?"), which Jesus basically repudiated but adapted to this particular context (Mark 9:35; 10:43 seq.; Luke 14:11; 18:14). Whether this be so or not, the passage must not be understood of the reign of God as present. In human effort and in his prophetic function on earth John is the greatest but everyone who is allowed a share in God's kingdom (it is not stated, indeed it is improbable, that John is not of their number) experiences an elevation in grace through God (Luke 14:11) that cannot be achieved by even the mightiest human endeavour.

There is another much debated passage in Luke 17:20 seq.: "And being asked by the Pharisees when the kingdom [reign] of God should come, he answered them and said, The kingdom [reign] of God cometh not with observation. Neither shall they say, Behold here or behold there. For lo! the kingdom [reign] of God is within you" (ἐντὸς ὑμῶν). One point is evident. Jesus is proposing an opinion opposite to that held by his questioners; it stops them in their tracks and makes them think. Their question is rooted in the nationalist and apocalyptic hope of a kingdom that looked and longed for as immediate a realization as possible. To this Jesus gives a negative answer in two sentences, the relation between which needs to be decided exegetically. Does the second explain the first? Or introduce a new point of view? Does Jesus intend to reject altogether the query about the When and Where? Or is he saying that men cannot calculate the temporal advent of the reign of God any more than they can determine it in space and place? The οὐδέ suggests a continuation of the thought so that the second interpretation is preferable. Jesus is well aware of the tendency (especially in circles influenced by the apocalypses) to calculate the When by means of portents. To this Jesus replies first that it is not a matter of observation and then that, even if it does come, men cannot look for it or establish its presence in this or the other place; his audience, in other words, has a completely false idea of the advent of the reign of God.

E. Percy[29] views the connection from a different angle because he does not interpret παρατήρησις in the sense of observation in time but in association with the expressions that follow it, with their spatial determinants. This leads him to render ἐντὸς ὑμῶν as "inwardly in you". But the word, the natural meaning of which is simply observation, can be employed in connection with temporal sequence (for example in observations of the heavens), as Percy admits. Such a connection is provided by the leading question of the Pharisees in Luke 17:20. It is unlikely that Jesus totally ignored it.

To substantiate his double negative (γάρ) Jesus now emphasizes his contrary position (ἰδού). "The reign of God is ἐντὸς ὑμῶν." The major controversy centres around this last expression.

Usually, ἐντός means "within, inwardly" but it may occasionally signify "in the midst of, amid", for example in Xeno-

[29] *Botschaft Jesu,* pp. 216–23.

phon (*An.* I, 10, 3; *Hell.* II, 3, 19); Herodotus (VII, 100,3), Arrian (*An.* V, 22, 4) and also Symmachus (Ps. 87:6; Lam. 1:3; Mich. 5:6; Hab. 3:2). Even if it does imply a delimited area (cf. Percy, pp. 219 seq.), Luke 19:21 could be read as follows: You need not go here and there, the reign of God is within your own range. And though a more recent suggestion, based on two passages in the papyri, which understands "at the disposition of" cannot be accepted,[30] this nuance could make itself felt in the passage: it is among you, and you can reach it if you wish. One can scarcely argue from the conventional sentence which follows (Luke 17:22).[31]

Since ἐντὸς ὑμῶν permits at least two renderings, namely "inwardly" and "among you", exegesis must make its choice. The old and spiritual interpretation that prevailed with the Fathers and throughout the Middle Ages referred it to an inner realm of grace within the heart; this was maintained by Luther among others in the Reformation era and has been held to our own times.[32] Its main weakness is that it does not fit in with the normal view of Jesus about the reign of God. For this reason most exegetes today accept very properly the version "among you". But this leaves us still with two possibilities: the eschatological, that is, the reign of God, when it appears,

[30] C. H. Roberts in *Harv.Th.R.* 41 (1948), pp. 1–8: this opinion is rejected by H. Riesenfeld in *Nuntius* 2 (1949), pp. 11 seq.; A. Wikgren, also in *Nuntius* 4 (1950), pp. 27 seq.; and J. G. Griffiths in *Exp.T.* 63 (1951), pp. 30 seq.; see also J. Gewiess in *Th.Rev.* 45 (1949), pp. 87 seq.
[31] This is not accepted by B. Noack, *Gottesreich bei Lukas,* pp. 39–50.
[32] For a history of this interpretation see Noack, op. cit., pp. 3–15. In the patristic period only one divergent interpretation is discovered, deriving from Cyril of Alexandria and developed more fully in Euthymius Zigabenus. For more modern exponents of the interpretation consult Kümmel, *Verheißung und Erfüllung,* p. 27, note 51; and E. Percy (note 29, above).

is among you all of a sudden; and the present, that is, that God's reign is already in your midst.

The defenders of the first view would be justified if the same situation continued in 21 b which existed in 21 a. Then, it might reasonably be qualified by "suddenly", "at once". But the connection is interrupted by ἰδοὺ γάρ. In 21 b Jesus is again speaking from his point of view. The double negative is followed by his positive answer which exposes two mistaken views, that of looking for portents to reveal when the reign of God will arrive and of seeking for it after it has appeared. The addition of "suddenly" in this context introduces the most important thought of all which Jesus could scarcely have left out. Therefore his answer should be understood literally, that is, in the present tense.[33]

This passage expresses, therefore, a presence of the reign of God which is at once a promise and a challenge; promise, in that its future advent is spoken of in other passages; challenge in so far as it compels men to take a decision and prepare for what is to come. It is the second of these which has here the greater weight. Jesus must have had this kind of pointed answer to these enquirers in mind (compare Luke 12:54–56).

There is a further expression, peculiar to Luke, that may create some doubt, namely to "announce" the reign of God. It occurs relatively often and with various verbs in the Greek text.[34] There is a parallel expression in the other synoptics, "to preach or announce the gospel" (Matt. 4:23; 9:35; 24:14; 26:13; Mark 1:14; 13:10; 14:1), deriving probably from the

[33] So among others, R. Otto, *Reich Gottes,* pp. 98–104; E. Stauffer in *Th.W.B.* III, p. 117, note 369; Kümmel, op cit. (with others) pp. 26–8; see also J. Bonsirven, *Règne de Dieu,* p. 55.

[34] With εὐαγγελίζεσθαι, Luke 4:43; 8:1; 16:16 b; with κηρύσσειν Luke 9:2; Acts 28:31; with διαγγέλλειν, Luke 9:60; with διαμαρτύρεσθαι, Acts 28:23.

traditional language of the early Church.[35] The special connection of "announcing" with the "reign of God" remains the prerogative of Luke. Does this denote that the future reign of God is being announced in the present or does the announcement suppose that in some way or other the reign is already there?

H. Conzelmann[36] sets the expression in the framework of Luke's eschatology, as he interprets this from the gospel and Acts. He is justified in placing John the Baptist in the series of prophets before the dawn of God's reign. Of Jesus he writes (commenting on Luke 10:18): "the kingdom proper comes only with the Parousia, and the present kingdom is merely its image. In the interval the apostles represent the Master (we see this in the Acts), they are prepared here for what is to come" (pp. 91 seq.). Of the *basileia* concept he writes that "the kingdom of God, far from being made concrete in history, recedes into the ontological distance" (p. 96). He interprets the phrase "announce the kingdom of God" as a sign that its commencement recedes into the distance. "Present and visible are only the Messianic manifestations (pp. 4, 18 seq.). In them salvation has revealed itself and become active. What is present is the message of the kingdom which Luke expressly distinguishes from the kingdom itself" (p. 104). Yet he also observes that "the kingdom has appeared in Christ" (p. 106). Other texts make it practically certain that Luke was concerned to keep a longer interval before the Parousia. But we are here dealing with his notion of the reign of God.

On the evidence of the *basileia* passages in Luke it would be insufficient to speak merely of a presence of salvation and

[35] See Mark 16:15; Gal. 2:2; Col. 1:23; 1 Thess. 2:9. Compare also "to preach the word"; see R. Asting, *Die Verkündigung des Wortes im Urchristentum* (Stuttgart, 1939), pp. 120–9; 164–70.

[36] *Mitte der Zeit,* pp. 96 seq.

a metaphorical presence of the kingdom of God. The sentence in Luke 16:16a, "From that time (the days of John the Baptist) the reign (kingdom) of God is preached" is followed by the sentence, "and everyone useth violence towards it" (16 b). It would be difficult to understand this except as a presence of the *basileia* in the preaching of Jesus and his apostles. In his significant tenth chapter Luke has stressed more markedly than the other synoptics the apostles' activity in the service of the *basileia*. The announcement, "the reign of God is at hand" occurs twice in their missionary instruction (vv. 9, 11), on the first occasion with the addition of "to you" (ἐφ' ὑμᾶς) and in the second, as a warning to the places that reject the disciples. The reign of God thus comes with the disciples' preaching to men. We are tempted to ask whether Luke did not understand the word ἤγγικεν as an arrival, since the addition of ἐφ' ὑμᾶς recalls 11:20. In any event, Luke also includes the assertion that the reign of God has reached mankind through the expulsion of devils by Jesus. And when the disciples on their return narrate how evil spirits were subject to them in the name of Jesus (10:17), this dynamic entry of God's rule must have affected their activity. It is from this point that the ἐντὸς ὑμῶν of Luke 17:21 has to be judged.

This leads us to conclude that the "announcement" should not tone down the idea of the "presence" of the reign of God but, from the viewpoint of an early Christian missionary (cf. Luke 9:60, 62), bring it into stronger relief. This is confirmed by texts from the Acts. The preaching of the *basileia* is intimately associated with the gospel of Jesus Christ (8:12; 28:23, 31), and though the future character of the *basileia* is not denied, its presence in the word and the miracles that proclaim it can scarcely be ignored. This does not mean that the reign of God is brought down into history and identified with the missionary

Church on earth or understood as interior salvation. It remains an eschatological reality that became operative with the advent of Jesus and continues to operate in the mission of the disciples. This last point is characteristic of Luke. The "historian" among the evangelists shows the development of the process of salvation but does not suggest that the present is merely a preparation for the future reign of God. For him too, its forces are active beforehand and manifest themselves in saving factors already present, in the first place in the Holy Spirit.

In Luke the reign of God also preserves its note of polarity between presence and eschatological fulfilment though Luke places marked emphasis upon the extending interval of the Church. And thus there is less urgency in the question whether in Jesus' challenge, "The kingdom (reign) of God is at hand", the ἤγγικεν signifies that it has already come or not yet come. The phrase is found in Mark 1:15 = Matt. 4:17, also in the address to the disciples when they are sent on their mission, Matt. 10:7 = Luke 10:9, 11, and finally in one place it is attributed to the Baptist, in Matt. 3:2 (see above section 9). The word itself and its normal usage compel us to believe that in these passages ἤγγικεν announces its near approach but not yet its definite arrival.

With his translation, "The kingdom of God has come", which fits in with his theory of a "realized eschatology"[37] C. H. Dodd has reopened this controversy. But it has been shown that in the Septuagint and the New Testament the word indicates in an overwhelming number of cases "come near"; we need not enter into individual instances.[38] It is important to note that the early Church also employed the eschatological

[37] *Parables of the Kingdom*, pp. 44 seq.

[38] For the Septuagint, see H. Preisker in *Th.W.B.* II, 330, 26 seq.; J. Y. Campbell in *Exp.T.* 48 (1936–7), pp. 9 seq.; K. Clark in *J.B.L.* 59

ἤγγικεν in a similar sense (Rom. 13:12; Jas. 5:8; 1 Pet. 4:7; cf. Heb. 10:25). So it too will have understood the call of Jesus to salvation in terms of the approaching reign of God.

It only remains to ask whether the context does not signify that the reign of God has already arrived.[39] In Mark 1:15 we read, "The time is accomplished", and the perfect ἤγγικεν at once follows. This refers to an event that has actually happened. But it is the special eschatological consciousness of Jesus that the time has come when the prophecies of the final era are realized but not yet the fulfilment. His own advent and operation fulfil the time and are a certain guarantee that the perfect reign of God is immediately at hand. A glance at Isa. 52:7 makes this even clearer. Jesus is the Messianic harbinger of joy who announces God's final kingship but he is only the harbinger.[40] As has been observed, the addition of ἐφ' ὑμᾶς in Luke 10:9 could mean that the reign of God is in one sense already there, because it is proclaimed, but this interpretation is not certain. The early Church understood ἤγγικεν in both senses according as it envisaged the perfect reign of God not yet achieved or its provisional existence. In fact, ἤγγικεν and ἔφθασεν are found in the same strand of tradition (Matt. 10:7 and 12: both from "Q") and they signify basically the same eschatological reality: namely, the orientation of the present towards the future and the retroactive influence of the future on the present. And so the differ-

(1940), pp. 367 seq.; for the New Testament see Kümmel, op. cit., pp. 13 seq.; Morgenthaler, *Kommendes Reich,* pp. 95 seq.

[39] M. Black in *Exp.T.* 63 (1952), pp. 289 seq.; also his *Aramaic Approach,* pp. 260 seq.; E. Percy, *Botschaft Jesu,* pp. 177 seq.

[40] F. Mußner in *Tr.Th.Z.* 66 (1957), pp. 257–75, sees this "nearness" realized in the activity of Jesus in Galilee, immediately following. In the passage from Mark the proclamation of Jesus has therefore its appropriate historical position. But was the later gospel any different?

ences that were justified on linguistic grounds lose most of their significance in actual fact. Under no circumstances must the gospel and challenge of Jesus be made to indicate a wholly realized or a purely future eschatology.

The remaining disputed passages lend themselves more readily to interpretation. The passages in which the reign of God is said in constructions with εἶναι and the genitive case to belong to definite individuals (as a saving grace) are all to be taken as future. For the Beatitudes (Matt. 5:3 and 10) this is made clear by the promises inserted between them.[41] The only doubt arises from the curious expression, "receive the kingdom of God as a little child" (Mark 10:15 = Luke 18:17). This could be understood as follows: "Whoever receives God's present reign as a child, will also enter into God's future reign",[42] yet in no other passage is the present reign of God regarded as a saving grace for individuals.[43] The nearest parallel to this striking phrase occurs in the missionary expression, "receiving the word (of God)."[44] It is possible that a saying of Jesus which originally was differently formulated was handed on in this form in the early Church. Perhaps this should be borne in mind also for Matt. 13:23 ("instructed in the kingdom (reign) of heaven") and Luke 9:62 ("fit for the kingdom (reign) of God"). On the other hand, we must put Mark 12:34 ("Thou art not far from the kingdom (reign) of God") with the passages that speak of entry and are evidently related to the future reign of God. The introductory formulae of the parables link their content with God's reign only in a general way so

[41] Cf. also J. Dupont, *Les Béatitudes* (Bruges-Louvain, 1954), p. 131.
[42] So V. Taylor. *Gospel acc. to St. Mark,* p. 115.
[43] See E. Lohmeyer, *Ev. des Markus,* on the passages.
[44] Luke 8:13; Acts 8:14; 11:1; 17:11; 1 Thess. 1:6; 2:13; Jas. 1:21.

that we have to decide their particular reference from the pictures they present, the emphasis they register and their recognizable points of comparison.

13. The Teaching of the "Growth" Parables

The so-called "growth" parables, those of the sower, the growing corn, the double parable of the mustard seed and the leaven, of the tares among the wheat (and the net full of fish) are of the highest importance for an understanding of the *basileia* gospel of Jesus. But they have been the theme of hot debate. They are at the heart of the animated discussion in modern times how the parables should be interpreted.

A. Jülicher cleared the way for modern research in his great work[45] when he freed the parables from a thick undergrowth of allegory. It is a sound methodological principle to accept allegorical or symbolical notes only when they force themselves on our attention and, as a general rule, to accept the parables strictly as parables, seeking between picture and content the *tertium comparationis,* the point of comparison on which both turn and which is the only point at issue. This is very evident in parables which describe circumstances from actual life but cannot be taken literally, as for example in those of the unjust steward (Luke 16:1–8), the judge without mercy (Luke 18:1–5), the helping friend (Luke 11:5–8) or the thief in the night (Luke 12:39 = Matt. 24:43). Jesus is concerned merely with one definite thought and his purpose is to encourage his hearers, by a comparison with men's behaviour – the conclusion is *a*

[45] A. Jülicher, *Die Gleichnisreden Jesu* (2nd edition Tübingen I, 1899).

minori ad maius – to reflect upon the divine action or to stimulate them to act.

But was there any fundamental difference between these and the parables drawn from the course of Nature? At this point, despite all his learning, A. Jülicher became one-sided. He held too closely to the Greek literary parable and failed to realize that certain fixed symbols are often found in Jewish parables, for instance that a king is in place of God and that servants represent men etc.[46] A further and more serious error of Jülicher was to educe only the vaguest religious ideas as the teaching of the parables, as though Jesus intended to put forward a doctrinal system like a Greek philosopher. This sort of abstraction from the historical and concrete and from the actual situation is foreign to the Jews and to the Bible. The *Formgeschichte* approach to the gospels encouraged interest in the actual, living setting and it is here that the work of C. H. Dodd on the parables of the kingdom has made a permanent contribution.[47] In his view, Jesus frequently borrowed his material from the direct experience of his audience, from day to day occurrences and special incidents and put it in a very actual form. This actual situation of Jesus can be most important in an interpretation of the parable but frequently it is overshadowed and obscured by the actual situation of the early Church which applied the parable to its own situation and possibly understood it differently. We can detect traces for instance not only of moralizing tendencies but also of the altered historical position after Easter, the missionary situation and the postponement of the Parousia.

J. Jeremias took over Dodd's material and suggestions and made a fresh study of the whole matter. By means of a careful

[46] See especially M. Hermaniuk, *La Parabole Evangélique* (Bruges-Paris-Louvain, 1947).

[47] C. H. Dodd, *The Parables of the Kingdom*.

examination of the linguistic basis (the Aramaic idioms) and of the Palestinian setting presupposed in the parables and with a very conscientious exegesis he was able to propose new interpretations, some of them quite surprising, from which to lay down the main themes and lines in the preaching of Jesus. This is not the place to assess the gains and limitations in this approach to the parables but a solid foundation has been laid so that subsequent discussion is concerned with detailed emendations and modifications. So far as the "growth" parables are in question recent research has taken the subject beyond J. Jeremias: a deeper study of the situation in which Jesus was actually preaching and his relations with his audience[48] and the concealed reference to his Messianic claim, in other words, the Christological character of the parables.[49]

Any interpretation must be tested textually to see if it is justified, that is relevant, and whether it meets the point of the parable. When a speaker wishes to elucidate an idea by way of a story, he places the accents of his story so that the audience sees where he is leading them. It is important, therefore, to recognize these accents and this is not easy in the "growth" parables, as is obvious from the various ways in which they have been explained. No key is provided to understand them. Two of them have explanations provided for the disciples by Jesus, those of the sower (Mark 4:13–20 par.) and the tares among the wheat (Matt. 13:36–43). But we must exercise caution because here if anywhere it might be to the interest of the early Church to

[48] N. A. Dahl, "The Parables of Growth" in *St.Th.* 5 (1951), pp. 132–66.
[49] E. Fuchs, "Bemerkungen zur Gleichnisauslegung" in *Th.L.Z.* 79 (1954), pp. 345–8; F. Mußner, "Gleichnisauslegung und Heilsgeschichte, dargetan am Gleichnis von der selbstwachsenden Saat" (Mark 4:26–29) in *Tr.Th.Z.* 64 (1955), pp. 257–66; W. Michaelis, *Die Gleichnisse Jesu* (Hamburg, 1956), passim.

intervene and apply the parable to its own situation. Indeed, linguistic examination (notions deriving from the early Church) and the strongly allegorical and moralizing manner of interpretation show such caution to be justified. Yet these interpretations do not necessarily miss the whole point of the original though it is prudent to study them carefully in detail. The Fathers insist that Jesus provided the explanation but they proceed to apply the parables to the circumstances and requirements of their own times. This basically is the same process which we suspect existed in the early Church. But is it unwarranted? Only if it falsified the preaching of Jesus. It will be shown that this does not obtain here, since the early Church presupposes the original interpretation and only then proceeds to a more specific application.

Both Mark 4 (which is followed by Luke 8:4–18) and Matt. 13 are literary compositions. In Mark 4, three parables are presented, though the text between the first and second is interrupted by other portions, while Matthew brings seven parables together. The three presented by Mark 4, those of the sower, the growing seed (peculiar to Mark) and the mustard seed are closely connected and certainly derive from an ancient traditional source anterior to Mark.[50] We will begin with these parables and then examine the others.

The parable of the sower (Mark 4:1–9 par.) has enjoyed a particularly wide range of interpretation. So far as the scene is concerned, it is clear from the other two parables that Jesus is not describing abnormal circumstances though they might be abnormal for us today. We find other instances of this method

[50] The continuation of the second and third parable through καὶ ἔλεγεν as distinct from Mark's normal formula καὶ ἔλεγεν (λέγει) αὐτοῖς can scarcely be accidental; see J. Jeremias, *Gleichnisse Jesu,* p. 8, note 1, where other references are given.

of sowing in the agricultural conditions of contemporary Palestine, especially in the infertile belt of Northern Galilee.[51] The connection between this parable and the other two leaves us in no doubt that it deals with the *basileia*. But what is the point it is making?

A little preliminary investigation will help us to understand the different ways in which it has been explained. We will confine ourselves to the main features with here and there a critical commentary.

i. L. Fonck, representing a conservative Catholic school of exegesis, believes that Jesus had a twofold objective. He wished first of all to show how the seed, that is tiny and imperceptible when it is committed to the earth, gradually develops. He wanted also to analyse the obstacles which oppose the seed, that is God's word, and explain the partial lack of fruitfulness in the ground.[52] The first of these two ideas is plainly influenced by the parable of the mustard seed but in neither of these parables is development emphasized. Here one can detect the long-prevalent notion of the *basileia* as a reality in the world, which develops historically and encounters opposition. It tends to be identified with the Church (though what is in question here is the word of God).

ii. This opinion is rejected by the logical eschatologists. These understand the parable much as A. Schweitzer does.[53] "In

[51] Jeremias, *Gleichnisse Jesu,* pp. 5 seq.; M. Rihbany, *Morgenländische Sitten im Leben Jesu* (4th edition, Basle), p. 123. A note of exaggeration creeps in only in the amount of the harvest: cf. G. Dalman, *Arbeit und Sitte in Palästina* III (Gütersloh, 1923), pp. 153–65; Jeremias, *Gleichnisse Jesu,* p. 131.

[52] L. Fonck, *Die Parabeln des Herrn im Evangelium* (3rd edition, Innsbruck, 1909), pp. 67–106, particularly pp. 85 seq.

[53] *Geschichte der Leben-Jesu-Forschung,* pp. 402 seq.

these parables it is not the idea of development that stands out but that of immediacy . . . . The parables stress to some extent the negative character of the initial moment which is followed as though miraculously and through divine power by the second moment at a definite time. They emphasize the miraculous and not the natural element." We note particularly that the time element is slipped in as though through a side-door, though there is nothing about it in the parable. And how does it arrive at its (early) glorious fulfilment? Schweitzer writes (though scarcely anyone follows him on this point): "The initial moment? Jesus can only refer to the movement of penance inaugurated by the Baptist and carried further in his own preaching. It forces the kingdom of God from the divine power as the seed a man sows wrings the harvest from the same infinite might."[54] But it is difficult to discover any trace of compulsion in the parable.

iii. The "realized eschatology" of C. H. Dodd represents a diametrically opposed view. Of this parable he writes: "But no farmer despairs because of such inevitable waste of labour and seed; it is to be expected; in spite of all, he may have an excellent harvest".[55] Dodd, however, sees the harvest in the present and attributes the losses chiefly to the small success of John the Baptist's preaching (pp. 182 seq.). The harvest is there, it is only the harvesters who are wanting. "All three (parables, those of the growing seed, the sower and the tares among the wheat) illustrate in various ways the coming of the kingdom of God in the ministry of Jesus under the figure of harvest" (p. 186). But precisely as a picture of the harvest (fulfilment!), this is false.

[54] Op. cit., p. 403.
[55] *Parables of the Kingdom,* p. 182.

iv. J. Jeremias classes the parable of the sower with the contrast parables. The contrast lies between the small beginning and the immense final success. The emphasis is on the abundant harvest which is being prepared and will be realized. For him, as for the others, it is fundamentally an eschatological parable which speaks also of the hidden beginnings in the activity of Jesus. The basic thought is that "despite all failure and opposition God will produce the glorious conclusion he has promised from a start that offered no hope" (p. 131). It is true that the contrast between beginning and end is striking and because of the rhythm of the story it is the end that receives the major stress. But surely the detailed account of the obstacles serves some special purpose.

v. N. A. Dahl criticizes Jeremias on this point and tries to pursue his interpretation further. In his opinion, we must pay greater attention to the historical situation of Jesus. Jesus has in mind the popular notions of the Messias. Men did not doubt that the reign of God would come; what they questioned was whether the words and deeds of Jesus had any connection with this. This is the crux of the problem: Jesus is having no success with his mission, and the parable is an answer to this.[56] But, we may ask, should not Jesus have given a much clearer answer to objections?

vi. This approximates closely to the Christological interpretation. W. Michaelis concentrates on the typical attitude of the sower.[57] He is inclined to identify the sower with Jesus himself (p. 33). Yet the sower is mentioned only once. For the rest, the parable deals with the fate of the seed, its failure and success.

To find a positive interpretation it is best to start with the

[56] Op. cit., pp. 152 seq. In his latest edition Jeremias has accepted and adopted these ideas of Dahl (p. 131).
[57] Op. cit., pp. 24–6.

ending which is also the culmination of the parable. If it is a *basileia* parable, then the rich harvest can only denote the perfect kingdom of God. But this end is prepared through the beginning. While Jesus is narrating this parable, the reign of God is already in a certain sense present. Whether we need to posit the alternative: reign of God, or only its proclamation, is uncertain. God's rule has made contact with men in the expulsion of devils by Jesus (Matt. 12:28) and surely also, in the teaching of Jesus. Preaching to the poor is on the same level as works of healing as a sign of the Messianic era (Matt. 11:5). In the parable the further statement is made that the beginning is modest and the full fruit not yet visible. The reason is also given, it is not properly received. Jeremias is right in insisting that what is emphasized is the contrast between the modest beginning and the glorious end and the certainty that this end will come despite all opposition. But on the other hand the inquiry into actual historical circumstances is imperative. Was it the purpose of Jesus to take issue with corrupt Messianic notions (Dahl) or prejudices (D. Buzy)?[58] It is more likely that he is speaking in the concrete situation. A large part of the people had already abandoned him or were about to do so. This is true of the final stage of his Galilean ministry and nothing prevents us from assigning the parable to this period. Jesus is declaring that a start has been made and the future kingdom draws inevitably near (nothing is said of nearness in time). Even under these conditions God guides his work to its end.[59]

[58] D. Duzy, *Parables,* p. 40: In his opinion, the parable is directed against the Jewish prejudice that the kingdom of God is a question of religion and race; in point of fact, it is a matter of virtue, the ethical attitude of the individual.

[59] See Ch. W. Smith, *The Jesus of the Parables* (Philadelphia, 1948), pp. 64 seq.

With this goes a stronger appeal to men to accept the gospel of Jesus, that is, to be converted and believe. The sower does not stand in the forefront of the story but Jesus can intend this as a discreet reference to himself, rising out of the situation. As the prophet of the reign that is at hand he withdraws behind his message and identifies himself with it. The mystery of God's reign (Mark 4:11, see below, section 15), that is operative and present through himself, implies also the mystery of his Messias-ship. And so in this parable Jesus is teaching something concerning the reign of God which is actually taking place. Only a few men listen to the gospel; yet that is sufficient to give certainty about the eschatological kingdom; the apostacy of the many cannot prevent God's plans, it is caught up in them. This gives the sower his confidence and warns the listeners to seize the saving hour. If the concluding warning (v. 9) may appear to be a minor addition of the evangelist (compare also v. 23), it is not without its meaning, in so far as Jesus told the parable to the whole people. Further, his intention is to summon and discover those to whom the mystery of God's reign has been revealed by God.

If the parable is understood in this way, the view of the early Church with its synthesis of tradition and even the explanation offered to the disciples (4:13–20) does not radically diverge from the intention of Jesus. To be sure, the basic reference to the eschatological kingdom is not included for even the rich harvest is made to serve a lesson. The intention of the early Church could indeed be a "warning to converts" (Jeremias p. 67). But is such treatment unjustified? The "mystery of the reign of God" was already revealed to the early Church and it proclaimed it to the faithful. With Jesus the reign of God has become present in an initial, provisional manner. With his Parousia it will be completely realized. In the meantime the faithful are in a situation similar to that of those who heard Jesus. They are summoned to a personal decision, to be made here and now in their whole religious and moral attitude. This explanation includes a reference to the early Church's pastoral methods, in which it employed the material of tradition for catechesis and preaching.[60]

To us nowadays this gives the impression of a forced use of allegory and of application of the parable. The three ways in which the seed is lost which serve as embellishments (in the narrative style of "threes", compare also the threefold yields in harvesting) are applied to three classes of men, identified not with the soil but with the seed itself. The incidental birds become Satan, the choking thorns become deceitful riches and so on. But this is a freedom of "applied instruction" which is conscious of the original meaning and presupposes it. The preachers who follow in the footsteps of Jesus do not feel obliged to provide an historical reconstruction of his life and to explain it to their audience. They "translate" it and apply it to their own hearers. If this be borne in mind, we may do fuller justice to the allegorical methods of the Fathers who made even wider adaptations to their own times. The degrees of harvest were applied by them to the married, monks or martyrs or in other similar ways. We must, of course, inquire what was the intention of the commentator and the meaning of his interpretation. But our confidence that the parables have been handed down as told by Jesus is not thereby in the least affected.

[60] Compare the appropriate sentences in J. Dupont, *Les Béatitudes,* 2nd edition I, p. 204: ". . . It is not sufficient for the evangelists to inform their readers of what the Master actually taught; they want this doctrine to be made concrete in life. The spirit that inspires them in this effort is precisely that of the early Church. There tradition is not regarded as an exact mechanical reproduction of the words of Jesus but as a testimony. The words of Jesus are a living ferment. The Church only hands them on enwrapped in her own life."

The parable of the seed developing with its inner vitality (Mark 4:26–9) presents similar problems, and again interpretations differ according to the basic approach. Even more obviously than that of the sower is it a parable about God's reign, though the introductory formula is not explicit. At the conclusion the harvest shows that the kingdom of God is made manifest. Till then, it is emphasized, the seed is ripening "of itself", that is, without the assistance of the farmer, "whilst he knoweth not". This negative aspect that no human co-operation is required and even that man has not the capacity to co-operate, demands the positive sense that God is at work to bring about his perfect kingdom. The power of growth in God's rule – unlike that in the image – must be supernatural. What is brought out in the parable is precisely this supernatural character of the perfect reign of God which is approaching irresistibly. "There is a plan and order determined for the eschatological chain of events that is illustrated in this process of growth. But what is taking place is no historical development guided by some immanent necessity but God's creative activity directing history towards its goal in harmony with his plan."[61] If we enquire what is the concrete application to the life of Jesus, we might see in it a rejection of a spurious human activity such as was expected from the political Messias. In this Jesus had disappointed his people (cf. John 6:14 seq.) and that is one of the principal reasons why he was repudiated, at the close of his Galilean ministry. Against the eschatologists who read into it a rapid approach of the last days we should observe the calm composure of the countryman. He waits quietly because he knows that the harvest will certainly come. That the harvest is not yet there (contrary to Dodd's view) is clear from the whole context, for at harvest-time no one bothers with the

[61] Dahl, op. cit., p. 145.

question just how it has come. Further, the individual phases of development, blade, ear, full corn (v. 28) are not stressed; they are merely descriptive details in the process by which the earth "of itself" brings forth the fruit. This rules out an interpretation of God's reign as part of an earthly process. The language itself fixes our attention immediately on the harvest (καρποφορεῖ v. 28 and correspondingly ὁ καρπός and ὁ θερισμός v. 29).

It may further be asked how far the parable has a Christological note. Many scholars would have preferred to call it the "parable of the patient and yet confident countryman."[62] Their argument is that the verbs are concerned principally with his action and restraint. He scatters the seed, sleeps and reawakens, scarcely observes the growth of the seed but eventually "puts in the sickle". The last clause is a quotation (Joel 3:13) which refers to the second part, namely the presence of the harvest. The evidence, however, hardly allows us to set the countryman so strongly at the centre of the story. In the concrete circumstances Jesus will certainly have thought of himself but only discreetly as in the parable of the sower. The parable's main theme is the "mystery of the reign of God" in itself, namely its concealed presence which by God's power will one day, gradually but inevitably, develop to its manifest glory. The mystery of the Messias is also included but only by way of allusion.

The last parable contained in Mark 4, that of the mustard seed (vv. 30–32) is also preserved in another channel of tradition ("Q") that is clearly more ancient. Luke 13:18 seq. has it in the form of a short story (a man plants the mustard seed in his garden) and he attaches to it a second parable telling of a woman

[62] So B. T. D. Smith, *The Parables of the Synoptic Gospels* (Cambridge, 1937), pp. 129–32; Jeremias, *Gleichnisse Jesu,* p. 132; Dahl, op. cit., p. 149; F. Mußner, op. cit., p. 265.

who mixed a little leaven in a large quantity of meal.[63] Matthew united both traditions (Matt. 13:31–33). Originally we have a double parable intended to present the one thought under a twofold image (of a man and a woman, cf. Luke 15:3–10). A different interpretation of the two parables has been suggested in terms of an extensive and an intensive development of God's reign. Yet this widely-accepted interpretation reads into it falsely an organic "process". In reality, we have a contrast between beginning and end. Despite the tiny and inconspicuous start, the glorious end is certain, and was intended throughout, the wide-spreading branches and the leavened mass of dough. These are new images for the kingdom of God! The tree in the shade of which "the birds of the air build their nests" easily suggested itself for already in Dan. 4:9, 11, 18; Ezech. 17:23; 31:6 it stands for a mighty realm.[64] The leaven simile is usually employed in a bad sense,[65] though not inevitably so. In Rom. 11:16 Paul uses two similar comparisons for the chosen people of Israel. Further, the large mass of dough (about 39. 4 litres) points to the plenitude of God's rule.[66] Here too, the point is not the gradual permeation by the leaven but the final state of things . . . "until the whole was leavened". The narrator is not reflecting on the natural process, the immanent force that hastens growth and permeates. He is judging by what he sees with his eyes. The great tree springing from the tiny mustard seed and the leavened

[63] Consequently Luke omits the parable of the mustard seed in chapter eight.
[64] It is questionable whether the birds symbolize the heathens as T. W. Manson tries to prove in *The Teaching of Jesus* (2nd edition, Cambridge, 1935, reprinted 1951), p. 133, note 1.
[65] B. T. D. Smith, op. cit., pp. 122 seq., doubts whether this is a parable of the kingdom and also whether the double form of the parable is original – but scarcely with reason!
[66] See Jeremias, *Gleichnisse Jesu*, p. 128.

mass, contrasted with the small measure of leaven, seem almost miraculous. This means in fact that the divine power can permit a glorious finale to crown an insignificant beginning. He provides the promise and guarantee that his kingdom will come. Again, this supposes that God's reign is present in the word and work of Jesus and that there is continuity between its commencement and its future realization, a continuity like that between the sowing season and harvest time. Manifestation on a cosmic scale is certain because God's rule is even now present and its power and reality can be sensed. The double parable does not contain an allusion to the person of Jesus – a warning not to force the Christological interpretation too far – but from the circumstances of his ministry we may conclude that its beginning is found in his activity.

These "growth" parables, therefore, supplement one another admirably and teach the same lesson, though with a difference of emphasis. Notwithstanding the depressing experience of the moment the reign of God is coming: it is coming by God's power. It will appear in glory, as surely as harvest time follows the sowing.

The theme is taken further and rounded off by two parables, peculiar to Matthew, those of the tares among the wheat and the fishing-net (Matt. 13:24–30, 47 seq.). It is possible that they were originally a double parable. Their design is even more markedly eschatological. The parable of the fishing-net, for example, leaves us in no doubt that it is focused upon an occurrence in the future. The drag-net has been thrown out, the catch brought in. Our attention is directed to the separation of the good fish from the bad. The parable of the tares again centres on the harvest. That is when wheat and weeds are separated. Yet growth is mentioned. "Suffer both to grow until the harvest" (v. 30). The reason for the sharp eschatological accent is certainly that the two parables answer the query why the wicked are still here, now that the reign of God has been proclaimed and the community of salvation is being formed.

Many commentators[67] find the concrete setting in the beliefs held by certain groups that Jesus would have to inaugurate the pure Messianic community by excluding sinners. There is no doubt that such notions were prevalent in contemporary Judaism, notably among Pharisees, Essenes and the Qumran community. But we must ask more precisely whether Jesus was rebutting the charge that he tolerated the unclean and sinners among his followers or the different accusation that he did not exterminate evil-doers. The first charge would have come from Pharisaic circles (Mark. 2:16 par.; Matt. 11:19 par.; Luke 7:39 seq.); the second could count on a wider echo from the people, especially since the preaching of John the Baptist.[68] The fact that Jesus addressed the parable to the people generally and that it contains no special mention of the Pharisees suggests that he is dealing with the objection that, if he were the Messias, he must at once "cleanse the threshing floor".

Both parables show us the main characteristics of the gospel of the *basileia*. Its appearance in the present takes place only in the form of salvation and postpones judgment. That is reserved for its full manifestation in the future. Till then evil men and oppressors may still wield power and threaten and do violence to the good seed that has been sown. The great division occurs

[67] B. T. D. Smith, op. cit., p. 198 (parable of tares); Dahl, op. cit., p. 150 (parable of fishing-net); Jeremias, *Gleichnisse Jesu,* pp. 188 seq. (both parables). The parable of the fishing-net does not describe how the net is thrown out and how it collects the good and bad fish; in other words, it is not concerned with the call of every type of man through Jesus; it mereiy insists that separation takes place at the end.
[68] See also Dahl, op. cit., pp. 151 seq., on the parable of the tares.

at the end. Men must, therefore, bear with evil provisionally and leave the judgment of evil men to God. Thus understood, these parables do not exclude a presence of God's rule. With Jesus' activity it has entered into this world, though this is still evil, and it finds itself confronted by the powers of evil, Satan and his followers. This co-existence of the forces of salvation and destruction should not confuse us as to the reality and power of God's rule in the present. The end will show who belongs to it. From the parable of the tares we can scarcely conclude that the work of Jesus was merely a preparation for God's kingdom in recruiting all men for the kingdom and collecting a Messianic community, but one which he could not, and indeed did not, yet wish to liberate from its links with the evil world and its contact with evil-doers. Whatever truth there may be in this, the reality of God's rule, already perceptible, must not be toned down. We must not use the similes of the tares and the fishing-net to interpret the remaining parables of growth as though the seed, the sowing and the planting were merely preparatory. They are more; they are a commencement out of which the future develops; they are a foundation and a promise of the glory that is to come.[69] The reason why these two parables force us to look at the end is that it is only with the end that we have the judgment, an aspect which is not stressed in the other parables.

The explanation of the parable of the tares given to the disciples in Matthew (13:36–43) – a later addition like that to the parable of the sower – (note the quotation in 13:35 corresponding to the passage about obduracy in 13:13–15 and also verse 36 referring back to verse 18) is recognizable as Matthew's in peculiarities of style and thought[70] and it again turns our atten-

[69] H. Ridderbos, *Koninkrijk,* pp. 124–42; E. Percy, *Botschaft Jesu,* pp. 202–11.

[70] Jeremias, *Gleichnisse Jesu,* pp. 69–72.

tion to the early Church. Evil-doers are now members of the community of salvation, that is, the Church. Eventually they will be cut off from the "kingdom of the Son of man" which is distinct from the "kingdom of the Father" (v. 43) and must be identified with the Church. For the rest we discover the same wide-ranging allegory as in the explanation of the parable of the sower. A warning note for the unfaithful and evil members of the community is frequently audible in Matthew: 7:22 seq.; 22:11–14; 24:38–51; 25:30. The explanation of the parable of the fishing-net in vv. 49 seq. is similar; it too has its connections with the concrete circumstances of the early Church.

As a result of these inquiries we maintain that the "growth" parables should not be employed to substantiate a wholly present or a wholly future concept of the reign of God but just that polarity between the beginning and the end, between sowing and harvest, between the unobtrusive present and the full future revelation of the glory of God's rule and kingship. There is also a continuous, unbroken relation between "now" and "then", not because of any immanent process due to earthly or human forces but through the intervention of God who manifests in the works of Jesus the kingly rule which one day will be shown forth in all its splendour. What happens in the present, despite every failure and opposition, is a promise of the future triumph. This will be seen when the forces of evil that now confront those of good will be destroyed, and evil men will be submitted to God's judgment.

The character of God's rule as actually "present" may be briefly described as follows. Jesus proclaims the eschatological kingship of God as something that is close and insistent, operative and tangible, bound up with his own person and activity and summoning his hearers to an inescapable decision. In this sense, it is present in him, in his words and works.

THE COMING OF THE PERFECT KINGDOM OF GOD

14. God's Future Kingdom and the Son of man

Notwithstanding the influence exercised by the eschatological kingship of God on the period when Jesus was proclaiming it and working his works of salvation, its main weight remains in the future. The gaze of Jesus is directed towards the future kingdom of glory. There are not two different kinds of divine reign proclaimed by Jesus but only the one same rule manifesting itself in his presence and then appearing on a cosmic scale. The great majority of references are to the future reign of God, as a general review will show.

i. The future "coming" of the reign of God:

In both Matthew and Luke the Our Father has as its central petition, "Thy kingdom (reign) come!" (Matt. 6:10 = Luke 11:2). Behind the peculiar reading of Codex D in Luke 11:2 ("to us") and also behind the prayer for the spirit which replaces in Luke that for the kingdom in some manuscripts and early Church references[1] there may well be a hint that this "coming"

[1] Minuscules 162, 170 (Marcion); Greg. of Nyssa, *De orat. Dom.* 3 (P. G. 44, 1157 C); Maximus Conf. on Matt. 6:10 (P. G. 90:840). For Marcion, see Th. Zahn, *Das Evangelium des Lucas* (Leipzig–Erlangen, 1913), Exc. IX, pp. 768–73 (prayer of the spirit and prayer for the

refers to an advance of the reign of God in grace and spirit in the Church; but originally, it could only have applied to the perfect kingdom of the future. This was what was meant among contemporary Jews (see Luke 17:20) when they spoke for the most part of the "appearance" of the eschatological basileia. The same future event is indicated by Jesus as the coming of the reign of God in power (Mark. 9:1; cf. Matt. 16:28; Luke 9:27 – on this point see below section 16). The additional clause "in power" merely confirms, it draws no distinction; otherwise, it would have been employed also in Luke 22:18, the ancient passage about the eschatological fulfilment, the association at table of Jesus with the disciples (see the other formulation in Mark 14:25; Matt. 26:29). In no passage is "coming" (ἔρχεσθαι) associated with the approach of the reign of God in the present.

ii. The statements about "entry into the kingdom of God": Matt. 5:20; 7:21; 18:3 par.; 19:23 par.; 21:31; 22:12; 23:13 par.; 25:10, 21, 23; Mark 9:47; John 3:3, 5. With these must be classed the opposite statements about "being cast out": Matt. 7:2 seq.; 8:12 (= Luke 13:28); 13:42, 50; 22:13; 25:30; cf. 24:51; 25:11.

iii. Kindred expressions:
This same approach is found in: *seek* the kingdom (reign) of God (ζητεῖν), Luke 12:31 = Matt. 6:33, namely seek or fight for admission (Luke 13:24); *inherit,* Matt. 25:34, or equivalently inherit (eternal) life, Matt. 19:29; Mark 10:17; Luke 10:25; 18:18; the image of the Promised Land, Matt. 5:5; *'give',*

kingdom); A. von Harnack, *Marcion* (Leipzig, 1921), p. 189 (prayer for the spirit in place of prayer for the kingdom). E. Klostermann, *Das Lukasevangelium* (2nd edition, Tübingen, 1929), considers the prayer for the spirit to be part of Luke's original text.

namely granted as a gift or reward through grace, Luke 12:32:[2] also, "be counted worthy of that world" (Luke 20:35) is identical;[3] *belong to* (εἶναι with genitive). God's future reign is assured as a saving possession and effectively conferred at the judgment (Matt. 25:34), so also Matt. 5:3, 10; Mark 10:14 par. The expressions "for the sake of the kingdom of God", Luke 18:29 (cf. Mark 10:29; Matt. 19:29) and Matt. 19:12 refer to the future kingdom. "Keys" and closure, Matt. 16:19; 23:14 (see section 17); future tenses with "in the kingdom of God", Matt. 5:19; 11:11 (= Luke 7:28 – see section 12); Matt. 13:43 (see next paragraph). In these passages the kingdom of God is partly identified with eternal life or with the "future aeon" in the Jewish manner. It is not certain what expression was originally employed but it is clear that the vision is directed towards the future.

iv. Images of the future reign of God:
The chief image is that already used by the Jews in an eschatological sense, namely the great banquet prepared by God: Matt. 8:11 seq. = Luke 13:28 seq.; 22:1–10 (cf. Luke 14:16–24); 22:11–13; 25:1–12, 21, 23 ("joy" signifies "meal of joy"); Luke 12:37; 14:10 (to be understood eschatologically, cf. also 14:11, 18:14); 14:15. We have examined the image of harvesting when dealing with the parables of growth (section 13): Mark 4:1–9 par.; 4:26–29; Matt. 13:24–30. In addition there are other pictures of fulfilment: the catch of fish, Matt. 13:47 seq.; the tree (or the grown bush), Mark 4:30–32; the leavened mass, Luke 13:20 seq.(= Matt. 13:33). The similes of the treasure and the pearl represent the supreme worth of God's reign: they culminate in the fulfilment of the perfect kingdom but they

[2] Matt. 21:43 on the contrary must be a later formulation with a reference to the parable of the vineyard.

[3] See Dalman, *Worte Jesu* I, pp. 97 seq.

remain an appeal to the candidate for it who sacrifices everything else for this one purpose and delights in its discovery.

A review of all this material leaves us with a large collection of sayings that are "dominated by the idea of entering into or failing to enter the kingdom of heaven. This idea is one of the most fundamental motives in the proclamation of the kingdom both by Jesus and the Christian community".[4] In this, Jesus was adopting thoughts deeply rooted in the Old Testament, such as the entry into the Promised Land and into the temple. But even in other images he delves into the rich treasury of the Old Testament and later Jewish ideas about eschatological salvation. There is no doubt at all that the still awaited, future kingdom is the guiding star of his preaching. It is no mere supplement or momentary aspect in the present but, on the contrary, the focal point from which his present assertions receive their direction, their mutual connection and their illuminative power.

There remains the question whether Jesus attributed any significance to himself with regard to the future and perfect reign of God. As we have seen, it is impossible to dissociate the realization of the *basileia* in the present from the person of Jesus and, in so far as there exists an indissoluble connection between the dawn of God's reign and its coming full manifestation in glory, the significance of Jesus for the perfect kingdom is evident. But we may ask further whether he will play a part in the "coming of God's reign in power" or does he merely announce it, prepare for it and establish its foundation. Is everything now to develop from some inner necessity and is his task fulfilled? Is he to make no appearance at its dramatic conclusion? This was certainly not the opinion of the early Church and we must examine whether its belief in the Parousia of the Lord,

[4] H. Windisch in *Z.N.W.* 27 (1928), p. 170.

bringing with him the eschatological kingdom of God, can be justified from the teaching of Jesus. Here we encounter a series of texts in which Jesus speaks of the Son of man who is to come.

Here we are concerned only with eschatological references to the Son of man. The two other series which announce his sufferings and the present claims of the Son of man, and which complicate the question whether and in what way Jesus used the title of Son of man, need not be dealt with in this context. Even radical critics do not deny that Jesus referred to the Son of man[5] though they doubt whether the term was applied to Jesus in person. Jesus was referring, they suggest, to the eschatological figure of the Son of man which he distinguished from himself. It was in their view the early Church that identified the Son of man with Jesus and multiplied the relevant passages. This opinion is logical enough if Jesus be denied all Messianic consciousness. Such an interpretation is very probably associated with W. Wrede's idea of the "mystery of the Messias". More recently, Ph. Vielhauer has denied that any statements about the Son of man were made directly by Jesus. "It is clear with a probability that borders on certainty that no statement about the Son of man who is to come derives from the historical Jesus."[6] We shall comment on this critical attitude when we consider individual passages but will not discuss its general approach. E. Percy has again emphasized the fact that these sayings do give rise to serious problems.[7]

But is it not possible that Jesus merely adopted the apocalyptic

[5] See R. Bultmann, *Geschichte der synopt. Tradition* on Luke 17:26 seq. par. (p. 123); Matt. 24:44 par. (p. 125); Luke 17:23 seq. (p. 128); Luke 12:8 seq. (p. 135); R. Bultmann, *Theologie des NT,* p. 4; G. Bornkamm, *Jesus von Nazareth,* pp. 161 seq.

[6] Ph. Vielhauer, *Festschrift für G. Dehn,* p. 71.

[7] *Botschaft Jesu,* pp. 245 seq.

expectation of his time or at least of many contemporary groups and understood by "Son of man" a person distinct from himself, the man who was to come with the clouds of heaven, "one like the Son of man" to whom "power and glory and a kingdom" were given by God, "an everlasting power that shall not be taken away" and a kingdom "that shall not be destroyed" (Dan. 7:13 seq.)?

The clear references in Mark 13:26 par., and 14:62 par. (cf. also John 5:27) make it sufficiently evident that Jesus and the early Church had this celebrated passage from Daniel in mind. Whether the reference was exclusively to Daniel's "Son of man" or included subsequent apocalyptic visions (for instance the Son of man in *The Book of Parables of Henoch* and in the *Fourth Book of Esdras,* 13) does not concern us here. It is sufficient to have observed that the Son of man was regarded as representing a definite eschatological expectation, if only among strictly limited circles of contemporary Judaism. For the rest, we must refer to recent publications.[8]

Certain considerations make the suggestion that Jesus drew a distinction between the "Son of man" and himself most improbable: i. It would be strange that Jesus did not bring the figure of this saviour more strongly into focus, as was done, for instance, in the *Book of Parables* of Ethiopic Henoch. ii. The relation between Jesus and the "Son of man" would remain completely obscure. Had Jesus to regard himself as the precursor and herald of that saviour and judge who would come from heaven? There is not the slightest hint of this. iii. Comparison with John the Baptist is illuminating. John

[8] E. Sjöberg, *Der Menschensohn im äth. Henochbuch;* E. Sjöberg, *Der verborgene Menschensohn;* O. Cullmann, *Christologie,* pp. 139–54; S. Mowinckel, *He that Cometh,* pp. 346–450.

announced the advent of one "stronger" than himself who was to judge (Matt. 3:11 seq.). This affected his assessment of his own person. He looked upon himself as unworthy to loosen the shoes of the one who was to follow him. There is no trace in Jesus of a similar attitude of reverence for the "Son of man"; on the contrary, it is through Jesus that God's deeds of salvation and power are wrought. iv. From the start the early Church identified the "Son of man" with Jesus in so certain and self-evident a manner that we would have to provide some explanation how it reached this conviction. In spite of arguments to the contrary, the more convincing reasons assure us that the early Church took this belief from the statements and the attitude of Jesus himself.

The radical assumption that all the passages which introduce the "Son of man" are to be attributed to the early Church, likewise runs up against serious difficulties. The chief of these is the fact that the evangelists only employ this title when it is put into the mouth of Jesus. "They never address him by it or introduce anyone else as using it. This would have been quite unintelligible if they had been the first to put it into his mouth. In effect, they have preserved the precise recollection that only Jesus spoke of himself in this way."[9] On the other hand, it is argued that in none of the synoptic passages about the "Son of man" is there any reference to the reign of God. "The reference to the 'Son of man' and the reign of God clearly belong to two different versions of our Lord's words."[10] Consequently, when we find a juxtaposition or relation between the two notions in the synoptics either individually or collectively, this must be attributed to the evangelists who associated the advent of

[9] O. Cullmann, *Christologie,* p. 158.
[10] Vielhauer, op. cit., p. 53.

the kingdom of God with the coming of the Son of man, identified with Jesus. Against this we need merely inquire; what other purpose can be attributed to the Son of man? Is not this association already contained in the genesis of this expectation of the Son of man? The facts have been observed correctly enough, but is the explanation of them not to be found in the fact that the passages about the Son of man emphasize the functions of the heavenly saviour and judge whereas the kingdom of God is looked for as the fullness of salvation after the drama of the last things? The best method is to study the texts themselves.

Two eschatological texts about the "Son of man" in Matthew may be set aside as of secondary character: it can be shown that the title was added subsequently. In Matt. 16:28 comparison with the other synoptics (Mark 9:1; Luke 9:27) shows that the author introduced "Son of man", probably in connection with the other passage in Matt. 16:27. In Matt. 13:41 the "kingdom of the Son of man" (as distinct from the "kingdom of the Father") is a reality of this present aeon, evidently to be identified with the Church. The catechetical language of the early Church may have influenced this interpretation (see section 13).

This may provide a handle for the critic to attack the originality of some other eschatological "Son of man" passages, notably in Matthew's gospel. This compels us to be cautious in our use of texts and to use only those logia of Jesus which enjoy the highest possible authenticity. Opinions about the authenticity of different passages diverge widely and we will not discuss them here. For a general view of the situation it should be noted that even E. Sjöberg who acknowledges Jesus as the "hidden Son of man" regards the following passages as "probably secondary": Mark 13:26 par.; Matt. 13:41; 16:27,

28; to Matt. 19:28; Luke 17:22; 18:8; 21:36 he gives the note "uncertain".[11]

One well-authenticated passage deriving from two sources is of great importance because it compares the attitude of men to Jesus with that of the men of the time when the Son of man is to come. Mark 8:38 (see Luke 9:26) reads: "He that shall be ashamed of me and my words ('in this adulterous and sinful generation' – only in Mark), the Son of man also will be ashamed of him, when he shall come in the glory of his Father with the holy angels (Luke: 'in his majesty and that of the Father and the holy angels')." An even older version is found in the tradition preserved in Matthew and Luke, and the most ancient of all in Luke 12:8 seq.: "Whoever shall confess me before men, him shall the Son of man also confess before the angels of God. But he that shall deny me before men, shall be denied before the angels of God."

In Matt. 10:32 seq. "Son of man" is replaced by the first personal pronoun; the identification of Jesus and the Son of man is taken for granted. In Luke the addition of "God" to "the angels" is a pleonasm (also in Luke 22:69) since "before the angels" is already a description of God, see 15:10. The expression, from the Matthew-Luke tradition, which has an older ring because of its parallel antithesis, portrays the Son of man not as a judge but as a witness before God. This also proves that the tradition is ancient and trustworthy. The logion in Mark 8:38 conforms to the picture of the Son of man in Daniel (and in the *Ethiopic Book of Henoch*). The positive aspect is omitted because the statement is employed as a warning. Not a few critics regard the second part of verse 38 ("when he shall come. . . .") as a later addition. But this does not affect the substance of the statement.

[11] *Der verborgene Menschensohn,* pp. 236 seq., note 2.

In theory, the statement might be interpreted as meaning that Jesus is distinct from the Son of man[12] but in this case it would lose its depth and force. The point is obviously this, that eventually a reverse situation occurs. If another person were introduced, an explanation would be required of the close relation between this person and Jesus. Consequently, the Matthean (and early Christian) interpretation is probable, that Jesus understands the "Son of man" as himself. The reason why he does not speak in the first person is the mystery of the Messias. He wanted to imply rather than reveal the identity of the Son of man, who would one day come in glory, with himself. The passage puts us in the same situation as his contemporaries who heard it. The sentence itself admits another interpretation but insinuates the identity of the Son of man with Jesus. This is in harmony with many other statements of Jesus, in which he refers indirectly to his actions as Messianic. They can be understood "at least as well in the hidden Messianic character of Jesus as in that of a non-Messianic proclamation"[13]. In Matt. 8:38 Jesus answers with a similar warning the unbelievers in the audience who clamour for a sign; they will be given the sign of Jonas, and this sign is – the Son of man (Luke 11:29 seq.; differently, Matt. 12:39 seq.).[14]

Other scholars also reject the passage Luke 12:8 seq. par. as unauthentic. In their opinion its contents suggests that it derived

[12] J. A. T. Robinson, *Jesus and His Coming,* pp. 53 seq., insists on the identification of Jesus with the Son of man but he emphasizes his function as a witness before the throne of God and excludes any relation to the Parousia.

[13] Sjöberg. *Der verborgene Menschensohn,* p. 234.

[14] Consult on this point A. Vögtle, "Der Spruch vom Jonaszeichen" in *Synoptische Studien,* Festschrift für A. Wikenhauser (Munich, 1954), pp. 230–77.

from the Christian community, possibly as a saying of early Christian "prophets" (who nowadays are thought of as the source of many such sayings). "Prophecy proclaims blessing and curse for believers and unbelievers in the community in so far as it applies to them the eschatological *jus talionis*."[15] From the juridical meaning of the term "confess" Ph. Vielhauer argues that Jesus never foresaw or foretold that the apostles would be persecuted and brought to judgment and, therefore, the passage reflects the subsequent situation of the Christian community.[16] Were this so, then many other sayings would need to be seen as reflections of the community. Our interpretation must rest on our general view of the teaching of Jesus. Much of this is made unintelligible unless we accept the later phase in which he speaks of his death and the suffering and persecution of the disciples (see section 15). This began with Peter's confession at Caesarea Philippi (Mark 8:27 seq.), and the fact that Mark and the early Christian tradition introduce here the Son of man passage with other passages reveals a sense and feeling for context and connections.

Matthew 25:31–46 contains a similar concept but in reverse, not prospective towards the Parousia but retrospective from the end. This great picture of the judgment, of whose authenticity not a few doubts have been entertained, has original Christian features and its bold conception reveals the master-hand of Jesus.[17] The Son of man, seated clearly as judge on the "throne of his glory" makes his judgment dependent upon the manner

[15] E. Käsemann, "Sätze heiligen Rechtes im Neuen Testament" in *N.T.St.* I (1954–55), pp. 248–60, this quotation is on p. 257.

[16] Op. cit., p. 70.

[17] See T. W. Manson, *Sayings of Jesus,* p. 249; J. Jeremias, *Jesu Verheißung,* p. 41, note 164; on the details, see Jeremias, *Gleichnisse Jesu,* pp. 172–4.

in which the men assembled before him have behaved to "the least of his brethren" (vv. 40, 45), in other words, not to himself but to the poor and needy whom he envisages as his brethren. These words ("brethren") certainly suppose, though they do not explicitly mention, that he himself once dwelt among them.

It must be admitted that there is some unevenness in the narrative. Verse 31 speaks of the "Son of man", from verse 34 onwards the subject is the "king". The Son of man appears here as judge, but in Luke 12:8 seq. and Mark 8:38 as witness. Verse 31 is clearly in Matthew's style as is shown by a comparison with Matt. 19:28, and elsewhere one finds traces peculiar to Matthew. But this gives us no right to present the whole as an early Christian composition drawn from Judaeo-apocalyptic material, inspired and enriched by sayings and ideas of Jesus, for example Matt. 7:21; 10:42; 18:5, as a "discursive elaboration of the theme given in 24:30, namely the final judgment".[18] That Jesus considered himself to be the eschatological judge follows from the expression "my brethren", which should be compared with the saying in Mark 3:35. Perhaps he spoke originally only of "king" and then Matthew added the introduction (v. 31). But we cannot exclude the possibility that the evangelist was using the term "king" to clarify the final office of the "Son of man" who bestows upon the elect the "kingdom" of God as their inheritance.

If this magnificent picture does derive from Jesus – no matter

[18] E. Klostermann, *Das Matthäusevangelium* (3rd edition, Tübingen, 1938), p. 204. J. A. T. Robinson has undertaken a new critical study in "The Parable of the sheep and the goats" in *N.T.St.* 2 (1955–6). pp. 225-37. He finds the source of this passage in a parable of a shepherd separating his flock with a series of antithetic sayings similar to Mark 9:37; Matt. 10:42; Luke 12:9 seq.

whether some of its expressions come from Matthew – there can be no doubt that Jesus claimed an active rôle in the final judgment. In this event, it is he who decides who shall have part in the eschatological kingdom of God (cf. Matt. 7:22 seq. = Luke 13:26 seq.).

The most significant passage, the authenticity and meaning of which are equally controverted, is Jesus' profession before the Sanhedrin, Mark 14:62 (= Matt. 26:64; cf. Luke 22:69, where the last portion is missing): "I am. And you shall see the Son of man sitting on the right hand of the power of God and coming with the clouds of heaven." Those who deny the historicity of this night session of the court naturally dispute this clear Messianic self-testimony before the highest tribunal of the Jews. Yet for this extreme position there exists no justification.[19] But even those who accept the scene as historical, interpret the answer of Jesus differently. Several modern scholars regard it not as a statement of the Parousia, as the advent of Jesus from heaven, as an implicit threat of judgment upon his earthly judges (as "visitation") but as an announcement of his coming elevation to the right hand of God and of a divine justification (as "vindication").[20]

J. A. T. Robinson who now places special emphasis on this in-

[19] J. Blinzler, *Der Prozeß Jesu* (2nd edition, Regensburg, 1955), pp. 86–9. G. Bornkamm in *Jesus von Nazareth,* pp. 150 seq. reiterates the familiar reasons for claiming that the scene is unhistorical.

[20] This interpretation is found in M. J. Lagrange, *Évangile selon S. Marc* (4th edition, Paris, 1928), and again in V. Taylor, *Gospel acc. to St. Mark,* at the appropriate passage. All reference to the Parousia is rejected by T. F. Glasson, *Second Advent,* pp. 63–8 and similarly by G. S. Duncan, *Jesus Son of Man,* pp. 175–7; for Robinson see next footnote. The opposite position is maintained by W. G. Kümmel, *Verheißung und Erfüllung,* p. 44, with note 102; also by H. K. McArthur, "Mark XIV, 62" in *N.T.St.* 4 (1957–8), pp. 156–8.

terpretation[21] understands the double quotation as a synonymous parallel, so that "coming with the clouds of heaven" is identical with "sitting at the right hand of God". But the sequence of the two should make us mistrustful of this. We recall that in Daniel. 13:7 seq. the appearance of the Son of man with the clouds and his presentation before the Ancient of days preceded the bestowal of kingly dignity. The fact also that the first part of the reply of Jesus takes up Ps. 109:1 and refers only to his elevation to God's right hand does not favour this explanation. Particularly does it fail to do justice to ὄψεσθε. How are the opponents of Jesus to experience his justification by God? "See" can hardly indicate anything other than a visible occurrence. This bears a close resemblance to a passage from the Matthew-Luke tradition of the discourses: "I say to you, you shall not see me henceforth till you say, Blessed is he that cometh in the name of the Lord" (Matt. 23:39 = Luke 13:35). The reference to the Parousia is indisputable. The only problem in the answer of Jesus to the high priests arises from the ἀπ'ἄρτι, in Matthew's text. A. Debrunner[22] suggests reading it as ἀπαρτί, that is, "certainly". But this would mean that Luke had misunderstood it and rendered it as the equivalent of ἀπὸ τοῦ νῦν, "from now on", and so changed and curtailed Jesus' reply. "From now on will the Son of man sit at the right hand of the power of God." Luke's version must certainly be regarded as secondary.[23] But Debrunner's suggestion appears to arise from embarrassment. Possibly the

[21] *Jesus and His Coming,* pp. 43–51.

[22] In *Festschrift für A. Fridrichsen Conf. Neoti. XI,* (Lund-Copenhagen, 1947), p. 48. The reverse is maintained by Kümmel, op. cit., p. 44, note 102; in *Th.W.B.* V, 865, note 50, A. Oepke expresses some reservation.

[23] This secondary form betrays itself in the unnecessary Θεοῦ, since δύναμις is already a circumlocution for God. Luke had to omit ὄψεσθε for he realized, better than the critics of today, that there can be no

ἀπ' ἄρτι (Matt. 26:64) is an early transference from Matt. 23:39, where it fits more easily into the context.

Others regard this self-testimony of Jesus exclusively as a prophecy of his Parousia, and for this there are grounds in the concrete situation before his judges who, as Jesus is aware, have decided upon his death. He thus professes his Messianic character in his humiliation but to his unbelieving judges he also proclaims his future triumph, as with the "sign of Jonas" (Luke 11:29 seq.) and the saying in Matt. 23:39 (= Luke 13:35). In the context it is not surprising that Jesus says nothing of the future kingdom of God, though this is implicit in the quotation from Daniel.

These passages allow us to state with confidence that the idea of the Parousia is part of the "foundation stone of the tradition of Jesus".[24] Consequently, we need merely enumerate the remaining passages that deal with the advent of the Son of man, without going into their detailed problems.

Threefold tradition: Mark 13:26 = Matt. 24:30; 21:27 (at the culmination of the eschatological discourse).

Twofold tradition: Luke 11:30, cf. Matt. 12:40 (sign of Jonas, see above).

Luke 12:40 = Matt. 24:44: "Be you then also ready; for at what hour you think not the Son of man will come."

Luke 17:24 = Matt. 24:27: The Parousia, the day of the Son of man, is like lightning.

Luke 17:26–30 = Matt. 24:37–39: The days of the Son of man (that immediately precede his advent) are like those of Noah (Luke and of Lot).

Single tradition: Matt. 10:23 b: "You shall not finish all the cities of Israel till the Son of man come" (cf. 16).

question of any "vision" of the elevation and justification of Jesus on the part of his present judges.

[24] A. Oepke in *Th.W.B.* V, 864, pp. 14 seq.

Matt. 19:28: "When the Son of man shall sit on the seat of his majesty, you also shall sit on twelve seats, judging the twelve tribes of Israel" (but see also Luke 22:29 seq.).

Luke 17:22: "The days will come when you shall desire to see one day of the Son of man, and you shall not see it."

Luke 18:8 b: "But yet the Son of man, when he cometh, shall he find, think you, faith on earth?"[25]

Luke 21:36: "Watch ye, therefore, praying at all times that you may . . . stand before the Son of man."

There remains one further query. Did Jesus speak also of "my *basileia*"? Only one text calls for consideration, Luke 22:29 seq., if we leave aside passages in which other persons employ the expression, "thy kingdom", clearly because of their Jewish Messianic expectations (Matt. 20:21 = Mark 10:37 "in thy glory"; Luke 23:42) and the two extracts examined above, Matt. 13:41 and 16:28, where we have the Matthean formula, "*basileia* of the Son of man."[26] In Luke 22:29 seq. Jesus says to the disciples at the Last Supper (and not, therefore, in public): "I dispose to you, as my Father hath disposed to me, a kingdom ("rule"), that you may eat and drink at my table, in my kingdom, and may sit upon thrones, judging (or "ruling"?) the twelve tribes of Israel."

This passage presents us with a number of problems of exegesis and derivation.

From the standpoint of exegesis it is not clear how we are to connect βασιλέιαν syntactically. Is it the object of διατίθεμαι (as translated above) and then the clause explains in what this co-

[25] See on this point Jeremias, *Gleichnisse Jesu,* p. 135, with note 5.

[26] Luke 1:53 belongs to another tradition, "and of his reign there shall be no end". Early Christian thought about the reign of Christ is reflected in the parable of the talents, for the "heir to the throne" (Luke 19:12, 15, 27) is evidently a reference to Jesus.

reigning consists (βασιλείαν without an article is a functional term)? Or does βασιλείαν belong to the καθώς clause ("in the same way that my Father has disposed a kingdom to me") and the ἵνα clause is the parting disposition which Jesus gives them as a reward for their faithful loyalty to him in his sufferings (v. 28)? Both are possible grammatically but the former corresponds more fully with normal usage and feeling for language.[27] There is the factual difficulty that association at table with Christ appears to denote a ruling function and this creates problems. As the result of some careful analysis H. Schürmann suggests these may be solved by treating verse 30 as a "secondary but pre-Lucan insertion".[28] In this case, the original form of the text is that Jesus disposes "authority" to his disciples as the Father has disposed it to him (the expression must be linked with the διαθήκη of verse 20). In the addition another idea emerges, already latent in verses 16 and 18, namely the eschatological fulfilment of a meal with Jesus in the kingdom of God. Verse 18 in which the vision of this ultimate table companionship remains undeveloped could originally have been more closely linked with verse 30 a.[29] Whether the turn of phrase "in my kingdom" derives as it stands from Jesus or was coined very early in tradition cannot be stated with complete certainty. Verse 16 calls it "in the kingdom of God" and the change may have been made because of the table companionship with Jesus. On the other hand, Jesus declares in verse 29 that the Father has given him "rule" and he could have spoken more openly with his disciples. Yet "rule" in verse 29 is not the same as "in my kingdom". Probably Jesus did not refer explicitly to his *basileia* even though this expression is justified from his sequence of thought.

[27] διατίθεσθαι is usually associated with an object in the accusative, cf. J. Behn in *Th.W.B.* II, p. 105.

[28] Schürmann, III, p. 54, cf. pp. 45–50. [29] Schürmann III, p. 61.

This indicates how difficult it is to assess all these passages, and presumably differences of interpretation will always remain according to the viewpoint of individual scholars. But, reserves apart, we may epitomize the idea of Jesus about the advent of the perfect, fulfilled kingdom in the following way. It will one day come, and unexpectedly, but in a form visible to all men, according to God's sovereign will and only through his all-powerful action. This will occur when the "Son of man", accompanied by the hosts of heaven, comes "with power". This "Son of man" is no other than Jesus himself. For the present, in the form of humiliation and to a certain degree in concealment, he is fulfilling his Messianic tasks on earth. But then he will manifest himself to all the world as possessed of kingly dignity and divine power to establish in God's name – the various individual eschatological acts are of no pressing significance – God's perfect, universal, cosmic reign.

15. The Jews Struck with Blindness, the Atoning Death of Jesus and the Future Kingdom

Since Jesus brings a gospel to his own age, which proclaims a divine intervention and compels his audience to make a decision, we must also examine his audience and its reaction. Once God attaches his salvific acts to history, we cannot ignore the manner in which men receive his message and respond to his challenge. From this consequences may arise for God's further action, not in the sense that God is dependent on human attitudes but because he adapts his measures accordingly. Man can neither hinder nor delay the advent of the kingdom of God which Jesus announced but the way in which it comes differs according as it finds, so to speak, an open door through which to enter or a door firmly bolted against it or again a situation in which some want to open and others to shut the door.

There is little doubt about the actual attitude of the audience of Jesus, at least in general lines, from the account of the evangelists. Their report merits historical acceptance since the outcome of the activity of Jesus is shown in precise historical data: the arrest of Jesus by the Jewish authorities, his delivery to the Roman tribunal, the process against him, and finally his execution on the cross. Several minor questions may be debatable, for instance, what was the status of the Jewish legal proceedings against Jesus, how the guilt for this judicial murder is to be shared between Jews and Romans, whether the leading sections among the Jews are alone responsible and to what extent the people, the followers of Jesus, and people who were not hostile to him, can be freed from all share in this guilt. From a theological point of view, it is enough to state as did John in his gospel: "And whereas he had done many miracles before them, they believed not in him" (12:37). The practical outcome of Jesus' preaching, supported by Messianic signs, was negative.

On closer inspection, both in the synoptic and in John's account, notable differences can be observed in the attitude of individual groups, and these, in spite of an occasional variation of emphasis, remain similar in all the evangelists. The people tend to believe more readily than their leaders but they do not arrive at any decisive acceptance of the Messias, not even a recognition of Messianism in Jesus' sense. They followed the Galilean healer and wonderworker, were astounded at his teaching of the Law and listened eagerly to his preaching. But they had no understanding for his implicit Messianic claim or, as at Nazareth, openly repudiated it (Mark 1:21; 6:6), looked upon him as John the Baptist reawakened from the dead,

Elias returned to earth or another of the prophets (Mark 8:28; cf. 6:14 par.) but not as the Messias in person. In John's gospel popular groups discuss whether he is or could be the Messias[30] but, if we leave aside an attempt to proclaim a political Messias after the multiplication of the bread (6:14 seq.) the opinion of the crowd continues to be divided, uncertain and undetermined, or the germ of belief is soon suppressed by the Pharisees and the fear of official authority (7:32, 47 seq.; 9:22, 34; 11:46, 57).

One marked distinction between the synoptic and the Johannine account is that in the former the attitude of the crowd remains practically the same, oscillating between admiration, misunderstanding, astonishment and unbelief, whereas in the latter we can trace a dramatic development with a peak and turning point in Galilee (chapter 6), disturbed doubts in Jerusalem (chapters 7–10) and a final wave of belief (chapters 11–12) because of the raising of Lazarus, and the particular enemies of Jesus, the influential (Pharisee) and leading (Sadducee) classes in Jerusalem are thrown into stronger relief in the tactical and eventually successful measures they adopt against him. The tragic *dénouement* of his conflict with the official leaders of Judaism (or simply with the "Jews") manifests itself as an instance of that dark reality, described in the prologue, that the "world" did not recognize the Logos at his advent, that "his own" did not receive him (1:10 seq.). The "elevation" on the cross, that takes the "Son of man" back into the glory of his Father and releases the energy of divine life for believers is a God-ordained necessity (3:14 seq.) to raise all men to himself in his heavenly sphere (12:32, 34). This Johannine vision of faith only strengthens and confirms the notion already present in the

[30] John 7:12, 26 seq.; 31, 40–43, 47 seq.; 9:16, 22; 10:19–21, 24, 41 seq.; 11:45; 12:11, 18.

synoptics that the "Son of man" must suffer cruelly and be rejected and put to death (Mark 8:31; 9:31; 10:33 par.). The early Christian stress on Jesus as the atoning Servant of God is unmistakably present in these prophecies of suffering but their kerygmatic formulation does not exclude Jesus as their original source. We cannot enter here into the much-debated question whether Jesus was conscious of himself in the rôle of the Isaian Servant of God but without such an assumption many of his words and his general attitude become completely unintelligible.[31]

A further problem arises how the teaching of Jesus about God's reign is related to the prophecy of his sufferings. Can they be reconciled? Is the humiliation of the Son of man, his sufferings in vicarious atonement only a consequence of Jewish unbelief or was it foreseen from the beginning in the teaching of the coming reign of God? This brings us again to the problem how the Son of man passages are related to the proclamation of the *basileia,* but this time not those which express his glory (see section 14) but his humiliation. Our approach to this set of problems is not from the Son of man texts of which we do not propose to give a critical analysis but from the *basileia* texts, and we ask whether they allow or create room for the atoning death. To do this, we must study the reaction of Jesus to the unbelief of the Jews.

But first another question must be examined, which may have only hypothetical value but is not without its importance for

[31] K. H. Schelke, *Die Passion Jesu in der Verkündigung des NT* (Heidelberg, 1949), pp. 60 seq.; M. Meinertz, *Theologie des N.T.* I, pp. 144 seq.; H. W. Wolff, *Jesaja 53 im Urchristentum* (3rd edition, Berlin, 1952); E. Lohse, *Martyrer und Gottesknecht* (Göttingen, 1955), pp. 116–29; J. Jeremias, article παῖς Θεοῦ in *Th.W.B.* V, pp. 698 seq., especially pp. 709–13.

the proclamation of the *basileia*. What would have happened had the majority of the people accepted the teaching of Jesus and had he not been hounded to death?

R. Guardini put this question and replied that, in that event, the reign of God would soon have arrived in glory.[32] He wanted, it seems, to solve the difficulty rising from the belief in an advent in the near future. He writes as follows: "When Jesus delivered the Sermon on the Mount – not only that but many another discourse in the same powerful and confident manner – there lay behind them a great possibility. All were related to the proclamation that "the kingdom of God is at hand" (Matt. 3:2). He had explicitly declared that it was near. This expression cannot have been merely an enthusiastic formula or a note of stern warning; "near" means in fact near. As far as God was concerned, the emergence of a new existence, announced in the prophecies of Isaias, might have been realized . . . . This kingdom would have come, if the message had encountered faith . . . . But this did not happen. Christ was rejected by his people and he turned away towards death."[33]

This hypothesis is carefully enunciated but can it be supported by the texts? The conditions in which the gospel was handed down make it impossible to fix individual passages as to time and setting. But there would be great difficulty in distinguishing two stages in the proclamation of Jesus, the first, in which supposing the acceptance of his teaching and prescinding from his way of death, he announces the coming of the kingdom of glory for the near future, and a second stage in which because

[32] *Der Herr,* pp. 46 seq.; 113 seq.; 259 seq.; 691. For Guardini this is at the same time an answer to the radical ethics of the Sermon on the Mount (pp. 109 seq.) and to the form of the Church which in that case would have been different from the form we now know.
[33] Op. cit., pp. 109 seq.

of the unbelief of the people or their leaders he becomes aware of his destined death and then proclaims another divine plan of salvation which in spite of the rejection of the Messias and indeed because of his atoning violent death, foresees and promises glory in the future. The texts which look most forcibly to a realization in the near future belong to the later portion of his activity, after the prophecy of suffering and death made at Caesarea Philippi (Mark 8:31–33: see also Mark 9:1; 13:30 par.). To say the least, the evangelists know nothing about an "original" plan for the establishment of the kingdom in the immediate future, that failed to be fulfilled because of unbelief. They have on the contrary so situated the promises that the reader has no doubts whatsoever that his road leads to death. Besides, the passages would have required the qualification, "If you believe, then the kingdom is near". The basic message is, however, an absolute one; "the time is accomplished; the kingdom (reign) of God is at hand" and from this arises the appeal to his audience, "Be converted and believe" (Mark 1:15).

The reign of God is certainly coming, and soon, but with complete independence of men's attitudes. All that men can do is to decide whether for them it will signify salvation or judgment (Luke 10:8–11). Finally, it is not certain at what period Jesus started to envisage his atoning death. It was only after Peter's confession at Caesarea Philippi that he began to initiate his disciples into the mystery of the sufferings of the Son of man, but this does not mean that he then became conscious for the first time of his destined death. It would be better to assume that since his baptism and temptation he had seen his Messianic rôle in the light of the "Servant of God" (Mark 1:11; Matt. 4:1–11 = Luke 4:1–13), even though it would be going too far to detect in the voice from heaven at the baptism a reference to the atoning death (Isa. 42:1). All we can assert positively is this. Jesus desired to fulfil his Messianic task on earth humbly and in obedience as the Servant of God and, conscious of the divine commission, he proclaimed the immediate dawn and the future realization of God's reign, himself ready to do and endure everything which the Father had ordained for this service. But when the assurance of his death as vicarious atonement was communicated to him, remains concealed in the mystery of his person.[34]

In consequence, the query what would have happened had the Jewish people believed in his message, remains purely theoretical because Jesus said nothing about it. We simply do not know, as we do not know in the concrete how the passion of the Messias would have been brought about had Judas not denounced and betrayed his master. A hypothetical theology of this kind was far from the mind of the early Church. What revelation says of the reign of God is stated without any "If" or "Had this been so" and it lends no substance to any twofold plan on God's part. The promise is absolute and not complex: its development is what continually uncovers new details. Jesus' proclamation of God's reign which is already its partial realization, wins new contours through the echoes and reactions it stirs in his hearers, and the answer of Jesus further reveals the manner in which God desires finally and fully to establish his reign. This calls for more detailed examination.

As regards these hearers, one statement of Jesus, relating to his use of parables, is of great significance. In Mark 4:11 seq. it reads as follows:

[34] No appeal can be made to Mark 2:20. We cannot fix its exact period with any certainty because it is set in the framework of controversy. Besides, it says nothing about a violent death but only very indefinitely, "when the bridegroom is taken away from you".

verse 11:
"To you it is given to know
the mystery of the kingdom of God [God's reign]
but to them that are without,
all things are done in parables."
verse 12:
"That seeing, they may see and not perceive,
and hearing, they may hear and not understand,
lest at any time they should be converted
and their sins should be forgiven them."

We may confine ourselves in principle to the Marcan text because the other two synoptics present a secondary form. This is clear in verse 11 in the replacement of μυστήριον by the plural, the source of which is the number of the parables; also from the addition of "to perceive" in verse 12 which shows that "given" refers to the faculty of spiritual understanding. The only doubtful point is whether τοῖς ἔξω in Mark belongs to the original. Matt. 13:11 has merely ἐκείνοις; Luke 8:10 in its turn τοῖς λοιποῖς (secondary). For the gospels Mark's expression in 4:11 οἱ ἔξω is exceptional, but it is often employed in Paul to denote those who are outside the Christian community (1 Cor. 5:12 seq.; Col. 4:5; 1 Thess. 4:12). But we have to be careful about accepting Pauline influence, since it is applied by Paul to unbelieving heathens whereas in Mark it refers to unbelieving Jews. In addition, the expression is possible from the Hebrew-Aramaic standpoint (cf. *ḥuṣ, ḥuṣa,* also adjectivally *ḥiṣōn* – the outsider). It must be admitted that τοῖς ἔξω is not essential for the parallel and it could be an explanatory addition of the evangelist.[35] This does not alter the fact that the parallel as such is

[35] If τοῖς ἔξω were original, then ἐκείνοις would be a superfluous demonstrative; this is a common Aramaic usage: see Jeremias, *Gleichnisse Jesu,* p. 9.

preserved only by Mark. A synoptic comparison shows that in verse 12 Mark's marginal references have toned down and shortened the text (see below).

This passage must first be studied in itself without regard for its present context because the chapter of parables shows signs of editorial composition, especially in the marginal remark in verse 10. This breaks into the situation which is created in 4:2 and reiterated at its close in 4:33, namely a discourse to a large crowd. "Those who were with him along with the twelve" clearly denotes a narrow circle (cf. verse 34 "his disciples").[36] Finally, the introduction of the passage by means of καὶ ἔλεγεν αὐτοῖς is a typical formula of Mark and it signifies the transition from one parable to another.[37] The parallel contains words that the evangelist rarely uses and this proves that he has taken an older logion and put it in the present context.[38] The two lines are constructed antithetically. "They that are without" correspond to "you" as does concealment through "parables" to the unveiling of the mystery.[39] Therefore the saying cannot be in its primitive and basic sense a justification offered by Jesus for his use of parables. It may have a direct reference to this proclamation of God's reign, since that is given in parable form both in this passage and in others. Its true significance is brought home only to those to whom God has entrusted the "mystery

[36] In point of fact, verse 10 can have no other meaning; the phrase is a pleonasm. According to Mark 3: 32, 34 those "around him" are his closest followers.

[37] See 2:27; 4:2, 21, 24; 6:10; 7:9; 8:21; 9:1.

[38] Jeremias, *Gleichnisse Jesu,* p. 8, note 5.

[39] See Matt. 7:17 with the same meaning. For the normal use of this expression cf. Jeremias, *Gleichnisse Jesu,* p. 10, note 1. In *Der verborgene Menschensohn,* pp. 224 seq., E. Sjöberg has criticized Jeremias' translation "all is mysterious", but with little justification. He himself admits the possibility of a Hebrew *"beth essentiae".*

of the *basileia*". The saying was thus introduced at this point by the evangelist but it suits the present context, since the meaning of the parables given is in fact withheld from "those who are without" (see section 13). Τὰ Πάντα hints at an even more general reference in the original. The whole teaching and even the activity of Jesus are "mysterious" to their minds.

The distinction between those who perceive and those who do not understand is referred (verse 12) to the will and plan of God. This is the much debated "hardening of heart". The theological problems which this raises do not call for treatment here but we may make this brief statement. Not without reason does Jesus choose words from the prophet Isaias. In what is happening he sees a typical realization of what the great prophet experienced and about which he was instructed in a revelation from God. We have also to bear in mind, therefore, the Old Testament situation and these three points emerge: i. The people are not guiltless; ii. Their hardness of heart has its temporal limits;[40] iii. A holy remnant continues to exist in this period of contumacy. Jesus must have understood the redemptive situation and God's plan for his hearers in a similar manner. Although the revelation of the "mystery of the reign of God" and the blinding of those "that are without" goes back to God's sovereign will, Jesus in his actual situation could regard this contumacy as a punishment for the people's unbelief and still leave room for possible conversion in the future.

This last suggestion would imply that the μήποτε clause in Aramaic originally meant: "unless . . . etc."[41] We must naturally

[40] This is a point of view brought out by Augustine which thus tempers his severe theory of hardening of heart; *In Joann. Ev.* tr. LIII, 11 (Corp. Chr. 36, 457); *Quaest. Septendecim*, Matt. XIV (P. G. 35 1372 seq.).
[41] So Jeremias, *Gleichnisse Jesu,* p. 11, from his understanding of the Targum and rabbinical interpretation (see Billerbeck 1, 662 seq.). T. W.

inquire about the way the evangelist and his Greek readers understood it. These could not have taken the clause as meaning "unless they be converted and their sins be forgiven them" but, at most, "whether perhaps . . . not . . . ."[42] If the conjunction is merely a reinforcement of μή ("in order that . . . not . . ."), the clause need not be understood as purposive, dependent upon the ἵνα sentence but it can be joined with this and repeat the same idea. This would justify its absence from Luke 8:10.

The continuation of a remnant is expressed and emphasized when the mystery of God's reign is entrusted to the disciples of Jesus ("to you"). In the actual situation we are dealing with, the gospel of Jesus had found acceptance only in a narrow and limited circle of believers, and this is an act of God's grace to them (note the use of the passive voice).

If this explanation be accepted, with its reminder of the Old Testament situation, reiterated at another level in the presence of Jesus, then Matthew's practice is neither arbitrary nor unjustified. His theological interpretation would be correct. The hardness of heart supposes the people's unbelief; he therefore alters the ἵνα into a ὅτι. At the same time, he did not wish to omit God's purpose in hardening their hearts, which had been eliminated from the saying, and he therefore introduced the substantial quotation from Isa. 9:6 seq. And so both motives find expression, the ground of the divine decree (the unbelief

Manson, *Teaching of Jesus,* pp. 76–80, looks upon the ἵνα as a misunderstanding of the Aramaic *"di"*; it originally denoted the relative pronoun: "All is mysterious to those outside, who see and yet do not see . . . ."The same author proposes a new and unconvincing interpretation of the whole passage in *Exp.T.* 68 (1957), pp. 132–5.

[42] This meaning is possible in an indirect question, see 2 Tim. 2:25; Bauer, *Wörterbuch*, p. 1027, 3 b; but it is foreign to this context.

of the people already in evidence) and God's design of further hardening. The situation created in the lifetime of Jesus becomes more sharply defined in the experience of the early Church for which the unbelief of the Jewish people, taken as a whole, was even more striking. The quotation from Isaias is found in other witnesses from the early Church, see John 12:40; Acts 28:26 seq. For the early Church as for Jesus this was the solution of the difficult problem of Jewish unbelief.

Mark's gospel does not expressly associate this saying of Jesus with a particular stage in his relation with the people. Only later do we learn in increasing measure of a special instruction for his disciples.[43] Jesus does not speak "openly" to the disciples about his passion and death till after the scene at Caesarea Philippi (Mark 8:32; also 10:38, 45; 14:8, 18, 21, 22–25, 27, 41). But the series of parables was outlined to the people and with it commenced the break away of those who did not understand, but only in connection with the *basileia* parables. These include no hint of the passion and death of Jesus and so there is no contradiction with 8:32. We can see how during the final portion of the Galilean mission when Jesus observed the inadequate faith of the people, he veiled the "mystery of the kingdom" (the "mystery of God's reign") in parables. But whether this saying was addressed to the disciples then or subsequently cannot be stated with assurance.

At any rate, with this remark Jesus' revelation of the reign of God enters a new phase that can be characterized as follows: i. Its mystery is revealed only to a small group; it remains hidden from the mass of the people. ii. Behind this is a divine plan, that only a minority is chosen to receive the gospel of

[43] "Privately" 6:31 seq.; 9:2, 28; 13:3; "in the house" 7:17; 9:33; 10:10; also 10:23–30, 35–45; 13 contain instruction for the narrow circle of disciples.

Jesus for the time being. iii. The "mystery" associated with it can scarcely be anything but its concealed presence in the operation of Jesus, to which those who are without are blind. iv. This hidden presence is followed by a subsequent manifestation in glory of God's reign. (The parables of growth in the same chapter fit in with this interpretation: see section 13.) Nothing is yet said about what is to happen between this present and this future. There is room for the atoning passion of Jesus but nothing is directly revealed, and no hint is given.

Other passages confirm the fact that Jesus distinguished between those to whom the mystery of God's reign is unveiled and those who did not believe or understand. In his prayer of praise Jesus thanked the Father that he had concealed this from the wise and prudent and revealed it to little ones (Matt. 11:25 seq. = Luke 10:21). The contrast is drawn slightly differently from that in Mark 4:11 where the wise must be the Scribes opposed to Jesus and the little ones are simple believers. These are, in the first place, the disciples of Jesus whose eyes see what the prophets desired to see and did not see (Luke 10:23 seq.). Matthew saw the affinity between this sentence and that about the mystery of God's reign because he introduced it at the appropriate place in his chapter of parables (13:16 seq.). In either case it treats of knowledge that salvation is present in the person of Jesus and this is confined to the close circle of disciples. Thus, the prayer of praise must be applied first of all to the disciples. It introduces only the two extreme groups but it does confirm that the revelation is limited to a narrow circle.

One may, therefore, doubt whether it is correct to join the prayer of praise with the solemn sending out of the disciples. The thanksgiving prayer does not fit in easily with the outcome of this mission because, in its general picture, there was little understanding of the *basileia* gospel, not as much as Jesus desired.

Luke chapter 10 is a Lucan composition and betrays Luke's missionary interests.

Luke 12:32 makes it plain that the company of those who accepted the gospel and persevered with Jesus was not large. "Fear not, little flock, for it hath pleased your Father to give you the kingdom (or dominion)." This sentence peculiar to Luke was used here as a stock phrase and belongs to a later setting (see Luke 22:28 seq.). It appears almost a general law that God reaches his objective with only a small company. The sentence, "Many are called but few are chosen" points in the same direction (Matt. 20:16; 22:14). It describes the significant reduction of the faithful to a small group of disciples. In itself, the appeal of Jesus was to all men; in practice only a few belong to the elect.[44]

Only after the scene at Caesarea Philippi, when the Passion was revealed to the disciples, do we come across several texts in which the atoning death of Jesus is associated with the realization of the perfect kingdom. This occurs clearly enough in his answer to the sons of Zebedee (Mark 10:35–40 = Matt. 20:20–23). To the petition of these apostles, among the first he had summoned, that they might have the first places in his kingdom he immediately replies, "you know not what you ask". He then speaks in a double simile of the fate that awaits him and which they also will share. In the context this can only mean that this mysterious event ordained by God ("drink the chalice" and "be baptized with a baptism") is the pre-condition for Jesus' rule, and correspondingly for his disciples' share in that

[44] The sentence does not therefore need to be understood in the sense of an absolute divine decree. Between the "call" of the many and the "election" of the few there is room for man's free decision. The sentence describes the situation as it actually is, after a long period of preaching: see I. Daumoser, *Berufung und Erwählung bei den Synoptikern* (Stuttgart, 1955), pp. 186–212, especially 202 seq.

rule. This is a precise application of the teaching developed after Caesarea Philippi that the Son of man must suffer severely and be rejected (Mark 8:31) and, in the mind of the evangelist who adds the following sentence, only then "come in the glory of his Father with the holy angels" (Mark 8:38), and that the disciples must be resolved to go the same way as their master (see Mark 8:34 seq.). Jesus clearly states in his reply to the sons of Zebedee what the evangelist is hinting at in his composition but he adds the limiting condition that even the distribution of places in the fully realized kingdom is reserved to the Father (Mark 10:40).

Yet this complete correspondence with the early Christian notion of the humiliation and elevation of the Son of man and of the disciples' path to glory through the cross casts suspicion on the answer of Jesus to James and John. E. Lohmeyer thinks it possible that the incident ended with the curt refusal, "You know not what you ask", all the more forcible the fewer reasons Jesus gives for it.[45] There follows an old double simile which presents problems of exegesis.[46] Yet despite the oracular statements made about it, it bears the stamp of genuine authenticity in its figurative form and in the twofold form preserved by Mark (Matthew has only the simile of the chalice). But in whatever way the two be interpreted, and both have an identical meaning, (G. Delling now holds them to signify God's judgment which Jesus takes upon himself) it is a scarcely-veiled prophecy of his

[45] *Ev. des Markus,* at appropriate point, p. 222; see R. Bultmann, *Geschichte der snpt. Tradition,* p. 23, and Supplement, pp. 7 seq.

[46] See G. Delling, βάπτισμα βαπτισθῆναι in *N.T.* 2 (1957), pp. 92–115, who distinguishes his position from previous exegesis. Against recent attempts to understand the sentence from the standpoint of Christian baptism, see O. Kuß, "Zur Frage einer vorpaulinischen Todestaufe" in *Mü.Th.Z.* 4 (1953), pp. 1–17, particularly 6–11.

Passion (which need not necessarily be understood as a prophecy of the deaths of the two apostles). But death is associated in his mind with the coming kingdom, for Jesus repudiates the false notions of his disciples about his Messianic kingdom, answers them from his knowledge of the *basileia* and looks towards this kingdom which is wholly subject to the Father's disposition.

The baptism simile is connected with a similar expression peculiar to Luke (Luke 22:50). This also creates exegetical problems because of its connection with the fire that Jesus will enkindle upon earth. A fuller analysis would take us too far and so we content ourselves with this as a confirmatory passage.[47] Mark's double simile is so clear that it leaves no doubt that Jesus was conscious of his destined death. Only after it – this is the Father's disposition – is the kingdom to be realized for him and his disciples.

There are other passages, for example Mark 9:12 par.; Luke 17:25, that reflect his announcement of his Passion and as formulated, they are secondary. For our purpose it is better to exclude them.

The words of Jesus at the Last Supper show in an even clearer light that in his formation of the disciples he placed the advent of the perfect reign of God after his death. Mark 14:25 (=Matt. 26:29) includes one of his sentences at this parting meal which lifted their gaze to the kingdom of glory: "Amen I say to you that I will drink no more of the fruit of the vine (Matthew also has: from henceforth) until that day when I shall drink it new (Matthew: + with you) in the kingdom of God (Matthew: of my Father)." The sentence is found in Mark and Matthew at the conclusion of the Eucharist account, in Luke on the other

[47] But see R. H. Fuller, *Mission and Achievement of Jesus,* pp. 59–62; G. Delling, op. cit., pp. 102–12 (not really convincing).

hand (in a somewhat altered form and duplicated), before it, namely in connection with the account of the Passover meal (Luke 22:16, 18). It would appear that the wording in Mark is nearest to the original but Luke's arrangement is preferable.[48]

Notwithstanding conflicting opinions among the Fathers,[49] there can be no doubt that Jesus is giving an image (see Luke 22:30a) of the future kingdom, in which he would be reunited with his disciples. The saying of Jesus which impressed even J. Wellhausen as being "very ancient"[50] and which in fact betrays an Aramaic linguistic basis,[51] presupposes a parting from the disciples and contains, notably in the twofold form in Luke 22:16, 18 a "mysterious prophecy of death" (Schürmann, p. 70). This much-controverted passage does not state that the death of Jesus has an immediate significance for the advent of God's reign but it does not deny it.[52] It can hardly be a "vow of detachment", through which Jesus wished to impress on the disciples how irrevocable was his decision "to pave the way for God's royal rule by means of his vicarious Passion";[53] for the form with οὐ μή is merely a strong guarantee.[54] It is highly

[48] Schürmann I, pp. 34–45. Schürmann thinks that Mark 14:25 provides the rudiments of what was originally a fuller passage, such as we have in Luke 22:15–18. Many commentators prefer Luke's arrangement.
[49] See H. J. Vogels, "Mark 14:25 und Parallelen" in *Vom Wort des Lebens, Festschrift für M. Meinertz* (Münster i. W., 1951), pp. 93–104.
[50] *Das Evangelium Marci* (2nd edition, Berlin, 1909), p. 118.
[51] V. Taylor, *Gospel acc. to St. Mark,* on the relevant text.
[52] Wellhausen, op. cit., p. 115: In his view, the kingdom will come without the co-operation of Jesus who hopes like all other men to have a share in it.
[53] J. Jeremias, *Abendmahlsworte Jesu,* p. 122.
[54] See similar passages with ἀμὴν λέγω ὑμῖν and οὐ μή which express the certainty of the prophecy: Mark 9:1, 41; 10:15; 13:30: on this point consult Blaß-Debrunner, *Grammatik des ntl. Griechisch* § 365.

improbable that Jesus was referring to the bitter chalice which he desired to drink in place of the festal wine.[55] But if we suppose this sentence to have been spoken prior to the institution of the holy Eucharist, it must receive new light from the words of institution. In these words Jesus gives to his death the character of vicarious atonement [56] and then the eschatological reference has the following meaning. Jesus will no longer sit at table with the disciples on earth but at a new meal in the coming kingdom of God. For this, the death he is awaiting is a necessary condition, since the disciples can partake of the eschatological banquet only in the strength of the atoning blood of Jesus (Luke 22:20, "that shall be shed for you"). Jesus is already applying this "new testament through his blood" to the company of disciples, and the parallel texts make it evident (Mark 14:24, cf. Matt. 26:28) that the saving power of the blood of Jesus, applied to the disciples, is not restricted to their number but that fundamentally his atoning death has a universal efficacy ("for many", that is for humanity, for all). In the passage about the eschatological companionship at the table of the elect, the disciples represent the elect who will share with Jesus in God's perfect rule, because of his atoning death (see more fully section 19). Thus, in his last hour, when death confronts him, inescapable but willed by God and deeply significant, Jesus expresses his firm confidence that God will inaugurate the kingdom he has proclaimed, not least by the sacrifice of his life, so rich in grace for all those who gain a share in the new covenant, established by Jesus.

At the close of Jesus' earthly course we can glimpse the divine plan of salvation designed by God in view of the unbelief of the

[55] R. H. Fuller, op. cit., p. 76.

[56] H. Schürmann in *L.Th.K.* I (Freiburg i. Br., 1957), pp. 29 seq.

Jews, the rejection of Jesus by the majority of the ancient people of God. Despite this rejection of his latest ambassador his perfect kingdom will not come as a universal destroying judgment but because of the death in vicarious atonement of his obedient Servant he will offer new possibilities of salvation for all men, even for the unbelieving Jews (see Apoc. 3:17–21).[57] The God who made his kingship flash forth and break through in the salvific operation of his Son but found attention and understanding only in a few men, offers once more an interval of grace. The history of salvation continues in this eschatological period (see below section 21). The tones of the gospel are heard again, God's eschatological kingship continues to be the glad tidings of peace and salvation for all who are converted and believe.

16. How Near was the Kingdom?

Whether Jesus expected and foretold the advent of the Son of man and the realization of God's perfect reign as an occurrence in the near and determined future is one of the most difficult problems for the New Testament exegete. Respect for truth compels him to avoid the specious arts of the apologist. Yet both his faith and the consideration of all available texts make it impossible for him to be satisfied with the rationalist assertion that Jesus deceived himself on this point and the early Church gave a different interpretation to this imminent expectation. However, these "awkward" passages lie in wait not only for the scholar who will not admit an error on the part of Jesus and who

[57] On the importance of the atoning death of Jesus for the coming kingdom see also T. W. Manson, *The Servant-Messiah* (Cambridge, 1953), pp. 76 seq.; H. Roberts, *Jesus and the Kingdom of God,* pp. 41 seq.; Fuller, op. cit., pp. 50–78 is particularly insistent.

regards the early Christian interpretation of his sayings as legitimate and consonant with essential facts; they also confront the "logical eschatologist" who claims that the prophecy of the end referred to the generation then alive.

The method often employed is illustrated in the work of E. Grässer.[58] In his view, the expectation of a near advent is taken for granted[59] and passages that contradict this *vi verborum* are attributed to early Church efforts to explain the delay of the Parousia. Texts that could refer to a nearer or more distant advent of the Son of man must arise from a period and from circumstances when men were uncertain how near the Parousia was. A passage such as Mark 13:32 must be attributed to the early Church without detriment to its Christological difficulty. As the Parousia became more remote, Luke advanced his theory of the progressive mission and continuous development of the Church. The same applies to passages which suppose a longer time for the preaching of the gospel (for example Mark 13:10). But what right have we to set forth the early Christian expectation of the Parousia in this manner? Are these various interpretations, historically speaking, consecutive and not rather contemporary? Cannot the early Church expect us to accept all the sayings she has preserved and examine them, rather than ascribe all the awkward passages to her? This question of "community formations" touches on the most controversial point. Anyone who studies the synoptic texts with these problems in mind realizes how difficult it is to assess the origin and original form and meaning of a passage. According as it is accepted as valid or invalid the general pattern of the teaching of Jesus is altered. It would be a sound principle to accept the verdict of tradition in cases

[58] *Das Problem der Parusieverzögerung* (Berlin, 1951).
[59] Op. cit., pp. 3–75.

that are doubtful, and strong reasons should be required to alter this assessment.[60] We shall study the relevant texts from this standpoint.

We have already seen that Jesus did in fact proclaim the near approach of God's reign. His preaching, his cures and the expulsion of devils are signs that it is breaking through and in a sense already here, but only in a provisional way, as a promise for the future, as a foretaste of its advent in glory. It has also been made clear that we may not attribute to Jesus a twofold notion of the *basileia* as though he were speaking of God's present reign as different from that of the future. We must not say that he speaks about the nearness of God's reign less definitely than about its presence because he was not so clearly aware of the future as of present reality. On the contrary, he was aware of what is to come and he saw it approaching in his redeeming acts and draw nigh to him and to men. Only thus can we understand the urgency of his appeal: The time is accomplished, the reign of God is at hand. This is the time for decision, be converted and believe. There must be no more delay and hesitation, no withdrawal. Anyone who desires to enter God's kingdom must be converted at once and do everything that God's holy will demands.

A large part of the teaching of Jesus can only be understood in this light. His warnings that men must watch and be ready[61] lose their meaning unless there is an urgent possibility that the last things will shortly be realized. The language of the parables is even more forcible. Man can be taken unawares by the last

[60] For a criticism of Grässer cf. O. Cullmann, "Parusieverzögerung und Urchristentum" in *Th.L.Z.* 83 (1958), pp. 1–12.

[61] "Be ready", Matt. 24:44 = Luke 12:40; cf. Matt. 25:10; Luke 12:47; "watch", Matt. 24:42 seq.; 25:13; Mark 13:33–37; Luke 12:37 seq.; cf. Mark 14:38 par.

things as was the generation of Noah by the flood (Luke 17:26 seq. = Matt. 24:37–39) and the inhabitants of Sodom by the disaster to their city (Luke 17:28 seq.). The contemporaries of Jesus who are skilled in reading the signs of weather in the sky do not know the signs of the hour of salvation in which they are living (Luke 12:54–56). Luke's picture of the enemy with whom a man should be reconciled on the way to the judge (12:57–59) is also understood by him as a simile of crisis; but the point of the picture of the rich landowner which he gives elsewhere (12:16–22) is that God says to this self-complacent man who has ignored him "Thou fool, this very night they (= God) shall require thy soul of thee." This is a warning. It can happen to anyone, because the eschatological hour has arrived. Luke has attached to the parable of the unfaithful steward (16:1–7) the particular warning, which appears to have been associated with this parable from an early date, that men must break away from Mammon (verse 9). In its earliest form the universal eschatological appeal was that men should be prudent and come to their senses in this final hour, as is shown in the concluding words of Jesus (verse 8). Luke's practical ethical application, suggested by the remarkably similar construction of the passage,[62] has not destroyed the original meaning even if it has narrowed and obscured it so that the parable is frequently interpreted as an exhortation to almsgiving without any reference to time. There is no mistaking the urgent eschatological appeal for conversion in the parable of the fig-tree (Luke 13:6–9) which is even more pointedly addressed to the Jewish people. In general, we observe how Jesus speaks to his hearers as concretely as possible and out of the concrete situation, for example in Luke 13:1–5; 23:28–31, also

[62] D. Buzy, *Paraboles,* pp. 691 seq. ("verse 9 does not belong to the parable; there is only a striking similarity of object and mode of expression").

perhaps in the parable of the housebreaker by night (Luke 12: 39 seq. = Matt. 24:43 seq.). Many other sayings and parables could be adduced that must refer to the threat of the last things and the crisis of the present hour, even when the interpretation is not always certain.[63] The general picture is clear enough; the teaching of Jesus contains an urgent, eschatological note (see above section 7).

The question remains how this expectation of a near advent is to be explained. In all the passages we have quoted no definite time is given; no temporal limits are fixed within which the advent in power of God's reign is to be awaited. Since we are dealing with the main body of the teaching of Jesus, and moreover with material whose authenticity is beyond question, we are compelled to say this is how Jesus preached, in this pictorial and urgent style that brings home to his audience the seriousness of the hour and the necessity to make a decision, without adding apocalyptic revelations or foretelling events that could be calculated. We have to give this fact its proper weight and not concentrate immediately on texts which appear to include a fixed term. To any inquiry what was the attitude of Jesus in this eschatological preaching, we must answer that he wanted to bring men to reflection and conversion, to awaken them from lethargy and trivial day-to-day preoccupations, and to spur them to a passionate religious search and attachment to God. His desire was to urge them to free themselves from sin and passions, from greed and lust for power and to strive towards a more unselfish love of God and their fellow-men. A share in God's kingdom that was to come and was indeed very near at hand is one of the strongest motives to arouse all the sound energies in man. But it is also a promise of consolation

[63] Dodd, *Parables,* pp. 154–74; Jeremias, *Gleichnisse Jesu,* pp. 139–67.

for the poor and for mourners, who have experienced the misery and wretchedness of this world (Luke 6:20–24). In the process Jesus is deliberately weaning his fellow-countrymen from a worldly and egoistic, a political and nationalist way of thinking so that they may recognize that guilt, hatred, hardness, lust for power and blindness are the real wretchedness and sickness of mankind. When a man seeks to bring his fellow-men out of their confusion, he must address them concretely, approach them in their actual situation and make his concern and aim a matter of urgency for them. In short, he must adopt the prophetic manner as all the great Old Testament prophets had done.

If we compare the prophecies, whether threats, warnings or consolations, of these men of God with the eschatological preaching of Jesus, we discover many closely-related features. Their manner resembles that of Jesus, not merely in bringing home to men their sin and guilt, but in setting the words of God in the actual situation, making God's demands a matter of practical urgency and bringing his promises home to them. Their prophecies are always directed to the appropriate time and historical setting, and the fulfilment is at times very different from the actual text of the prophecy. "Since the primary task of all prophecy concerns its contemporaries for whom it explains God's will in the historical situation, prophecy enters into this task by making the purpose of God's intervention visible and intelligible for the particular time and its particular concerns. To do this, it has to assume a concrete temporal form; it must penetrate into the assumptions, ideas, knowledge, needs and problems of its time and, therefore, include many factors of time and place that restrict it, for without them it could not speak in the language of the age."[64] How often do the prophets

[64] W. Eichrodt, *Theologie des A.T.* I, p. 342.

speak in precisely the same style as Jesus of the "nearness" of the day of the Lord and of judgment![65] And how the pictures themselves fluctuate between temporal tribunals and the final judgment! Yet we must always stress the fact that in its content the teaching of Jesus essentially transcends that of the prophets. With him the time of fulfilment is there, through him God's eschatological work is in operation. God not only contemplates thoughts of salvation (Jer. 29:11 seq.), he is putting them into effect, and the abiding promise is based not only on the words of Jesus but also on the deeds wrought through him. But could Jesus not have employed the prophetic style to describe the future promise? Could he too not have shortened the perspective? The certainty of the promise would not have been affected and the addition would be true, for with Jesus the eschatological future has already begun.

We must examine from this point of view the greatest prophecy of Jesus, the "eschatological discourse" (Mark 13 and parallels). In its present form it shows many signs of editorial revision and it provides a number of obscure points. A comparison of the synoptics shows the freedom with which they arranged their material and presented it to their readers, notably when we pass from Mark to Luke.[66] But neither of them has obscured the actual intention of Jesus. The master is not revealing a cryptic apocalyptic doctrine to his disciples but arming them for what is to come. The whole of this coherently constructed discourse is shot through with warnings and motives

[65] Compare the texts which speak of a "near expectation" in Isa. 13:6; 51:5; 56:1; Jer. 48:16; Ezech. 7:1-13; 12:21–25; 30:3; Joel 2:1; Soph. 1:7, 14–18. On this subject see J. Schildenberger, *Bib.* 24 (1943), pp. 107–24; 205–30, especially pp. 121 seq.

[66] See on this matter the commentaries of J. Schmid on Mark 13 and Luke 21.

for comfort, Mark 13:5–27: a warning against deception (vv. 5 seq.), encouragement for a bold profession of faith (vv. 9–13), the open announcement of the great abomination and yet security of mind because he has foretold it (vv. 14–23), a renewed warning about false Messias and false prophets (vv. 21–23) and, to conclude, the final occurrence, at once object of desire and means of freedom, the Parousia (vv. 24–27). The eschatological tension, heightened through the sayings which follow and to some extent contradict one another (compare v. 30 with v. 32) leads to the threefold final appeal to be watchful (vv. 33, 35, 37). This is the eschatological preaching of Jesus which is taken up into the eschatological teaching of the early Church.

The basic interpretation of this "synoptic apocalypse", as it has been mistakenly called, differs considerably even on the Catholic side. Three hypotheses are recognized: one, a logical explanation in terms of the final judgment; the second, purely temporal and applied to the destruction of Jerusalem; and a third which combines both of these in a balance between historical and eschatological passages. The third hypothesis, which long remained in favour, was based on the "prophetic perspective" that beheld the immediate and the remote in one vision. And this explained the existence of different passages side by side for they are blended to form one whole. But if the prophetic spirit is invoked in support of this hypothesis – and this scarcely does justice to the structure of the discourse – then can it not also be used to substantiate the hypothesis that the whole discourse in Mark 13:5–27 is a purely eschatological vision, partly coloured (in the section, vv. 14–20) with historical elements, as is the case with the Old Testament prophets, though in fact it is wholly concerned with the last things (see v. 19)? If this be accepted, could not Jesus have made these future events appear near in the prophetic manner? He could have taken the language of prophets and apocalyptists and enriched it, as in another way the seer of Patmos did in the New Testament apocalypse. This vivid style which at once prophesies, brings concretely present and drives home with urgency needs further attention and must be more closely studied.[67]

There are, however, several texts which give a definite term. Strictly speaking, they define the time limit as the generation which was then living, or that of many of their contemporaries.[68] Form and the history of tradition tell us that these are logia whose original context we can no longer establish. This warns us to be careful in explaining them. We can certainly exclude the view that the passages which describe the "advent of the kingdom of God (in power)" or of the "Son of man" refer to a phase preceding the final occurrence, to something that prepares and foretells the cosmic triumph of God or Christ. However we apply these difficult texts to the destruction of Jerusalem, Christ's Resurrection, Pentecost, the powerful expansion of the Church down to the present time, there is no evidence in the gospels that Jesus taught such a progressive coming of the *basileia,* that he ever understood the advent of the *basileia* and of the Son of man as anything other than the final eschatological manifestation. As regards the time-indication given in Matt. 10:23; Mark 9:1 par. and also Mark 13:30 par., it would best

[67] In addition to the passage, already referred to, from J. Schildenberger, a number of points of contact are provided in the work of F. Gils, *Jésus Prophète d'après les Évangiles synoptiques* (Louvain, 1957). He insists that the "prophetic visions of the future destiny of the kingdom" (pp. 126–33) require to be studied with greater exactness. But his concept of the kingdom of God is a doubtful one. Can one speak of the "earthly destinies of the kingdom"? (pp. 100–26).

[68] See especially W. G. Kümmel, *Verheißung und Erfüllung* (principal thesis of the book); further G. R. Beasley-Murray, *Jesus and the Future,* pp. 183–91; the same author, *Commentary on Mark XIII,* pp. 12 seq.

correspond historically with the destruction of Jerusalem and the temple in A. D. 70,[69] but there is no proof that, though Jesus did foretell this event (Mark 13:2 par.; Matt. 23:37 seq.; Luke 13:34 seq.; Luke 19:43 seq.), he spoke of it as a "coming of the Son of man" or of the "reign of God (in power)". It is, of course, another question whether the early Church saw in it a sign and presage of the cosmic triumph of Jesus. Yet even for this we have no indisputable evidence. But let us study the texts in closer detail.

Matt. 10:23: "When they shall persecute you in this city flee into another. Amen I say to you, you shall not finish all the cities of Israel till the Son of man come." This logion is peculiar to Matthew and it stands out in contrast to the verses which immediately precede (vv. 21–22) and which have their parallel in the eschatological discourse (Mark 13:12 seq.; see Luke 21:16 seq., 19). This fact and the compositional character of the whole "mission discourse" in Matt. 10 dealt a death blow to A. Schweitzer's theory that Jesus expected the Parousia prior even to their return from this mission.[70] In this form the theory of the "logical eschatologists" scarcely calls for consideration. As H. Schürmann has shown recently,[71] verse 23 was in all probability joined originally with verses 19 seq. which find their parallel in Luke 12:11 seq. It must have been part of the common source and merely omitted by Luke. He warns them not to seek refuge in flight from persecution and gives them a new motive for comfort when they are to appear before tribunals. This should

[69] So many Catholic authors, see M. J. Lagrange *(Études bibliques);* D. Buzy *(La Sainte Bible,* ed. Pirot-Clamer), P. Benoit *(Jerusalem Bible),* K. Staab *(Echterbibel)* at appropriate text.

[70] *Geschichte der Leben-Jesu-Forschung,* pp. 405 seq.

[71] H. Schürmann, "Zur Traditions- und Redaktionsgeschichte von Matt. 10:23" in *B.Z.N.F.* 3 (1959), pp. 82–8.

solve the exegetical problem whether the flight of the disciples through the cities of Israel or their presupposed mission to Israel will be finished before the advent of the Son of man (cf. vv. 11–15).[72] It is a picture of flight. A certain echo of this is discernible in Matthew 23:34 ("persecute from city to city"), an expression that has become a stock phrase in Matthew (but otherwise in Luke 11:49). This passage about the persecution of the prophets which is realized in the disciples of Jesus and will be "avenged on this generation" (23:36) is followed by the announcement of the destruction of Jerusalem (vv. 37–39; in Luke in another context, 13:34 seq.). This may indicate that the evangelist had it in mind also in Matt. 10:23. As for its original setting we may recall the other flight description in Matt. 24:16–21 (= Mark 13:14–8) in which Jesus depicts the eschatological situation (before the Parousia) and adds the comfort that they will be rescued from their grim distress (see also the shortening of the time, Mark 13:20 = Matt. 24:22).

Mark 9: par.: "Amen I say to you that there are some of them that stand here who shall not taste death till they see the kingdom (reign) of God coming (or come) in power" (Matt. 16:28 . . . "till they see the Son of man coming in his kingdom [kingship];" Luke 9:27: . . . "till they see the kingdom of God"). The changes in Matthew and Luke show that the Marcan text raised difficulties and this tempts us to suspect it as a subsequent addition from the Christian community at a period when they wanted to

[72] If verse 23 be taken literally and applied to Christian missionary effort, then we could accept the interpretation that the conversion of Israel would not be complete before the Parousia. So, Hilary of Poitiers; Matt. 10:14 (P. L. 9, 971 s); in modern times, J. Knabenbauer, *Evangelium sec. Matthaeum,* 2 vols. (Paris, 1892–3), notably I, pp. 397 seq.; E. Walter, *Das Kommen des Herrn,* II, p. 98. Yet this interpretation would not harmonize with Rom. 11:25–32.

revive the idea of a near advent.[73] But surely it would have been presumptuous to fix a terminus so close. It is harder to fix the place of this saying in the history of tradition than it is with Matthew 10:23. Mark at any rate separated it from the preceding passage by means of a new clause ("and he said to them"). The explanation of the Fathers that the prophecy was realized in the Transfiguration which occurred shortly afterwards (Matthew/Mark "after six days"; Luke "about eight days") may be looked upon as a theological interpretation of the evangelists;[74] it is highly improbable that it was the original meaning. Even if it be granted that the word "see" could denote a prevision of God's reign, there remains the difficulty that the Transfiguration is not associated with the kingdom of God. Luke's abbreviated form leaves the possibility of recalling the Resurrection, Pentecost and the impressive expansion of the Church. Matthew clearly linked the verse with the preceding verse that refers to the coming of the Son of man with his angels. But could he have understood differently the coming of the Son of man "in his glory"? In the light of Matt. 10:23 the evangelist could have recalled the catastrophe of Jerusalem. If the expression "kingdom of the Son of man" be emphasized, it might be interpreted from Matt. 13:41 as referring to the devel-

[73] So among others G. Bornkamm, *Die Verzögerung der Parusie: In memoriam E. Lohmeyer* (Stuttgart, 1951), pp. 116–26, on this point pp. 118 seq. ("It is an ancient Christian prophetic statement which tradition made into a saying of the Lord"); E. Grässer, op. cit., pp. 131–7. W. Marxen, *Der Evangelist Markus* attributes the statement to Mark's editorship and his desire to explain 8:38, without discussing the authenticity of the passage *Studien zur Redaktionsgeschichte des Evangeliums* (Göttingen, 1956), p. 140, note 1.

[74] See J. Schildenberger, *Bib* 24 (1943), pp. 213–18; F. J. Schierse, *Historische Kritik und theologische Exegese der synoptischen Evangelien*, Commentary on Mark 9:1 par., *Schol.* 29 (1954), pp. 520–36.

opment of the Church, perhaps after the destruction of Jerusalem. Consequently, we can scarcely determine what the evangelists had in mind when they recorded this passage. Perhaps the saying was a puzzle even to the early Church which nevertheless carefully handed it on. But we could provide an adequate or even partial explanation of its meaning in the mind of Jesus[75] only if we understood the setting and circumstances or at least the context in which tradition has handed it down.

Mark 13:30 par.: "Amen I say to you that this generation shall not pass until all these things be done" ("all" missing in Luke). The difficulty would disappear if γενεὰ αὕτη did not signify or stress the contemporary generation but was merely a qualifying term for the evil and rebellious race of the Jews.[76] This qualifying note is certainly present in all the gospel passages that contain the expression. But at the same time there is the definite reference to contemporaries which may emerge more forcibly because of the context (see Matt. 12:41 seq. = Luke 11:29; Mark 8:38; Matt. 23:38) as is the case also in the Old Testament (Jer. 7:29; 8:3; Ps. 78:8; 95:10). One possible inter-

[75] J. A. T. Robinson, *Jesus and His Coming,* pp. 89–91, explains the passage as follows: Despite the general principle that the disciples must follow Jesus in death (8:34–38), many of those in the crowd would see the coming of the kingdom as an objective reality even without sharing in the death through which alone its glory can break through. This is most improbable.

[76] So J. Knabenbauer, F. Prat *(La Sainte Bible),* J. Schniewind *(German N.T.);* K. H. Rengstorf *(German N.T.* on Luke 21:32); W. Marxsen, op. cit., p. 133 (for Luke only); especially M. Meinertz, "Dieses Geschlecht" im N.T. in *B.Z.N.F.* I (1957), pp. 283–9. In *Was lehrt Jesus über das Ende der Welt?* (Freiburg i. Br., 1958), p. 64, F. Mußner declares: "The existence of the Jewish people throughout history is the great sign for other peoples of the truth and truthfulness of the words of God and Jesus."

pretation would be that the Jewish people, this evil and faithless race, "must appear at the Parousia with the whole human family before the Son of man"[77] but throughout the Parousia discourse the antithesis between Jews and gentiles does not appear, and in verse 30 it is not obvious that any stress is placed upon the Jews. It would, therefore, appear that the historical accent predominates in the passage.[78] Not a few exegetes who apply γενεά to the contemporary generation would like to see in it an allusion to the destruction of Jerusalem (Matt. 23:36). That may well have been true of the passage in its original form. But it would be difficult in the context of the eschatological discourse since ταῦτα πάντα seems to comprehend all the things previously enumerated, including the Parousia.[79]

All remaining passages that might be adduced contain no such definite indication of time. When in Matthew 23:38 seq. (= Luke 13:35) the "desolation of the house" of the Jews is followed immediately by the vision of the Parousia, or when the Son of man at his Parousia is to be a sign (of judgment) for the Jews who demand a sign (Luke 11:30; but see Matt. 12:40) or when Jesus proclaims before his Sanhedrin judges the coming of the Son of man (Mark 14:62 par., see section 15), this can be a prophetic perspective or it can assume the resurrection of the present generation (see Matt. 12:41 seq. = Luke 11:31 seq.). Luke 18:8b is one of the texts that foretell a near advent. It is Mark 9:1 par. that continues to cause the greatest difficulty.

[77] M. Meinertz, *Theologie des N.T.* I, p. 51; *B.Z.* 1957, p. 289.
[78] So F. Büchsel in *Th.W.B.* I, p. 661; J. Schmid, E. Lohmeyer, V. Taylor and others on this passage; Beasley-Murray, *Commentary on Mark, XIII,* pp. 99 seq.
[79] This is not the place to comment upon an interpretation of the whole discourse, proposed by A. Feuillet, but in my opinion quite untenable, which refers it all to the historical events that culminated in A.D. 70.

May one conclude from these passages with definite indication of time-limits that the expectation of a near advent of Jesus was narrowed and circumscribed to the generation then living, both as regards place and time, and that Jesus also suffered from this illusion, even though what mattered in his eyes was not the precise time but the certainty of what was to come? This is the opinion of not a few Protestant exegetes.[80] But there are exegetical as well as theological objections to this opinion. In a number of passages Jesus expressly repudiated any calculation and knowledge of this terminus (Matt. 13:32 par.). For methodological reasons we refrain from appealing to passages which suppose a long period of activity, a mission to the gentiles (Mark 13:10 par.; Matt. 28:18–20; Luke 24:47) because their genuineness and meaning have been questioned and it would take too long to discuss the objections. Other extracts which cannot seriously be impugned are sufficient. From Luke's passage in 17:20: "The kingdom (reign) of God cometh not with observation", one thing is certain, Jesus was not and had no desire to be an apocalyptist. He kept deliberately clear of apocalyptic questions, including that of prophetic calculation.

This assertion may seem to contradict the presence of portents in the eschatological discourse. But the events there described are not intended to provide tangible data; their purpose is a practical one. Sufferings, persecutions and temptations to disbelief are to come upon the disciples and they must be prepared to confront them. It is only the additional simile of the fig-tree, with its practical application to the disciples (v. 29) that seems to present the events described as genuine "portents". Yet is this

[80] See particularly T. W. Manson, *Teaching of Jesus,* pp. 277–84; O. Cullmann, *Le retour du Christ,* pp. 25–27; W. G. Kümmel, *Verheißung und Erfüllung,* pp. 133–47; G. R. Beasley-Murray, *Jesus and the Future,* pp. 183–191.

its original meaning? Perhaps it referred, as did Luke 12:54–56, to signs already evident in the operations of Jesus that could reveal the nearness of the reign of God to all who could see (note the term ἐγγύς).[81] Emphasis on signs of the future is first laid in verse 29 which gives the impression of being secondary: cf. the ταῦτα, further ἐγγύς . . . ἐπὶ θύραις (here the Christ of the Parousia seems to be indicated).

If we are thus compelled to bring out the prophetic quality in the preaching of Jesus, it is just as necessary to absolve him from all typically "apocalyptic" tendencies. We have a proof of this, actually at the close of the eschatological discourse – together with Luke 17:20 it is a vital passage for his prophecy of the future – namely the saying in Mark 13:32 (= Matt. 24:36): "But of that day or hour no man knoweth neither the angels in heaven nor the Son but the Father."

Doubts about its genuineness must founder on the difficulty of the passage for Christian ears. Such an admission of ignorance on the part of Jesus could not have entered the mind of any Christian at the middle of the first century. There were reasons why Luke omitted the passage. There are no grounds for striking out the final words ("nor the Son but the Father") as long as we accept the genuineness of Matt. 11:27 = Luke 10:22.[82] The idea that God alone knows the end of time is mentioned but only incidentally in Zach. 14:7; *Ps. Sal.* 17:23;

[81] So Jeremias, *Gleichnisse Jesu,* pp. 102 seq., who connects v. 29 with the simile and comments: "Who is it who stands at the door? The Messias." The contrary opinion is held by Beasley-Murray, *Commentary on Mark* XIII, 9, pp. 94–8. If verses 28 and 29 are taken as an original unity we can scarcely question the reference to future signs. One would then have to ask whether Jesus was postulating genuine signs by which the Parousia could be recognized or only the certainty that the end would come.

[82] E. Sjöberg, *Der verborgene Menschensohn,* p. 231.

Syr. Baruch 21:8. There is no likelihood, therefore, that it was taken from some Jewish apocalyptic text.[83]

There are two possible explanations of the passage. The ignorance could be understood absolutely or only relatively. If the latter be accepted, the argument runs as follows. According to Mark 13:30 the only interpretation is that Jesus cannot give the exact day and hour of the Parousia within the time limit provided by the generation then living. In favour of this is the distinction in the expression "of that day or (alternatively and) hour".[84] Further, "that day" is a familiar Old Testament term for the "day of Yahweh" and "the hour" is merely a synonym (especially in the Marcan text "or"). Parallel expressions are found in Matthew 24:50 = Luke 12:46, see also Matthew 25:13. But, apart from this, there are other passages which describe the end as absolutely uncertain, namely Matt. 24:44 = Luke 12:40; Matt. 24:50 = Luke 12:46; Matt. 25:13. That also corresponds to the sudden unexpected onset of the events of the Last Days (Luke 21:34 seq.; see 17:26–30, 34–5 and parallel passages in Matthew). Tradition thus gives us a solid basis for believing that Jesus left the time of the Parousia or the end in complete obscurity. The day and hour are not merely indefinite within a certain period of time; knowledge of them is reserved wholly to the Father.

It is quite another question how Mark 13:32 is to be reconciled with 13:30 in the arrangement of the eschatological discourse. Did the evangelist understand verse 32 after verse 30 only as relative ignorance of the time? A more likely solution is that

[83] So Bultmann, *Geschichte der synoptischen Tradition,* p. 130 and elsewhere; but on the contrary, Kümmel, *Verheißung und Erfüllung,* p. 36 (also note 79); V. Taylor, on this text.

[84] Beasley-Murray, *Commentary on Mark XIII,* pp. 107 seq.; see Marxsen, op. cit., p. 127.

early tradition has brought together these two divergent sayings and thus created a dialectical antithesis. There are other instances of this method of question and response in the early Church. We may compare the universal expectation of a Parousia in the near future with texts like Acts 1:7; 1 Thess. 5:1 seq.; Apoc. 3:3; 16:15.

We have arrived at the following position. A broad stream of tradition testifies that Jesus announced the coming of God's reign, and correspondingly of the Son of man, for a near future but without further specification of the time, indeed with an explicit refusal to provide more precise details. Against this, only a few passages contain a definite time reference, to the generation then alive. It was not possible to explain these passages. It would seem that the early Church was uncertain how to fit these awkward pieces neatly into the eschatological discourse of Jesus. This attitude of the Church may well point to the best method for ourselves: namely, to nourish a living eschatological hope from the urgent prophetic preaching of Jesus without drawing false conclusions about that prophecy from individual passages. The early Church did not admit any mistake on the part of Jesus. Nor need we do so, if we adopt a careful attitude towards tradition as a whole and pay attention to the manner, the significance and the purpose of Jesus' preaching.[85]

[85] We part company here with Protestant theologians who admit a mistake on Jesus' part but consider it of no importance for his own position. What we are attempting to do is to specify the character of his sayings and determine their literary style and thus throw light on their proper contents. This is the method advocated by Pope Pius XII in the encyclical, *Divino Afflante Spiritu,* September 30th, 1943: (C.T.S. transl.) "If the Catholic exegete is to meet fully the requirements of modern biblical study he must, in expounding Sacred Scripture and

To approach these questions critically we shall have to abandon our empirical notions of time, which envisage time in our Western thinking as a continuously moving line, divisible into measurable sections ("spaces"). Biblical thought about salvation, on the other hand, asks what occurs in time and what "fills" it, and enquires what action of God gives every time its character and significance. It is in this sense, again prescinding from our spacial view of time, that the sentence, "With God one day is as a thousand years and a thousand years as a day" (2 Pet. 3:8), has its validity. Since Jesus proclaimed his eschatological gospel, the whole of time is near to the fulfilled *basileia,* because this has become tangible and certain in Jesus, penetrates through him into "this aeon" and works upon men, is in a certain sense already present and awaits only its manifestation in glory. This sets a seal on this whole period in the history of salvation and communicates to it its orientation towards the end, regardless of our position, whether at the "beginning" or at the "end" of that era. Now that Jesus has sown the seed and since his ministry, God's reign is irrevocably present though as yet only in a provisional way, the harvest is there at the door, and the Last Things draw near to us forcibly and insistently. Fundamentally, the two perfect tenses used in Mark 1:15 tell us everything: the time of eschatological fulfilment is here and God's kingdom of glory is near. Both are irrevocable realities firmly established through the coming of Jesus. All that happens from now on, develops, it is true, in this world of space and time and is experienced by men as history and therefore as temporal succession but stands in the shadow of the ever-abiding sign of

vindicating its immunity from all error, make prudent use also of this further aid: he must, that is, ask himself how far the form of expression or literary idiom employed by the sacred writer may contribute to the true and genuine interpretation . . ."

salvation brought by Jesus and at the dawn of the "day of the Lord". Jesus' call to conversion and belief was re-echoed by the early Church and must be repeated by every Christian preacher to his generation, and with the same insistent urgency of the eschatological hour, which is always a "today", till God sets an end to this "penultimate" era of salvation (see Heb. 3:12 seq.). This particular eschatological consciousness, the mood that reflects our eschatological "interval", was derived by the great theologians of the early Church from the preaching of Jesus and impressed upon their faithful (see in particular 1 Cor. 7:29–31; 1 Thess. 5:1–11). And in this they certainly grasped and preserved the innermost and fundamental intention of the eschatological teaching of Jesus.

THE REIGN OF GOD AND THE REDEEMED COMMUNITY OF JESUS

17. The Community of Jesus in the Light of his Gospel of God's Reign

In God's redemptive plan Jewish unbelief was one reason for the atoning Passion and death of God's servant, Jesus. This prompts the question whether the form and development of the community of Jesus were not influenced in their turn by the factual, in general negative, response to his gospel of God's reign. We cannot, it is true, make the founding of his community depend exclusively upon his rejection by his people. For there is little doubt that he began early to gather disciples, as early as the great and successful Galilean ministry and that he then formed his inner group of the twelve (Mark 3:13–19).[1]

According to Mark the intention of Jesus was that "they might be with him and that he might send them to preach; and he gave them power to heal sicknesses and to cast out devils". In addition to sharing his way of life they are to take over and extend his activity, naturally in association with and in subordination to himself. The twelve are to proclaim (κηρύσσειν) in par-

[1] Recently this has been challenged once again by Ph. Vielhauer, op. cit., pp. 62–4 (particularly in association with J. Wellhausen). For the contrary view see K. H. Rengstorf in *Th.W.B.* II, 325–8; also G. Bornkamm, *Jesus von Nazareth,* p. 138.

ticular the gospel of God's approaching reign (see Mark 1:14 seq., 38 seq.) and "drive out devils", that is to restrain the power of Satan, as a sign that God's reign is already dawning (see Mark 3:23–27; Matt. 12:28 seq. par.; Luke 10:18). Their activity like that of Jesus is directed to the people of Israel. The very choice of twelve as messengers and associates is clearly symbolic. In a kind of prophetic parable Jesus is making a claim on the people of the twelve tribes, the whole of ancient Israel to whom were made the promises of salvation, as is shown in Matthew 19:28; see also Luke 22:30 b. He envisages the chosen people as the prophets had declared it would be finally reconstituted[2] and he takes the first steps to reconstitute it. In consequence, the limiting of his mission to the "lost sheep of the house of Israel" (Matt. 10:5 seq.; 15:24; see also Matt. 7:23) is made fully intelligible.[3] The formation of a community is not, in the first place, a response to Jewish unbelief but on the contrary it is a precondition for the coming kingdom. God will exercise his full sovereignty not in general "over the world" or over a transfigured earth but concretely over his chosen people, to whom, of course, the remaining (gentile) peoples are to be added (see section 9).

It was a serious error to suppose, as was done especially at the time of Adolf von Harnack, that Jesus had no intention of forming a community and that this was far from his mind, on the grounds that he was inculcating a new relation to God and announcing a kingdom of God that was to come immediately. It was argued that the intention of establishing a Church was first ascribed to him after the early Church had come into existence. Such an interpretation completely misunderstands the

[2] See Isa. 11:12 seq.; Jer. 3:18; 23:3 seq.; 30:8 seq.; Ezech. 16:60 seq.; 34:11–16; 37:15–28; Amos 9:11; Abd. 17; Mal. 3:19–21. For late Judaism see Volz, *Eschatologie*, pp. 342 seq.

[3] Consult on this point J. Jeremias, *Jesu Verheißung*, pp. 16–8.

Messianic and eschatological thought of Israel, in which eschatological salvation can never be dissociated from the people of God and the community of God belongs necessarily to the kingdom of God. The future achievement of salvation is to be the consummation of all God's action throughout history, and this includes the choice of Israel as his people. This reality was never denied or ignored in the prophecies, and both the pattern and development of God's salvific plan demand also the ultimate existence of a community of salvation and even the fulfilment of the special promises made to Israel.[4] Consequently, Jesus turned to Israel to form the community for the final period and when Israel as a whole failed, he could not abandon the thought of the eschatological community. It is another question, of course, whether Jesus desired to establish a special group in Israel. The concrete evidence of the gospels emphatically denies this; but that is scarcely the meaning of the debated "original establishment of the Church" (Matt. 16:18 seq.). A comparison with similar enterprises and now in particular with the Qumran group shows that Jesus repudiated these splinter tendencies to form a circumscribed and holy remnant from among the people (see section 9). This is not the place for a detailed study of this many-sided problem.[5] We are concerned only with the relation of God's reign announced by Jesus to the company of disciples and the community of faith, which he actually established.

Because the teaching of Jesus and his apostles was rejected by the people, contemporary Israel could no longer be considered as the eschatological community, or as its root. Here again, we

[4] Paul saw this clearly in spite of his conflicts with unbelieving Jews, Rom. 9–11.

[5] A. Vögtle intends to publish a study of this question. Meanwhile, consult his rectorial address, *Das öffentliche Wirken Jesu auf dem Hintergrund der Qumranbewegung* (Freiburg im Breisgau, 1958).

must avoid the conjecture, what would have happened had the gospel of Jesus found acceptance. Would the conversion of contemporary Israel have been followed by the reconstitution of the ideal Israel of the twelve tribes, to be taken into the kingdom of God as a redeemed people, with whom the gentiles would have become associated? The gospels provide no answer to this point but we do learn that a small group of believers from Israel remained with Jesus (Luke 12:32).

We find here the idea of a "remnant" but it is very different from the exclusive groups in the Judaism of that period. Jesus had in mind and made his appeal to the whole of Israel though the "little flock" is the practical outcome. He prescribed no particular "purity" laws to protect the "holy" remnant but demanded only attachment to his person. With all his concentration on the group of disciples and their interior formation he had no intention of withdrawing an élite from Israel. Everyone is still summoned to a share in belief. God reaches his goal by a new path; the old covenant is transformed into a "new covenant" (Luke 22:20; Mark 14:24), established through the blood of Jesus and setting up a new community. The stock grows to a "holy seed" (see Isa. 6:13) in a manner wholly new and not confined to ancient Israel. The redemptive power of Jesus' atoning death provides both the possibility and the existence of a new people of God.

We may take it for granted that the faithful who gathered around the group of apostles and were almost fused with it (Luke 22:28, 31 seq.) had a definite significance in the plan of Jesus and God. But there is no dearth of positive statements. To begin with, the parables of growth (see section 13) show Jesus' conviction that the kingdom of God would come in spite of Jewish unbelief and every obstacle and that nothing could hinder or delay it. He assures the "little flock" that it has pleased the Father "to give them the kingdom" (Luke 12:32). He "disposes" authority to the disciples who have persevered with him in his trials, as the Father has "disposed" it to him that they may "sit upon thrones, judging the twelve tribes of Israel" (Luke 22:29 seq.). Finally, he promises them a new table companionship in the kingdom of God (Mark 14:25; Luke 12:16, 18, 30 a and also see section 12 above). These passages that belong to the last phase of his ministry make it plain that the reduced company of disciples on earth is to be the core of the redeemed community in the future kingdom. They will not constitute the whole of that community. Jesus' promises to all who fulfil the conditions for entry into the kingdom remain in force; they are a universal prophecy without regard to person or origin. Yet we should note the ruling and judging function which Jesus has reserved for the twelve (Luke 22:30; and see Matt. 19:29) in the coming kingdom.

This passage recorded differently by Luke and Matthew has been challenged more than once and is not interpreted only in one sense. But the formation of the apostolic group and this promise support one another. If Jesus intended through the twelve to make a claim on the chosen people, a claim which he confirmed by sending them out to preach, the readiest explanation would be that "because they were repudiated by the Jews, they become in early Christian tradition their judges and play a decisive part in the judgment".[6] However, we should not confine ourselves to contemporary Judaism which then embraced merely two and a half tribes; the eschatological office of the twelve must extend to all twelve tribes. The idea of the reconstitution of the ideal Israel must have been in their minds and it is possible that Matt. 23:39 is suggesting a final conversion of

[6] K. H. Rengstorf in *Th.W.B.* II, 327, 35 seq.

Israel, which is expressly taught by Paul (Rom. 11:25–32). It is improbable that "Israel" in this passage denotes the new people of God for we have no other evidence that Jesus spoke of the "new Israel". It is, however, possible that the early Church understood the word in this sense. In that case, believers from ancient Israel are included (see Apoc. 7:4–8; 21:12 cf. below section 25). One query remains, whether the authority which Jesus "disposes" to the twelve is exhausted by their judicial office over the twelve tribes of Israel, or is this only a special instance of a broader sharing of Christ's rule?

The gentiles also belong to the redeemed as is clear from Matthew 8:11 = Luke 13:28 seq. (see section 9) and also from Matthew 25:32 seq. and the universal character of the banquet parable. If Jesus repudiated the current picture of the future community, he never destroyed the basic ideas on which it was built. The people of God will stream into the kingdom of God, once it has been purified in the great judgment from all the unworthy and from evildoers (Matt. 13:30, 48; 22:11–13; 25:32 seq.). The "elect" will be assembled from all quarters of the heavens and brought into the perfect kingdom (Luke 17:34 seq. = Matt. 24:40 seq.; Mark 13:27 par.). In God's plan the atoning death of Jesus has a decisive significance for the redemption of the "many" (Mark 10:45; 14:24) and for the gathering of God's scattered flock (Mark 14:27 seq.), to which the early Christians were convinced that the gentiles belong (see John 11:51 seq.; 10:16 seq.; 12:24, 32). The success of its mission to the gentiles brought home more strikingly to the early Church what was in principle contained in Jesus' description of the gentiles at table with the Jewish patriarchs (Matt. 8:11 par.). We must insist that Jesus never abandoned the notion of a community of the redeemed, particularly in the context of the proclamation of the eschatological kingdom.

Attention must be given to certain texts which speak of a gradation or hierarchy in the future kingdom, for example Matt. 5:19; 11:11 (= Luke 7:28; see section 12); 18:1 (differently, Mark 9:34; Luke 9:46). The first portion of Matt. 5:19 a, "one of these least commandments", reveals a Jewish rabbinical formulation[7] and the second portion may well express the same mentality. A person's deviation in teaching is punished with a lower place in the kingdom but he is nonetheless admitted, and this reminds us of the "scribe instructed in the kingdom of heaven" (for God's reign) exclusive to Matthew (Matt. 13:52). We must accept this as a Matthean formula referring to teachers in the community. The idea stressed in verse 19 b that deeds are what really matter finds a parallel in Matthew 7:21 (see Luke 6:46). The original saying of Jesus which the evangelist is framing and interpreting for his Jewish Christian readers will have insisted that the will of God must be fulfilled wholly and radically by everyone who desires to enter God's kingdom.

Jesus does not completely reject the plea of the sons of Zebedee for the first places in his kingdom. He observes that it is not his responsibility to allot them but that they belong to those for whom they are "prepared" by God (Mark 10:37, 40). Behind this the idea of the ruling office of the twelve could still be preserved (see Luke 22:29, 30 b) and this would explain the expression, "least in the kingdom of God" (Luke 7:28 = Matt. 11:11). It seems that Jesus did envisage a certain hierarchy for the community of the redeemed in the future kingdom but, as always when he is speaking eschatologically, this is kept in the back-

[7] See J. Schmid on this passage; D. Daube, *The New Testament and Rabbinic Judaism,* pp. 119 seq. Note also the remark of G. Dalman, *Worte Jesu* I, p. 94: "In a similar way Jesus envisaged different levels among those who would participate in God's reign. But the principle by which these levels would be assigned differed from that of the rabbis."

ground and expressed figuratively. For the rest, he explicitly condemns striving after special places and stresses the paradox that the man who humbles himself (on earth) will one day be elevated (by God) (see Luke 14:7–11; 18:14) and that his disciples have another commandment imposed upon them, to make themselves servants and the least of all, that they may (one day) be great (Mark 10:43 par.). The standard is completely altered. A share in God's kingdom is the "elevation" which men must strive for and that God will grant.

What is the relation of the group of disciples, formed by Jesus on earth, to the eschatological community of the redeemed that is to share in the reign of God? Is this company of men who accept the gospel of Jesus and await God's kingdom merely a preparation? Or is it already a preliminary, an anticipation and a provisional form of that perfect company of the blest? Can we detect and recognize a certain penetration of God's kingly rule in its earthly existence and activity?

W. G. Kümmel in particular feels compelled to deny this suggestion. He is convinced that "Jesus never described God's reign as present and operative in the circle of his disciples and followers" and that the twelve were not the "core of the new people of Israel".[8] This fits in with his thesis that "Jesus never stated or suggested that the future reign of God would show its presence in the community of disciples between his death and the Parousia. Jesus envisaged the presence of God's rule, before the Parousia, viewed as imminent, only in his Person and his works. He knew no other manifestation of eschatological fulfilment."[9] Kümmel maintains therefore that Matt. 16:18 seq.

[8] "Jesus und die Anfänge der Kirche" in *St.Th.* 7 (1953) pp. 1–27, notably p. 4 and p. 7.
[9] *Verheißung und Erfüllung,* p. 132.

cannot be part of the oldest tradition of Jesus.[10] We are thus left with a gulf, a vacuum between the dawn of God's reign in the person of Jesus and its fulfilment in the Parousia. The disciples in the meantime are a group of men who are simply waiting. Can this conceivably be correct? The significance of the disciples has to be sought elsewhere.

We can remark pointedly that the company gathered around Jesus the Messias is just as much a sign of the powerful presence of God's reign as his words and deeds, the forgiveness of sins, the expulsion of devils and the cures. God made known to the disciples the mystery of the inauguration of this reign with Jesus (Mark 4:11); he revealed this to little ones (Matt. 11:25). God is therefore collaborating in forming this company, since revelation in the context involves acceptance into the company of Jesus. We have to look at the disciples' vocation in this light as a call of God through Jesus and, while they must make their decision to follow him, the challenge and demand derive from God. The disciples' vocation is both consequence and fruit of the saving gospel of Jesus (see Mark 1:16–20, after 15). This is most fully grasped in John's gospel where Jesus declares that believers are given him by the Father (6:39), that no man can come to him unless the Father attracts him (6:44) or if it is not given him by the Father (6:65).

Jesus thanks the Father in the Upper Room for all those he has given him "out of this world"; "thine they were and thou gavest them to me" (17:6). Behind this is the picture of the flock entrusted to the Messianic shepherd. The forming, existence and perseverance of this faithful flock are a proof also of God's

[10] Ibid. See also an earlier work, *Kirchenbegriff und Geschichtsbewußtsein in der Urgemeinde und bei Jesus (Symb. Bibl. Ups.* I), 1943, pp. 27 seq.; further, *St.Th.* 7 (1953), pp. 17 seq.

eschatological work of grace. In this sense, it is a "final community" if not yet a "perfect community".[11] In other words, it belongs to God's reign that dawns with Jesus just as does the company of the blessed in the future kingdom. This further denotes that the company of the disciples is not itself and does not represent the reign of God. Any identification of the Church with the provisional reign of God is to be ruled out in principle by this feature of the earthly life of Jesus. The group of disciples, to be sure a preliminary to the Church, remains attached to earth whereas God's reign, despite its penetration into this realm of earth, is never wholly absorbed in it, at least in the present era. As soon as it penetrates completely, we have the eschatological and cosmic kingdom of glory. It is better not to speak of the Church as a "manifestation of the kingdom of God" (B. Bartmann and others) or the "contemporary form of God's kingdom" (E. Walter).

In addition to their subjection to God's rule, the disciples have also their part and responsibility. They take over Jesus' preaching, they have a share in his powers. They are not only to be assistants in the Galilean ministry; they are to continue his mission to Israel. Otherwise, the prophecies about suffering and persecution are unintelligible. Apart from this, why should they be dragged before Jewish tribunals? (Mark 13:9 par.; Luke 6:22 seq. par.; John 16:1 seq.). Their preaching with Jesus' authority means that the existing forces of God's reign are still operating. The disciples take over Jesus' task; they replace him. Even prescinding from the disputed "mission" passages which state this explicitly,[12] a passage like Luke 12:11 seq. = Matt. 10:19

[11] H. D. Wendland, *Eschatologie des Reiches Gottes,* p. 160.

[12] Matt. 10:16 = Luke 10:3; Matt. 10:40 par.; Luke 10:16; John 13:20. Bultmann in his *Geschichte der synoptischen Tradition,* pp. 152 seq., holds that these passages originated with the Christian community because it

seq. (cf. Mark 13:11; Luke 21:14 seq.) not only presupposes missionary work among Jews but proclaims the assistance of the Holy Spirit and also of Jesus.[13] Are we to suppose that this has no reference to the influence in the present of the *basileia?*

W. G. Kümmel misrepresents Jesus' view of his group of disciples after his departure when he writes: "Jesus certainly expected his disciples to gather for a common meal without him (Mark 14:25); he certainly thought they would be persecuted after he had left them and would have to suffer (Luke 17:22; Matt. 10:28; Mark 8:34); and he most certainly thought they would have to wait for his coming (Mark 13:33–36; Luke 12:36–38). But this does not in the least imply that Jesus expected his disciples to form themselves into a special community."[14] But were the disciples to celebrate his memory and await his advent as an esoteric group? We treat this question far too narrowly if we regard the disciples as merely forming a closed group during Jesus' lifetime, the germ of a particular sect.[15] The intentions of Jesus embraced the whole of Israel and, so far as the future was in question, they were not directed towards any community alongside or outside Israel but towards the people of God as such. It is not surprising that the boundaries of those who responded to his summons were flexible. Even the "little flock" that remained faithful did not require to be a closed society, and the number of preachers could be increased without prejudice

is the Risen Christ who speaks in them, and that the words were perhaps taken from a Jewish source and adapted.

[13] C. K. Barrett, *The Holy Spirit and the Gospel Tradition* (London, 1947), pp. 130–2, considers Luke 21:14 seq. to be the original form of the declaration. The Holy Spirit was introduced by the Christian community after its experience of the outpoured Spirit.

[14] *St.Th.* 7 (1953), pp. 15 seq.

[15] Ibid., pp. 4 seq. and 16.

to the special status of the twelve. The sending out of the seventy in Luke 10 sets, it must be granted, some problems of its own.

Our problem is to discern the character of this community which gathered round Jesus and which he desired. His purpose was to attract the whole of the chosen people of old. If in effect a new community developed from Israel and beyond Israel and became the rival of the greater part of contemporary Jews who refused belief, this was a factual development, a further stage in the history of salvation. But could Jesus not have foreseen this development in the light of his estrangement from the people and have viewed it thenceforth as a necessary development? The famous yet disputed passage of Matt. 16:18 seq. cannot be made prior to this stage of development, to the turning-point of Caesarea Philippi; it must be considered later.[16] Is it impossible that Jesus decided to establish his community in some other way at a moment when the chosen people had repudiated his following? We have to remember that for Jesus "his community" simply referred to the people of God that he was preparing for the kingdom to come.[17]

Assuming as we shall now do without further argument that

[16] See A. Vögtle, "Messiasbekenntnis und Petrusverheißung" in *BZ. NF* I (1957), pp. 252–72; 2 (1958), pp. 85–103.

[17] For the concept of ἐκκλησία as God's community, whatever Hebrew or Aramaic word may be its basis, see K. L. Schmidt in *Th.W.B.* III, 528–30; O. Michel, *Das Zeugnis des N. T. von der Gemeinde* (Göttingen 1941), pp. 5–26 (with special consideration of the *Damascus Document*); O. Betz, "Felsenmann und Felsengemeinde" in *Z.N.W.* 48 (1957), pp. 49–77, in particular pp. 57–9 (dealing with the Qumran texts). Attention is drawn to his conclusion: "The titles סוד and עדה adopted by the Qumran sect can refer to a community that is determined from its first beginning to its final end, namely the ultimate community of those chosen by God. This is also the significance of ἐκκλησία in the New Testament, and particularly in Matthew 16:18" (p. 58).

Matt. 16:18 seq. is not impossible in the mouth of Jesus after the negative attitude taken up by the majority of the Jews, this passage become highly significant for the relation of this community of Jesus, later to be the Church, to God's reign and the future kingdom. It is from this point of view that we intend to examine it. Jesus wishes to give to Simon Peter "the keys of the kingdom of heaven" (v. 19a). Does this *basileia* refer to the present reign of God or the perfect reign of the future? Evidently the latter, since this is confirmed by the metaphor of the keys which signify the handing over of full authority (see Isa. 22:22) and in particular entry into the kingdom of God, participation in God's perfect reign. This is clear from Matt. 23:13, where Jesus accuses the Scribes and Pharisees of shutting God's kingdom to men; they do not themselves enter nor do they permit those who want to enter, to do so.

This saying is one of the "entry statements" that must all be referred to the future kingdom (see sections 7 and 14). Judaism also thought that salvation culminated in a share in the "future aeon". This was secured through a faithful observance of God's law, and the Scribes as its official exponents had the grave responsibility of showing men the way. Yet Jesus charges them with blocking this way through their perverted legalistic interpretation and their behaviour. In the parallel passage Luke speaks of the "key of knowledge" (11:52). This is probably τῆς γνώσεως, a genitive of apposition; key to the kingdom of God, one that consists in knowledge. This must have had reference to the teaching of the law. In point of fact, it is not merely knowledge since the legal decisions made by the Scribes also affected salvation.[18] The key also denotes authority,

[18] Cf. J. Jeremias, Art. κλείς; *Th.W.B.* III, 743–53; more precisely 750, 11–27; rabbinic extracts also in Billerbeck 1, 736 seq.

as is shown in Apoc. 3:7, which is referred to Christ. He possesses the Messianic power to open or shut God's house (= kingdom of God) at the end of time. But in Matt. 16:19 Jesus transfers this authority in its earthly competence to Simon Peter.

This chosen apostle is presented not as door-keeper of the Church (see v. 18) or "of heaven" (v. 19b) but as one with authority to determine who shall enter into the future kingdom. The purpose of this solemn declaration of Jesus is then made clear. Jesus' community that can never be destroyed by the powers of death, is established upon Peter, the rock, in order that men may attain to the kingdom of God. In contrast to the Scribes Peter will have the capacity and power to lead men in effect into God's kingdom. The purpose and mission of this community founded upon Peter as rock foundation, the Messianic community of God, is one day to enter as the complete and perfect community of the redeemed into the kingdom of God. "Peter is to lead the people of God into the kingdom of the Resurrection."[19]

The authority promised in terms of the key is immediately specified (v. 19c) as power to "bind and loose". Prescinding from the long discussion of this expression, it is sufficiently evident that it includes not merely an authority to teach but a power to guide and judge, functioning in the main though not exclusively in the forgiveness of sins.[20] In this sense John 20:23 is an allusion to and legitimate interpretation of the authoritative guarantee given by Jesus to Peter (Matt. 16:19) and the other apostles (Matt. 18:18). Because Peter (mentioned separately owing to the promise made individually in Matt. 16:18 seq.)

[19] O. Cullmann, *Petrus, Jünger – Apostel – Märtyrer* (Zürich, 1952), p. 229.
[20] See F. Büchsel in *Th.W.B.* II, 59 seq.; J. Jeremias, ibid. III, 750 seq.

can "bind" and "loose" in such a manner that God acknowledges his decision ("in heaven" means "with God"), he is able to provide for the redeemed an entry into God's kingdom. Consequently, this power is related to "the authoritative proclamation and communication of the grace of God's reign" and comprises the "acts of proclaiming and teaching, binding and directing, that operate grace and judgment."[21] Forgiveness of sin is especially stressed. This is the first eschatological act of Jesus, a sign of the salvation that has now dawned, a proof that God's rule is present and operative. Jesus transmits this authority to Peter and correspondingly to the apostles and enables the eschatological forces of salvation to develop more widely. The double formula, bind or loose, retain or forgive, makes it clear that we have here a power of decision, a juridical function.[22]

The second ἐκκλησία passage from Matt. 18:17 fits in well with this explanation. The sinning brother who will not listen to a personal appeal or to the warning of two or three witnesses and not even to the admonition of the community is threatened with expulsion from it (this formula would be understood by the Jews). In the background, as is evident from the following verse 18[23] is the thought that this decision is recognized by God. The obdurate sinner will be dismissed from

[21] A. Vögtle in *L.Th.K.* II (1958), pp. 480–2, particularly p. 482.

[22] Jeremias in *Th.W.B.* III, 750, 35–38 thinks that this loosing granted by God, namely acquittal, does not take place until the final judgment, but this explanation does not carry conviction. For a contrary view see A. Oepke, "Der Herrnspruch über die Kirche Mt 16:17–19" in *St.Th* 2 (1948), pp. 110–65 seq.: "The meaning is simply this, that human judgment is recognized as binding before the highest tribunal, whether this happens in the present or the future aeon."

[23] For the relation between these two passages see J. Schmid, op. cit.

the community of the redeemed which has been promised a share in God's future kingdom.

The founding of the ἐκκλησία upon Simon Peter and the promise that it would never be overcome make it certain that Jesus is thinking of the earthly community ("the pilgrim people of God") and not of the perfect eschatological society. A distinction has to be made between the two "communities" because the judgment will bring into the redeemed company of the perfect *basileia* other men who did not know Jesus in their lifetime (Matt. 25:34–40) and who evidently were not members of his visible Messianic community, and on the other hand unfaithful and unworthy members will be cast out (Matt. 7:22 seq.; differently, Luke 13:26 seq.; Matt. 13:24–30, 36–43, 47–50; 22:11–13, at least in the interpretation of the early Church). After all, the promises of Jesus in the entry-passages are made unconditionally (see Matt. 7:21). But it is also accepted in principle that those who look for the kingdom of God belong to the earthly community of Jesus.

What consequences can be drawn about the relation between the reign of God and the Ecclesia?

i. God's reign and the earthly community of Jesus are not identical but there is a relation between them. Because God's eschatological reign was already present in the person and action of Jesus and will manifest itself in power and glory at the Parousia, the community established by and attached to him has a share in the saving graces of the present and the promises for the future.

ii. The main significance of the community of Jesus consists in its orientation towards the future kingdom; it is one day to become God's community of the perfect *basileia* but only after the test and discrimination of Judgment. The Ecclesia is the community of those who look for the kingdom of God, the "threshold of the βασιλεία, because its members have the promise that, if they persevere to the end (Matt. 13:18) they will have a share in God's reign."[24]

iii. The forces of God's present reign are active in Jesus' community as in Jesus himself on account of the powers Jesus communicated to his disciples and especially to Peter. They have the authority to teach and forgive, they have received the word and spirit of God, and those who despise the salvation they offer will be excluded from God's future kingdom. We might even say that their juridical office of the future is already presaged in their power to judge on earth (Matt. 19:28).

iv. Jesus assures his community founded upon Peter, the rock, that the "gates of hell", that is, the forces of death, will never prevail against it. This signifies that it will endure till the advent of the cosmic reign of God. It must, however, filled with the vitality of God's rule, fight against the powers of evil, against Satan and his satellites (see Luke 10:19; 22:31 seq.) and must suffer affliction and persecution, especially in the period before the end. It is an *ecclesia militans et pressa,* an *ecclesia crucis.*

v. Membership of this eschatological community founded by Jesus does not in itself guarantee acceptance into the future kingdom. Its members must persevere in loyal observance of God's will (Matt. 7:21), in resolution through the eschatological trials and calamities (Mark 13:12 seq. par.) even to martyrdom (Mark 8:35 par.), in discipleship to Jesus (Mark 8:34 par.; Luke 14:27 par.) and in their confession of faith in him (Mark 8:38 seq. par.).

vi. The basic thought, uniting present and future, must be that of the eschatological people of God. This people is considered as assembled – but also, from another point of view,

[24] J. Jeremias in *Th.W.B.* III, 750, note 70.

as God's flock scattered in the world – yet genuinely God's flock over which God exercises his sovereignty. The Ecclesia is the assembly ground of the elect (ἐκλεκτοί) who still have to endure their earthly combats. Again, it is the flock of Jesus, the Messianic shepherd who not only gathers them around himself at God's instance (Mark 6:34; 14:28) but gives his life for their salvation (Luke 22:20; Mark 14:24; John 10:11).

We should make a brief comparison between this possibly slightly premature explanation (see section 19) and a number of answers, on both the Catholic and Protestant sides, to the problem of the relation between "Church and kingdom of God". Some Protestant theologians come to conclusions which resemble ours. Recognizing the genuineness of Matt. 16:18 seq. they admit the founding of a visible "church" or "community" which they try to explain from the standpoint of the people of God. F. M. Braun speaks of a "new consensus" and his review of the question can be recommended.[25] These Protestant theologians lay more stress on the fact that the Church of Jesus in this aeon remains an *ecclesia militans et pressa,* but so does R. Gro-

[25] *Neues Licht auf die Kirche,* pp. 93–102 (especially with reference to Kattenbusch, K. L. Schmidt, G. Gloege, W. Michaelis, H. D. Wendland, A. Fridrichsen, F. J. Leenhardt, O. Cullmann, W. A. Visser't Hooft). With these the Swedish theologians are to be associated who have expressed their views in the joint volume, *Ein Buch von der Kirche* (Göttingen, 1951); it includes G. Lindeskog's study, *Gottesreich und Kirche im Neuen Testament,* pp. 145–57; see also O. Michel, op. cit., pp. 26–30, in particular p. 30: "The foundation of the community can only be understood as a further establishment and building up of God's present and future reign. After Good Friday and Easter it is only through the actual community that the forces of the heavenly kingdom operate. The charismatic presence of God's kingdom is completed and fulfilled in the community. Both these realities are mutually interrelated and they both are orientated towards Jesus Christ."

sche, a Catholic, along similar lines.[26] In fact, Catholic and Protestant theologians often agree about the fundamental distinction between these two things and the relations between them. Where they differ is about the structure and constitution of the Church (primacy, succession, etc., but this lies outside the framework of this book).

Even Catholic theologians are frequently uncertain how to determine the relation between the Church and the present reign of God. R. Grosche underlines the strictly supernatural character of God's reign, he warns us against any sleight of hand in "turning the kingdom of God into a kingdom of men".[27] From this point of view it is doubtful whether we should speak of the Church as a "bearer of the kingdom of God"[28] or a "manifestation of God's kingdom".[29] The "essential presence" of God's reign in the Church[30] is sufficiently safeguarded if we recognize in it the forces and graces of salvation in the Biblical sense. But God's reign is not so associated with the Church that we can speak of it as a "present form of God's kingdom",[31] since this would suppose an amalgamation with the Church's history on earth. God's reign as such has no organization and goes through no process;

[26] *Reich Gottes und Kirche,* p. 68. [27] Ibid., p. 46. [28] M. Meinertz, *Theologie des N. T.* I, p. 70.
[29] V. Schurr, *Paulus* 23 (1951), p. 25. [30] Ibid., p. 23.
[31] E. Walter, *Das Kommen des Herrn* II, p. 43; adopted by V. Schurr, op. cit., p. 25. F. M. Braun proposes a dialectical solution: "The Church is the kingdom in so far as here on earth it is permeated with the power of the kingdom and its whole being is directed towards the future kingdom of glory and fulfilment. Correspondingly, the kingdom is the Church in so far as the power of the kingdom, poured forth by Jesus in the form of spirit, grace and eternal life, operates chiefly and normally – though not exclusively – in the community of the faithful established by the twelve" (op. cit., p. 153). But this reciprocal formulation easily leads to misunderstandings.

it does not embrace the just and sinners, it is in no sense dependent upon earthly and human factors. It is not "built up" by men and thus brought to its goal. Yet all this can be said of the Church in its mundane form. Whether we should apply terms like "organ" of God's reign to the Church will be clarified later when we treat of the situation in the history of salvation and revelation after Easter (see part III).

The relation of Church to *basileia* is clearly and beautifully brought out in the *Didache*: "Be mindful, O Lord, of thy Church, rescue her from all evil and perfect her in thy love, and bring her together from the four winds, her whom thou hast made holy, into thy kingdom which thou hast prepared for her" (10, 5).

18. The Significance of God's Reign for the Community of Jesus

We have frequently remarked that the opposite is also true, namely that the reign of God has an important place in the consciousness of the community of Jesus. The Ecclesia is aware that she was called into being to receive the elect (ἐκλεκτοί) and to conduct them to the kingdom of glory. We have adduced many passages that reflect the early Church's interest in what Jesus says about God's reign. It is no accident that these references are found principally, though not exclusively, in Matthew's gospel. This is more markedly a "Church" gospel than the other two synoptics (see merely the two ἐκκλησία passages) and to this it owed the high esteem in which it was held in the early Church.[32]

[32] See E. Massaux, *L'influence de l'Évangile de S. Matthieu sur la littérature chrétienne avant S. Irénée* (Louvain, 1950); for what follows consult also G. Bornkamm, *Enderwartung und Kirche*.

It will be useful to study Matthew's method in greater detail. How did the early Church employ the idea of the *basileia* to understand its existence, character and tasks?

There is, first of all, a well-defined group of texts in which the morally exigent character of God's reign gives its support to the Church's exhortations. The whole Sermon on the Mount appears from Matthew 5 to 7 as Christ's New Law which must be fulfilled for entry into the kingdom of God. The beatitudes, the first and last of which are subordinated to the idea of the *basileia* (5:3, 10) are different in their Matthean form from that in Luke, a list of ethical dispositions for those who look for the kingdom (note particularly those concerning the merciful, the pure of heart and the peacemakers, which are absent from Luke 6). If we confine ourselves to the entry passages, we discover in Matthew 7:13 seq. a saying that in comparison with Luke 13:23 seq. has been characteristically enlarged. In Luke's clearly original form it calls for the greatest effort in the metaphor of the narrow door. Matthew introduces the two paths, Jewish in origin but adapted for Christian teaching (*Didache* 1–5; *Barn.*18). The *basileia* theme gave them a valuable application. A broad way trodden by the many leads to destruction; a narrower way, found only by the few, to life, that is to the kingdom of God.

In the *Discipline Roll* of the Qumran community the emphasis is placed upon predestination to one or the other way. The children of justice walk on the ways of light, the children of destruction on the ways of darkness (IQS III, 20 seq.). Naturally, the "angels of darkness" and "all spirits of his lot" attempt to lead the children of justice astray but the "God of Israel" and the "angels of his truth" assist all the children of light (III, 22–25). The early Church seems also to have speculated about the number of the elect (see the introduction to Luke 13:23) but the moral summons of Jesus in his *basileia* gospel set limits to this apocalyptic question (compare *Fourth Book of Esdras* 7:51 seq.; *Syr. Bar.* 75:6; *Apoc. Abr.* 29:17).

The passage about those who call on their "Lord, Lord" in Luke 6:46, uttered as a warning of Jesus to his contemporary audience, becomes in Matthew 7:21 a general "entry passage"; there is no doubt that the Christian community is also addressed: it is not enough to invoke the name of Jesus, moral behaviour must accompany this. It is not sufficient to appeal to the Lord and to one's association with him. The passage that follows, describing an eschatological scene in Luke 13:26 seq. and spoken by Jesus to the contemporaries who ate and drank with him and heard his discourses, is expressly adapted by Matthew to his Christian readers. Christian prophets and wonderworkers who appeal to their extraordinary deeds in the name of Jesus will be repudiated as evildoers by the eschatological judge if they have offended morally.

We have discussed earlier (see above, section 13) the application of the parables of the sower, the tares amid the wheat and the net with the fish, which transfers the gospel situation at the time of Jesus to its setting in the early Church. Perhaps the warning against those who cause scandal in Matthew 18:6 seq. (compare this with Luke 17:1 seq. and Mark 9:42) was consciously applied by the evangelist to disturbing elements within the community. The man without a wedding garment (that is, one washed clean), who is dismissed from the festal hall, is a warning to men streaming into the Church who show themselves unworthy of the call, that is, of baptism. The blend of the two similes of wedding feast and wedding garment (Matt. 22:1–10; 11–14) is probably the work of the evangelist or the Church tradition used by him, since the invitation to the wedding feast was concerned originally not with adherence to the Church but with the call to God's future kingdom. In its earliest form the parable of the wedding garment dealt simply with the moral prerequisites for those who awaited the kingdom of God.

To conclude, it is easy to see that where Jesus employs the term "brethren" for his fellow Jews, but always with a religious undertone, Matthew is thinking of his Christian brethren, the brethren in the community of Jesus (see Matt. 5:22 seq., 24; 7:3–5; 18:21, 35; compare with v. 15) – a proceeding which he adopts and justifies by Jesus' reference to his "spiritual" brethren (Mark 3:33–35 par.). From this derive earnest and concrete admonitions to brotherly love and readiness to be reconciled and to forgive. Nor is the eschatological note of warning lacking (Matt. 18:35).

In a second group of texts the early Church uses the idea of the *basileia* to remind heads of the community of their responsibility. Matthew 18:1–20 generally interpreted as "community rules", must have been composed mainly with this end in mind. From the dispute among the disciples (vv. 1–3) verse 4 draws this conclusion, found in this form only in Matthew: "Amen, I say to you, whosoever shall humble himself as this little child, is the greater in the kingdom of heaven", obviously influenced by the passage, "Whosoever shall exalt himself, shall be humbled (by God), and he that shall humble himself, shall be exalted (by God)" (Matt. 23:12; see Luke 14:11; 18:14).

Matthew 23:8–12 gives us an insight into the evangelist's method. Jesus' original attacks on the presumptuous Scribes are turned into a warning for Christian teachers (v. 8) and catechists to develop a brotherly attitude (v. 8 at end, "You are all brethren"). With this he associates the expression, "the greatest among you shall be your servant" (v.11, see Mark 9:35; 10:43 par.) which certainly derives from Jesus' instruction to the disciples, and the other passages about being humbled and exalted (v. 12).

Here the thought of the kingdom of God becomes a dominant

motif. In Matthew 18:1, the introductory question is "Who is the greater in the kingdom of heaven?" whereas in Mark 9:34 = Luke 9:46 the disciples are merely disputing which of them (that is of their present company) is the greatest. Matthew understood this quarrel about the leading rank on earth as also a query about privileged places in God's kingdom (see Mark 10:37 par.), an indication perhaps that he regarded the community of disciples on earth as a foreshadowing of the perfect community in the future kingdom. In that case, he has grasped the meaning of Jesus' paradox that in this preparatory state the man who desires to rule must serve. Luke seems to have borne the circumstances of the early Church even more pointedly in mind when he allows the dispute among the disciples to flare up once more during the Last Supper. The mention of earthly rulers who oppress the peoples is linked by Matthew and Mark (Mark 10:42 = Matt. 20:25) with the passage about the sons of Zebedee. Luke attaches it to Jesus' answer in the first dispute (22:26; see 9:48b in another context), and then adds a reference to the company at table: "For who is greater, he that sitteth at table or he that serveth? Is not he that sitteth at table? But I am in the midst of you as he that serveth" (v. 27). This is surely a reminder to those presiding at the Agape to serve the poor with love.[33]

The parable of the lost sheep which follows in Matthew 18:11–14 is illuminating. Jesus employs it, according to Luke 15:4–7, to justify the message of divine grace which he is proclaiming to sinners and his own attitude to these "lost ones". In Matthew 18:11–14, the parable is made a warning to leaders of the community to be genuine shepherds especially of their

[33] H. Schürmann, *Der Abendmahlsbericht Luke* 22: *7–38 als Gottesdienstordnung, Gemeindeordnung, Lebensordnung* (Leipzig, 1955), pp. 74 seq.

"little ones", that is the insignificant and feeble, the errant and sinning members of the community.

There are many other indications that sayings of Jesus are applied with special reference to leaders in the community. The simile of the servants waiting for the master to return from a feast (Luke 12:35–38), originally a summons to eschatological watchfulness (Mark 13:34), becomes a special warning for the disciples. Luke's series of parables and sayings culminates in the parable of the steward (Luke 12:42–46; Matt. 24:45–51), to which Luke appends a discussion about the lesser or greater guilt of such a servant (v. 47). In Matthew's version of the parable of the talents (Matt. 25:14–30; see Luke 19:12–27) the *basileia* motif again appears, since the faithful servants are to partake of their master's feast and banquet of joy (vv. 21 and 23). Luke, on the other hand, in his (originally independent?) account of the "heir to the throne" has a more marked allusion to the Christ of the Parousia. The subsequent verse shows that the third evangelist uses the notion of the blind leading the blind as a warning for the disciples (6:39 seq.; see Matt. 15:14), just as with him, the simile of the leaven (Luke 12:1) signifies the purity of intention of the preacher.

In a third series of texts we can see the mind of the early Church turning to the conversion of the heathen. In view of Jesus' great prophecy in Matthew 8:11 (= Luke 13:29) it felt justified in detecting this promise of its Lord in many details of the parables which were, to begin with, merely part of the picture. The parable of the royal marriage feast (Matt. 22:1–10) and that of the great banquet (Luke 14:16–24) must have been narrated later – in a different context, as is seen by comparing Matthew and Luke – so as to make clear the reference to the call of the gentiles.

A different method is employed in the two contexts. Matthew

first describes how punishment is meted out to those first invited, understood as the Jews, especially the leaders, whose city will be destroyed (v. 7). The substitutes from the "byways" he interprets as the gentiles. In Luke's account the poor in the city are contrasted with the distinguished guests who were first invited (v. 21) and they are listed as in verse 13, where Jesus recommends us to practise hospitality not to relatives and wealthy persons but to the "poor, the feeble, the lame and the blind". Here the evangelist is underlining the call of Jesus to the poor and wretched (see Luke 6:20 seq.). A messenger is then despatched a second time to bring in more guests from the highways and byways outside the city, and by this second group of substitutes Luke could only have meant the gentiles. We need not enquire here what was Jesus' original intention. The early Church at any rate thought itself justified in adopting this interpretation in view of its actual circumstances in preaching.

Similar to this is the parable of the evil vinedressers, which is given by all three synoptics (Mark 12:1–12; Luke 20:9–19; Matt. 21:33–46). In this much discussed parable[34] we are concerned only with the question whether and in what way the early Church applied it to the gentiles. That it did so is evident from one verse of Matthew who was universal in outlook in spite of his Jewish Christian readers: "Therefore I say to you, the kingdom (reign) of God shall be taken away from you and shall be given to a nation yielding the fruits thereof" (21:43).

[34] Leaving Catholic exegetes aside, the authenticity of this parable, despite subsequent recensions, is firmly held by J. Jeremias, *Gleichnisse Jesu,* pp. 59–65; E. Lohmeyer, *Das Evangelium des Markus,* p. 249; V. Taylor, *Jesus and his Sacrifice* (London, 1937, new printing 1955), pp. 106–08; V. Taylor, *The Gospel According to St. Mark,* pp. 472 seq.; E. Sjöberg, *Der verborgene Menschensohn,* pp. 170 seq.; W. Michaelis, *Die Gleichnisse Jesu,* pp. 113–25.

The meaning is clear. God's ancient people will be rejected because it repudiated God's messengers (only Matthew has the plural; the "servants" are obviously the prophets) and also his Son, and a new "people" enters, the new Israel, to which the gentiles too belong. What is surprising is the way this is formulated and the idea of the "reign of God" that underlies it.

"To take away the kingdom (reign) of God" is a curious expression in the New Testament and it compels us to understand the *basileia* as a reality already present in the history of Israel, a notion that contradicts the normal eschatological concept of the *basileia* in the gospels (see section 7). We are familiar, however, with the rabbinical notion (see section 5) that in the past the "kingship" was with Israel but that it was "taken" from them when they sinned and "given to the peoples" in their stead (*Midr. Est.* 1, 2). But they were not referring to God's reign, though Israel's political sovereignty was closely connected with God's action. The verse in question would seem to be influenced by views and expressions of this kind, now transferred to "God's reign". The term, rarely found in Matthew, βασιλεία τοῦ Θεοῦ (instead of τῶν οὐρανῶν) suggests that it was taken over by Matthew, possibly from Jewish Christian sources. We are reminded of the explanation of the parable of the tares (see section 13). Strictly speaking, the *basileia* should not be identified with the vineyard for this represents Israel (the evil vinedressers are its leaders) but such lack of precision is apt to occur in "applied" interpretations. The idea expressed in Matthew 21:43 cannot be dissociated from Jesus. In Matthew 8:12 the peoples stream in and receive a share in God's kingdom while the "sons of the kingdom" (in Luke 13:28, "you"), the unbelieving Jews, are excluded.

The missionary outlook of the early Church can be detected in slighter details. Matthew 13:38, interpreting the parable of the tares says that the field in which the seed is scattered is the world. With the image of the light upon its standard Luke may be hinting at the conversion of the gentiles. In the two instances in which he introduces it (8:16; 11:33) it is essential that those who are entering see the light. Matthew may well have realized how the idea of the *basileia* helped the missionary when repeating a passage from Mark 13:10, he speaks explicitly, of the "gospel of the kingdom" (24:14; see 4:23; 9:35; 13:19).

A fourth group of texts reveals the keen interest taken by the early Church in the Lord's Parousia, by means of which the kingdom of God will be brought about with power. Here it adopts in the main the monitory attitude of Jesus (Be ready! Be alert!) but it seems mindful as well of its particular importance in the history of salvation.

We purposely avoid the phrase, "delay in the Parousia" because it supposes what would have to be proved, namely that Jesus foretold the Parousia for the near future (see section 16). But even while we reject the thesis of "logical eschatology", we may ask whether the early Church as it longed vehemently for the Lord's coming ("maranatha!") and saw the passage of the years, may not have formulated the tradition to a certain extent in the light of its own situation. This would be true particularly of Luke.

This expectation of the Parousia may have made the early Church introduce a more marked Christological accent into many of the parables. It applied that of the thief in the night (Luke 12:39 = Matt. 24:43), in reality a spur to eschatological watchfulness, directly to the Christ of the Parousia (compare Apoc. 3:8; 16:15) and in the heir of the parable of the talents, journeying to a far country to inherit kingly status and power it saw the Lord for whose return it was waiting (Luke 19:12–27).[35]

[35] It is generally accepted that the form and features of this heir are

As is clear from the marginal remark in verse 11, his disciples believe that the kingdom of God is to appear immediately because they are drawing near to Jerusalem. The early Church can, however, draw the lesson that God's reign, to be established by Christ, is still in the future, since the heir to the throne has journeyed into "a far country". More important than the nearness of the kingdom are the tasks he has given his servants during the interval. Matthew placed his corresponding parable of the talents with his other Parousia parables (chapter 25) and added that the Lord of those servants would return "after a long time" (v. 19), without, however, laying special emphasis on this.

Two further parables contain a reference to this delay. In that of the steward, entrusted with the charge of the other servants, the evil servant, reflecting on his master's delay, treats his fellow servants shamefully and leads a corrupt life (Matt. 24:48 seq. = Luke 12:45); the Lord returns at a time "which he hopeth not" and punishes him severely. But this may be merely an incidental feature suggested by the imagery. The fundamental idea is the rewarding of the good and the punishment of the bad servant. There is a similar remark in the parable of the ten virgins, that the bridegroom is delaying his arrival. This makes the situation a possible one, for only so can we understand that both foolish and wise virgins fall asleep, and their situation when the bridegroom suddenly enters (Matt. 25:5 seq.). The additional comment, "Watch you, therefore, for you know not the day nor the hour" (v. 13) does not quite match the situation for it is not a

taken from the Hasmonean Archelaus who journeyed to Rome in 4 B.C. to win Roman approval for his tetrarchy of Judaea and on his return took a bloody revenge on his enemies (Fl. Josephus, *Ant.* XVII, 229 seq.; *Bell.* II, 80). In consequence, the allegory cannot be transferred quite simply to the Christ of the Parousia.

question of watching but of being prepared. These warnings have become stereotyped and interchangeable (compare Luke 12:40 with 37; Matt. 24:44 with 43 – the opposite case). It might be easier to detect a particular Church interest in the elaboration in Luke 12:38; Mark 13:35 where different hours of the night are given as possible moments of arrival; yet this is part of the imagery and there is no hint of an allegorical interpretation in terms of periods. The idea is that the Lord of the house may come suddenly; therefore, be on the watch (Mark 13:36 seq.). In Luke it should be observed that the question "When" is expressly put four times and each time it is rejected (Luke 17:20; 19:11; 21:7; Acts 1:6). This is no accident.[36]

In all these images that melt into one another[37] there remains one fundamental question: were they, to begin with, parables of the Parousia and not rather "crisis" parables, intended to depict the sudden inrush of catastrophe and of the eschatological distress prior to the end, the approach of the judgment, in the same way that the flood surprised, divided and judged the generation of Noah (see Luke 17:26 seq. = Matt. 24:37 seq.)? This is claimed by C. H. Dodd for the four parables of the faithful and unfaithful servants, the servants waiting for their master, the thief in the night and the ten virgins.[38] J. Jeremias accepted this view and added the parable of the talents or the *minae*.[39] Each parable needs to be examined separately. Granted that Jesus

[36] See H. Conzelmann, *Mitte der Zeit,* pp. 103 seq.

[37] The porter who remains awake for the master coming home at night; the servants who await the indefinite day of their lord's return; the servants with definite responsibilities during his absence: all of these seem special characteristics; originally they may have been independent similes which were later amalgamated; see Mark 13:33–37; Luke 12: 35–38, 42–46.

[38] *Parables of the Kingdom,* pp. 154–74. [39] *Gleichnisse Jesu,* pp. 40–55.

scarcely wished to depict himself as coming like a housebreaker by night and that this was originally a crisis parable addressed to the obdurate, we may still ask whether it makes sense and is likely that the catastrophe should be presented in the form of a bridegroom appearing for a wedding. In the corresponding parable of the servants awaiting their master (Luke 12:36 seq.) there is no warning or threatening note but only, "Blessed are those servants whom the lord when he cometh shall find watching". Cannot Jesus have concealed himself behind the figure of the home-coming lord and that too of the bridegroom even if, or in fact precisely because, the metaphor of bridegroom was not commonly employed by the Jews for the Messias? May he not have intended to preserve his "Messianic mystery" in this way, that is, to reveal it only to those who understood? At the conclusion of the parable of the virgins the bridegroom evidently takes on the traits of the eschatological judge, when he repudiates the foolish virgins with the words, "Amen, I say to you, I know you not" (Matt. 25:12; see 7:2). Unless we regard the parable as fashioned by the Christian community[40] – and for that there exists no compelling reason[41] – we must accept it as a Parousia parable narrated by Jesus himself.[42]

For the rest, the distinction between "crisis" and "Parousia"

[40] See R. Bultmann, *Geschichte der syn. Tradition,* p. 125, pp. 190 seq.; W. G. Kümmel, *Verheißung und Erfüllung,* pp. 50–2; G. Bornkamm, *Die Verzögerung der Parousie,* In memoriam E. Lohmeyer (Stuttgart, 1951), pp. 119–26; E. Grässer, *Problem der Parousieverzögerung,* pp. 119–27.

[41] J. Jeremias, *Gleichnisse Jesu,* pp. 157–60; M. Meinertz, "Die Tragweite des Gleichnisses von den zehn Jungfrauen" in *Synoptische Studien,* Festschrift für A. Wikenhauser (Munich, 1954), pp. 94–106; W. Michaelis, "Kennen die Synoptiker eine Verzögerung der Parusie?:" ibid., pp. 107–23, particularly pp. 116–20.

[42] See A. Oepke in *Th.W.B.* V, p. 864, and also note 47.

parables has merely a relative importance for those who do not deny that Jesus proclaimed the Parousia, as J. Jeremias notes with refreshing clarity in the latest edition of his work: "Actually there is no difference in the expectation of Jesus and the early Church; both expect the turning point to be reached with the final period of distress and the display of Satanic power over the world, and both of them – Jesus and the Church – are certain that this final distress will conclude with God's triumph in the Parousia. The only difference is in this that Jesus, speaking to the multitude emphasized the sudden onrush of this era of distress . . . whereas the early Church fixed its gaze on the end of the period of distress."[43]

Because of his hypothesis of a "realized eschatology" Dodd has to treat every Parousia parable as a crisis parable. In them he sees "a situation reflected in the ministry of Jesus when the crisis he had provoked was hastening towards uncertain and unexpected developments, which called for the utmost alertness on the part of his followers",[44] and he finds these developments in Jesus' Passion and death. His system leaves no place for the Parousia. As he sees it, Jesus appeals to men "to recognize that the kingdom of God was present in all its momentous consequences and that by their conduct in the presence of this tremendous crisis hey would judge themselves as faithful or unfaithful, wise ort foolish".[45] Basically, the "inaugurated eschatology", advocated nowadays by J. A. T. Robinson which also denies to Jesus all prophecy of the Parousia is in the same position.[46] It is merely a

[43] *Gleichnisse Jesu,* pp. 42 seq. [44] *Parables of the Kingdom,* p. 171.
[45] Ibid., p. 174. For criticism of this view see R. Morgenthaler, *Kommendes Reich,* pp. 9–33; R. H. Fuller, *Mission and Achievement of Jesus,* pp. 20–35; H. Roberts, *Jesus and the Kingdom of God,* pp. 33–6; 102–07.
[46] *Jesus and his Coming,* passim, especially pp. 81 seq.; 100 seq. For criticism, see above section 14 (on Mark 14:62).

modified version of "realized eschatology" since it leaves no room for any future expectation after the Resurrection of Jesus.

It is, therefore, certain that the early Church centred its expectations for the future more firmly in the Parousia. The Lord will come as judge and saviour to his community and will receive the faithful into the kingdom of God. At any time he may appear, suddenly and unexpected. The time is uncertain but the event, even if it be longer delayed, is certain. With this Christological emphasis, Jesus' gospel of the *basileia* exercises a significant influence on his community after his death.

A fifth group includes a number of texts that need examination, in which can be sensed the growing self-awareness of the Christian community. Matt. 21:43 is an instance. The early Church is conscious of itself as the new people of God, bringing forth the fruits of God's reign. It develops a more profound understanding of itself in its missionary work undertaken at the commission of the Risen Lord to make all peoples his disciples. For this purpose after his enthronement in heaven he transmitted his power to the Church and promised it his assistance (Matt. 28:18–20). The fact that the Christian missionaries embraced and carried on the mission of the first disciples allowed many sayings of Jesus to his disciples to be extended to all who proclaimed the faith. The mention of a reward for the man who provides a drink of water in the name of a disciple was obviously adapted in favour of the earliest travelling missionaries. In Matthew's phrasing, perhaps the earliest, ("to one of these little ones") the expression occurs at the end of a series of sayings that refer to the apostles (10:40–42). Mark 9:41 makes this plain: "Whosoever shall give you to drink a cup of water in my name . . .",[47] but in Matthew the passage occurs with many

[47] The text may have been originally ἐν (τῷ) ὀνόματί μου S *DW Θ

others in the great "Mission discourse" (chapter ten), the whole of which becomes a compendium for Christian missionaries. Christ's messengers – an obvious parallel with the outstanding members of the Jewish community – are known as "prophets, wise men and scribes" (Matt. 23:34; but compare Luke 11:49), and the persecutions waged against them by the Jews bring down God's judgment on the guilty (Matt. 23:35 = Luke 11:50 seq.).

The interior religious self-consciousness of the Christian community attached itself to sayings like that of the Lord's presence among those gathered together in his name (Matt. 18:20) or of his continual assistance till the end of the world (Matt. 28:20). The reward promised to all who have left family and possessions for Jesus' sake consists according to Mark 10:30 (see Luke 18:30; not so in Matt. 19:21) not only in eternal life but also in a substitute even "in this life". Mark's version that shows the interpreting influence of the early Church[48] signifies that the whole-hearted followers of Jesus find a new and larger family in their brothers and sisters in the faith (Mark 3:34 seq.).

From this commentary, by no means exhaustive, it has been clearly shown that the *basileia* gospel of Jesus exercises a very concrete formative influence on the early Church, on its ideas and aspirations, its preaching and catechesis, and that it is also to a certain extent transformed though not, we are convinced, distorted and falsified. The thought of the *basileia* makes the community of Jesus realize its nature and dignity, its responsibilities and duties. The eschatological character of God's reign is not forgotten, hopes for the future remain strong and

al. lat. sy$^{hmg\ pal}$; ὅτι Χριστοῦ ἐστε (quia Christi estis, because you belong to Christ) may derive from an early copyist (see Lagrange on the text).

[48] See J. Schmid, on this text.

centre upon Christ's Parousia. Yet the intervening period, in which the Church has to fulfil her obligations on earth, comes more strongly into the foreground, and in this historical situation many a saying of Jesus is seen in a new light. Consequently, there is and indeed there must be a change in the preaching of the gospel, in its concepts, terms and expressions. We shall be able to appreciate this more fully when we pass from Jesus' proclamation of the *basileia* to the kerygma of the early Church (see part. III).

19. The Eucharist in the Christian Community and the Concept of God's Reign

We must not underestimate the significance of the institution at the Last Supper both for the *basileia* gospel (see section 15) and for the establishment of the Christian community, as also for that community's consciousness of its character and mission. It is a focal point round which the thoughts of Jesus crystallized at the close of his ministry and on the eve of his willingly accepted death. The advent of God's perfect reign, the necessity of his atoning death, the application to his disciples of his blood, at once destroying sin and establishing a covenant, the vision of table-companionship in the future kingdom: all this is present to Jesus' mind in that farewell hour and it finds simple yet profound expression in his sacred actions and their accompanying words.

It is outside the scope of this book to enter into all the exegetical and theological problems connected with the institution of the Eucharist or to inquire more fully what was the original form of words, whether the Mark-Matthew account is prior to that of Luke-Paul, and other historical questions.

The literature on the subject may be consulted.[49] Our concern is with the theological content of the institution at the Last Supper as this was understood, and we maintain legitimately, by the early Church.

We find confirmed what we have discovered earlier (section 15). After the failure of his preaching to the Jews, Jesus regards his Passion as a necessary precondition for the coming of the perfect kingdom. He is certain that his table-companionship with the disciples will be realized in God's future kingdom in a new and perfect way (Luke 22:16, 18, 30b; Mark 14:25 = Matt. 26:29). How this will be possible in spite of and precisely on account of his death is shown in his words over the Eucharistic cup. This represents the "new covenant" to be established through the blood of Jesus (Luke 22:20; 1. Cor. 11:25); its content is Jesus' "blood of the covenant" (Mark 14:24; Matt. 26:28).[50] The blood is the symbol of violent death.[51] The blood of Jesus, however, acquires an atoning power (ὑπέρ ...) and in the background are ideas from the theology of the martyrs (2 Mach. 7:37 seq.; 4 *Mach.* 6:28 seq.; 12:17; 17:21 seq.; *Eth. Hen.*, 1 seq.; rabbinic texts in Billerbeck II, 279 seq.),[52] but especially Jesus' own interpretation of his Passion and death in the light of Isaias 53.

If the two Last Supper traditions verbally diverge (Luke-Paul

[49] See the literature in Schürmann, I–III.

[50] The objection frequently raised that it is impossible to translate τὸ αἷμά μου τῆς διαθήκης back into Aramaic is disputed, and rightly so, by J. A. Emerton, *The Aramaic Underlying* τὸ αἷμά μου τῆς διαθήκης Mark XIV, 24 in *J.Th. S.* 6 (1958), pp. 238–40.

[51] H. Schürmann II, p. 98; A. Vögtle in *L.Th.K.* ²II (1958), pp. 539–41.

[52] H. W. Surkau, *Martyrien in jüdischer und frühchristlicher Zeit* (Göttingen, 1938), pp. 9–74; E. Lohse, *Märtyrer und Gottesknecht* (Göttingen, 1955), pp. 66–110. In *Die Abendmahlsworte Jesu*, p. 111, J. Jeremias observes correctly that in view of the widespread Jewish ideas about the atoning

"for you"; Mark-Matthew "for many"), each includes the decisive word "for" (that is, "in favour of", but also, "in place of"). If Luke's form is original, as Schürmann suggests with sound reasons,[53] Jesus has first of all in mind the actual participants but not in any exclusive "particularist" sense. The reference to the disciples is a distributive formula through which the redeeming force of the blood is applied to them. The Mark tradition would have brought out more definitely the underlying idea that Jesus was conscious of being the atoning Servant of God (Isa. 53:11 seq.) for all mankind ("many" equals "all"), and the universal significance of Jesus' saving death is more forcibly stressed. The gentiles are included in the "many" of whom Jesus is speaking.[54]

Intimately linked with this is the notion of the (new) covenant. For the community this is the dominant and emphatic note. Again, the decisive word "covenant" is found in both traditions. In Mark and Matthew the idea is rooted in the old covenant of Sinai, sealed with the "covenant blood" of animals (Exod. 24:8); this is replaced when the new covenant is established at the Last Supper by Jesus' own blood. The covenant of Jesus is the fulfilment, elevation and perfection of the old covenant which God once bestowed on the people of Israel. The word "new" is not used but it is a new, eschatological institution. The form of the Luke-Paul tradition recalls directly the prophecy in Jeremias (31:31–4) of an eschatological "new" covenant. The words of Jesus then reveal that this promised covenant is to be realized through his bloody death and to be made effective for those who partake of this meal. He will not unfold his full glory

power of blood we can and must attribute this thought to Jesus and have no need whatsoever to bring in a later "community dogma".

[53] II, pp. 75–8.

[54] J. Jeremias, *Abendmahlsworte Jesu,* pp. 108–11.

until the disciples share in God's full reign in the perfect kingdom; but Jesus assures them of this full share in God's reign because of this institution of the covenant in the Upper Room (compare Luke 22:29 with 20).[55]

The theological significance of the new "covenant", founded in the blood of Jesus and applied to the disciples at this farewell meal, follows somewhat different lines in the two traditions, but these lines move closer to one another than might at first appear. For Mark and Matthew it should be observed that "Servant of God" and "covenant" are related notions in the prophecy of Deutero-Isaias (see Isa. 42:6; 49:6, 8; 54:10; 55:3; 56:4, 6; 59:21; 61:8).[56] Even though the "people's" and the "peace" covenant, as understood in the Old Testament, signifies the renewed covenant of God with Israel, the very same passage leaves a door open to the gentiles who attach themselves to Israel (see 42:6; 49:6; 55:4 seq.; 56:7). In the Luke-Paul tradition the emphasis rests upon the re-establishment of the covenant and its final eschatological form. But this also is found in Deutero-Isaias (see particularly 59:21; 61:8) and it is most fully developed in Jeremias 31:31 seq. Consequently, both forms of Jesus' words over the chalice present the thoughts of the departing Lord in a striking manner. The peace covenant of God's grace (Isa. 54:10), the saving covenant resting upon forgiveness, which brings undisturbed communion between God and his people (Jer. 31:31 seq.) is actualized by Jesus'

[55] We have already commented on the probable connection of διατίθεμαι Luke 22:29 with the διαθήκη of verse 20 (see above p. 144). See also R. Otto, *Reich Gottes,* p. 234; R. H. Fuller, op. cit., p. 74 thinks that Jesus spoke more fully of this in the preceding *Haggada.*

[56] This is also stressed by R. Otto, *Reich Gottes,* pp. 235 seq.; O. Cullmann, *Christologie,* pp. 63 seq.; J. L. Price, "The Servant Motive in the Synoptic Gospels" in *Interpretation* 1958, pp. 28–38, especially p. 37.

blood, by the sacrifice of the life of God's Servant. God himself decreed and fulfilled this (note the passive ἐκχυννόμενον); through the blood of Jesus he established his saving covenant with God's people of the Last Days.

Because this new covenant is eschatological it comes very close to God's perfect reign. The two concepts cannot, however, be reduced to one. Each has its own range of application in the Old Testament. The new covenant, established through the death of Jesus and applied to his community in the Eucharist, finds its goal in full communion with God in God's kingdom. "The one goal of fulfilment is depicted in both notions, 'God will rule' and 'the new order of God prevails', the order which finally determines God's relation to them."[57] To this final covenant in Jeremias 31:33 belong the perfect fulfilment of God's law by his people and their acceptance into full communion with God; first of all God pardons his people their guilt (v. 34). In its New Testament realization God first forgives sins because of the atoning death of Jesus (see the explanatory clause in Matt. 26:28 εἰς ἄφεσιν ἁμαρτιῶν) but he does not grant eschatological sinlessness. The final covenant is effective but not yet complete. There is a parallel with the reign of God, operative in the present but manifest in glory only in the future.

If Jesus sees the new covenant established in his blood and at the same time awaits God's perfect kingdom, the only explanation is that his saving death guarantees the advent of the eschatological kingdom and makes it possible for him to anticipate its essential content, the full order of and communion with God, and he applies this to those who share this meal in the new covenant. As covenant, this sacred institution of Jesus is at once a sign and expression, anticipation and guarantee of God's

[57] J. Behm in *Th.W.B.* II, p. 137, 7–9.

eschatological reign. When his community celebrates the Eucharist, it receives the blessings of the new covenant and so experiences something of the glory of the future kingdom.

This view is confirmed if we study the sequence of events at the Last Supper. The Lord does not merely set the chalice with his blood before the disciples as a symbol and guarantee of the covenant; he hands it to them so that all may drink. He thus actually applies to them the power of the covenant established in his blood. Because of the gifts it gives, the Eucharist is not merely a symbolic but a sacramental event and in its relation to the kingdom of the future it not only prefigures, it gives a foretaste, naturally in a form adapted to the preparatory condition of the people of God. Those who partake receive eschatological salvation initially and provisionally, as it were on trial; they are given a real title to the kingdom of God but it has to be maintained through their own efforts. We might say that God's eschatological reign is present and operative in a special manner in the Eucharist and presents itself as the new covenant which, founded in the blood of Jesus, retains its force and significance till the coming of the kingdom of glory.

A look at the Christian community after the death of Jesus, commemorating his farewell feast, shows something far removed from a group of survivors or eschatological enthusiasts waiting for the Parousia and the perfect kingdom of God. What we see is the people of God, gathered by Jesus and now attracting other men, the new people of God building itself up on a new foundation after the unbelief of the old people of God. It has become of no importance to belong to the earthly Israel, though it is from Israel that the core derives, thus keeping continuity with the chosen people of old. The community that celebrates the Eucharist is the Ecclesia established by Jesus and belonging to him (Matt. 16:18, see section 17) and its true essence emerges in this celebration; it is the community of the redeemed called to the coming kingdom. The promise that it will never be overcome by the powers of death (Matt. 16:18), that it will persevere to the end of this era of the world (Matt. 28:20), receives new light from the institution of the Last Supper, as it were a concrete outline and confirmation. The new covenant founded in the blood of Jesus is to continue and to dispense its saving vitality till it is finally consummated in the kingdom of God.

This naturally presupposes that the Last Supper with its sacred acts was more than a special farewell feast for the loyal disciples of Jesus, that it was in fact a genuine institution for the future when he would be separated from them. Such an intention on Jesus' part is to be seen not merely in the injunction that they are to repeat this, in Luke 22:19, for the bread, and 1 Cor. 11:24 seq., for bread and wine, and this does not lose its force even if the phrase be regarded as "secondary", that is, as not present in the earliest tradition. Luke 22:16–8 makes it clear that the disciples in contrast with Jesus go on celebrating the "Pasch", naturally a "transformed" Christian Pasch (H. Schürmann). In the Mark-Matthew account the word ὑπὲρ (or περὶ) πολλῶν points to the widest possible range of men who receive in the Eucharist the universal salvific power of the blood of Jesus. To conclude, there are many grounds, in the first place the practice of the early Church itself, for accepting the historic genuineness of the command to repeat the Eucharist. Its absence in Mark and Matthew can be understood from the fact that their Eucharistic account had to be fitted into that of the Passion which had an orientation of its own.[58]

Granted that Jesus instituted the Eucharist with this intention, it can no longer be said that he made no provision for the period

[58] See H. Schürmann II, pp. 123–9.

after his death. He was careful to make the most important provision of all, namely that the powers and graces of God's reign communicated to his followers since the beginning of his ministry should remain with them; even more, that they should be communicated now in the full measure won by the shedding of his blood, the atoning force of his death and God's abiding readiness to forgive which that death had secured.

We can detect the mind of the Christian community as it celebrates the Eucharist in the accounts of its institution but these accounts are none the less reliable historical testimonies of what Jesus did at the Last Supper. This is even more marked in the "breaking of bread" and the "Lord's supper" of the post-Easter community. A glance at the Acts and epistles will be helpful. For the "breaking of bread" which must bear a Eucharistic sense in the account of Acts 2:42–6 and at the Sunday service in Troas (Acts 20:7, 11)[59] and was celebrated in connection with a community meal[60] the eschatological joy (ἀγαλλίασις) is characteristic. These Christians were conscious of themselves as the community of the redeemed, to which the eschatological promises belonged and which had already been realized in one respect: the liturgical presence of their ascended Lord and the eschatological gift of the Holy Spirit. They had every right

[59] See J. Gewiess, *Heilsverkündung,* p. 152; O. Cullmann, *Urchristentum und Gottesdienst* (Zurich, 1950), pp. 17–20; M. Meinertz, *Theologie des N. T.* I, p. 132; G. Delling, *Der Gottesdienst im N. T.* pp. 124 seq.; 131 seq.; Ph. D. Menoud, "Les Actes des Apôtres et l'Eucharistie" in *R.H. Ph.R.* 33 (1953), pp. 21–36 (he interprets all three passages as Eucharistic); A. Wikenhauser, *Die Apostelgeschichte* (Regensburg, [3]1956), pp. 55 seq.; M. Fraeymann, "Fractio panis in communitate primitiva" in *Coll. Brug. Gand.* I (1955), pp. 370–3; J. Dupont, "Le repas d'Emmaüs" in *Lum. Vie* 31 (1957), pp. 77–92 (he accepts the passages as Eucharistic).
[60] See Acts 2:46 μετελάμβανον τροφῆς; 20:11 γευσάμενος.

to rejoice and be exultant.[61] For the "supper of the Lord" which might be misunderstood and abused in the Hellenistic world as an extravagant ritual meal, we have the apostle's commentary, appended to his description of the institution: "For as often as you shall eat this bread, and drink the chalice, you shall show the death of the Lord until he come" (1 Cor. 11:26). Paul draws a contrast between a falsely conceived joy and the serious nature of the Christian ceremony which, whatever its eschatological reference, was also the memorial and representation of the Lord's death. He preserved thereby all the essential features of the Lord's supper and placed its saving significance between the death of the Lord and his Parousia. In consequence, the Eucharist reveals its unique and irrevocable links with past and future; it is the liturgical representation of the unique historical event, the death of Jesus on the cross, and the liturgical anticipation of perfect communion with the Lord when he returns.

The Lord's supper is also a sacramental event. It gives a share in the body and blood of the Lord (v. 27; see 10:16) and it brings together all who enjoy the one same bread into the "body of Christ" (10:17; also 11:29?). For Paul the sacraments as gifts and means of salvation always include obligatory tasks and motives (see 1 Cor. 10:1–13; Rom. 6:2–14). Therefore, the "body" of Christ received in the Eucharistic bread and represented in the Christian community and realized in a new manner, becomes a stern admonition to fraternal love (1 Cor. 11:29). The community of Jesus, now the community of Christ, grows aware in the Eucharist of its true character and its distinction

[61] See Matt. 5:12; Acts 16:34; 1 Pet. 1:6, 8; 4:13; Apoc. 19:7. See also R. Bultmann who writes in *Th.W.B.* I, p. 20, 12 seq.: "What is characteristic is the way in which the Christian community is conscious of itself as the congregation of the final era constituted through God's salvific action;" further consult O. Cullmann, *Gottesdienst,* p. 19.

from the still existing liturgical community of the Jews (see 1 Cor. 10:18, 32). It and it alone is the genuine "community of God" because it is the community of the Messias, purchased through the blood of Jesus, linked with the triumphant Lord and summoned to enter at his Parousia into the perfect kingdom as the eschatological people of God. Without exaggeration we may say that Jesus' institution at the Last Supper is one of the principal bases of this awareness of the early Church, the bridge that links Jesus' company of disciples and the Christian community after Easter, and an ever-flowing fountain for the interior life of God's people of the New Testament.

III

God's Reign and Kingdom in Early Christian Teaching

THE CONCEPT OF GOD'S REIGN IN THE POST-PASCHAL COMMUNITY

20. From the Gospel of Jesus to the Gospel Concerning Jesus, Messias and Lord

WHEN THE apostles took over the preaching and mission of their master, we might have expected that after his death they would have proclaimed the coming reign of God which had already showed itself, as their central theme. What we actually find is an astonishing change, at least at first hearing. God's reign recedes into the background of the apostolic preaching until it is scarcely noticeable. A second theme occupies the stage, the gospel of Jesus, Messias and Lord. This very significant change in the history of revelation emerges from the account given in Acts and from Paul's epistles. We shall examine the relation of these epistles to the idea of the *basileia* in the second chapter, so that we may here limit ourselves to the Acts. Yet we must not set the great apostle of the gentiles apart from the general tradition of early Christian teaching. He himself adopts it and conversely we can discover features and accents similar to those of Paul in the kerygma before him and in his time. However, a methodological distinction is recommended between the two lines of tradition.

We are presupposing that the account of the Acts merits

acceptance. It is not difficult to detect the hand of Luke in its composition, as a comparison with his gospel shows, especially as regards his theological ideas. His second work, a description of the life, development and mission of the early Church, allowed him freer room for composition than did the gospel, where he was compelled to remain closer to tradition and the available sources. His historical and theological outlook is expressed more freely in the Acts than in the gospel where he was limited to arranging and editing the text. His basic concept of the triumphant march of the gospel "from Jerusalem . . . to the uttermost parts of the earth" (1:8), only apparently hindered by persecutions, with scarcely any preoccupation with internal problems (chapter 15), driven mightily onwards through God's chosen instrument for the conversion of the gentiles, the apostle Paul, is fully elaborated. At its conclusion, the gospel is being preached by the imprisoned apostle in the imperial capital "with all confidence, without prohibition" (28:31). Yet the Acts must not be regarded as an historico-theological composition with many legendary elements. In chapters 1 to 15 it is based upon a manifold tradition and perhaps actual sources too, that merit credence.[1] The discourses in the first part contain a scheme of missionary preaching which comparison with the oldest portions of the Pauline epistles (especially 1 Cor. 15:3–5) and the basic form of the gospels, shows clearly to be the kerygma of

[1] See A. Wikenhauser, *Die Apostelgeschichte und ihr Geschichtswert* (Munster, Westphalia 1921); for the sources of chapters 1 to 15 consult J. Dupont, *Les problèmes du Livre des Actes d'après les travaux récents* (Louvain, 1950), pp. 35–49; E. Trocmé, *Le "Livre des Actes" et l'histoire* (Paris, 1957), pp. 154–214. The critical position represented by E. Haenchen, following the researches of M. Dibelius and underlying his detailed commentary (Göttingen, 1956) is summed up in his article, "Tradition und Komposition in der Apostelgeschichte": *Z.Th.K.* 52 (1955), pp. 205–25.

the apostles.[2] We can use Peter's discourses and that of Paul at Antioch (13:16–41) to discover the kernel of early Church teaching.

Linguistic examination reveals that the centre of gravity has shifted from God's reign to the gospel of Jesus, the Messias and Lord. Only once is the *basileia* made the object of εὐαγγελίζεσθαι (8:12); the person of Jesus occurs more frequently (5:42; 8:35; 11:20; 17:18) or other closely related expressions: the word (8:4), the word of the Lord (15:35), peace through Jesus Christ (10:36), the promise fulfilled in Jesus (13:32 seq.). The same is true of the parallel and related word κηρύσσειν (on two occasions with βασιλεία, namely 20:25; 28:31; otherwise with different phrases 8:5; 9:20; 10:42; 19:13). Frequently God's reign is proclaimed in conjunction with Jesus Christ. Philip preaches God's reign and the name of Jesus Christ (8:12); Paul witnesses to God's reign and tries to convince the Jews at Rome that Jesus is the promised Messias (28:23; see 31).[3] It is even more significant that the reign of God is no longer mentioned in the missionary discourses. In the whole of the Acts it is introduced only seven times[4] as against thirty-nine times in Luke's gospel.[5] On the other hand, the theme of Christ, that is the gospel of Jesus' redeeming ministry from his baptism, and of his crucifixion and Resurrection, is the central motif of these discourses.[6]

On examination, the *basileia* references seem to have lost something of their vigour. They have become general in character, they offer no detailed explanation of this *basileia* of God and in consequence many exegetes apply them to the Church rather

[2] J. Gewieß, *Heilsverkündigung;* C. H. Dodd, *Apostolic Preaching.*

[3] There is an interesting reading for 20:25: "kingdom of Jesus" or "of the Lord Jesus": D gig Lucif sa.

[4] 1:3; 8:12; 14:22; 19:8; 20:25; 28:23, 31.

[5] Or even on forty-one occasions if 19:12, 15 are also included.

[6] 2:22–36; 3:13–16; 4:10–12; 5:30–32; 10:36–43; 13:26–39.

than to the eschatological reign of God.[7] Yet the first of these references does not justify this new interpretation.[8] In 1:3, the Risen Christ instructs his disciples about "what concerns the reign (kingdom) of God" τὰ περὶ τῆς βασιλείας τοῦ θεοῦ; the author is establishing the connection between his gospel and his second work. When the disciples ask (1:6) whether the Lord will now re-establish the kingdom for Israel, there is a clear parallel with Luke 19:11 seq. In both instances the disciples are looking for the prompt appearance of the kingdom of God in the sense of the Jewish national eschatology, though not necessarily in a political form.[9] In the gospel Jesus indicates in the parable of the *minae* that he must first depart and win his dominion (19:12–15), at least as the evangelist understands it. Possibly the Risen Christ is also suggesting that he will return only after a considerable period to bring the perfect kingdom (Acts 1:11). The disciples are not to know the times and hours which the Father in his power has fixed; they are to receive the power of the Holy Spirit when he descends upon them, to be witnesses to Jesus and to carry out their missionary tasks (1:7 seq.).

It is no accident that the gospel of the *basileia* is again mentioned at the close of the book (28:23, 31). Luke's intention is to

[7] J. Knabenbauer, *Comm. in Actus Apostolorum* (Paris, 1899); E. Jacquier, *Les Actes des Apôtres* (Paris, 1926); J. Renié, *Les Actes des Apôtres* (Paris 1951); see also A. Steinmann, *Die Apostelgeschichte* (Bonn, [4]1934), and other Catholic commentators on the passages. On the Protestant side see K. Lake-J. Cadbury, *The Beginnings of Christianity,* Part I, Vol. IV (London, 1933), on 1:3 and elsewhere. The expression was employed for the Church in the Acts but its eschatological meaning was never excluded.
[8] See A. Wikenhauser, "Die Belehrung der Apostel durch den Auferstandenen" in *Vom Wort des Lebens,* Festschrift für M. Meinertz (Munster, Westphalia 1951), pp. 105–13. He refutes the view that this was the clear opinion of the Fathers.
[9] J. Gewieß, op. cit., pp. 101–06.

hold fast to the central theme of Jesus' teaching and to give no other kerygmatic character to his second work, but in point of fact Jesus is the main subject of discourse and proclamation. The general characterization of the apostolic preaching as an announcement of God's reign (see 8:12; 19:8; 20:25) sounds more like a convenient label or formula. The passage in which Paul, speaking to the presbyters at Miletus, declares he has moved among them as a herald of the kingdom (διῆλθον κηρύσσων τὴν βασιλείαν) (20:25) recalls the description of Jesus' ministry in Luke 8:1 (peculiar to Luke): "He travelled (διώδευεν) through the cities and towns, preaching and evangelizing the kingdom (reign) of God; and the twelve with him." This is what Paul was doing. In 14:21 the kingdom of God appears as an object of hope, and indeed under the most familiar image of the gospels: "Through many tribulations we must enter into the kingdom of God." All these passages contain the same notion as Luke's gospel, that of the eschatological reign of God, but it has lost some of the freshness and originality it had in Jesus' teaching. It does not disappear from the apostolic preaching, even from that of Paul[10] but it is no longer the central theme. This is now Jesus, in whom the scriptures are fulfilled (18:28; 28:23; see Luke 24:26), the crucified Messias resurrected by God and assumed into heavenly glory, the Lord.

In portraying Jesus as exalted after his Resurrection to the right hand of God (in accordance with Ps. 110 [109]:1) and thus established in dominion (see 2:33–35; 5:31; also 13:33, following Ps. 2:7) Luke is using a very early, perhaps the earliest Jewish Christian Christology. The phrasing of 2:36 reveals a Jewish conception of the Messias: "Therefore, let all the

[10] The Lucan expression πείθειν, employed for missionary preaching (13:43; 17:4; 18:4; 19:26; 26:28; 28:23 seq.) should be noted, therefore, in 19:8.

house of Israel know most certainly that God hath made both Lord and Christ, this same Jesus whom you have crucified." The Jewish mind thought of the Messias as the mighty representative and vicegerent of God (see *Ps. Sol.* 17; also *T. Jud.* 24:5 seq.; *T. Lev.* 18:9; *Eth. Hen.* 45:3; 46:4 seq.; 51:3; 55:4 etc). In such a perspective Jesus became Messias in the full sense only after he had been established in divine power. This ancient "Elevation Christology" does not deny the Messianic character of Jesus on earth but sees its fulfilment in his status as Lord.[11] This status as ruler is taken seriously: "now in fact rule is assigned to him."[12] The Jewish mind takes it for granted that the Messias exercises sovereign rule over his people.[13] This is illustrated in the Acts when the apostles work wonders " in the name of Jesus Christ" (2:43; 3:6, cf. 13; 4:10, 30; 5:12; 6:8; 9:34; 16:18) but bear fearless witness to Jesus, and the Lord appears on their behalf (see 4:29; 5:41 seq.; 7:55 seq.) and through his Spirit directs his community on earth (5:9) and their mission (16:7). The Spirit, God's great eschatological gift, does appear as an independent reality but is still the Spirit of Jesus. Luke 24:49 makes it clear that it is Jesus who sends the "promise of the Father" to his disciples and all those who believe in Jesus receive the same Spirit in baptism (Acts 2:38). "Even if Paul had a more profound and broader concept of the relation of the Spirit of the Risen Christ with that of Christians, he is in complete agreement with the apostolic belief that the Spirit of God indwelling within the faithful was intimately linked with Jesus, the Messias, as he walked upon earth and now reigns as Kurios, Lord."[14]

[11] E. Schweitzer, *Erniedrigung und Erhöhung,* pp. 60–74; 88; O. Cullmann, *Christologie,* pp. 222 seq.
[12] O. Cullmann, op. cit., p. 223. [13] E. Schweitzer, op. cit., p. 96.
[14] J. Gewieß, op. cit., p. 91.

This belief that Jesus as the exalted Lord exercises a real rule, concealed for the time being in heaven but effectively guiding and protecting his community on earth is a most important development in the history of revelation that we shall trace in the other early Christian testimonies in the New Testament, especially in Paul. From Luke's two works we discover that in the gospel he brings out the present rule of Christ as forcibly as circumstances permit. Jesus' entry into Jerusalem is not only the approach to the place where the prophets were murdered and where the earthly destiny of the Messias is to be fulfilled (Luke 13:32–3); it is also a triumphant entry leading him to the glory of God. At the beginning of the so-called "journey narrative" (9:51) occurs the mysterious expression "assumption" (ἀνάλημψις) which in the light of Acts 1:11 (ἀναλημφθείς) signifies his assumption by God into heaven. Jesus' sorrowful words over the Jerusalem that had slain the prophets and the announcement of the punishment of God's ancient city are followed by a vision of his return in glory (13:35; see Matt. 23:39)[15] and Luke's Parousia discourse adds the further note that prior to this "the times of the nations shall be fulfilled" (21:34). Luke's version of Jesus' reply to the high priest is particularly striking (22:69; see above section 14). In contrast to Mark-Matthew it omits the reference to the Parousia and stresses the enthronement soon to take place (ἀπὸ τοῦ νῦν) of the Son of man at the right hand of God. Finally, the instruction given by the Risen Christ to the two Emmaus disciples assumes that after his Passion and death, foretold by the prophets and decreed by God, Jesus will have entered into divine glory (24:26).

The important turning point is brought out clearly. For the

[15] T. W. Manson, *Sayings of Jesus,* pp. 127 seq. rightly compares Zach. 14:2 with 5 and 9.

post-Easter community God's reign is operative in a new way, namely in the rule of Christ who has been raised on high. God's perfect reign remains a reality of the future but it is being realized here and now in Christ's rule. Prior to the Resurrection and Ascension nothing could be said about this sovereignty since Jesus remained the hidden Messias, not yet invested with power. Consequently, this elevation represents an actual "increase in power" (J. Gewieß) for Jesus. Historically, it denotes a new phase in God's salvific action. In the reign of the Messias which has already begun, the graces necessary for salvation are there and are bestowed upon believers, namely forgiveness of sins and the Holy Spirit; they are communicated through the one Saviour, Jesus Christ (Acts 4:12; 5:31; 10:43; 13:38 seq.; 15:11). Seen from the gospel account, this is now already an era of fulfilment. Salvation, incarnated in the Saviour (Luke 1:69, 71, 77; 2:11, 30; 3:6) is given to everyone who believes and receives baptism (compare Acts 2:38). The Holy Spirit, present personally and operative in Jesus since his baptism (Acts 10:38) is poured out upon all the faithful.

The blessings of this reign of Christ are before Luke's eyes from the beginning of his two books; an arch links the account of the infancy (Luke 1–2), which derives from its special sources, with the history of the apostles. Besides the passages already mentioned in which "salvation" and "saviour" occur, the words of the angel in Luke 1:33 call for particular attention. The reign of Jesus here appears as that of the promised scion of David (v. 32) and is to be imperishable. Early Christian theology adopted this Christology of the Son of David, as is shown by texts from varying sources.[16] David's Messianic kingdom is, of course,

[16] Acts 2:30 seq., 34 seq.; 13:22 seq.; 15:15–18; Rom. 1:3; 2 Tim. 2:8; Apoc. 3:7; 5:5; 22:16.

introduced in a sense unfamiliar to the Jews but for this early Christian thought it is realized with power in the Resurrection and exaltation of Jesus. How strongly the early Church was affected by this idea of David and his Messianic descendant can be noted particularly in Peter's Pentecost discourse, in which this Christology is drawn out in detail (Acts 2:25–26). The Risen Jesus is raised to God's right hand and mounts the throne of David; this he will possess for ever, as the angel had proclaimed. The same sequence of ideas occurs in Acts 13:22 seq. and 34 seq., where we also find the term characteristic of Luke, "Saviour" (σωτήρ 13:23), which he employs to bring home the Jewish notion of the Messias to his gentile Christian readers.

But does this early Christology of the Son of David have a foundation in the teaching of Jesus? The question is hotly disputed. Jesus' reserve about this Messianic title most familiar to the Jews is well known. Yet he did not repudiate it when the blind Bartimaeus so addressed him (Mark 10:47 seq.) and at his entry into Jerusalem similar acclamations seem to have been shouted (Mark 11:10; Matt. 21:9 – Matthew extends the use of the title, see also 9:27; 12:23; 15:22; 21:15). The question depends upon the interpretation of the small pericope about the Son of David (Mark 12:35–37), whether it is to be accepted as genuine or as a later formula from the Christian community. Besides other scholars[17] who have defended the tradition as trustworthy, D. Daube appears to have thrown fresh light on the exceptional sequence of ideas. He considers that the query put by Jesus concerns a so-called *Haggada* question designed to

[17] R. Otto, *Reich Gottes*, pp. 193 seq.; E. Lohmeyer, *Ev. des Markus*, on passage, p. 263; E. Lohmeyer, *Gottesknecht und Davidssohn* (Göttingen, [2]1953), pp. 75–84; V. Taylor, *Gospel acc. to St. Mark*, p. 493.

harmonize an apparent contradiction in scripture.[18] The objection may be raised that Jesus does not introduce two such apparently contradictory passages. But we may retort that this Messianic sonship of David was referred to in many scriptural passages and that Jesus selects the one instance in which the relation of David to the Messias is treated differently. In any case we can defend its original use by Jesus under the heading of "Messianic mystery" since Jesus provided other instances of his personal use of scripture (see Mark 10:6–9 par.; 12:26 par.) in meanings that were unfamiliar or inconvenient to the official teachers.[19]

Did Luke consider that Christ's reign is actualized in the Church? Materially, his account of Christ's elevation and the working of the Holy Spirit points to this, as may be illustrated from Acts 9:31: "Now the Church had peace throughout all Judaea and Galilee and Samaria; and was edified, walking in the fear of the Lord, and was filled with the consolation of the Holy Ghost." But Luke does not speak formally of the reign of Christ nor does he consider the Church under this concept, all the more so because the term ἐκκλησία in the Acts usually refers to local communities. The idea of Church is differently formulated and is most clearly expressed in 20:28, where the Holy Spirit is said to have appointed leaders of communities to be "overseers" (ἐπισκόπους) to "rule the Church of God which he hath purchased with his own blood" or "the blood of his own, i. e. Son"?[20] Christ appears exclusively as the saving mediator for the Church, not yet as head of the Church.

[18] *The New Testament and Rabbinic Judaism* (London, 1956), p. 160; J. Jeremias, *Jesu Verheißung,* p. 45.

[19] J. Jeremias, see note 18 above; V. Taylor on text; O. Cullmann, *Christologie,* pp. 132–4.

[20] R. Schnackenburg, "Episkopos und Hirtenamt" in *Episcopus,* Festschrift für Kardinal von Faulhaber (Regensburg, 1949), pp. 66–8.

In Luke 22:30 we find a general reference to Christ's eschatological reign, that begins with his elevation but becomes manifest only with his Parousia. And in his parting instructions he gives the apostles a share in this eschatological function of ruling (see above sections 14 and 19). As regards the plea of the penitent thief, if the reading "when thou shalt come into thy kingdom" (εἰς τὴν βασιλείαν σου) is the original one, the evangelist must have been thinking of the heavenly realm of Christ: but the correct reading is probably "when thou shalt come with thy royal power" (that is, as king) (ἐν τῇ βασιλείᾳ σου) and the former reading is the interpretation of early copyists.[21] On the other hand, we saw (above section 14) that Matthew in two places (13:41; 16:28) refers to the "kingdom of the Son of man" and has in mind, at least in 13:41, the Church. To some extent, as is evident from 21:43, he has placed God's reign in the concrete setting of history (see section 18). We find ourselves, therefore, in a transitional period, in which the idea that Christ exercises his rule in and through his community on earth and thus in a certain measure actualizes God's reign is beginning to assert itself. Luke in his two works prepared the way for this idea but did not himself pursue it.

To that extent H. Conzelmann is correct in denying that Luke "historicized" the idea of the kingdom of God;[22] but compare his purely eschatological interpretation of Luke's *basileia* concept as a result of the delay in the Parousia with section 12 above. The Catholic exegete, D. M. Stanley, on the other hand over-simplifies.[23] In his view, both Luke and the

[21] The first reading (εἰς . . .) is found in BL c e f ff² I vg Or (lat) Hil.; the second (ἐν . . .) in S A C Θ K and the majority of MSS. In favour of the second rather than the first reading are M. J. Lagrange, on text; J. Jeremias in *Th.W.B.* V. 768, note 47. [22] *Mitte der Zeit,* pp. 96–102.
[23] "Kingdom to Church": *Th.St.* 16 (1955), pp. 1–29.

Greek Matthew text maintained that God's reign is realized in the Church, Luke through the design of his two works, the first evangelist through the whole cast of his gospel (or his handling of his material). The Acts describe the extension of God's reign by the apostolic witness under the direction of the Holy Spirit,[24] but as we have already noted, Luke does not employ the concept of βασιλεία τοῦ θεοῦ in this sense. The Greek Matthew text, according to Stanley, reveals a profound view of the realization of God's reign in the Church. The five great discourses are influenced by this idea and draw a parallel between the experience of the apostolic age and that of Jesus' life on earth. The organization of the Church is an integral part of the advent of God's reign.[25] This view is sound in many ways but it is still not entirely correct since even in Matthew's gospel the majority of the texts indicate and hold fast to the eschatological kingdom. It is perhaps more likely that in reporting the sayings of Jesus, Matthew, where possible, introduced this theme from his own Christian way of thinking (see section 18). But we must always remember that the first responsibility of the evangelists was to hand on tradition; they were only to a very limited degree interpreters of Jesus' gospel. The American Jesuit boldly establishes this change in the character of Christian preaching ("Kingdom to Church") but he does not examine the foundations and the legitimacy of the early Christian procedure.

[24] Ibid., p. 3.

[25] Ibid., pp. 23 seq. A similar view was held earlier by F. J. F. Jackson and K. Lake in *The Beginnings of Christianity,* part 1, vol. i, (London, 1920, reprint 1942), p. 331.

21. Development in the History of Salvation

Did the early Church remain true to the eschatological gospel of Jesus? Did not a process soon set in which people like to term the "development of early Catholicism" and by which are meant a release from eschatological tension, the division of the history of salvation into periods, the adaptation of Christianity to the world, the toning down of the radical moral demands of Jesus and the setting up of an ecclesiastical organization? We have to examine this objection in the context of the *basileia,* because this less pronounced stress on God's future reign, in favour of fuller self-consciousness on the part of the Church, is regarded as symptomatic. As has been indicated, the change of kerygma is an indisputable fact. The question remains whether this development was a break with and away from the gospel of Jesus or a logical consequence not opposed to his intention. We have to enquire how the early Church accepted and handed on Jesus' statements about the future and the demands which arose from them.

The existentialist interpretation of Jesus' message by R. Bultmann and his school has brought a fresh actuality to this problem. Whereas earlier Protestant theologians thought they could detect the "break" after the apostolic era, it is now put back into the New Testament itself. In H. Conzelmann's studies, Luke appears as a representative of early Catholicism and E. Haenchen pursues the same line of argument in his commentary on the Acts. H. Conzelmann assesses Luke's eschatological position as follows: "Luke is faced with the situation of the Church now that the Parousia is delayed and the history of the Church in the world has begun. It is this he is attempting to deal with in his history."[26] In a subsequent article Conzelmann goes further,

[26] *Mitte der Zeit,* p. 6.

glances from Luke to Mark and argues that even Mark tends to view the history of salvation in stages. "There are indications that he is thinking of different periods, but they are sporadic; there is no deliberate and closed division into past, present and future."[27] The literary composition of the "gospel" rests upon a theological process that presupposes the early Church interpretation of Jesus' teaching.[28]

According to these theologians this interpretation does not do justice to the eschatological position of Jesus. They speak of the "break" existing "between the historical Jesus and the Christian community which is accentuated by his death and the experiences after Easter" and they challenge "the possibility of drawing a continuous line between the consciousness of Jesus and the faith of the Christian community".[29] The sharpest point in the controversy is how the gospel of the historical Jesus is to be understood, and particularly whether and in what sense the passages about the Son of man should be attributed to him (see above, section 14). On this point, the matter we are here considering does not touch the problems raised by those theologians. If, however, it is shown that the eschatological outlook of the early Church was basically uniform, we must ask in all seriousness whether the Church was deceiving itself in thinking that its eschatological hope was part of Jesus' gospel or whether, as is far more likely, the new interpretation of the historical Jesus is not a gross error?

The Parousia is rarely mentioned in the Acts. The scanty references (3:20 seq.; 10:42; 17:31) could be looked upon as Luke's development of the apostolic kerygma in the service of his historical theology. But we must remember the purpose of

[27] *Z.Th.K.* 54 (1957), p. 292. [28] Ibid., p. 293.
[29] Ibid., pp. 279 seq.

the first Christian preaching, in order to realize there was no need to talk about the Parousia. The early Church was concerned with proving that Jesus, the scion of David, was the Messias, prophesied in the scriptures. This argument achieved its purpose when it demonstrated that the crucified Jesus had been justified and enthroned in power by God. His Parousia was not a part of the argument but a consequence of belief in this elevated Messias. What most struck the Jewish ear in the early Christian portrayal of the Messias was the statement that the Messias "must suffer and so enter into his glory" (Luke 24:26). This and this alone had to be brought home to the Jews as a divine decree of salvation, till then concealed. The Parousia of the elevated Messias, his "coming in power and glory" was only the proper fulfilment of his Messianic office. Paul's preaching, with its orientation towards the Parousia – it is taken for granted and cannot be removed from his teaching – is the best proof of this. It shows how a Jew, once he believed in the crucified and resurrected Messias, now with God, had to follow this reality of faith and salvation to its ultimate consequences. When it became clear that the Messias proclaimed by the Christian community did not fit into the usual Jewish framework of the Davidic Messias but could be understood only as the Son of man, dwelling invisibly with God (the actual title is not important), men were practically compelled to expect his return in the future.[30] The Parousia expectation cannot therefore be regarded as a later stage of early Christian Christology; it belongs to the portrait of the Christian Messias as it was presented from the beginning.

[30] See Volz, *Eschatologie,* pp. 201–03; 204–06; Sjöberg, *Der verborgene Menschensohn,* pp. 44–54; Mowinckel, *He that Cometh,* pp. 358–61; 388–93.

T. F. Glasson and J. A. T. Robinson deny that Jesus expected a future with dramatic final happenings of an apocalyptic kind and consider that his vision extended only as far as his justification by God and his heavenly enthronement.[31] They must therefore offer some explanation for this early Christian belief in the Parousia and they appeal to the influence of Old Testament passages (that originally referred to the manifestation of God and were transferred to Jesus), the penetration of apocalyptic notions from the Judaism of the time and the development of Christology. But this process must have taken place between A.D. 30 and 50 (see Thessalonians). This sets a severe time limitation, since Paul proclaimed his doctrine from the start (1 Thess. 4:15, with its reference to a saying of Jesus), and the ancient invocation *maranatha* (1 Cor. 16:22) takes us back to the Aramaic-speaking Church of Palestine. Any gradual growth of belief in the Parousia in the early Church is thus unintelligible. The "break" between Jesus and his community would have to be placed immediately after Easter, when the disciples "became convinced through the apparitions of their Risen Master after the crucifixion that he still lived and was elevated to the glory of God".[32] It is an interesting point that these English theologians do not deny that Jesus envisaged his "vindication" by God and his elevation to heaven.

Other sources besides Luke testify that the early Church was convinced that the process of salvation, even though it had now entered upon its final ("eschatological") phase, continues. Mark's version of Jesus' discourse about the last things (Mark 13) does indicate a possible near term for the Parousia but it also

[31] T. F. Glasson, *Second Advent,* pp. 151 seq.; J. A. T. Robinson, *Jesus and His Coming,* pp. 83 seq.; 118 seq.

[32] Ph. Vielhauer, op. cit., p. 79; this is expressed differently by H. Conzelmann in *Z.Th.K.* 1957, pp. 282 seq.

leaves open the possibility of a more distant date; and it particularly paves the way for a mission to the gentiles, involving time (v. 10). However this great discourse be considered, in its present form it is a proof that Mark and the tradition he was using took for granted different intervals of time, to follow one after the other: verse 7, not yet the end; verse 8, beginning of afflictions; verse 19, the great distress; verse 24, subsequent events leading to the Parousia. Luke may have deliberately lengthened the interval (21:8, 24, conclusion), given prominence to the persecutions that would occur in it (v. 12, beginning), recommended more strongly the quality of patience (21:19; compare 8:15) and stressed the exhortation by a warning against worldly living and the counsel to persevere in prayer (vv. 34–36). But the basic characteristics of the interval are already present in Mark. Mark's version indicates at least that the historical process of salvation may be more prolonged. He left a door open, through which Luke, in his own situation and with his own outlook, then passed.

Matthew also, it is evident, divides the history of salvation into stages. This is true of the period before Christ, since he discovers in the parables of the wicked vine-dressers (21:33–41) and the royal wedding feast (22:1–10) a brief historical account of the obdurate people of Israel who greeted the prophets repeatedly sent them (note plural used for the messengers) with disdain and persecution.[33] Both parables indicate in Matthew's own manner that the first evangelist regards the history of salvation as still unfolding in the New Testament era, with his glance at the mission to the gentiles (see above section 18). Does he differ here fundamentally from Luke who leaves an indefinite interval free for the "proclamation of God's reign"?

[33] See J. Jeremias, *Gleichnisse Jesu,* pp. 57 and 60; J. Schmid, on passage.

We ought not appeal to the great concluding scene in Matthew's gospel to see in the heavenly enthronement of the Risen Christ the culmination of Christ's history, behind which there lay originally no further peak, in the Parousia.[34] If Matt. 28:18–20 was composed according to the threefold design of heavenly assumption of power, proclamation of sovereignty and promise of protection for his messengers,[35] the eschatological note ("to the consummation of the world") which in other passages Matthew associates with Parousia and Judgment (13:39, 40, 49; 24:3) cannot be eliminated.

The "proclamation" to the peoples presupposes the period of the gathering together of God's eschatological people. Christ's emissaries are "to go out" and make the peoples "disciples", that is, bring them into the saving discipleship of Jesus by means of baptism (v. 19b) and its obligation to follow Christ (v. 20a). It is a period of wandering, beneath the protection and help of the *Kurios,* now enthroned in power, and one day it will reach its goal and end. "The words that began with the existence of the end, become merged in the vision of the coming end of this world era."[36] The epoch of the Church in sacred history, as it was understood in the early Church, is thus brought out in strong relief. Christ's eschatological reign is established but not yet fulfilled; God's final people are gathering together, saved and equipped for final salvation, yet still summoned to discipleship and trial; the cosmic realization of God's reign is certain though not yet manifest. How long this period is to last

[34] According to J. A. T. Robinson, op. cit., pp. 131 seq., the scene was originally a description of the Parousia, the direct fulfilment of the promise made in Galilee (Matt. 28:7, 10, 16).
[35] O. Michel, "Der Abschluß des Matthäusevangelium" in *Ev.Th.* 10 (1950), pp. 16–26; J. Jeremias, *Jesu Verheißung für die Völker,* pp. 32 seq.
[36] E. Lohmeyer, *Das Ev. des Matthäus,* p. 423.

for God's pilgrim people is a matter now purely in the background.

Paul's historical approach which sees Christ "between the ages" and the Church as proclaiming Christ's gospel to the gentiles "until the fullness of the gentiles should come in" (Rom. 11:25) is so evident that we need adduce no individual passage. We merely recall several characteristic extracts to illustrate the dynamic of this process of sacred history as Paul envisages it and his eschatological position. In Rom. 13:11 our salvation is "now" nearer than before, when we first believed. Even within the era of Christ's reign (see 1 Cor. 15:25), that commenced with Jesus' accession to power (Rom. 1:4) "progress" is registered. The "now" of salvation (2 Cor. 6:2) is neither an uncertain interval nor a provisional completion but a period striving and hastening towards a Parousia and a fulfilment, itself urged on and urgent (see 1 Cor. 7:29–31). While there is little to say about times and terms for the final events, as the day of the Lord comes "like a thief in the night" (1 Thess. 5:1 seq.), nevertheless watchfulness, sobriety and preparedness are necessary to win final salvation (1 Thess. 5:6–9).

This is the missionary era and one senses the yearning of the apostle of the gentiles to bring salvation to those to whom it has not been preached (Rom. 15:16–24). The call to the gentiles, their equal share in salvation, is a mystery of God, decreed from all eternity, which is now, in the age of eschatological fulfilment, to be revealed by the Church, and Paul considers himself to be the chosen servant and preacher of this economy of salvation (see Col. 1:25–27; Eph. 3:1–10). But each community and every individual Christian should remain without blame until the day of Jesus Christ, till his "manifestation" (1 Thess. 3:13; 5:23; 1 Cor. 1:7 seq.; Phil. 1:6, 10). Christians must "redeem", that is, use for their salvation, the time that is always encompassed and threatened by the powers of evil (Eph. 5:16). All this indicates that the present course of the world is determined eschatologically in Paul's eyes, not only in the sense of a new possibility of existence through faith, through existence "in Christ" but also in the historical sense, in so far as God's action is directed towards the final term of redemption and the fulfilment of the world. It is right and proper to bring out the historical challenge in Paul's preaching, its concrete vital claim upon the man to whom it is communicated. But it would be false and dangerous to deny its vision of the whole process of salvation, that runs from creation to the end of the world. Only when these two elements are taken together can the fundamental situation of the Christian in his (present, provisional) condition of salvation be properly described according to the mind of Paul (see Gal. 1:4; Phil. 3:20).

But, it may be asked, did not John abandon this historical dynamism and rediscover the real attitude of Jesus? Does he not show that the whole dramatization of the future and the apocalyptic trimmings are superfluous and that what matters basically is the eschatological decision to which every man is summoned by the kerygma? Or does he not preserve an independent tradition that has retained the earliest Christology and eschatology, in fact the genuine message of Jesus? The Parousia has been realized with the Resurrection of Jesus, not as a final event but as a continual permeation of the day-to-day life of the disciple and the Church, as a Parousia from now on which relates us permanently to God's eschatological coming.[37] This is not the place to examine and give a general assessment of eschatological thought in John's gospel. We select merely a few

[37] J. A. T. Robinson, op. cit., pp. 162–80, especially p. 176.

points of view which show that even here the blend of historical and eschatological thought is not abandoned.

i. John's gospel presupposes that the era of Jesus and that of the Church follow one another and are mutually related and that this relation is essential to their understanding. The saving graces of the Son of man who descended from heaven will not be fully operative, that is, in the sacraments, till his ascent into heaven and the sending of the Holy Spirit (3:5–8; 6:27, 53, 62–63a; 20:22 seq.). The Spirit sent from the Father by the glorified Christ fulfils the promises of Jesus and continues his work (14:16 seq.) in illuminating the revelation of the word (14:26; 16:13 seq.) and as a witness against the unbelieving world that resists God (15:26; 16:8–11) as also in communicating life to the faithful (7:39; 6:63a). As he appears in this gospel, Jesus addresses his hearers in their actual situation but always with the consciousness that he will soon be exalted and glorified. This emerges from the expression, "the hour cometh, and it is now here" (4:23; 5:25) and the general indifference to divisions of time prior to his exaltation (12:23; 13:1; 16:32; 17:1). The Church is never explicitly mentioned but throughout and especially in the farewell discourse, its existence is taken for granted.[38]

ii. The Church's missionary situation is present by implication and can be sensed. Many sayings clearly reflect the subsequent missionary activity, for example 4:38; 10:16; 11:52; 17:18, 20. It might be asked how far an actual interest of the evangelist lies behind the Samaria episode.[39] John, of course, understood that the Christian mission never consists in a mere backward

[38] N. A. Dahl, *Volk Gottes,* p. 172.

[39] O. Cullmann, "Samaria and the Origins of the Christian Mission" in *The Early Church* (London, 1956), pp. 183–92.

glance at salvific acts but always in addition in a forward striving towards eschatological fulfilment.

iii. Because in the Johannine Christology all the graces of salvation are present in Jesus on earth though they are not yet released, and this release of his power after glorification (17:2) has become a reality for hearers and readers of the gospel, the fullest emphasis can be placed on Christ's immediate gifts which rescue the faithful basically and finally from the realm of evil, the dark world of death (5:24; 8:12, 51; 10:28; 11:25 seq.). But this does not exclude the future eschatological fulfilment, the resurrection of the body. John had not moved so far from Semitic thinking that he could allow the bodily share in the divine life of glory to lapse. There is never a hint in his gospel that the Greek doctrine of immortality, the mere survival of the soul, has replaced the Semitic concept of life (see 12:25).[40]

It would be arbitrary to ascribe the texts that speak of resurrection on the Last Day (5:28 seq.; 6:39, 40, 44, 54) to subsequent editing by the Church. John 12:26; 14:3; 17:24 declare that the disciple will follow his risen and transfigured Lord into heavenly glory. Certainly the thought of reunion with Christ and the vision of his glory so predominate that the bodily transformation of the individual seems much less important but

[40] See H. Pribnow, *Die johanneische Anschauung vom "Leben"* (Greifswald 1934), pp. 139–41; F. Mußner, ΖΩΗ. *Die Anschauung vom "Leben" im vierten Evangelium unter Berücksichtigung der Johannesbriefe* (Munich, 1952), pp. 140–9. For the whole question consult: G. Stählin, "Zum Problem der johanneischen Eschatologie": *Z.N.W.* 33 (1934), pp. 225–59; B. Aebert, *Die Eschatologie des Joh.-Ev.* (Dissertation, Breslau) (Würzburg, 1936); E. Gaugler, "Das Christuszeugnis des Joh.-Ev.", in *Jesus Christus im Zeugnis der Hl. Schrift und der Kirche* (Munich, 1936), pp. 34–67, particularly pp. 57 seq.; W. F. Howard, *Christianity according to St. John*, (London, 1943, reprint 1947), pp. 160–28.

the general early Christian conviction is in no wise abandoned and finds expression in these passages.

iv. The same is true of judgment. Judgment, according to 3:8 (see also 5:24) certainly comes about through unbelief. The unbeliever brings it on himself *ipso facto* through his repudiation of the Son of God. Yet this present judgment neither replaces nor displaces future judgment; it only anticipates this in the encounter with Jesus. The sentence, "the Father hath given all judgment to the Son" (5:22) covers both points of view, the eschatological judgment of the future and the present judgment of unbelief. In the background stands the old notion that God hands over the judgment to the Son of man (see 5:27) but since the eschatological judge is already present in Jesus, the Son of God, the issue of salvation is decided in this encounter with him, in belief or unbelief. There is no hint of an original Christology recognizing only the justified and exalted Christ. The ancient Christology of the Son of man is interpreted in a fresh light which still leaves room for the office of the future judge. The general statement in verse 22 is developed logically in two stages: communication of life in the present over against judgment in the present (vv. 24 seq.); then follows the future re-awakening to (full, even bodily-transfigured) life and judgment (of real death) (v. 28 seq.). The curious phrasing used by Jesus that the word he is now pronouncing will emerge on the Last Day to judge unbelievers (12:48) confirms this opinion.

v. Where Jesus is no longer introduced as speaking during his life on earth but the subject is the glorified Christ, namely in John's first epistle, the eschatological note comes out more strongly. Even if we did not have the Parousia passage of 2:28, there is the typically Johannine text of 3:2 that rounds off a thought from the gospel (17:24). The vision of (Christ and)

God receives fulfilment and completion only through resemblance to (Christ and) God. But this is realized in the Biblical sense which is not forsaken in favour of a Hellenistic "transfiguration through vision" but through the bestowal of "doxa", linked with bodily resurrection.[41] The whole misunderstanding of the Johannine eschatology rests upon an unwarranted "spiritualizing" from which John like all early Christianity is far removed. This does not, however, deny that the Johannine theology has transferred its accent from future to present. What the decisive reasons for this were, is another question. What interests us is that John should not be looked upon as an exception who had jettisoned the historical thinking of the early Church or represented the genuine "eschatological" position of Jesus as against other teachers who misunderstood it.

After this account of John who is claimed as an exponent of a "demythlogized" eschatology no further examination of the other New Testament writings is necessary, since they remain to be dealt with in connection with the *basileia* concept (see chapter three). What stands out is that the continuance of the history of salvation was an essential basis for the thought of the first Christians who after Easter and Pentecost had the mission of explaining Jesus' gospel. The "era of the Church" was for all Christian preachers and theologians a necessary continuation, even in a sense a fulfilment (see John) of the era of Jesus. But the "era of the Church" was regarded also as an intervening period prior to complete fulfilment with the Parousia. Yet the Church was a reality on earth that had to attend to its earthly tasks and adapt itself even to the point of external organization. To what extent it may have succumbed to a spirit of worldliness is again

[41] See R. Schnackenburg, *Die Johannesbriefe* (Freiburg im Breisgau, 1953), on this passage.

another question. The only verdict we can pass on Luke and the other early Christian theologians as they developed their eschatological positions, each after his own manner, is that in their eyes it was no "theory" but a matter of faith that with the elevation of Jesus to glory a new epoch in the history of salvation had commenced, the epoch of Christ's reign manifest in heaven though still concealed on earth, but actual and operative, realizing itself in and through the Church, with its goal in God's perfect kingdom of the future.

THE KINGDOM OF GOD AND THE REIGN OF CHRIST IN ST. PAUL

22. Kingdom of God, Reign of Christ and Church

The thought of the apostle Paul is Christocentric. Its centre is in Christ and from there it permeates and captures every part of the Christian gospel. In his eyes the present operation of the *Kurios* Jesus dominates everything. This living Risen Lord has "laid hold of him" and attached him to his company. From now onwards the apostle knows only the one purpose to "lay hold of Christ", to know him and the power of his resurrection and the fellowship of his sufferings" (Phil. 3:10 seq.). Even in the universal vision of the great paean to Christ, Philippians 2:6–11, the pathway of the Son of God leads through self-renunciation and obedience unto death to the throne in heaven at God's right hand. From there, enthroned, proclaimed and empowered by God, he reigns over all the powers of the universe. The strongest possible emphasis, stronger than that of the early apostolic preaching, is placed upon the present exercise of Christ's sovereignty. It is, therefore, all the more remarkable that the perfect kingdom of the future does not disappear from Paul's thinking.

The passages in which Paul speaks of the "kingdom of God"

are infrequent (there are ten formal references to which 1 Cor. 15:24 may be added) but they are illuminating. The chief epistles include on four occasions the expression "inherit the kingdom of God" (1 Cor. 6:9, 10; 15:50; Gal. 5:21). Here there is an unmistakable connection with the "entry statements" of Jesus, whatever opinion may be held about the use that Paul makes of Jesus' sayings.[1] The expression sounds like a stock formula but it is employed deliberately as a serious moral admonition. In this use of "inherit" rather than "enter" Paul may have been influenced by the Septuagint with which he was familiar, where the formula occurs fifty times, especially in Deuteronomy. The notion of inheriting the promised land lies at the origin of the expression used by Jesus (see Matt. 5:5) and Paul would have been aware of and familiar with this theological background since he had also read in Deutero-Isaias of the eschatological "inheriting the land" (Isa. 57:13; 60:21; 61:7; 65:9). Besides, Paul adopted this notion of inheritance in a Christological sense. The followers of Christ are made by Christ sons of Abraham and heirs of the promise (Gal. 3:16, 29; 4:7), but in these texts Paul does not associate this inheritance with the kingdom of God. In general, he looks upon "inheriting the kingdom of God" as a strong ethical motive with which to challenge the vicious (1 Cor. 6:9 seq.; Gal. 5:21). There is one passage in which he employs the phrase in a genuinely eschatological sense, namely that flesh and blood, that is men in their natural existence on earth, cannot inherit the kingdom of God just as corruption (= the dead)cannot inherit incorruption. At the resurrection living and dead must be transmuted into that radiant mode of being that corresponds to the glorious condi-

[1] See C. H. Dodd, Ἔννομος Χριστοῦ in *Studia Paulina,* Festschrift für: J. de Zwaan (Haarlem, 1953), pp. 96–110 (his view goes too far).

tion of the future world.[2] The "kingdom of God" in all these passages is understood exclusively as the eschatological reality of the future, as it was by Jesus.[3]

The influence of Christology with its idea of Christ's present reign becomes apparent in Ephesians 5:5. The context is similar to those of 1 Corinthians 6:9 seq. and Galatians 5:21, namely a warning to the vicious, but the formula now reads, "has no inheritance in the kingdom of Christ and of God". In the first place, the unusual double reference "kingdom of Christ and of God" is striking but so also is the altered form, "have inheritance". This leaves room for and even suggests a transcendent existence of the kingdom in the present. If we bear in mind the general tenor of Ephesians (see 2:6), the sentence can and perhaps must be interpreted as meaning that the kingdom of Christ and of God already exists, even though still concealed in heaven, and that what matters most is not to lose one's rights as citizens and heirs.[4] The kingdom of God is thus brought closer out of its eschatological remoteness. The double reference for the "kingdom" which is not two consecutive stages in the realization of sovereignty but indicates one reality, implies that God's eschato-

[2] J. Jeremias, "Flesh and blood cannot inherit the Kingdom of God" (1 Cor. 15:50); *N.T.St.* 2 (1955–1956), pp. 151–9.

[3] It is, therefore, better to avoid the expression "heavenly inheritance" which L. Cerfaux uses (*Recueil L. C.* [Gembloux, 1954], II, pp. 367 seq.). Cerfaux rightly refers to its Old Testament roots and its eschatological significance but he appears to attach a certain importance to the mystical explanation of Philo. For the contrary view see A. Wikenhauser, *Kirche,* pp. 41 seq.

[4] See H. Schlier, *Brief an die Epheser,* p. 235: "The κληρονομία which the vicious do 'not have' in the kingdom of Christ and of God is the βασιλεία τοῦ Χριστοῦ καὶ Θεοῦ still to be revealed and openly realized in the future, but already anticipated in hope. But as such, it is already there, even though it is hidden, and even now men can 'have an inheritance' in it."

logical reign is already realized in the rule of Christ. God rules through Christ and consequently the kingdom of God may also be termed kingdom of Christ (see also section 23).

Before turning to Colossians and Ephesians, in which we must expect a more advanced theological doctrine, we should like to review other texts from earlier epistles. Two passages from Thessalonians prove that Paul has adopted the eschatological concept of God's kingdom. 1 Thess. 2:12 states that God has called us "into his kingdom and glory", and again this is converted into an ethical motive. The men he is addressing are to "walk worthy of God". The synoptic gospels show us that for the early Church "kingdom of God" (or of Jesus) and "glory" (δόξα) are synonymous terms (compare Mark 10:37 with Matt. 20:21; Mark 8:38 with 9:1). For Paul δόξα is heavenly radiance and eschatological transformation, a grace in which the Christian faithful can partake only in the future world.[5] The beginning and end of God's salvific will are concentrated upon this "being called to the kingdom of God". Similarly, 2 Thess. 1:5 declares that the Thessalonians who have been tested in persecution and distress (v. 4) shall be considered worthy "of the kingdom of God". The kingdom of God as reward, as the generous reward of grace ("be accounted worthy"[6]) and in particular because of patient endurance of persecution for Jesus' sake – this recalls Jesus' own preaching (Matt. 5:10, 11 seq.; Luke 6:22 seq.). "To suffer for the kingdom of God" does not denote human co-operation in achieving the kingdom but an effort to have a share in it; it is the same idea that Paul

[5] See 2 Thess. 2:14; Rom. 8:18, 21; 1 Cor. 15:43; 2 Cor. 3:18; 4:17; Phil. 3:21; Col. 3:4; 2 Tim. 2:10.

[6] See Luke 20:35, "they shall be accounted worthy of that world and of the resurrection from the dead". Except for these two passages καταξιοῦσθαι only occurs in Acts 5:41.

frames Christologically, "we must suffer with him (Christ) that we may be also glorified with him" (Rom. 8:17; see 2 Tim. 2:12).

The phrase in Col. 4:11, "helpers in (towards . . . εἰς) the kingdom of God" must be understood in an eschatological sense. Paul could scarcely have said that his fellow preachers were working at the kingdom of God (this would have demanded the genitive); he means that they are toiling in the service of the coming kingdom by proclaiming it (see Acts 8:12; 19:8; 20:25; 28:23, 31), by making it possible for men to partake of it, and for its sake taking all possible burdens upon themselves.

Associating this text with 2 Cor. 8:23 (εἰς ὑμᾶς συνεργός) we might think of it as a field for activity;[7] but βασιλεία τοῦ Θεοῦ is never used elsewhere for an area, a place available for human activity. A more suitable comparison would be with Luke 9:62, "fit for the kingdom of God", where the manuscripts hesitate between the simple dative ἐν and εἰς. The phrase is an abbreviation for the proclamation of the reign of God. Actually, Col. 4:11 should mean the same as 1 Thess. 3:2, "minister of God in (ἐν) the gospel of Christ".

The profound view of the kingdom of Christ which we discover in Colossians (1:13 – see below) in no way compels us to understand in this sense the kingdom of God, referred to in a series of greetings. This was an old habit of speech, adopted by the missionaries, even by Paul.

On the other hand, two passages from the principal epistles call for another interpretation. 1 Cor. 4:20 informs us that "the reign of God is not in speech but in power". This curt sentence can be understood only in the context in which the

[7] So Bauer, *Wörterbuch*, Sp. 1559.

epistle was composed. Paul is threatening certain "puffed up" members of the community that he will soon come and examine whether this is mere talk or a matter of (divine) power (v. 19). These Corinthian Christians, because of their pneumatic gifts or their "gnosis" (see 1:5; 8:1 seq., 10 seq.; 13:2, 8; 14:6) are claiming that they have already secured the promised share in Christ's reign and already possess the future gifts. The apostle counters them by saying that God's reign manifests itself, where it is genuinely operative, not in speech but in divine power.

The chatter of these "puffed up" individuals (v. 6) is illustrated in the partly ironical (v. 8) and then serious and shaming sentences of the apostle (v. 9). Among other things, they must have said, "we are now full; we have become rich; now we reign without the apostle" (v. 8a). Paul seizes upon this word "reign" (βασιλεύειν) and observes, "I would to God you did reign, that we might also reign with you" (v. 8b). He then insists how it is precisely the apostles, the men most called to reign with Christ, who experience contempt, privations and persecutions(vv. 9–13). Therefore, the time for "reigning" and glory has not yet arrived; it is the era of the way of the cross. Βασιλεία τοῦ Θεοῦ in verse 20 can hardly be referred to the future. The very form excludes this interpretation. All we could do is to supply the copula (cf. Lietzmann on this passage) and ἐν would then signify character and manner.[8] To translate it as meaning that the man who belongs to God's kingdom (of the future) can be recognized by the working of God's power in

[8] See Bauer, *Wörterbuch,* under εἰμί III, 4 (Sp. 446) and under ἐν III, 2 (Sp. 517). In the papyri the conjunction of εἰμί with ἐν and an abstract notion is a common substitute for a verbal construction; E. Mayser, *Grammatik der griechischen Papyri aus der Ptolemäerzeit* II, 1 (Berlin-Leipzig, 1926), p. 224, note 1, and II, 2 (1934), p. 398.

him, would not do the sentence justice.[9] There is no contradiction with verses 8 seq., for there Paul is pursuing another line of argument. Both points of view are tenable. The apostles' experience proves that God's manifest reign and this reigning with Christ are not yet there; yet God's reign is already showing itself in the power of God's spirit (cf. 2:1–5; Paul must have had this in mind in using ἐν δυνάμει).

Accordingly, Paul preserves the polarity in the idea of the *basileia* which we have established in the teaching of Jesus. As a visible kingdom God's eschatological reign is still awaited, yet it already announces its coming in powerful gestures which the apostle, and with him the whole of the early Church, is experiencing, particularly in the operation of the Spirit of God (cf. 2:4).

This opinion is confirmed by another and a very similar passage in Romans 14:17. Warning them to have consideration for the "weaker brethren" in the matter of food and drink, because they wrongly consider many things to be unclean and are persuaded to eat and drink against their conscience, Paul declares that "the kingdom of heaven is not meat and drink; but justice and peace and joy in the Holy Ghost". This particular combination of subject and predicates creates difficulties. Does the apostle merely mean that the man who wishes to attain to God's kingdom must qualify not through meat and drink but through these spiritual qualities?[10] This is highly improbable since "justice, peace and joy in the Holy Ghost" clearly denote fruits of the Spirit (Gal. 5:22) that should be manifest and develop, present graces bestowed on us and marking our

[9] W. G. Kümmel in an addition to H. Lietzmann, *An die Korinther* I–II, (Tübingen, 1949), p. 173.

[10] So W. Michaelis, *Reich Gottes und Geist Gottes,* p. 24; W. G. Kümmel, see above, footnote 9, p. 173.

redeemed condition (see Rom. 5:1 seq.).[11] They are regarded not as conditions for God's future kingdom but as his manifestations in the present.[12] "It is a matter of the revealing of God's reign in the present" (O. Michel). The meaning of the passage is that it is not meat and drink that matter but those spiritual fruits, in which God's reign already shows something of its future radiance.

Paul recognizes also an operation and tangible presence of God's reign here and now, notably, if we have not misunderstood him, in the presence and operation of the Holy Spirit. This should not be termed a "mystical presence" of the properties of God's kingdom, we should not suggest that the "riches of heaven are as it were reproduced in every soul though in a slighter and less intense degree."[13] With regard to that dynamic and pneumatic presence of the rule of God, Paul is thinking rather of the community, where the Holy Spirit operates in every member. For Paul God's reign never becomes a mystical, interior reality; the epistles never speak of this.

Paul's ideas about Christ's reign are new and theologically they mark a distinct advance. The actual expression is infrequent, occurring only in 1 Corinthians 15:24; Colossians 1:13; Ephesians 5:5; 2 Timothy 4:1, 18. The two extracts from the pastoral epistles do not belong strictly to this category. The solemn admonition in 4:1 calls attention to Christ's ruling office that in the end will manifest itself: his office as judge of living and

[11] M. J. Lagrange, *Épître aux Romains* (Paris, 1931) (= 1950); O. Michel, *Der Brief an die Römer* (Göttingen, 1955).
[12] The proximity of Gal. 5:21 and 22 should not lead to false conclusions. The motive of "inheriting the kingdom of God" is addressed only to the vicious. The Spirit and his fruits are gifts that have been already given.
[13] L. Cerfaux in *Recueil* II, pp. 378 seq.

dead, his "manifestation" (ἐπιφάνεια) and his "kingdom". His royal power will be manifested at the Parousia (note the term "epiphany"), his reign will be perfect and will endure. This eschatological "kingdom" of Christ is not distinguished here from the kingdom of God. The whole passage envisages the union of God and Christ (ἐνώπιον τοῦ Θεοῦ καὶ Χριστοῦ), the exercise of divine power by Christ (as judge), the glorification of God through Christ. This is the normal outlook and way of speaking of the early Christians; these are "formulae from an ancient Christian creed" (J. Freundorfer). The second extract will be considered later (section 24 below).

We are concerned here with the Pauline concept of Christ's rule in the present. For this, two passages, 1 Corinthians 15:24 and Colossians 1:13 are both important and sufficient; 1 Corinthians 15:24 because it presents in compact and sharply outlined form Paul's whole concept of the process of salvation and the reign of Christ and God, and Colossians 1:13 because it provides a bridge to the ideas of Colossians and Ephesians with their strongly marked orientation towards heaven.

1 Corinthians 15:24–28 treats of the final handing back of Christ's dominion to the Father "when he shall have brought to nought all principality (ἀρχή) and power and virtue" (v. 24c). The difficulty of the passage is recognized; it is best taken as a short eschatological fragment within the framework of the chapter on the resurrection; there is a certain parallel in 15:54 seq.

There are two conflicting explanations of the whole picture. Some authors[14] take verses 23 and 24 together and hold that

[14] Among commentators J. Weiß. A. Loisy, H. Lietzmann, A. Schlatter, H. D. Wendland; further A. Schweitzer, *Die Mystik des Apostels Paulus* (Tübingen, 1930), pp. 67 seq.; 94 seq. 304; W. Michaelis *Versöhnung des Alls,* p. 83; M. Rissi, *Zeit und Geschichte,* pp. 162–5; H. Bietenhard, *Das*

three separate divisions (τάγματα) are being described: Christ as firstborn, then Christ's followers at the Parousia, and finally the remainder (τὸ τέλος) or the rest of mankind when Christ surrenders his royal power.[15] Others[16] start a fresh sentence with verse 24 and admit only one resurrection; nothing is said about the resurrection of non-Christians. The second explanation is preferable. For details readers are referred to the relevant literature.[17]

A few points need to be made for a general understanding of the passage: i. ἕκαστος in verse 23 does not take up πάντες of verse 22 unconditionally nor does it divide it into three groups; for in that case Christ once risen would not again be mentioned. Verse 23 must clarify preferably the relation between Christ, the first fruits of the dead, and his followers. Christ must first be reawakened, then those associated with him can follow at the

tausendjährige Reich, ²1955, pp. 56 seq. These scholars admit to some extent that τὸ τέλος cannot directly mean "the rest" (see following footnote) and they translate it by "the end" or "finally" but they still consider this to contain a silent reference to the resurrection of the remainder of mankind. On the problem of the resurrection of Christians and non-Christians see H. Molitor, *Die Auferstehung der Christen und Nichtchristen nach dem Apostel Paulus* (Munster in Westphalia, 1933) particularly pp. 34–53.

[15] J. Héring has attempted to demonstrate in *R.H.Ph. R.* 12 (1933), pp. 300–20 that τὸ τέλος cannot denote "the remainder". In his *Wörterbuch* (Sp. 1607, 2) W. Bauer thinks that this meaning is possible but he does not recommend it for 1 Cor. 15:24.

[16] So all Catholic commentators and also J. Moffatt, J. Héring (see previous footnote and also *Royaume de Dieu,* pp. 175 seq. and in commentary [Neuchâtel-Paris, 1949]); W. G. Kümmel (in appendix to Lietzmann's commentary).

[17] See particularly the excursus in E. B. Allo, *Première Épître aux Corinthiens* (Paris, 1956), pp. 438–54; F. Guntermann, *Eschatologie* pp. 314–7; H. Molitor, op. cit., pp. 44–53.

Parousia. The resurrection guaranteed to Christ's followers in Christ has its definite place, namely at the Parousia. ii. The destiny of non-Christians is not considered by the apostle throughout the chapter, and it would be astonishing if it were dismissed with a mere allusion without more detailed examination. Even in verses 50–55, at the peak point of Paul's discussion, he is dealing with Christians who were dead and reawaken, and with living Christians. iii. Verses 54 seq. are particularly significant for it is in the reawakening of Christians that Paul beholds the victory over the power of death. This triumph is portrayed in such absolute terms that he is clearly thinking of the ultimate victory (v. 54 κατεπόθη ὁ θάνατος). This must be the same event described in verse 26, "and the enemy death shall be destroyed last".[18] Paul could scarcely have remained silent about a further "general reawakening", at which the complete annihilation of the power of death would take place. For Paul the reawakening of Christians is the fulfilment of verses 54 seq. The coincidence of Christ's victory with the resurrection of Christians is of particular importance for the interpretation that now follows.

The statement that Christ will reign and, by God's will, must reign (v. 25) does not lay down a fixed temporal starting point. But this must certainly be taken as Christ's Resurrection and elevation. Only in the hypothesis of a first and second resurrection could a final "interval kingdom" be envisaged, beginning with the Parousia and concluding with the surrender of power to the Father; but this does not emerge directly from the

[18] It is true that καταργεῖν can denote "disarm" but in this eschatological context it must certainly be understood as "annihilate" or "overcome", see Bauer, *Wörterbuch* Sp. 825, 2; G. Delling in *Th.W.B.* I, 454, pp. 22–5. One can hardly suggest a further stage since death disappears completely (in answer to W. Michaelis, *Versöhnung des Alls,* p. 117).

passage. There is no need for such an explanation if, as we believe, there is question only of one resurrection, that of Christians. A firm argument that in Paul's view Christ exercises his sovereignty immediately after his ascent to heaven is the use of Psalm 109:1 in verse 25.[19] This psalm was employed in early Christian theology to prove the ruling status of the Risen Christ (Acts 2:34) and it provides an important foundation for the theology of Colossians and Ephesians (Eph. 1:20; Col. 3:1). Is not this a uniform line into which our present passage can be fitted? The association of Psalm 109:1 with Psalm 8:7 as we discover it in 1 Corinthians 15:25, 27 reappears in Ephesians 1:20, 22. The thought that Christ is enthroned as Lord and Ruler in heaven is the supreme peak of the hymn to Christ in Phil. 2:6–11. Every knee, of those in heaven, on earth and under the earth must bow before him and acknowledge his sovereignty.

The epistles of the captivity are not the first to speak of the subjection of these spiritual forces and powers. 1 Corinthians 2:8 also alludes to their overthrow. If the princes of this aeon who are reduced to nothing (2:6) had known the hidden wisdom of God, they would never have crucified the "Lord of glory". An understanding of Paul's preaching of the cross and resurrection leaves us in no doubt that in his eyes the crucified became at the Resurrection the "Lord of glory". He secured this divine predicate when he was elevated to the right hand of God, and in Christ enthroned in power the "princes of this world" have to acknowledge their folly and the sign of their annihilation. Accordingly, Christ once enthroned in heaven reigns over the

[19] Among the alterations in the phrasing of the psalm, made by Paul (in comparison with the Septuagint) we notice particularly the addition of πάντας; this was important for Paul's argument.

powers hostile to God, and he must continue to reign till God has laid all enemies at his feet.[20] Although normally the power of death does not belong to the ranks of these spiritual powers, the apostle associates them in this context; it will be annihilated as the "last enemy" (v. 26; the same expression as in verse 24). It sustains its complete defeat when Christ's associates attain to bodily resurrection (vv. 54 seq., 57); it loses all its power, when the Christians "reign in life" (Rom. 5:17). The connection is so clear throughout Paul's thought (see also Rom. 8:11; 2 Cor. 5:4) that the annihilation of the power of death is not an act distinct from the resurrection of the dead.

On this ground O. Cullmann's hypothesis is to be rejected, that the final struggle against the forces and powers will be triumphantly won only after the Parousia and that the Son will not surrender royal power to the Father till he has gained it. According to Cullmann this portion of the Regnum Christi that has existed since the resurrection projects into the future aeon and is the "realm of a thousand years" of the Apocalypse.[21] He thus establishes a harmony between 1 Corinthians 15:24 seq. and Apocalypse 20:4 but he misunderstands the meaning of the passage from Corinthians. Literally, the text could suggest that the annihilation of the power of death (v. 26) followed the resurrection (v. 23). But if the line of thought changes in verse 24 and εἶτα does not continue the ἔπειτα of verse 23,[22] these two acts can in fact refer to the one event. Nor does 1 Thessalonians 4:14–17 suggest that the Parousia, at which the dead rise again

[20] For the reference of the subject to God in both passages in the Psalms see F. W. Maier, "Ps. 110: 1 and its connection with 1 Cor. 15:24–26" in *B.Z.* 20 (1932), pp. 139–56.

[21] *Königsherrschaft Christi,* pp. 14 seq.

[22] Εἶτα can also indicate a logical step, see H. G. Liddell - R. Scott, *Greek-English Lexicon* (9th edit., Oxford, 1940 [1948]), 1, 498.

and the living meet the Lord, will be followed by any struggle with the powers hostile to God. 1 Corinthians 15:52 is related to this earlier passage (compare the setting, the trumpet, the resurrection of the dead, the transformation of the living) and there follows at once the paean of triumph over the conquered power of death (vv. 54 seq.). To be sure, it is not unambiguously clear that this power of death is irrevocably annihilated, but this supposition is more probable than the other which repeats in a concluding act "in concentrated and final form" what has already happened[23] (see also section 25).

In this passage Paul is merely stating in a more clear-cut and decided manner what is contained in the rest of his Christological statements, that Christ as the exalted Kurios exercises a genuine rule, makes subject the evil powers of the cosmos till, when he annihilates the "last" and most characteristic power of evil, namely death, his victory will be manifest to the whole world. His salvific action through history will be then fulfilled. Then he will have completely overcome the evil brought into the world by Adam (Rom. 5:12) and have given the superabundant fullness of the future aeon to those who adhere to him. This is the significance of the "surrender of royal power" to the Father. Christ brings to his Father a mankind wholly redeemed and a universe restored to its due order. The new world is inaugurated surpassing the old creation, in which God is "all in all" – an expression of plenitude that in fact signifies the perfect reign of God. There exists no contradiction, not even a conscious distinction, between a "kingdom of Christ" and a "kingdom of God": βασιλεία here indicates the function of ruling, and precisely in its salvific relation to the period between the Resurrection and the Parousia, with all the eschatological acts that

[23] Cullmann, op. cit., p. 14.

belong to it, and cannot be separated or temporally differentiated from it. From another point of view this rule of Christ here and now can be termed God's rule (cf. 1 Cor. 4:20. Rom. 14:17), in so far as God exercises his government through Christ, and God's future kingdom can also be called the kingdom of Christ (2 Tim. 4:1), since Christ is not displaced as heavenly ruler or joint ruler (σύνθρονος). He will no longer officiate as Saviour, for the era of salvation will have reached its end and goal. Paul's whole concept of the process of salvation is concentrated in the idea of the *basileia* in 1 Corinthians 15:24–28, and we must use it to understand the great ideas of Colossians and Ephesians.

Colossians 1:13 tells us that God "hath delivered us from the power of darkness and hath translated us into the kingdom of the Son of his love". This *basileia* of the Son is therefore an existent reality in which Christians have a share.[24] In contrast to 1 Cor. 15:24 seq., it would seem to be not merely an exercise of sovereignty but, at least metaphorically, a place. It is tempting to think of it as the Church which, as the body of Christ (Col. 1:18, 24), is directed by its heavenly head. But it is questionable whether we are justified in making this identification. To grasp Paul's thought, we must include the preceding verse 12 which declares that the Father had made the Colossians "worthy to be partakers of the saints in light". The two verses are distinguished by the change of grammatical construction (participle – relative clause) and of the personal pronoun (ὑμᾶς – ἡμᾶς), but the contrast between "light" and "darkness" shows that they are intimately connected. In giving them a share in "the lot of the saints in light" God has snatched them from the realm of darkness. It is a genuine vocation which because of baptism

[24] This view is opposed to that of W. G. Kümmel on 1 Cor. 4:20 (in appendix to Lietzmann, *An die Korinther,* p. 173).

(2:12) bestows on them even now real salvation, a share in the risen life of Christ and at least in a hidden sense (3:1–3) in his heavenly glory. This is the most likely meaning of the phrase "into the kingdom of the Son of his love". The "saints in light" are not the brethren who have been sanctified in Christ on earth but the heavenly throngs that delight in God's glory. The old query whether the term "saints" is applied to men or angels cannot perhaps be answered with certainty. A comparison with the remarkably parallel passages in the Qumran texts suggests it is more probably angels, though the just are not necessarily excluded.

These texts are striking and we have to assume a common background of late Jewish ideas. The relation is provided by the notion of "Lot", rarely found in the New Testament but extremely common in the Qumran texts. This passage gives us pleonastically (hendiadys) μέρις and κλῆρος together (see Acts 8:21). We find μέρις again in 2 Corinthians 6:15 which has a decidedly Qumran ring, while κλῆρος occurs in Acts 26:18 closely akin to Colossians 1:12. In the third account of Christ's appearance on the way to Damascus the word might be taken by Luke from Paul's preaching or it might go back to an early Christian topic, the conversion "from darkness to light" (see the fragment of a baptismal hymn in Eph. 5:14; further, 1 Pet. 2:9; 1 Thess. 5:5 seq.). In the Qumran texts גורל ("Lot") has a larger and more extensive place by comparison with the Old Testament and it has different meanings:[25] among them, the notion of being called to heavenly communion with the "saints". Here are some characteristic extracts: IQS XI, 7 seq.: "God has given his elect a share in the lot of the saints and he has united his

[25] See F. Nötscher, *Die theologische Terminologie der Qumran-Texte* (Bonn, 1956), pp. 169–73.

company with the sons of heaven to form a council. Their assembly will be in the holy city as an everlasting plantation." IQM XII, 1 seq.: "For a throng of angels is [for me] in heaven and hosts of angels under thy holy rule, and thou hast set the elect of thy holy people beneath [. . .]. . . . to muster the [hosts of thy elect] in their thousands and tens of thousands together with thy saints." Ibid., XIII, 4: ". . . but the lot of God is (destined) to light." IQH III, 21 seq.: "Thou hast cleansed the disordered soul from many sins that he might set himself with the host of saints and enter into the company of the sons of heaven. Thou hast bestowed on man an eternal lot with the spirits of knowledge that he may praise thy name in the company of God." Ibid., XI, 9 seq.: ". . . to distribute the lot of thy holy ones that this worm, man, may be lifted out of the dust to the height of eternal things".

The goal of God's vocation is therefore acceptance into God's heavenly community that abides in God's realm of light. The thought that Christ is enthroned as Lord in the midst of this exultant community is very ancient. But his realm also embraces the Christians still on earth, the object of whose hope awaits them in heaven (Col. 1:5). This view is confirmed and clarified in Ephesians. Through baptism God has made us alive and raised us up with Christ and has established us in heaven in Christ Jesus (2:5 seq.); those who were once heathens have thereby become "fellow citizens with the saints and the domestics of God" (2:19). The context of this last passage shows that Christians possess their heavenly citizenship as members of the Church. Consequently, there is a close relation in actual fact between the "kingdom of the beloved Son" and the Church, in which for Christians it is realized on earth. Yet in Colossians 1:13 Paul is right to speak not of the Church but of the kingdom of the Son; he is considering the sphere of power and glory of the elevated Son who has rescued Christians from the sphere of influence of all the powers of darkness (compare the "powers of angels" and the "elements of the world" of Colossians). The heavenly kingdom of Christ and his eschatological kingdom cannot in this respect be separated.

"Kingdom of Christ" is, therefore, a more comprehensive term than "Church". In the Christian's present existence on earth his share in Christ's kingdom and his claim to the eschatological kingdom (see also Phil. 3:20) find their fulfilment in the Church, the domain in which the graces of the heavenly Christ are operative (Col. 1:18, 24). But Christ's rule extends beyond the Church (see below, section 23) and one day the Church will have completed her earthly task and will be absorbed in the eschatological kingdom of Christ or of God. The reign of the Risen Christ is not only one of grace and blessing over the Church; it is one also of force and subjection over the spiritual powers (Col. 2:10, 15; Eph. 1:20 seq.; 4:8–10). Christ is the head also of these powers and the epitome of all things (Col. 1:20; 2:2, 10, 19; Eph. 1:10). The expression "kingdom of his beloved Son" in Colossians 1:13 was chosen by contrast with the "realm of darkness" and preserves its relation to the heavenly realm of light (v. 12). The same sequence of ideas can be recognized in Ephesians 2:1–7; the establishment of those redeemed by God's grace "in the heavenly places through Jesus Christ" (v. 6) is perhaps the best commentary on Paul's meaning in Colossians 1:13.

The notion of the sovereignty exercised by the exalted Christ is thus deepened and made concrete. The later epistles bring out not only the fact but also the manner of this present exercise of power (1 Cor. 15:25). Two factors perhaps were particularly responsible for this: Paul's reflections on the cosmic significance of Christ, provoked by the false doctrines of the Colossians, and the growth of an ecclesiology, stimulated by the call of the gentiles and the establishment of a community of salvation, containing Gentiles as well as Jews (Ephesians). We must now examine the resulting problem how Christ's rule is realized in the Church and over the cosmos and what is the relation between these two realms and functions.

23. Christ's Rule over Church and World

From the beginning Pauline theology presents Christ as the "Lord" of his earthly community but to begin with only as the *Kurios* liturgically honoured (Rom. 10:9; 1 Cor. 12:3; Phil. 2:11), to whom it owes salvation and life, whom it encounters in a special manner in the Lord's supper (1 Cor. 10:21) and looks for at the Parousia (Phil. 3:20 seq.). His present activity of supremacy and grace within the Church, which can very appropriately be called a "rule", emerges more definitely when he is spoken of as "head" of his body, the Church, and is known in the full dimensions of this dignity and power; that is, in Colossians and Ephesians. It is well known that the "theology of the body of Christ" is described differently in the major community epistles (1 Corinthians and Romans) and those of the captivity. The leitmotif for 1 Corinthians 12 and Romans 12:4 seq. is the union of the members, their unity and solidarity, "in Christ" or, "in the body of Christ" and in 1 Corinthians 6:15–17 this is seen in concrete detail and used for moral exhortation. In 1 Corinthians 12:13 (baptism) and 10:16 seq. (Eucharist) the sacramental foundations of this real union with Christ and with one another are made clear, as had occurred in Galatians 3:27 seq. without the actual term "body of Christ". In Colossians and Ephesians there is, however, a new element, a concept of "head" and "body" which it is difficult to interpret merely as an organic development of the earlier notion of body of Christ.

The attempt to explain the "body of Christ" in 1 Corinthians and Romans as the individual body of the exalted Lord "permeating" the Church by means of the Holy Spirit and "assuming" Christians as its members[26] is unconvincing in the light of the texts. Is this not a projection of the σῶμα doctrine of Colossians and Ephesians into the text of Corinthians and Romans? The relation between the individual Christ enthroned in heaven with his own transfigured body and his body developing in the Church on earth and at most to be "identified mystically" with his heavenly σῶμα would have to be explained, as is done in the κεφαλή — σῶμα doctrine of the captivity epistles. The passages in 1 Corinthians and Romans illustrate rather than explain, though they are to be understood in a thoroughly real sense when applied to the communion with Christ of all the baptized (Gal. 3:27: all are one in Christ Jesus).[27]

The relation Christ – Church, as represented by the related terms "head" – "body" (Col. 1:18, 24; 3:15; Eph. 1:22 seq.; 4:11–16; 5:23, 30) includes both association and difference, the subordination of the Church to her Lord in heaven and also the Church's significance for his rule as it extends over the cosmos. To begin with the characteristic and almost paradoxical extract from Ephesians 5:23, Christ is the head of the Church, he, the saviour of his body. Paul exhorts Christian wives to be subject willingly to their husbands, and for a motive tells them that the husband is "head" of the wife in a manner similar to that of Christ's

[26] So most recently, J. Reuß in *B.Z. NF.* 2 (1958), pp. 103–27, in particular pp. 104–13 where other advocates of this explanation are mentioned.

[27] For the distinction between the two σῶμα concepts, see particularly H. Schlier, *Brief an die Epheser,* pp. 90–6.

relation to the Church. But in expressing this thought he is aware of the exceptional manner in which Christ gained this position. He delivered himself up for the Church (v. 25) and made it his own by his redeeming act of love. The Church belongs to him more intimately than the wife to the husband; the Church is indebted to him for existence, holiness and glory (vv. 26 seq.).

Another passage gives an even more profound basis for the Church's origin in Christ. According to 2:16 Christ's intention was to reconcile the two halves of humanity, Jews and Gentiles, "in one single body" with God through the cross. The old exegetical controversy whether the reference is to Jesus' physical body which shed blood on the cross (Col. 1:22) or the body of the Church, is badly stated, for the context shows that both are included. The explicit mention of the cross and the glance backwards to ἐν τῇ σαρκὶ αὐτοῦ (v. 14) are a clear reference to the individual body of the crucified, who was a sign and means of peace for both halves of humanity estranged from God and who moved God to be reconciled with the whole of mankind. The formation in Christ of "a new man" from the two separated halves (v. 15) and the correspondence of ἐν ἑνὶ σώματι (v. 16) with ἐν ἑνὶ πνεύματι (v. 18) show just as clearly that the body of the Church is also included and is represented and from this standpoint already present in Jesus' body of flesh and blood.[28] As in verses 23, 25–7, the Church appears as an existent reality at the death of Jesus on the cross. Chapter 2:14–8 leaves us with no practical doubt that the "body" of the Church is envisaged with Christ's individual body. One and the same body of Christ

[28] The passage is interpreted in this way by M. Dibelius – H. Greeven, *An die Kolosser, Epheser, an Philemon* (3rd edit., Tübingen, 1953); J. Reuß, op. cit., p. 119; H. Schlier, *Brief an die Epheser,* p. 135 (where supporters of other opinions are also listed).

that died on the cross and rose to transfigured life is built up in a new manner in the Church by Christ, the head. It is in a real sense the "body of Christ", the concrete body on earth of Christ, its head in heaven, truly "his" body, belonging to him as the physical body belonged to Jesus on earth and the glorified body to the Risen Christ, indeed "the" body of Christ, which is no second body in addition to the individual body of the transfigured Lord but is "mystically identified" with it (L. Cerfaux) or whatever other expression be employed.

How this point of view is to be explained has been much debated but this does not concern us here. All we need say is that speculation about Adam is behind it. This is shown by the "new creation" (κτίσῃ) to a "single new man" (ἄνθρωπος). The Semitic notion of a "corporate personality" offers the readiest explanation, namely that all the followers of Christ are thought of as represented by and incorporated in Christ, the new Adam, the ancestor of a new humanity. He really does represent those who will be united with him in faith and baptism; in this view, his body of flesh is already the body of the Church. The terms ἄνθρωπος and σῶμα in this context, the association of the "head" in heaven with the "body" on earth, the peculiar self-construction of the body from its head, the "development" of all into the "perfect man" (4:12 seq.), among other notions, compel us to recognize a taking over and adaptation by Christians of Gnostic ideas and images, as has been demonstrated judiciously but convincingly by H. Schlier in his commentary, without damaging the Christian originality of the apostle.

The cosmic status of this "body of Christ" is brought into prominence in Ephesians 4:11–16. The body is considered in process of formation (v. 12) and this is directed by the head, by the Christ who has ascended above all the heavens (v. 10) and who bestows his "gifts" upon the Church for its formation and growth. As such (interpreting the quotation from Ps. 67:19 in verse 8) he mentions those who have pneumatic offices, apostles, prophets, evangelists and teachers (v. 11) because, being equipped for this purpose by the Spirit from on high, they assist the building up of the body in a special way; they perform the "work of service" for the perfecting of the saints.[29]

It is then shown that not only the men with a special office but all members (οἱ πάντες v. 13; πᾶν τὸ σῶμα v. 16) have their part in this building up of the body in so far as they grow in truth and love (vv. 14 and 15). However difficult it may be to interpret some of the details, one thing cannot be doubted: this body of Christ is on earth, is contained and fulfilled in the Church, is formed by its heavenly head and forms itself through the collaboration of its members, it is an operation in and upon the cosmos. In the first place, all those comprised within this body of Christ are being led towards their heavenly and eschatological destiny. And therefore the universe in need of redemption is brought to God, is restored in Christ to its pristine order and placed under the divine rule (1:10).

This concept is expressed formally in this passage if Schlier is right in translating 4:15 thus, ". . . (that we) may speak the truth in love and so help the cosmos to grow towards Christ who is the head". In contrast to the usual rendering, " . . . (that) doing the truth with charity we may in all things grow up in Christ who is the head" which makes αὐξάνειν intransitive and takes τὰ πάντα as an accusative of relation, Schlier can justifiably argue that, in this case, nothing new is added to verse 12 seq. and that τὰ πάντα, placed emphatically at the end should here as elsewhere signify "the cosmos". Less convincing is his view

[29] For an understanding of the three prepositional turns of phrase πρός . . . εἰς ἔργον . . . εἰς οἰκοδομήν which allow different grammatical explanations, see Schlier on the passage.

of the ἵνα clause, vv. 14 seq. which must refer to an objective going beyond that of verse 13; this is not the case with the first half (v. 14) and verse 15 can be only a positive enlargement of the same thought. There are other difficult points, notably verse 16. In Schlier's interpretation Christ is described in verse 15 simply as the head, not only of the Church but of the whole cosmos. But if verse 15 envisages the return home of the cosmos, then it is difficult to imagine how verse 16 can revert to the body of the Church without mentioning the cosmos. Schlier himself is aware of this and he, therefore, proposes (p. 209) a new rendering for verse 16, in which πᾶν τὸ σῶμα to start with refers to the body of the Church and again commemorates its growth from the head, but the αὔξησις τοῦ σώματος directed by the whole body of the Church is connected with the elevation of the cosmos to Christ which accompanies the building up of the Church. The second σῶμα towards the end of the passage would be the "body of the world" – in itself an explanation worth considering if compared with Colossians 2:19. This interpretation of verse 16 would be disturbed through the concluding purpose εἰς οἰκοδομὴν ἑαυτοῦ ἐν ἀγάπῃ, which clearly refers to the body of the Church. This removes the "cosmic" eminence towards which the whole argument was directed. It will be better, therefore, to apply verses 11 to 16 to the body of the Church in process of development. Indirectly, it expresses also the cosmic significance of the Church, for verse 10 tells us that the Christ who has ascended above all the heavens shall "fulfil all things" and according to verse 11–16 he appears to make use of his Church for this.

Christ's "rule" over the Church consists, therefore, in a generous bestowal of "gifts" (v. 11), a powerful construction in grace of his own body (v. 12), his direction of all who are united in faith towards heavenly, eschatological fulfilment (v. 13). Christians under his most gracious rule must collaborate in the interior development of the Church, this growth of the body towards its head, in so far as their faith becomes strong and mature (vv. 13 seq.) and expresses itself in love (v. 15). Love is the essential law of the "body of Christ", by means of which it forms itself (v. 16) and draws near to its head. For the Church is born from the love of Christ (see 5:2, 25) and by it is "nourished and cherished "(v. 29). The more its members grasp and respond to this love of Christ that surpasses understanding, the more they will be "filled" until they become wholly the "fullness of God" (3:19). Christ's reign over the Church is accomplished by the streams of grace deriving from Christ's love which continually overflow from the "head" to the "body". The Church subjects herself in receiving and begging for his gifts and saving graces (3:16 seq.; 6:10), in efforts to secure deeper knowledge and greater love (4:15) and in moral behaviour which is in contrast to the works of darkness (see Eph. 5:6 seq.; Col. 3:5 seq.).

What of Christ's reign over the world? It is established through his victory on the cross that took away their power from the rebel "princes of this world" (1 Cor. 2:8), who appear in Colossians and Ephesians under different names but are always cosmic powers and spiritual forces. Colossians 2:15 informs us that God disarmed and stripped them when he overcame them in Christ. The image here latent of a triumphal procession into heaven is presented in Ephesians 4:8–10 on a grander scale. Christ leads the captive powers to the heights as spoils of war and mounts above all the heavens "that he might fill all things", i. e. administer with sovereign power.[30] The outcome is his enthronement in heaven "above all principality and power and virtue

[30] See J. Gewieß, "Die Begriffe πληροῦν und πλήρωμα im Kolosser- und Epheserbrief" in *Vom Wort des Lebens,* Festschrift für M. Meinertz (Münster 1951), pp. 129–41.,

and dominion and every name that is named, not only in this world but also in that which is to come" (1:21).[31] At the same time, no doubt with reference to late Jewish angelology, Christ's unlimited and unshakable grasp and exercise of power, by divine commission (1:19 seq.) in and over all things is described.

Christ's basic victory over all the powers that brought rebellion and disorder into the world (Eph. 2:2; Col. 1:20) and his authority over them and consequently over the world can neither be challenged nor shaken, even though this is not yet fully proclaimed and Christ's redeemed must continue the struggle against these more than human forces but in the strength and armoury of God (Eph. 6:10–17). Christ's cosmic rule, in contrast to his guidance and direction of the Church through grace, exerts compulsion in so far as it controls and subjects these enemies of God, permits them no more despotic rule over men and for all their seeming freedom of movement denies them effective victory and triumph. While in 1 Corinthians 15:24–8, 54–7 our gaze is directed towards Christ's ultimate victory over the last enemy, death, no longer in doubt because of the Resurrection and enthronement of Christ, the whole emphasis in Colossians and Ephesians is placed on the victory now obtained and the sovereignty already won, which cannot be called in question by the activities still permitted to the conquered (see also Rom. 8:37–9).

This subjection of the powers of evil accounts for only one aspect of Christ's rule over the cosmos. The real significance of his reign is a positive one, described most briefly and beautifully in Ephesians 1:10, namely to bring all things in Christ under one head, to recapitulate them in him and raise them to the pristine

[31] For a more detailed interpretation see the commentaries; also, F. Mußner, *Christus, das All und die Kirche*, pp. 41 seq.

and now perfect order of God.[32] The eschatological order has its basis and scheme in the order of creation. This emerges more clearly from the hymn to Christ (Col. 1:15 seq.) than from the opening words of Ephesians, especially verse 4. In Christ all things, in heaven and on earth, were created, visible and invisible . . . All things were created by him and in him (v. 16). Redemption has brought about the return and full renewal of creation that was directed towards Christ and through Christ towards God. Through Christ all things are reconciled "unto himself" (to Christ? better, perhaps, to God) (v. 20), and the spiritual powers are here included.[33] "God's two decisive acts, creation at the beginning and redemption at the end, have their purpose in Christ."[34]

The precise significance of Colossians 1:20 is difficult to determine and it has received a wide variety of interpretation, as can be seen from the monograph of E. Testa.[35] For men who need and are prepared for redemption the "reconciliation" of all things with God is certainly a genuine "peace-making through the blood of his cross"; but what is it for the angelic powers of heaven? The answer depends strictly upon what beings are understood in this expression. If it refers to the rebellious enemies of God who in the last resort are "irreconcilable" powers, "reconciliation" can mean only "constraint" and "subjection". The act which brings men to redemption, leads those powers to an acknowledgement of the sovereignty of Christ

[32] The expression itself is rich in meaning and this is all suggested by the context, see the commentaries; further, H. Schlier, in *Th.W.B.* III, pp. 681 seq.; E. Percy, *Die Probleme der Kolosser- und Epheserbriefe* (Lund, 1946), pp. 423 seq.

[33] Compare the εἴτε τὰ ἐπὶ τῆς γῆς εἴτε τὰ ἐν τοῖς οὐρανοῖς of verse 20 with verse 16.

[34] Dibelius-Greeven, on this passage.

[35] *Gesù pacificatore universale* (Assisi, 1956).

and God. Consequently, it sets the world again "in order" and in subordination under God.[36] Yet even explained as the establishment of peace, the term "reconciliation" does not provide a satisfactory answer.[37] But there is no certain basis either in Paul or the rest of the New Testament for real "reconciliation", a final "reconciliation of all things".[38]

E. Testa pursues a different line. He considers these heavenly powers as angels in conformity with late Jewish (Jewish Gnostic) views confirmed by the Qumran literature. These observed strictly the exigencies of the Law and defended them even against the mercy and patience of God; their demands were "appeased" by Christ's death on the cross and they were brought to rest themselves and to peace with God.[39] This suggestion deserves respect since it avoids the impasse of "good or bad angels" and takes into consideration the Jewish-Gnostic errors of the Colossians and Pauline notions that we find elsewhere (see Gal. 3:19 seq.; also 3:13), but difficulties remain. Surely the "powers and forces" of Colossians 2:15 (the same as in 1:16, 20) are regarded as defeated enemies?[40]

[36] See J. Michl, "Die 'Versöhnung'" (Kol. 1:20): *Th.Q.* 128 (1948), pp. 442–62; E. Käsemann, *Eine urchristliche Taufliturgie,* in Festschrift für R. Bultmann zum 65. Geburtstag (Stuttgart, 1949), pp. 135-145 in particular p. 139; J. Dupont, *La réconciliation dans la théologie de St. Paul* (Bruges–Paris, 1953), p. 37, note 39; Dibelius–Greeven, on the passage.
[37] F. Büchsel in *Th.W.B.* I, pp. 29 seq.
[38] This is contrary to the position held by W. Michaelis, *Versöhnung des Alls,* which is based upon Colossians 1:20 (pp. 24–30) and then tries to establish a doctrine of the reconciliation of all things for the whole of the New Testament; see M. Rissi, *Zeit und Geschichte,* pp. 161 seq.; for further criticism see J. Schneider in *Th.L.Z.* 77 (1951), pp. 158–61.
[39] Op. cit., pp. 119–43; 147 seq.
[40] Consult also H. Schlier, *Principalities and Powers in the New Testament* (Freiburg im Breisgau, 1958), in particular p. 14, note 13.

This is indeed a cosmic and universal reflection, in terms of the history of salvation, comprising heaven and earth, creation and fulfilment, in which Christ is seen as the mediator of creation and redemption and as the goal of history. He is the hidden meaning of the world's history under God's guidance, the head of creation and of all its domains, the ruler in the perfect kingdom of redemption.

The question arises how Christ's rule over the world and his rule over the Church are related to one another, for obviously they cannot subsist without links and relations. What evidence have we in the texts? In Colossians 1:15 the apostle passes from the description of the cosmic significance of Christ with a simple καί to an ecclesiological reflection. Verse 20 shows, however, that he has not yet abandoned the cosmic horizon. Similarly, we observed in Ephesians 4:8–16 that after Christ's overthrow of the spiritual powers and his sovereign fulfilment of all things (vv. 8–10) his gifts to the Church and the building up of his body are described (vv. 11–16). This immediate sequence certainly denotes a sequence of ideas. The mighty permeation of all things is realized in grace within the Church.[41] In Ephesians 1:21–23 also we find Christ's elevation to sovereignty over the spiritual powers and then his "establishment" as head of the Church. But how does this come about? The addition of ὑπὲρ πάντα to κεφαλήν is striking; the interpretation "to the head towering above everything" leaves out of account the unmistakable relation to πάντα in verse 22 a. We have to assume a condensed, abbreviated connection of ideas: God has given Christ "as the head who has been established above all things

[41] Nothing is said about the geographical extension and the spread of the Church unless there is an allusion to the Church's mission in the mention of messengers and preachers (apostles and evangelists) in verse 11.

(also as head) to the Church."[42] The union between the cosmic and the ecclesiological statements is even closer in verse 23. There the apostle describes the Church as the body of Christ and the "fullness" of him that is "all in all".[43] The "fullness" of Christ (and ultimately the fullness of God, see Col. 2:9; Eph. 3:19) has established itself in the Church, and this is the same presence and fullness of God's power which operates in another manner in the cosmos, namely in the subjection of the angelic powers (4:10). The same thought is found in Colossians 2:9 seq.: "You are filled in him who is the head of all principality and power." The fullness of God that dwells corporeally in Christ (v. 9) passes through Christ also into Christians, but at the same time Christ, ruling the cosmos, also chooses the Church as his direct sphere of operation, into which his divine blessings stream. We must, therefore, conclude that Christ's reign over the world is realized in a special manner in the Church and becomes there a concrete reality of grace. In the Church the cosmic influence of the "powers" is taken from them, and in the measure in which the Church is built up by her heavenly head, so is the power of these forces lessened. Through the Church Christ wins increasingly his dominion over all things and draws them ever more powerfully and completely beneath himself as head.

This does not, however, imply that Church and cosmos are identical,[44] but the Church gains a cosmic significance. Church

[42] See J. Gewieß, *Die Begriffe* πληροῦν *und* πλήρωμα, p. 140; further, Ch. Masson, *L'Épître de S. Paul aux Colossiens* (Neuchâtel–Paris, 1950), who translates thus: "*. . . qu'il a donné en qualité de Tête dominant toutes les créatures à l'Église*"; H. Schlier, on this passage.

[43] Schlier, *Brief an die Epheser,* p. 99, wants to understand ἐν πᾶσιν as masculine; but this is scarcely feasible if τὰ πάντα denotes the All (and not the Church); on this point see Gewieß, op. cit., p. 134. 'Εν πᾶσιν must be merely another way of saying "fullness" (see 1 Cor. 15:28).

[44] This is the justified opinion of Mußner (op. cit., pp. 166 seq.).

and cosmos are not two separated spheres beside or opposed to one another, having nothing in common except their subordination to the exalted Christ.[45] It is in and through the Church that the cosmos is grasped by Christ – attracted or compelled. By its very existence the Church has a task in regard to the world; to this must be added the activity imposed by the Lord in accordance with the Church's nature. This is most profoundly expressed in Eph. 3:10 . . . "that the manifold wisdom of God may be made known to the principalities and powers in heavenly places through the Church". Because the Church appears before the world and proclaims its gospel of Christ, Christ's cross through which the rulers of the world thought they had triumphed, moves into a new light, is illuminated by Christ's Resurrection, and to this the Church bears witness through her existence and her kerygma. And thus God's wisdom hidden from all eternity is revealed "which none of the princes of this world knew" (1 Cor. 2:8). In this kindred passage in First 1 Corinthians the apostle continues that God has revealed his mysterious wisdom to "us", believers in Christ, through his Spirit (2:10 seq.). In Ephesians 3:10 he develops the thought implicit in 1 Corinthians 2:8 b, that God's manifold wisdom, the development of his hidden design of redemption, has been made known to the rebellious powers through the Church (see v. 9).[46] This is done especially by the preaching of the apostles but the apostle is only, we may say, the mouthpiece of the Church which by its very existence shows forth the divine wisdom and the escha-

[45] This is against the view of Mußner, op. cit., p. 168; for a discussion of the two views see V. Warnach, *Kirche und Kosmos,* pp. 182 seq.

[46] This idea is found also in the Johannine theology. The "conviction of the world" takes place through the Paraclete (John 16:8–11); but he makes use of the Church for his witness, 15:26 seq.; 1 John 5:7 seq.; see R. Schnackenburg, *Die Johannesbriefe,* on the passage.

tological fulfilment of the redemptive design and thus exposes the spiritual powers and the feebleness that has come upon them. The Church is "the manifestation of God's wisdom"; it "brings home by itself and in itself and through itself the wisdom of God to the powers and forces" (H. Schlier).

The "conquest" of the world for Christ takes place in and through the Church in a twofold way; within by means of its growth in grace and outwards through its mission. Both functions are intimately associated: by being built up in love, the Church, directed and nourished by its Lord and head, bears witness to the reign of Christ, the defeat of the powers and the return of man's world to God's order; and as, growing stronger, it proclaims all this to the world and summons men to accept Christ's rule, it widens its influence and sphere of action in the cosmos, it forces back the cosmic powers and takes their sphere of activity away from them. The Church's interior sanctification, its self-development in charity under Jesus Christ, the head, made possible through the Holy Spirit, receives the greater stress in Ephesians. The Church "embraces the whole universe in its mainly sacramental action and draws it into its own reality that is filled with Christ".[47]

Nor must its immediate missionary duty to the world be overlooked. Paul is conscious of being the minister of the gospel "which is preached in all the creation that is under heaven" (Col. 1:23), for with the world of men the whole of creation will be brought again under Christ's headship (see Rom. 8:22 seq.). The gospel is to "bring forth fruits and grow" through the entire world (Col. 1:6) precisely as Christians are to "bring forth fruits and grow" in the knowledge of God (1:10). This means that external and interior growth correspond and must go hand

[47] V. Warnach, op. cit., p. 189.

in hand. God's mystery is already active among the gentiles and is operating as a "hope of glory"; but it is being further proclaimed by the apostle to "present every man perfect in Christ Jesus" (Col. 1:27 seq.). There would seem to be an inner connection between the theology of the two captivity epistles and Christ's commission in Matthew 28:18–20. In the authoritative word of the Risen Christ conscious of his enthronement, there is an echo of his claim to reign over heaven and earth (v. 18); to realize this, he employs his apostles whom he sends to all the peoples. They are to "make disciples" of all[48] the nations, that is, bring them to his saving reign,[49] and this is to happen through the bestowal of baptism and insistence upon Jesus' commandments (v. 19). We have here in different language what is expressed in Ephesians. Here the apostle pictures inclusion under Christ's rule as follows. In baptism God has made us alive with Christ and associated us with his Resurrection and Ascension, but with the obligation of attesting the gift of grace by a manner of life consonant with it (Eph. 2:5–10). But we must also observe that in Matt. 28:18 seq. Christ's attainment of power over the world is realized by winning men for disciples and that the whole passage issues in a missionary commission. A point of view that is contained but not properly developed in Colossians and Ephesians now comes into greater prominence, namely that the Church's mission is necessary and willed by Christ to bring the world of men and with this the whole of creation under his rule.

This more profound and broader cosmic ecclesiology of the

[48] See O. Perels in *Th.L.Z.* 76 (1951), pp. 391–400: he remarks that apart from the commission to baptize in Matthew, πᾶς occurs nowhere else in the New Testament as repeatedly as in Colossians and Ephesians.
[49] On μαθητεύσατε see E. Lohmeyer, *Evangelium des Matthäus* p. 418, note 2.

Pauline epistles that we have been studying, throws light on the special attitude that was seen by and imposed itself on the early Church as soon as it grasped the notion of Christ's position as Lord, his heavenly exaltation and establishment in sovereign power and reflected upon all its consequences. Christ's rule here and now over Church and world is the manner in which the kingship of God is realized in the present era of salvation between fulfilment and completion, in the field between the polarities of this aeon and the future aeon, in this mixture of "light" and "darkness". The relations between Church and cosmos under the reign of Christ are, however, the hidden ground and the background in sacred history of those phenomena which we experience in the foreground as "world history".

THE REIGN AND KINGDOM OF GOD IN THE LATER BOOKS OF THE NEW TESTAMENT

24. The Transcendent and the Eschatological Kingdom

In Pauline theology as we have been examining it, Christ's rule, established through his exaltation and enthronement in heaven, has been revealed in its rich aspects but one could scarcely expect a sharply defined and uniform terminology. As the theology developed, this lack of precision or even a certain confusion of conceptual expression makes it difficult to grasp the exact significance of the thought. Such development is fairly well known in the second century with the Apostolic Fathers, in particular with the Alexandrines.[1] Even in the later New Testament writings we come across a number of new terms that require clarification. Naturally, they do not express new ideas; but they contain accents and nuances of importance for the theological development of early Christianity.

In 2 Timothy 4:18 Paul expresses the hope that the Lord will deliver him from every evil work and preserve him unto his heavenly kingdom. The phrase is curious even though the adjective "heavenly" (ἐπουράνιος) is Pauline enough.[2] As an

[1] R. Frick, *Die Geschichte des Reich-Gottes-Gedankens,* pp. 27 seq.; 82 seq.

[2] It occurs four times in 1 Corinthians 15, five times in Ephesians (in the

attribute of the *basileia* it need not surprise us since, as we have seen, the "kingdom of Christ" in Colossians 1:13 (cf. 12) has its true and appropriate place in heaven. But the thought in Colossians 1:13 and Ephesians 2:6 is different from that in the pastoral epistle. In the captivity epistles Christians, members of the Church, have already, on earth, been given a share in Christ's heavenly rule. But in 2 Timothy 4:18 the apostle is contrasting his existence on earth, beset with danger, with Christ's heavenly kingdom which he hopes to attain after death. This contrast ought not be interpreted as opposition, for in Ephesians 5:5 there is already the suggestion that we should think of an inheritance waiting in heaven and, therefore, understand the "kingdom of Christ and God" as a transcendent reality in heaven that will be finally manifested in full glory at the eschatological fulfilment (see also Col. 3:3 seq.). It was natural that this idea, latent in the great conception of the captivity epistles, namely that Christ's sovereign rule, comprehensive though it is, nevertheless possesses a special sphere in heaven where it is manifest in glory, should come to the fore in the last epistle to Timothy. We can understand this from Paul's premonitions of his own death. In 2 Corinthians 5:8 he consoles himself for the possibility that he may not see resurrection immediately, with the desire "to be absent from the body and to be present with the Lord" and in Philippians 1:23 he yearns "to be dissolved and to be with Christ". None the less the expression "heavenly kingdom of Christ" is a novelty that makes a "Hellenistic" impression.

As we remarked at the beginning (section 1), the Hebrew mind represented God's kingship not as a spatial "kingdom"

stereotyped phrase ἐν τοῖς ἐπουρανίοις – in heaven); Phil. 2:10 (the heavenly powers; otherwise only in Matthew her 18:35; John 3:12) and six times in Hebrews: see C. Spicq, *L'Épître aux Hébreux* II (commentary) (Paris, 1953), on the passage; H. Traub in *Th.W.B.* V, pp. 538–43.

but as an exercise of royal rule, and this way of thinking determined the usage of the New Testament βασιλεία τοῦ Θεοῦ. Spatial images emerged only for the perfect eschatological reign of God and were all the more justified since then no further spheres more or less subordinate to God can be distinguished but God is "all in all". If Judaism believed that God's will is fulfilled perfectly in heaven and God is king in heaven[3] in a special way, heaven was still not called his "kingdom" but mostly his "dwelling" or something similar.[4] It was reserved for the Hellenistic Book of Wisdom to inform us with an allusion to his vision in Bethel that Wisdom showed Jacob the "kingdom of God" (10:10), that is, permitted him a glance into God's transcendent world. But although Paul – if we accept the authenticity of 2 Timothy – formulates this expression from another point of view, because of his belief in the exalted Lord of heaven, a certain Hellenistic influence cannot be denied.

This expression, innocent in itself, was to have awkward consequences. Where Greek thinking prevailed, "Christ's kingdom" became identified with heaven. Subsequent centuries interpreted "kingdom of heaven" in Matthew as simply "heaven", unaware of Matthew's original meaning. The results for the history of theology and devotion are well known. The emphasis was shifted from general cosmic eschatology to the individual hope "to enter heaven" after death, to attain "the next world". To this there would be no objection if faith had retained the depth and vitality of Paul who saw in this the fulfilment of union with Christ that was incomplete on earth and if the faithful had remained conscious of eschatological salvation and the world's

[3] G. Dalman, *Worte Jesu* I, pp. 314–21.

[4] H. Bietenhard, *Die himmlische Welt im Urchristentum und Spätjudentum* (Tübingen, 1951), pp. 8–10.

fulfilment. These notions were, however, spiritualized to so alarming an extent that they disappeared altogether and became mere phraseology. We must, therefore, insist that the heavenly transcendent kingdom of Christ is not at the centre of New Testament thinking and, when it does emerge, it continues to receive all its light, its colours and its strength from the awaited eschatological kingdom of Christ and God.

We have already examined the characteristic and probably secondary reading of Luke 23:42, "when thou shalt come into thy kingdom" (see above p. 267). This Jewish malefactor will have been thinking of the Messianic kingdom ("when thou shalt come as king") and of mercy in judgment. To this glance towards the future Jesus opposes his "today" (v. 43) which not a few of the Fathers connect for reasons of apologetics with "I say to you". Here, as in Luke 16:19–31, "individual eschatology" comes on the scene, not from the standpoint of the *basileia* but from that of Paradise.[5] In Luke 23:42 seq. the history of the text is really that of theology.[6]

In point of fact, such an interpretation of "kingdom of Christ" or "of God" can be shown to be more or less contemporary, though in isolated instances. Hermas, *Similitudes,* IX, 16:2–4, indicates that the (Old Testament) dead have already "entered into the kingdom of God". The *Letter to Diognetus* (X, 2) tells us that God has promised "the kingdom of heaven" (τὴν ἐν οὐρανῷ βασιλείαν) to men. Justin in *Apology* 10, 2 envisaged a "reigning" with God after death (see 42, 4). In a later addition to the *Martyrium Polycarpi* Pionius expresses his hope that "the Lord Jesus Christ with his elect will conduct him into his heav-

[5] J. Jeremias in *Th.W.B.* V, pp. 768 seq.

[6] E. Fascher, *Textgeschichte als hermeneutisches Problem* (Halle, 1953), pp. 57–60.

enly kingdom" (22, 3 – reminiscent of 2 Tim. 4:18?). Generally, the eschatological notion of the kingdom of God is preserved, but as an abstract formula.

The "heavenly kingdom" of Christ in 2 Timothy 4:18 certainly does not displace the eschatological kingdom (4:1). But as well as the horizontal view of the history of salvation another becomes increasingly prominent, the vertical.

The blend of these two views is typical of the Epistle to the Hebrews. This book, permeated with Alexandrine (Jewish-Hellenistic) spirituality, regards all "heavenly" things as the true and proper realities. Things of earth are only "shadows" of the things of heaven (8:5; 9:23; 10:1 ὑπόδειγμα and σκία); the "heavenly" is what is "better" and "abiding" (10:34; 7:19, 22; 8:6; 9:23; 11:16, 35, 40; 12:12, 27; 13:14). At the same time, these truly good things, present in their full reality in heaven, are the "future" things awaited by Christians (1:14; 2:5; 6:5; 9:11; 10:1; 11:20; 13:14). Christians partake of them in their present possession of salvation, in the Holy Spirit, in the mystery of worship and the sacraments. They "taste", to use the old expression, already the "heavenly gift" and the "powers of the world to come" (6:4 seq. – "heavenly" and "future" are again connected). They stand already in the new order of salvation which is not like the old order, a "shadow of the good things to come" but possesses the "image" (εἰκών), that is the completely real image of the things themselves (10:1). The author with his particular approach has associated "the archetypal world of heaven and the eschatological re-creation", he has linked a spatial and a temporal scheme.[7] The *basileia* reappears in this context, in the revealing expression "immovable kingdom" (12:28). The adjective is suggested by the preceding verse which deals with the

[7] F. J. Schierse, *Verheißung und Heilsvollendung*, pp. 62–4; 92 seq.

eschatological "convulsion" of heaven and earth (referring to Agg. 2:6). The final event leads to a transformation (μετάθεσις) of the movable things (that is created things) "that those things may remain which are immovable" (v. 27). The *basileia* is one of those heavenly realities that are immovable. Then, finally, Christians who already belong to it, will "receive" it, take effective possession of it and reign within it.[8]

Mention of the *basileia* may be conditioned by this eschatological context, but verses 22 to 24 prepare for it and illuminate it. There we learn that the Christians are (already) "come to mount Sion and to the city of the living God, the heavenly Jerusalem" (v. 22). They, therefore, belong to that saving reality which will emerge openly and completely in the perfect eschatological kingdom. Verse 23 mentions in addition to myriads of angels the "church of the first born who are written in the heavens" and we will not be far wrong in regarding this as an "apocalyptic picture of Jesus' community" (O. Michel) that embraces also the faithful living upon earth. Basically, this is the "heavenly Church", the Church considered in her true nature, her heavenly destiny, her union with her heavenly Lord. The Church, as the eschatological people of God, is to enter into heavenly "rest" (4:1–11); and this rest, in the last resort, is nothing but the "future world" (2:5), the "promised land" (11:9), the "city of God" (11:10, 16; 12:22), the longed-for "city" and "home" (13:14; 11:14). All this is the object of God's promises and of the hope of the faithful (4:1; 6:11

[8] Παραλαμβάνειν is certainly to be understood as the assumption of rule, as is made clear by the reference to Daniel 7:18: the saints of the All Highest παραλήψονται τὴν βασιλείαν; this signifies something over and above the certain "grasp" through faith. See Bauer, *Wörterbuch* Sp. 1229, 2b; O. Michel, *Der Brief an die Hebräer* (Göttingen, 1949), on the passage (against C. Spicq).

seq.; 9:15; 10:36), it is always the same beneath varying images.[9]

Among them is the "immovable kingdom"; the kingdom too is part of the promised inheritance (9:15; 6:12, 17) or, rather, it is the hoped-for objective seen from one particular point of view. Those who are one day to inherit the *basileia* are already citizens of the city of heaven, which as "kingdom" will manifest its glory. Fundamentally, if we prescind from the particular style of Hebrews, this is the outlook of Ephesians and practically all the images we have mentioned appear in the earlier epistle. Hebrews places a stronger emphasis on the pre-existence and presence of the kingdom that one day will be eschatologically revealed, and the connection between the Church on earth and the heavenly city of God is both more pronounced and intimate. Both constitute the one reality, still divided during the course of this aeon, in which the people of God, holding fast in faith, make pilgrimage towards the goal of their desire (13:14). But God's pilgrim people have the promises as a sure possession, and have a foretaste of future salvation (6:4 seq.). It inherits only what belongs to it already; takes only what is prepared for it. Consequently, the "kingdom" is already there as a heavenly reality, abiding and unshakeable; its citizens need only reach it to reign therein.

This kingdom could also be termed "eternal", if by that we understand a quality or property rather than indefinite temporal extension. "Eternal" is applied to what is divine, heavenly, of the next world; in Hebrews "salvation" is "eternal" (5:9) as are "judgment" (6:2), "redemption" (9:12), "inheritance"

[9] E. Käsemann, *Das wandernde Gottesvolk, Eine Untersuchung zum Hebräerbrief* (2nd edition, Göttingen, 1957) (= 1938), pp. 18 seq.; F. J. Schierse, op. cit., passim.

(9:15) and the (new) "covenant" (13:20). On one occasion we even discover the expression "eternal kingdom" in the New Testament, namely in 2 Peter 1:11. There is no doubt that this document, strongly permeated with Hellenistic spirituality, refers to the eschatological kingdom, and the phrasing recalls the "entry passages" in the synoptic gospels. If Christians bestir themselves to "make sure of" their calling and election, there will be an "entrance ministered to [them] abundantly into the everlasting kingdom of our Lord and Saviour Jesus Christ". Then the "most great and precious promises" are fulfilled for them (1:4).

In what, however, does this ultimate fulfilment consist? In "sharing the divine nature". This Hellenistic phrase which recalls our future divinization and transformation, suggests that even the "eternal kingdom" has lost its original pictorial vigour, its portrayal of the cosmic kingdom of glory, and has become a more or less formal term for eternal salvation, the "salvation of souls" as it is already called in 1 Peter 1:9. The Jewish-Christian inheritance of the "promises" is preserved (2 Pet. 1:4, 19 seq.; 3:2, 4, 9, 13) but in spite of the imagery it has taken over, the fulfilment is made more spiritual and Hellenistic. It is true that the author still expects "a new heaven and a new earth" (3:13) but he adds, "in which justice dwelleth". And so the "eternal kingdom" becomes the imperishable glory of heaven which the Christians will enjoy after the Parousia of their Lord (see also 1 Pet. 5:4, 10), when the "eternal day" dawns (2 Pet. 3:18).

The philosopher and martyr, Justin, also refers in his *Dialogue with Tryphon* to an "eternal kingdom" which, foreshadowed in Daniel 7 Jesus Christ will establish after his return (*Dial.* 31). This kingdom (or this reign) belongs to Christ, as the scriptures indicate, and Christians are to share in it (116, 2). After the

Resurrection God will translate "some of them into this eternal and indissoluble kingdom where they will be incorruptible, immortal and impassible, others he will despatch to the everlasting punishment of fire" (117, 3). In this debate with his Jewish opponent, the Jewish way of thinking about the history of salvation generally prevails but, as the last passage shows, the Hellenistic belief in immortality is beginning to assert itself. Justin's "eternal kingdom" is the promised eschatological kingdom of God, in which Jesus reigns eternally for ever but it is also the region of changeless blessedness and immortality for the just.

Jesus' assertion of his kingship before Pilate has to be viewed in the light of other theological presuppositions, John 18:36 seq. On the surface, there is no question of a "kingdom" or "sphere of rule" but of a kingly dignity and of Jesus' claims to sovereignty; yet in the background there must also be the notion of the exercise of royal power and a domain of royal action.

Exegesis must not be confined to Jesus' "defence" of his unpolitical kingship. In view of the question of the Roman judge, "Art thou the king of the Jews?" (v. 33), Jesus certainly intends to make clear the unworldliness of his kingship but to stress at the same time his royal dignity, as he understands it. Jesus had always declined kingship in a political sense (see John 6:15) and before the representative of earthly power he can easily dispose of the accusation on the grounds that, if he had such power, his servants would have fought for him (v. 36). This negative delimitation apart, which was imperative at his trial, the query, "Therefore thou art a king?" gives Jesus the opportunity of asserting his kingship positively. He confesses that he is a king (v. 37a) but a king who has come into the world "to give testimony to the truth". Verse 37b is a parallel to Jesus' answer in verse 36 and in its last sentence it contains an allusion to his subjects. "Everyone that is of the truth heareth my voice" (and subjects himself to my kingship).

For the kingly claim of the Johannine Jesus it is significant that in two passages he does not repudiate the royal title. He accepts the confession of Nathanael (1:49) and of the pilgrim crowds at his entry into Jerusalem (12:13) but on each occasion he is greeted not as "king of the Jews" but as "king of Israel". He is willing to be the saving king of the people of God but not king of the "Jews" who have become opponents of God and even representatives of the "world". Jesus' declaration before Pilate gives a more profound basis for his kingship than is expressed in the title of honour "king of Israel" (which Pilate understood falsely or not at all). Jesus is king as the ambassador from on high, the heavenly revealer and mediator of divine life. The title "king" for this unique office occurs once in the Johannine writings but it is not remote when we consider passages like 3:35; 5:27; 10:28; 13:3; 17:2. In this scene with the Roman magistrate, it is not only fixed by the situation and by tradition: it is chosen deliberately to confront the representative of earthly power and a worldly outlook.

Jesus' kingly "witness to the truth" is best explained by 3:31–36. He is the only one who has come from "above", from the region of heaven and God; in that capacity, he is "above all" and has a dignity that is without parallel. "What he hath seen and heard, that he testifieth", namely divine reality and truth, which he alone knows from immediate communion with the Father(1:18). This he can reveal supremely because he possesses the Spirit "without measure" and the Father "hath given all things into his hand". These phrases show that Jesus' possession and power of communication of divine nature, of "truth" and "life", are understood as royal, that is unlimited, authority. With revelation is indivisibly associated the gift of divine life to all who believe (3:36; 5:24). Although before Pilate Jesus speaks only of his coming into the world, we have at the same time to envisage his return to heaven: that is part of the pattern of John's thought (3:13; 6:62; 16:28) and here, as in his "sacerdotal prayer" Jesus is speaking with a consciousness of his glory (17:1 seq., 24). The bestowal of revelation and life on the faithful is only fulfilled with his "elevation". Then he will "draw all things to himself" (12:32); then he attains his full salvific power over all flesh to bestow eternal life on all whom the Father has entrusted to him (17:2). All who understand can find in Jesus' reply to Pilate a claim to royal power (ἐξουσία); it provides a vision of his sphere of sovereignty (perhaps referred to in βασιλεία). Raised aloft and glorified, he exercises over all "who are of the truth", who have their origin and character in God and belong to God through vocation and decisive response, an activity which (through the Spirit) illuminates his truth (16:13) and dispenses life (17:2 seq.; 14:17, 19) but is also his sovereign rule convicting the "world" (16:8–11). Fundamentally, this presents in other categories Paul's concept of the rule of Jesus Christ. In John's special theological style it is only followed further back and linked eventually with his heavenly origin, his eternal co-existence with the Father, but with John it remains also connected with the history of salvation, because Jesus attains his full saving power only after his "elevation", his return to the Father.

This analysis disposes of the false assumption that the "unworldly" kingship of Jesus has nothing to do with the "world", as the theatre of the historical process. Even though his "kingdom" is not of this world, Jesus' claim to rule is always directed to the world and will assert itself in it or against it. For this purpose Jesus sends his messengers into the world (17:14–18;

20:21).[10] But it seems that Paul's profound concept and John's different but equally penetrating concept of Christ's reign as not of this world but none the less making its claims upon it and embracing it, were subsequently to lose much of their vigour.

25. The Idea of the Basileia in the Apocalypse of John

It is with no slight surprise that the student of theology finds himself in the concluding book of the New Testament taken up to a lofty mountain from which he can look down and observe again many notions of the *basileia* and gaze with delight upon the ocean of God's eschatological kingdom as the seer of Patmos depicts it in his last great visions. For this reason alone it would be a great loss not to have John's Apocalypse in the canon of the New Testament.

We cannot enter here into critical literary questions. Even though the present form of the work raises various doubts about its unitary character and suggests a critical examination of its sources, its final edition, about 96, has given the book a unified and constructive character and therefore for the purposes of our biblico-theological study we do not require to take into account possible differences of strata in its composition.[11]

Right at the start we hear something of Christ's present reign and our share in his kingship, not developed theologically as with Paul but in short titles and allusions to Old Testament passages in the apocalyptic style. Jesus Christ is called in 1:6 the "faithful

[10] H. Schlier, "Jesus und Pilatus" in *Die Zeit der Kirche,* gesammelte Aufsätze (Freiburg im Breisgau, 1956), pp. 56–74, in particular pp. 62–5.
[11] A. Wikenhauser, New Testament Introduction, p. 540; W. Michaelis, *Einleitung in das Neue Testament* (2nd edition, Berne, 1954), pp. 306–08.

witness, the first begotten of the dead and the prince of the kings of the earth". This sequence of ideas is a clear allusion to his Resurrection and his heavenly enthronement. Whereas Paul associates Jesus' exaltation particularly with the overthrow of the cosmic spiritual powers, the visionary John emphasizes the overlordship of Jesus Christ over the kings of the earth. In the Apocalypse these are wholly in the service of Satan and his accomplices; they "fornicate with the harlot", Babylon (17:2; 18:3, 9) and they fight in alliance with Antichrist (19:19). But the Christ of the Parousia who issues to join decisive battle with them bears written on his cloak the words, "King of Kings and Lord of Lords" (19:16) and his victory is never in doubt (17:14). This prominence given to the earthly-political powers reflects the cruel experience of early Christianity which had come into contact with the pagan State, with Rome and its vassal kingdoms, a State which in emperor-worship assumed divine honours and became an enemy of God. Christian faith defies this to its face: Jesus is the ruler of all rulers, and so the final consequences of Christ's rule are drawn even for the political realm. But these Christians, persecuted for their faith and exposed to further persecutions are conscious of their dignity; they know they are loved and redeemed by their Lord who still exercises his rule of the world in a hidden way in heaven; and even more, that they have been elevated to the rank of kings and priests (1:5 seq.).

This declaration is again conveyed in the language of the Old Testament. In Exodus 19:6 God inspires Moses to address his people of Israel as follows: "you shall be to me a priestly kingdom (kingship of priests) and a holy people". The author of the Apocalypse who presents a different text from the Septuagint[12]

[12] The same textual form βασιλείαν, ἱερεῖς is attested by Symmachus

and so comes very close to the original[13] meaning, lays stress on each word: Christians also are to exercise kingly and priestly functions. This is confirmed by the chant of the ancients at God's throne (v. 9 seq.) who praise the Lamb that has redeemed men of all nations and origins, "and hast made us to our God a kingdom (= kings) and priests, and we shall reign on earth". The kingship of the redeemed is thus no mere title of honour, it is a promise of actual rule with Christ. This is realized according to the Apocalypse in a twofold way. The martyrs who persevere (and confessors?) will be "priests of God and Christ and shall reign with him for a thousand years" (20:6). However the special reward of these true witnesses to Jesus is to be assessed in detail, there is no doubt that they partake of Christ's eschatological reign. In his description of the heavenly Jerusalem, God's fulfilled kingdom, the seer says of all that belong to it, "The Lord God shall enlighten them and they shall reign for ever and ever" (22:5). In retrospect we may remark that, referring to baptism, Paul declared that God has established us in heaven in Christ Jesus (Eph. 2:5 seq.); the first epistle of Peter described our spiritual and priestly service in God's temple, the Church (2:5–9), and employed the phrase "kingly priesthood" from Exodus 19:6 LXX.[14] The seer on Patmos takes these ideas and images for granted and unveils a vision of eschatological fulfilment.

The Apocalypse also portrays Christ as subjecting to himself

and Theodotion; similarly in the *Book of Jubilees* 16, 18 in the Syriac version ("kingship and priests") and the Onkelos-Targum ("kings, priests"). See R. H. Charles, *The Revelation of St. John,* 2 vols. (Edinburgh, 1920), on the passage.

[13] J. Bauer, "Könige und Priester, ein heiliges Volk (Ex. 19:6)" in *B.Z.F.* 2 (1958), pp. 283–6.

[14] See on this point J. Blinzler, "'Ιεράτευμα. Zur Exegese von 1 Pet.

the world, but it would appear that this cosmic rule is not regarded as in the Pauline theology as a present subjection of powers hostile to God, a progressive permeation of the world for God's order but rather as a clash, in which for the time being the powers of evil, namely the pagan State with all its instruments of force, are permitted free rein. But all this activity against God will be ended with one stroke through the victory of the Lord when he returns, and the old corrupt world will be replaced by a new heaven and a new earth. The contradiction is merely an apparent one. The seer envisages the last period of dread prior to the end, for Paul also foretold a rebellion of the powers opposed to God (see especially 2 Thess. 2:3–12). Further, the oppressed and persecuted Church, in John's vision, plays more than a passive rôle in the final drama. Not only is she intimately linked with the triumphant company of heaven and God's hosts; in spite of every need and distress (cf. the "signing" of the servants of God, 7:2 seq.), she has an unshakeable faith in victory.[15] Through steadfast profession, through the word and blood of her every member, she also bears "witness" (2:13; 6:9; 11:7; 12:11, 17; 17:6; 20:4), as Jesus himself bore "witness",[16] and (through his death), became the "faithful witness" (1:5; 3:14).

The Church's witness continues the witness of Jesus that proclaims to the world God's design of salvation and God's reign. For the forces that resist God, this is the announcement of

2:5 und 9" in *Episcopus,* Festschrift für Kardinal Faulhaber (Regensburg, 1949), pp. 49–65.

[15] See the assertions of victory in chapters 2 and 3; the pre-vision of 7:9–17; and also the chants in 5:9 seq., 12; 11:15, 17 seq.; 12:10–12; 15:3 seq.; 19:1 seq. 6–8.

[16] Note the subjective genetive μαρτυρία Ἰησοῦ, 1:2, 9; 12:17; 19:10; 20:4; on this point see H. Strathmann in *Th.W.B.* IV, pp. 506–08.

defeat and of judgment passed upon them. In the word and blood of Jesus' witnesses, even the satanic forces behind the kings of the earth must acknowledge that they have forfeited mastery and victory. This emerges clearly from the hymn of triumph in 12:10–12. The great accuser before God, Satan, who seduced the whole world (v. 9) is overthrown and hurled from heaven to earth through the victory of Michael and his angelic hosts (vv. 7–9). This fall from heaven, the complete disarming of the ancient corrupter of mankind, was the consequence, as John saw it, of the cross and exaltation of Jesus (v. 5; also, John 12:31); but Satan's overthrow is further revealed and realized through the brave profession and courageous death of Jesus' witnesses. "They overcame him by the blood of the Lamb and by the word of their testimony" (v. 11).

The roots of this idea of witness go back as far as the teaching of Jesus himself. The instructions to the disciples in Mark 6:11 par. tell them that they are to abandon a place where men will not receive them and listen to their message and they are to shake its dust from their feet "for a testimony to them" (εἰς μαρτύριον), that is, as a witness against them at God's judgment. The same idea is found in Jesus' statement that they will be persecuted and brought before seats of judgment for his sake (Mark 13:9 par.). John's gospel develops the idea further. The Paraclete and also the disciples will give testimony to Jesus (15:26 seq.), a testimony that will unmask, convict and condemn the unbelieving world (16:8–11).

The inerrancy of Jesus' witnesses, the "patience and faith of the saints" (13:10) becomes an active contribution of the Church on earth in the conflict with the enemies of God, even if the final reason for their destruction lies in the blood of Jesus (12:11). The defeat of the "saints" in the war unleashed by Antichrist (13:7) is merely apparent, superficial and permitted by God (cf.

ἐδόθη αὐτῷ). In this campaign waged with all earthly means of force and satanic cunning and propaganda, the Church of Jesus Christ stands always beneath God's abiding protection and his promise of victory (chapter 14).

The ultimate focal point in all trials, persecutions and distress is God's great victory at the close. The author of the Apocalypse concentrates on this event, which at once lights up and dispels all the darkness of the fearsome eschatological period and blends its light with his sombre descriptions, letting the hymns of praise and triumph be heard ever and again between the prophecies of disaster. In those hymns we discover how significant in his eyes is God's kingship, in the sense of God's all-embracing and active reign. The hidden meaning and purpose of the history of salvation is to restore this divine government of the world, as it was at the start of creation, to surpass the original order in the radiance of re-creation. Rule over the world is also the ambition of the powers rebelling against God and in the last days they make one final desperate attempt with the help of all their earthly satellites and auxiliaries to save their failing and indeed broken power and to obstruct God's cosmic kingship. This attempt is bound to fail; God's victory is already decided. "And the seventh angel sounded the trumpet; and there were great voices in heaven, saying: The kingdom (= rule) of the world has become our Lord's and his Christ's, and he shall reign for ever and ever" (11:15).

The full significance of this heavenly proclamation of victory can already be detected in the announcement at the seventh trumpet peal, given by a mighty angel descending from heaven, who swears by him that lives for ever, "who created heaven and the things which are therein; and the earth and the things which are in it; and the sea and the things which are therein. That time shall be no longer. But in the days of the voice of the seventh angel, when he shall begin to sound the trumpet, the mystery of God shall be finished, as he hath declared (εὐηγγέλισεν) by his servants and prophets" (10:6 seq.). This epitomizes God's design for the world and for salvation. The solemn invocation of the Creator is to remind us that God will round off his salvific work with the same power with which he called creation into existence, but it suggests also that the eschatological fulfilment is a re-creation of the created order. And in the angel's voice there are the accents also of God's historical pattern of redemption that is now on the point of eschatological completion. God revealed his mystery to the prophets; here it finds a final unveiling and fulfilment. God's eschatological kingship is seen here clearly as the completion of creation and the summit of redemption.

The proclamation of the world rule of God and his Anointed is followed as by a responsory by the thanksgiving prayer of the twenty-four ancients: "We give thee thanks, Lord God Almighty, who art and who wast and who art to come, because thou hast taken to thee thy great power and thou hast reigned" (11:17), and the individual acts are named in which God realizes his assumption of royal power: his anger at the wrathful pagan nations, the judgment of the dead, reward for his servants, the destruction of the powers that have corrupted the earth (11:18). All this is reiterated, in a somewhat different order, in 19:17–20:15. Here too God's kingship is seen as action and only in the final state does it lead to the new creation, the heavenly Jerusalem and the kingdom of God that abides for ever (21:1–22:5).

A new note is heard in the hymn of the martyrs who have passed through the persecution of Antichrist and now dwell in heaven (15:3 seq.). They praise God as the "king of the nations" whom all will glorify "for all nations shall come and adore in thy sight". Not all the gentiles will permit themselves to be misused as instruments of Satan and his associates; many will be converted and honour God as their Lord. Here the prophet is reviving the old notion of the peoples' pilgrimage to mount Sion (with a literal reference to Ps. 85:9) which Jesus also introduced into his picture of the *basileia* (Matt. 8:11 seq.). But this universal character of God's perfect kingdom could be recognized in the prophetic vision of 7:9 and it is brought out explicitly in the description of the heavenly Jerusalem. "The nations shall walk in the light of it (the city of God) and the kings of the earth shall bring their glory and honour into it" (21:24, cf. 26); the leaves of the tree of life serve "for the healing of the nations" (22:2).

The hymns of praise, 11:15 and 12:10, paid honour to "his Anointed" at God's side. The active rôle played by Christ in the setting up of God's eschatological kingship is revealed during the course of these last things. He leads the hosts of heaven to the final, decisive battle against God's foes, smites the peoples with the sharp sword out of his mouth, rules them with a rod of iron and treads the winepress of God's wrath ("Battle of the Messias", 19:11–16). A grandiose portrayal of the Parousia in which Christ is seen in full Messianic majesty but again he appears only as the one who carries out the divine decrees and as God's vicegerent. At his side are found "the called and the elect and faithful" (17:14; cf. 2:26).

A further image brings Christ into even more intimate association with God's eschatological kingdom. The final event is the "marriage of the Lamb" (19:7–9; 21:9). War and its alarms are over; a feast of joy is being celebrated. "Blessed are they that are called to the marriage supper of the Lamb" (19:9). This is the other aspect of Christ's eschatological victory: the bringing home of his bride, the Church, its reception into the perfect kingdom, the heavenly city of God (21:9 seq.). The prophet foresees the close of the ecclesiological series. The Church, seen to begin with in its form at once of earth and heaven, passes now after all its trials and sufferings on earth wholly into eschatological fulfilment. The community on earth joins the community of heaven, and the Church entire solemnizes its marriage with its bridegroom, Christ. This image in its turn recalls previous images, notably Paul's statement about the "chaste virgin", espoused to one husband, namely Christ, who will be led to him (at the Parousia, 2 Cor. 11:2) and also concerning the bond of spiritual "marriage" between Christ and his Church (Eph. 5:22–23); then even further back, Jesus' pictures of the wedding feast and banquet, in which he outlines the glory of God's future kingdom (Matt. 22:1 10, 11:13; 25:1–12); and finally, the Old Testament picture of the "marriage" of Yahweh with his people (Osee 1-3; Jer. 2:2; 3:1–3; Ezech. 16:7 seq.; Isa. 54:6–8; 62:4 seq.), which, applied at a higher level to Christ and the saving community of the New Testament, finds its typical realization.[17]

The interplay and development of these images is conditioned by the historical process of revelation and salvation. Even in the Apocalypse no uniformity is reached. Now the community on earth is the bride of Christ, yearning to be led home by its heavenly bridegroom (21:17; cf. 19:9); now it would seem to be the transfigured community of heaven that has the wedding festival with the Lamb (19:7; 21:2, 9), and this second picture blends with that of the heavenly Jerusalem, the perfect kingdom of God (compare 21:9 with 10 seq.). In this the various aspects of the Church are unveiled. She is provision-

[17] L. Cerfaux, *The Church in the Theology of St. Paul* (English transl.) p. 297; J. Jeremias in *Th.W.B.* IV, 1094–9; J. Schmid in *R.A.C.* II, pp. 544–7.

ally divided into an earthly and a heavenly community and yet is fundamentally one. The earthly community belongs in essence and destiny to heaven, and the heavenly community consists only of the portion of the earthly Church of martyrs and confessors that has attained blessedness. Eventually, they will form one whole, the heavenly bride, led home by Christ. The transition from the image of bride to that of heavenly Jerusalem shows us, however, that the Church as God's people (purified from all the unworthy and evil) enters into and indeed is absorbed in God's perfect kingdom, so that it is better to speak of it as the city or kingdom of God. Only in eschatological fulfilment do "Church" and "kingdom" become identified. But "cosmos" and "Church" also become one, for God's kingdom is also "the new heaven and the new earth", the "All" eschatologically renovated and complete (21:1, 5). The switching of imagery in Apocalypse 21–22 for the same reality is significant and of the highest theological importance. In God's fulfilled reign Church and cosmos become one, but only then. Till then, the distinction between Church, cosmos and the reign of God or Christ retains its actual force.

To conclude, what is the relation between the reign of God and that of Christ or, in terms of realization, between the kingdom of Christ and that of God? The accounts of the heavenly world and the last things show in many ways that in this intervening period God exercises his rule with and through Christ to the end. A few examples will suffice. In the great opening vision (1:9–20) the prophet beholds the "Son of man" enthroned in the glory of heaven, and he applies images and predicates to him that belong to God. He is the "first and the last" (1:17) as God is "Alpha and Omega" (1:8; see also 2:8; 22:13 with 21:6). After the great vision of God's throne in chapter 4 we read in verse 6 that "in the midst of the throne and of the four living creatures and in the midst of the ancients" stands the Lamb, standing as it were slain, and that he has "seven horns and seven eyes, which are the seven spirits of God, sent forth unto all the earth" – in the symbolic language of the Apocalypse these are signs of the fullness of Christ's power and his rule that permeates the earth. Towards his communities this expresses itself in care, formation and sound correction (see the letters in chapters 2–3); but to the world that opposes God it appears as a fearsome power (6:16 seq.). Only the Lamb is worthy to loose the seven seals of the book and so discover and fulfil God's decrees for these final times (5:5, 9). Consequently, the hymn of praise of those who dwell in heaven is offerred to him who sits upon the throne and also to the Lamb (v. 13; see also 11:15; 12:10). Even though Christ sallies forth only at the end to destroy the army that combats God (chapter 19), all the actions and chastisements which lead up to this are the consequences of his victory on the cross (7:14; 12:11) and a sign of his ultimate triumph (15:3 seq.).

In the period of the Church between Christ's exaltation and his return, the reign of Christ and the reign of God therefore, coincide; the final victory still belongs to God and his Anointed. But it then appears that there is still a particular kingdom of Christ, the famous "kingdom of a thousand years" (20:1–6). The exegesis of the passage has a lengthy history behind it and in the form of Chiliasm it has itself made history.[18] Even today we are a long way from any uniform and satisfactory interpretation. This must always depend upon the basic explanation

[18] H. Leclercq, "Millénarisme" in *D.A.C.L.* IX, 1181–95; W. Bauer, "Chiliasmus" in *R.A.C.* II, p. 1073–8; A. Gelin, "Millénarisme" *D.B. Suppl.* V, 1289–94; J. Michl, "Chiliasmus" in *L.Th.K.* II, 2nd edition, p. 1058 seq.; for the history of the idea, see in particular L. Gry, *Le Millénarisme dans ses origines et son développement* (Paris, 1904).

of the Apocalypse and the theological background of the individual. It is impossible for us to deal adequately with this complicated set of questions within the framework of this work.

Both Catholic and Protestant exegesis is confronted here with extremely great difficulties. The monograph of H. Bietenhard gives the best account of attempted solutions by Protestants.[19] We cannot (or can no longer) regard the explanation of the millenium as the whole span of the Church, from the Resurrection to the Parousia, as "the" Catholic interpretation.[20] This view, deriving from Augustine (*De civ. Dei* XX, 7 seq.) has been very influential and still has its advocates.[21] More recent French exegetes have proposed a variant on this theme and they recognize this kingdom (or this reign) of Christ in the Church since the collapse of the Roman Empire; the Church's victorious advance in the world is really the rule of Christ and the saints in heaven over the earth.[22] But this explanation in terms of world and Church history becomes impossible if 19:11 seq. is a description of the Parousia, and this can scarcely be called in question.[23] From then onwards it would appear that only strictly eschatological

[19] *Das tausendjährige Reich,* pp. 144–64.

[20] So Bietenhard, op. cit., p. 82.

[21] E. B. Allo, *L'Apocalypse* (3rd edition, Paris, 1921, [3]1933), Exc. 37; J. Bonsirven, *L'Apocalypse de S. Jean* (Paris, 1951), pp. 287 seq., especially p. 295.

[22] H. M. Féret, *L'Apocalypse* (Paris, 1946), pp. 297 seq.; M. E. Boismard in the *Jerusalem Bible* (Paris, 1953), p. 81; A. Gelin, op. cit., p. 1292; see also J. Sickenberger, *Erklärung der Johannesapokalypse* (2nd edition, Bonn 1942), and E. Schick, *Die Apokalypse* (Würzburg, 1952), on 20:1–3; they interpret these verses as a prophecy of a peaceful, blessed era of the Church.

[23] See A. Wikenhauser, *Offenbarung des Johannes* (Regensburg, 1947), on this passage.

events are recorded: a glance backwards to the time before the Parousia in 20:1–3 is highly improbable.

How then are we to interpret the vision? Millenarism, in the exact meaning of the term, the hypothesis of a Messianic interregnum of Christ prior to the Last Judgment, whether in the crass form of a realm of the elect with worldly power or in the milder form of a spiritualized and happy reign of Christ over the earth after the Parousia, has been rightly repudiated by the Church.[24] O. Cullmann and his pupil, M. Rissi, suggest that the *Regnum Christi* that commenced with the Resurrection continues into the initial stage of the future aeon and that the "kingdom of a thousand years" will be the Church of this final period.[25] But can Satan be let loose again in the future aeon and kindle a war of the peoples (Gog and Magog) against the saints and their city (Apoc. 20:8–10)? H. Bietenhard has critical remarks[26] to make on all the texts adduced by Cullmann with the exception of 1 Corinthians 15:24 (Matt. 19:28; Apoc. 5:10; 20:4; 2 Tim. 2:12; 1 Cor. 6:2 seq.) but he arrives at a similar solution except that it is in reverse and he allows the future aeon to penetrate into the present era: "If we assume that the risen live during the thousand years in heaven or on earth, the life of resurrection and transfiguration commences already in this aeon." In his view, God concludes and fulfils the history of this world and this aeon in the kingdom of a thousand years; this means in the concrete that the history of Israel is brought to an end in the millenium.[27] Catholics interpret the "first resurrection" either symbolically as a special reward of the

[24] See the document from the Holy Office, dated April 11th, 1941 (Denzinger 2285).

[25] O. Cullmann, *Königsherrschaft Christi,* pp. 22 seq.; M. Rissi, *Zeit und Geschichte,* pp. 151–8.

[26] Op. cit., pp. 83 seq. [27] Op. cit., p. 152.

martyrs[28] or as a real vision reflecting a spiritual reality (similarly, the special reward of the martyrs) and not an actual fact.[29] Here again there are difficulties, in the first hypothesis the symbolic meaning of "live" (ἔζησαν) in verse 5; in the second, the fact that the judgment described afterwards (20:12 seq.) with the general resurrection of the dead must be understood as an actual event. On closer examination there would seem to be no place even in the Apocalypse for an interregnum of Christ. These few observations make no claim to provide a satisfactory solution to this problem.

In considering the approach of the "end", which must be identified with the Parousia, we have to realize that the space-time dimensions of the old world, "of this aeon", cease altogether and the new order commences, and this we cannot represent. Even the eschatological events that take place on the frontier of the old and new worlds but are basically "unworldly" in character, can no longer be grasped in essence and sequence by means of our earthly human concepts. Jesus made this clear in his reply to the Sadducees' question about the resurrection of the dead, when he pointed to the entirely different condition of risen bodies and also to God's incomprehensible power (Mark 12:24 seq.). This basic principle is reflected in the very "realistic" visions and descriptions of the seer of Patmos. He has to describe as a human being for human beings the whole eschatological process in spatial and temporal categories, and this he does unaffectedly using many images and colours in temporal sequence with a dramatic climax. If we consider the course of events as they are described, the plagues and the last things proper, we have to recognize in it a language of symbolism,

[28] So Sickenberger and Schick, on this passage.

[29] So Wikenhauser, *Offenbarung des Johannes,* pp. 129 seq.

enriched with many Old Testament and Jewish apocalyptic images and symbols (colours and numbers) and also that the time-sequences are an artificial construction.[30] To return from general considerations to our specific theme, the following observations may be made which suggest even if they do not actually prove in the strict sense that the prophet can scarcely have been thinking of an actual interregnum.

i. In the previous proclamations and hymns of praise there is no hint of a special kingdom of Christ prior to the real kingdom of God. God's eschatological kingship comes into view immediately. In 11:15, "The kingdom (= rule) of this world has become our Lord's and his Christ's", God's rule is at the same time Christ's rule. Similarly in 12:10 God's reign and the power of his Anointed are praised together. The song of Moses and the Lamb, 15:3, glorifies God as the "king of the nations".

ii. 11:17 seq. is particularly conclusive because here the hymn appears to allude to the general onslaught of the "peoples" in 19:15, 19–21. With this "battle of the Messias" the "kingdom of a thousand years" is associated in 20:1 seq. But 11:17 simply states that God has assumed his great power and become king. Further, verse 18 mentions other events in the eschatological process, namely the judgment of the dead (= 20:12 seq.), the reward for God's servants (= 20:4–6? or 22:3–5?) the destruc-ion of those that corrupt the earth (19:20; or 20:10?). Neither the sequence nor the connection between events is clear. There is no mention of a double campaign and a separate destruction

[30] St. Giet, *L'Apocalypse et l'histoire* (Paris, 1957), wants to interpret Apoc. 4:1 to 19:9 as historical. Even if he were correct in this opinion, it would be impossible to lay down any precise sequence for the escha-tological events, as Giet himself demonstrates when he deals with the author's method. (See particularly pp. 146–85; 222–9.)

of Antichrist (and the false prophets) and of Satan. What room is left for a special kingdom of the Messias? The only passage which can be adduced, namely 5:10, [31] is hardly a reliable one. It is part of a hymn of praise to the Lamb: "Thou hast made them (those redeemed through thy blood) a kingdom (= kings) and priests, and they shall reign on the earth." Does this mean more than that they will share in the reign of the Lamb when this completely embraces the earth as well?

iii. 16:13–16 must be an anticipatory description of the "battle of the Messias" (19:11–21). There too the demons spring out of the mouth of the dragon, the beast and the false prophets, to assemble the kings of the whole earth for war on the "great day of God". This is the only campaign mentioned and the dragon is named as its instigator. We hear nothing of a later war of the peoples (Gog-Magog, 20:8), stirred up by Satan.

iv. Perhaps the outline of a positive explanation emerges from this. The doubling of events in 19:11–21 and 20:7–10 may have taken place for descriptive reasons. The final destruction of all God's enemies, those on earth and the Satanic forces behind them, required a successive description to create a strong impression. Chapter 20 rounds off the circle that we enter in chapters 12 and 13. In chapter 12 Satan acquired power against the Church and began to attack her (v. 17); but in chapter 13 he made use of the "beast" from the sea and from land (Antichrist and the false prophets). The eschatological destruction of these enemies is narrated in chapters 19 and 20 in reverse order. The victory of Christ starts with Satan's accomplices on earth and finishes with Satan himself. Antichrist with his army is defeated by Christ, Satan (with all the peoples he has corrupted) is annihilated by God himself through fire from heaven. Satan is hurled into the

[31] O. Cullmann, op. cit., pp. 22 seq.

sea of fire (20:10) like Antichrist and his assistant (19:20), and the seer expressly remarks, "where are both the beast and the false prophets". The two destructive battles at the end are fastened together and marked as one concluding act. But are not these events which the prophet views as a sequence, in reality only one and the same event?

v. A study of the descriptive style in 19:11 to 20:10 reveals many traditional Jewish and early Christian images. This has been sufficiently proved for the "kingdom of a thousand years".[32] However, the account in Apocalypse 20:1–6 is far removed from the concrete (and late) Jewish concept of a Messianic interregnum before the "future aeon" is inaugurated, and should be explained rather in terms of Christian ideas. These too are clad in imagery and symbolism that must go back in the main to Ezechiel chapter 37 onwards.[33] But what is the Christian idea in this visionary setting? According to the peak of the vision in verse 6 it must be the rule of the previously humiliated martyrs (12:11; 13:7–10, 16 seq.) with Christ; their superiority to Satan (12:11 seq.), their special closeness to Christ, their dignity and worthiness to receive a special reward may have found significant expression in this intervening vision which represented no interval in actual fact.

vi. If the "kingdom of a thousand years" were really regarded as an interregnum or an era of rule by the Church in the future aeon, we should have to ask what its relation to the "marriage

[32] See particularly A. Wikenhauser, "Das Problem des tausendjährigen Reiches in der Johannesapokalypse" in *R.Q.S.* 40 (1932), pp. 13–25; the same, "Die Herkunft der Idee des tausendjährigen Reiches", ibid. 45 (1938), pp. 1–24; the same, "Weltwoche und T. R." in *Th.Q.* 127 (1947), pp. 399–417; also H. Bietenhard, op. cit., pp. 33–51.

[33] See in particular Wikenhauser in *R.Q.S.* 40 (1932), pp. 13–25; also Rissi, op. cit., pp. 151 seq.

of the Lamb" is. What further fulfilment would be denoted by Christ's taking home his bride, the Church, over and above the thousand year kingdom? The Church awaits her Lord until the Parousia but then all her yearning is assuaged. No room is left for an interval of rule between the Parousia (19:11 seq.) and the marriage of the Lamb (19:7, 9; 21:2).

vii. Finally, God's future kingdom represented under the image of the celestial Jerusalem descending from heaven (21:10) denotes no new phase in contrast to a "kingdom of Christ". The Apocalypse knows nothing of a handing over of rule by Christ to the Father at the end of time. On the contrary, we discover in 22:3 that the "throne of God and the Lamb" will be found in the eschatological city of God and there God's servants will fulfil their "priestly service", behold his countenance and reign for ever (22:4 seq.). For John the seer the future fulfilment of the world and the future aeon are one whole; there is only one kingdom of God and of Christ. If he employs different pictures, succeeding and blending with one another, this is merely to bring out different points of view. In spite of all the problems of exegetical detail that remain (into which we have been unable to enter) the fundamental explanation of 20:1–6 must lie in the direction that the vision is a symbolical description of the martyrs' victory and their special, appropriate reward.

All the lines of the Apocalypse converge in the end upon the great concluding picture of the city of God (21:1 – 22:5), which illustrates the perfect cosmic kingdom of God. There are good theological as well as personal reasons why this is depicted as a city, as his city, Jerusalem. The seer is able to compress into this vision all his thoughts and images of fulfilment: the return of Paradise, God's dwelling, the light of glory, perfect communion with God, the acceptance of the converted gentile nations, the vision of God, the perfect temple, the priestly service of the blessed, the heavenly liturgy. We need develop this no further. What is important for our reflection is that in this picture God's perfect reign appears in fact as a "kingdom", since God now permeates the whole world, a new world, with his will and being, his holiness and glory and has become really "all in all".

SUMMARY

THE BIBLICAL notion of God's kingship has had an historical development of its own. It has also played a dominant part in the history of revelation and salvation. The main purpose of this book has been to illustrate this. The notion appears early in the Old Testament though it is not precisely formulated till the period of the monarchy and it reaches its culmination in the eschatological teaching of Jesus. In this process through several centuries God's kingship is pictured in varying ways, and already in the Old Testament a number of additions can be discovered. Yahweh, and Yahweh alone, is to rule over his chosen people but he admits an earthly monarch as his representative. He is also the Lord enthroned in heaven who as Creator rules over the whole world and claims dominion over the remaining peoples. God's kingship is commemorated particularly in religious worship and ritual, so that his guidance of Israel through history is always made present and is also a promise for the future. The immediate point of contact for the preaching of Jesus is the declaration of the prophets that in spite of all the rebellions of Israel and its temporal punishments, God will establish his eschatological kingship which will bring complete and final salvation to Israel and to all the peoples that are associated with her.

In later Judaism two parallel lines of eschatological ideas can be discovered: the "national" hope of a revival of the ancient theocracy, of a Messianic kingdom of Israel, and the "universal" and "cosmic" expectation of a renewal of the whole world. These two currents penetrate one another and intermingle, for instance in the notion of a temporary Messianic kingdom that will be followed by the era of final salvation: see, for example, the two apocalypses at the end of the first century A. D., the *Fourth Book of Esdras* and the *Syriac Apocalypse of Baruch*. Rabbinic schools elaborated their own concept of salvation: God had previously established his rule over Israel but in their periods of unfaithfulness he had handed over the lordship of the world to other peoples. At present Israel enjoyed only a hidden rule of God to which devout Jews should subordinate themselves through exact observance of the Law "to bring the Messias near". Only at the end of time will God's kingdom be manifested in its full glory to the joy of Israel. This apocalyptic approach blended many fantastic elements with a genuinely religious yearning for the perfect cosmic kingdom.

In contrast with these various Jewish hopes the gospel of Jesus that the kingdom of God is at hand brings a new and special revelation. Jesus explicitly repudiates the idea of a kingdom that is purely national and affected by dreams of political freedom. He shares the apocalyptic notion of a universal cosmic kingdom which God of his pure grace will inaugurate but he dissociates himself from all calculations and imaginative descriptions. He is at one with the Pharisees in insisting that God's rule imposes serious moral obligations on men but he rejects the Pharisaic interpretation of the Law and its legalistic piety. He will have nothing to do with any particularism and is, therefore, distinguished from any special sects of the élite. He is conscious that he has been sent particularly to call sinners. His teaching of salvation which links up with the preaching of the prophets, especially that of Deutero-Isaias, may be characterized positively as the definite proclamation of God's reign, as God's greatest and last offer of salvation, which calls, of course, for men's response in conversion and belief in the gospel (Mark 1:15), undivided service of God and earnest moral effort in order to "enter into the kingdom of God".

From the eschatological point of view, Jesus does not proclaim that God's kingdom is already fully there ("realized eschatology") or that it is as yet wholly absent but is to be awaited in the near future (Eschatologism). It is truer to say that God's eschatological reign is inaugurated in the teaching and action of Jesus, in the forgiving word and the promise of full salvation. Even if the kingdom of God is now present only in an initial and scarcely discernible form, it will one day arrive in all its glory despite every obstacle; consider the parables of growth. The *basileia* that Jesus heralds has both a "present" and a "future" significance, and this should be indicated by the distinction between "reign" and "kingdom". The preaching of Jesus cannot be separated from his person. He is conscious of himself as possessing from God the full authority of Revealer and Saviour as well as the status of "Son of man", with whose advent in glory the perfect kingdom will be inaugurated.

The unbelief which Jesus met with from the greater part of the Jewish people and the growing hostility of the Jewish authorities which encompassed his death introduce a new revelation of God's salvific will. God will introduce his kingdom for the salvation of all peoples on the basis of Jesus' atoning death. Jesus reveals this saving design of God in his parting institution of the Eucharist which proclaims his blood shed for many to be the "blood of the covenant" but at the same time permits us a glance at the future kingdom (Mark 14:24–5 par.). Therewith the Old Covenant is dissolved by the New, and a new people of God is constituted, no longer bound to the old Israel but comprising all those who are redeemed in the blood of Jesus.

The question arising here concerning the relation between "community of salvation" and "kingdom of God" is not easy to answer. It is certain that from the time of the election of Israel God's kingship supposes a community and it is God's resolve to fashion an eschatological "people", belonging wholly to himself. Once Israel had refused belief, it is historically tenable that Jesus intended to found a new community, his community (Matt. 16:18 seq.). We should not, however, identify this community, the subsequent Church, with the kingdom of God proclaimed by Jesus. It is his foundation for the interval between the dawn of God's rule and the advent of the perfect kingdom. In it the powers of God's kingdom are already operative. Jesus' disciples are commissioned and empowered to lead men into the future kingdom of glory (Matt. 18:18; John 20:21 seq.). But the earthly community includes many who are unworthy and who will be cast out at the final judgment: it cannot yet be identified with the community of the redeemed in the future kingdom. The early Church was aware of this problem and had its own situation in mind when handing down the words of Jesus.

After Easter and the descent of the Holy Spirit Christ's new community of salvation comes to effective life. With this God's rule rises to a higher level. Jesus is now the Lord, raised to God's right hand and he directs his Church on earth through his Spirit and wishes by its means to win mankind for God's reign and kingdom. The kingship of God is thus administered and realized in the rule of Christ. We can understand how in the preaching of the early Church the accent moves from God's reign to the rule of Christ on high. Not that the Church forgets Jesus' gospel of the future kingdom of God: but the gospel of Jesus, Messias and Lord, comes into the foreground.

Paul has illustrated with great clarity how God's present rule is realized in Christ's exercise of dominion over Church and world. In his eyes, the Church is the domain in which Christ's saving rule is fully developed ("Body of Christ", "Fullness of Christ"). It is also the instrument to bring all men back to God (through preaching and missionary work). Forces hostile to God are still active in the world, even though in principle they have been overcome through Christ's victory on the cross and are condemned to collapse. During this our eschatological interim till the Parousia, they are contained and repelled through Christ's rule, again by means of the Church. Christ's salvific reign over the Church operates the destruction of these forces of evil. The might of whatever opposes God is broken through the Church, her word and witness, her sacraments, her service in love and her sufferings, and the rule of Christ and of God is strengthened. The stronger her faith and charity, the more men she brings back to God and his obedience, so much the more widely is Christ's rule spread throughout the cosmos. But Christ must rule till the last enemy is overcome, in order then to hand back the rule to God the Father (1 Cor. 15:24–28).

This idea of the rule of Christ and God is expressed differently by the other theologians of the early Church. They speak at times of the heavenly, that is transcendent, kingdom of Christ, without, however, losing their eschatological vision. The future kingdom of glory is represented in various images and awaited with varying degrees of vigour and urgency. Frequently the presence of Christ comes to the fore, in which all salvation consists and in which his gifts and saving graces are received, as in John's theology. At other times, the emphasis is rather on yearning for his Parousia and the perfect kingdom. Yet the early Church is always conscious that beneath Christ's gracious rule it is still on the way, that it is the pilgrim people of God (Hebrews), "strangers and sojourners" in this world (1 Pet.), still oppressed and persecuted, yet certain of its hope (Apocalypse). It is highly probable that the Apocalypse, the prophetic work of the New Testament, does not envisage an interim eschatological kingdom (the "kingdom of a thousand years," Apoc. 20:1–6), similar to the Messianic kingdom which according to some Jews was to precede the future aeon. The forms in which the idea is expressed vary but the basic notion remains the same: it is now the era of Christ's hidden rule which in its turn is to prepare the way for and bring about the manifestation of the perfect cosmic kingdom of God.

NOTE ON THEOLOGICAL TERMINOLOGY

IN THE Foreword we drew attention to the lack of complete agreement about a good theological terminology. As we conclude this study it is perhaps in order to offer a few suggestions (they are nothing more) for a more biblical manner of speaking in theology and preaching.

In general it is preferable to refer to the "reign" or "rule" of God rather than the "kingdom of God". The translation "kingdom of God" is required only for certain metaphorical expressions: for instance, "to enter into the kingdom of God", "to sit at table in the kingdom of God". But there is a theological basis for speaking of the perfect cosmic *basileia* as the "kingdom of God", and this should have emerged especially from the latter portion of this study. That is why we chose for its title: God's Rule and Kingdom. We should on no account call the *basileia* in its present form "kingdom of God" because in English this suggests something objectively completed and realized. If we were to adopt this distinction, then many unbiblical phrases such as "building up the kingdom of God" or "spreading the kingdom of God on earth" could be done away with.

The rendering *Königtum Gottes* or "kingship of God" proposed by H. Schürmann, deserves consideration because of its biblical origin (*Das Gebet des Herrn*, Leipzig 1957, pp. 41 seq.) and it has the advantage of providing a single comprehensive term but to me it appears not to fit in with our contemporary English or German usage. *Königtum* or kingship suggests royal dignity and power rather than kingly rule or a kingdom. *Königtum* or kingship is suitable for summing up the Old Testament declaration that Yahweh is king. But *es komme dein Königtum,* "thy kingship come" sounds rather strange. It is probably better to abandon the notion of a single term to be employed in all contexts.

It is theologically sound and suitable to apply the expression "reign or dominion of Christ" to the period between the Resurrection and the Parousia. Here again I should employ the phrase "lordship" or "sovereignty" of Christ for his dignity and power and "reign or rule of Christ" for the actual exercise of sovereignty (see 1 Cor. 15:24 seq.). "Kingdom of Christ" would signify only its perfect state, either the "heavenly kingdom of Christ" (2 Tim. 4:18, and in this case the adjective "heavenly" should be retained) or the eschatological "kingdom of Christ" which is identified with the "kingdom of God".

We should distinguish the "Church" from the reign both of God and of Christ. The close relations of the Church with the reign of God in the present, in the context of the history of salvation since the Resurrection, are best explained in terms of the reign of Christ. For God's present reign is expressed in the concrete by the reign of Christ. This is not, however, restricted to the Church. It extends to the entire cosmos. It includes not only the bestowal of the gifts and powers of grace upon the Church but also the subjection of the powers of evil, opposed to God, until the last enemy is annihilated. To do justice to every aspect of the Church (this was not our purpose in the preceding study) it would be advisable to complement this approach from above from the concepts of the reign of God and Christ with another approach from below: that of the earthly existence and constitution of the Church, its relation to the cosmos and its heavenly "presence". The concept of the Church may be suitably linked with the Pauline doctrine of the "Body of Christ" and the idea of the "people of God" which runs through the Old and the New Testaments, and there are various images which help us to amplify it, for example, those of planting, building, temple, betrothal, marriage. At once earthly and heavenly, the Church requires different categories from the purely eschatological and supernatural categories of the "reign of God".

Yet we are not here concerned with neat theological distinctions and divisions. Biblical ideas stand in varied and often very close relation to one another. Each has, however, its own sphere of application, as may be learnt from the key notions of the Old Testament, "kingship of Yahweh", "covenant", "people of God". There must be synthesis as well as analysis. But it will be easier to make a synthesis, the more individual concepts have been understood in their theological significance. A New Testament synthesis can be greatly assisted by a redemptive and eschatological approach, for in the last resort all theological lines come to a common focus. The Church, her earthly tasks fulfilled, is merged in the kingdom of God; the Messianic community of the final period, after testing and separation, is transformed into the perfect community in the glory and happiness of God. When mankind is fully redeemed, when the powers of evil are overcome and the cosmos is brought home, Christ delivers his royal power to the Father.

God's eschatological reign, which since and through Christ's mission has been operating in this aeon, which has found in the Church a special realm of influence, and which through Christ and the Church has been mighty also in the cosmos, now attains to its true goal: it comprises the universe entire, it subdues or destroys all that is hostile to God; it brings happiness and communion to all those who belong to God; it fashions a new world, wholly subordinated to God and transformed in his splendour: in short, it becomes the universal, cosmic kingdom of God.

SUPPLEMENT: RECENT DEVELOPMENTS

Since the first edition of this book in 1959, when it was so kindly received not only in Catholic circles but also in the world of critical scholarship at large, a number of years have gone by. This new edition, consequently, is intended to take into account the literature which has grown up around the various topics concerned. However, since this book was written only to provide a stimulating over-all picture for theology and teaching generally, based on the utterances of Scripture, and not for the purpose of dealing in detail with all of the technical problems involved — a task which was scarcely feasible at any rate in the face of the broad extent of the biblical and theological areas touched upon — it seems to be advisable again at the present to avoid dwelling upon any particular problems. Thus the work as a whole remains unchanged, so that the emphasis might remain as it was clearly upon the historical aspect of revelation and its consequences for exegesis and theology. The bibliography given at the end is meant to assist the critical reader in forming his own opinion of the current fundamental conceptions and approaches, as well as of the treatment of individual problems. I would, however, like to mention here several larger works, together with one or other critical point in this discussion, and to point out some new perspectives. I would also like to set forth very briefly some modifications of my position and to indicate several points which I have learned since that time.

1. With respect to the history of the most recent research on the idea of "the rule and kingdom of God", we now have two works which are helpful in an assessment of the present discussion, each in its own way. The work of G. Lundström which appeared in 1947 in Swedish is now available to a wider circle of readers in an English translation[1]. This work also includes an additional chapter which treats in detail the relevant material appearing since its first edition. The twelve chapters which deal with the history of research on this subject presented in the first edition, ranging from A. Ritschl up to the second World War, show with a copious use of references how ideas on this topic have changed over the years.The work attempts to trace the larger lines of historical development in the method of approach (among other things, the break-through of the "eschatological" interpretation of J. Weiss and its effects); it also attempts to group the scholars together according to their various conceptions (this latter section appears to me to be questionable in part). In his treatment of the newer works which have appeared between 1947 and 1962, the Swedish author comes very close to the standpoint taken up in the present book, namely in the treatment of the present-and-future character of the *basileia*-preaching of Jesus and its relation to his own person. He characterizes this Christological basis as "a strong tradition among Scandanavian exegetes" (p. 278). Such extensive agreement is all the more welcome as it does not spring from any common confessional presuppositions or traditions.

1 *The Kingdom of God in the Teaching of Jesus* (Edinburgh, 1963).

The work of the American exegete N. Perrin[2] deals approximately with the same period, though it was written independently of Lundström and differs from him in that it is extensively orientated towards the "eschatological question". His similarly knowledgeable treatment, which also incorporates the results of American exegetical work (cf. the chapter "Jesus as a Prophet", pp. 148–57), nevertheless centres around different points. He deals more at length with the Son of Man problem and the Bultmann school, for example, and concludes by formulating three precise subjects for the further study of the topic: the rule of God in the Apocalypses and in the teaching of Jesus; the relation between present and future in the teaching of Jesus on the Kingdom; the relation between eschatology and ethics in the teaching of Jesus. We shall see that these are just the questions which have received greater attention in the exegetical and theological preoccupations of the respected scholars.

2. With regard to the OT chain of ideas concerned with the rule and kingdom of God, it has become much clearer that the *title* "king" was applied to Jahweh only later when Sion-Jerusalem was elevated as the "royal throne" of Jahweh,[3] and not without the influence of Canaanite ideas. It is also clearer that "the kingly position of a god was only established and assured by the building of a temple".[4] Just as the Canaanites revered the "highest god" who

[2] *The Kingdom of God in the Teaching of Jesus* (London, 1963).
[3] Cf. the work of J. Schreiber, *Sion-Jerusalem, Jahwes Königssitz* (Munich, 1963), which carefully examines and explains the whole question.
[4] W. Schmidt, *Königtum Gottes in Ugarit und Israel* (Berlin, 1961), p. 57; cf. also H. Schmid, "Jahwe und die Kulturtraditionen von Jerusalem", in *Z.A.W.* 67 (1955), pp. 168–97; H. J. Kraus, Psalmen I (Neunkirchen, 1960) pp. 197–201; id., *Gottesdienst in Israel* (Munich, 2nd edition 1962), pp. 237 seq.

was enthroned upon the sacred mountain, so did Israel honour Jahweh who proved himself to be a powerful God and a leader when he brought Israel out of Egypt and helped them to take possession of the land. Israel finally also designated him as the "great king over all the earth" (Ps. 46:3), and "highest" (Ps. 82:19) who is "above all other gods" (Ps. 96:9). It is still firmly held that Jahweh's rule and kingdom is before all else a dynamic exercise of kingship[5] which during the high period of Israelitic history, in the early time of the kings with their splendid cult upon Sion, was praised as a kingship over all the world.

Thus one must treat of "Jahweh's Kingship in Liturgy", as it is presented above (pp. 21–30), even more markedly from the historical *Sitz im Leben*, from the choice of Sion as the centre of the cult by David, and from the imposing building of the temple by Solomon. In German exegesis preoccupation with the "feast of the enthronement of Jahweh" seems to have been abandoned at last;[6] at least the acclamation *Jahwe malakh* according to more recent study[7] almost certainly is to be translated as

[5] This is also shown by the study of T. Blatter, *Macht und Herrschaft Gottes* (Freiburg, Switzerland, 1962); on the kingdom of God see Blatter, pp. 96–108; Whether ἡ βασιλεία τοῦ θεοῦ designates a spatial or dynamic idea is still controversial; cf. S. Aalen, "'Reign' and 'House' in the Kingdom of God in the Gospels" in *N.T.St.* 8 (1961/62), pp. 215–40. A different view is expressed by G. E. Ladd, "The Kingdom of God – Reign or Realm?" in *J.B.L.* 81 (1962), pp. 230–8.

[6] Cf. H. J. Kraus, *Gottesdienst in Israel*, pp. 239–42; J. Schreiner, *op. cit.*, pp. 210–14; also K. H. Bernhardt, *Das Problem der altorientalischen Königsideologie im Alten Testament* (Leiden, 1961), pp. 252–61.

[7] Cf. L. Koehler in *V.T.* 3 (1953), pp. 188 seq.; J. Ridderbos, *ibid.* 4 (1954), pp. 87 seq.; for a detailed study see D. Michel, "Studien zu den sogenannten Thronbesteigungspsalmen" in *V.T.* 6 (1956), pp. 40 to 68; H. J. Kraus, *Gottesdienst in Israel*, pp. 240 seq.; J. Schreiner, *op. cit.*, pp. 194–7.

"Jahweh *is* king". The kingship of God is thus something which is present, which always was, and which in the future is only to manifest itself more and more over the whole world, which in worship is considered and praised in all its aspects. Whether the psalms of Jahweh-as-king at least in part presuppose the later prophetic preaching (Deutero-Isa.; cf. p. 24), is still a subject of dispute. A consequent "eschatological" interpretation thus remains as problematic as a purely cultic interpretation which tries to explain the "eschatological view" from the cultic enthusiam of the early period of the kings.[8]

3. The rule of God in the preaching of Jesus has received more attention in NT studies and is treated in most of the studies upon the gospels. Besides mention in the works given above on the history of recent study, the theme has been treated separately by the Dutchmen H. Ridderbos[9] and Tj. van der Walt,[10] and by the American G. E. Ladd.[11] These authors also are quite close to the treatment in this book. Van der Walt takes a moderately critical position (pp. 26 seq.) in the question of the genuineness of the "logia" of Jesus; he places special emphasis on the presence of the kingship of God in the person and activity of Jesus and he attempts

[8] H. Schmid rejects the "eschatological" interpretation in *Z.A.W.* 67 (1955), pp. 185 seq.; H. J. Kraus, *Psalmen* II (Neukirchen, 1960) considers Psalm 92 (pp. 647 seq.) and Ps 98 (pp. 682 seq.) to be pre-exilic, though for Ps 94–97 he accepts a dependence upon Deutero-Isa. (pp. 665 seq., 671 seq., 677). J. Schreiner thinks that the dependence of Ps 95 and 97 (pp. 205, 206 seq.) can be explained by their common relation to the cult language.

[9] H. Ridderbos, *The Coming of the Kingdom* (Philadelphia, 1962). Unfortunately my attention was drawn to this great work too late for it to be taken into account. Ridderbos also defends the present-and-future aspect of the *basileia.*

[10] Tj. van der Walt, *Het Koninkrijk van God-Nabij!* (Kampen, 1962).

[11] G. E. Ladd, *Jesus and the Kingdom* (New York, 1964).

to solve the eschatological problem by the central place he gives to Christology: In Christ past, present, and future converge pp. 312 seq.). The result at which Ladd arrives in the question of the preaching of Jesus is almost the same as the one proposed in this book: The kingdom of God was, for Jesus, the dynamic rule of God which permeated history in his person and mission, and which would again reveal itself at the end of the world, in order to bring this very messianic redemption to its fulfilment (p. 303). In its purpose and method, however, this work is somewhat differently orientated, since the author in "biblical realism" accepts the text simply in its direct sense with consideration of the historical background, but is less interested in the reception of the message of Jesus in the early Church and the implied questions concerning eschatology and the difficulties these raise for our present understanding.

It is precisely here that new efforts have been made, and on the Catholic side as well. This has resulted partly from an examination of the gospel of Jesus itself: is it actually as strongly coloured by the eschatological perspective as it appears to be? The conviction which was held almost unanimously by exegetes since the beginning of the century that the teaching which Jesus brought was above all an eschatological one — about the coming of the reign and kingdom of God — is being questioned anew as to its unity and importance. What is perhaps the strongest statement of this has been made by H. Schürmann in a contribution to K. Rahner's *Festschrift*.[12] He wants to "direct our view to the proximity and combination of two types of utterances among the logia of Jesus:

[12] H. Schürmann, "Das hermeneutische Hauptproblem der Verkündigung Jesu", in *Gott in Welt* I (*Festgabe* for Karl Rahner, Freiburg i. Br., 1964), pp. 579–607; cf. his contribution to the *Kampmann-Festschrift*, also to be found in K. Schubert, ed., *Vom Messias zum Christus* (Vienna, 1964), pp. 203–32.

the eschato-logical and the theo-logical" (p. 581), and thus to a "polarity in the teaching of Jesus" (p. 582). Without denying the eschatological nature of the preaching of Jesus, he wishes to find a deeper basis for the real concerns of Jesus, namely in the "knowledge of the absolute holiness of God which leads to a final theocentrism" (p. 592). "Besides, in, and over the knowledge that the eschaton of God brings forgiveness and salvation, Jesus places the knowledge of the fatherly love of God" (p. 593). What Schürmann is concerned with, therefore, is what one might call the relative value of the eschatological texts; he wishes to diminish their importance in relation to the truly "theo-logical" utterances of Jesus which are concerned with a new and direct relationship to God which is both near to children and totally demanding of men. It is of course a risky thing to allow the teaching of Jesus as we have received it to disintegrate into two series of disconnected though proximate texts, something like "wisdom logia" or timeless "teaching" or an "eschatological gospel"; but if one stresses, as Schürmann does, the "central fusion of eschato-logical and theo-logical utterances in the gospel of Jesus" (pp. 597 seq.), then one can find in this approach a decisive hermeneutical tool for the solution of "the eschatological problem". This same concern is apparent in the work of E. Neuhäusler on the instructions of Jesus.[13] Of course, the problem of texts dealing with the expectation of the imminent end is not thereby solved, but must be dealt with at greater length according to special textual interpretation (cf. p. 213 above).

On the Protestant side various paths are being purseed in order to provide an answer to the eschatological question for our present-day needs an understanding. The "existential inter-

[13] E. Neuhäusler, *Anspruch und Antwort Gottes* (Düsseldorf, 1962); cf. my article in *B.Z., N.F.* 8 (1964), pp. 123–6.

pretation" of the Bultmann school is particularly influential; the articles of H. Conzelmann may be taken as representative of this approach. For him, Jesus "overcomes the apocalyptic question about dates by concentrating upon the present meaning of the proclamation of the kingdom: present and future are so related that the kingdom of God has been preached and has been made comprehensible in the actions of Jesus. Its proclamation is in this way closely bound to the presence of Jesus. And so, with respect to the salvation which is offered to us today, utterances referring to the future and the present are given a unified meaning: Time has come to an end, insofar as it is *our* time; what remains is a respite for repentance. In this way is *our* time; what remains is a respite for repentance. In this way the apocalyptic problems about the exact time of the coming disappear. The kingdom, its nearness, etc., are no longer considered from the viewpoint of an apocalyptically conceived world-situation, but conversely the world-situation is interpreted from the perspective of the coming kingdom. The movement leads from the kingdom of God to us, and not the other way around."[14] Against this, W. G. Kümmel[15] and O. Cullmann[16] make a point of the significance of time in the Basileia-gospel of Jesus. According to Kümmel, we cannot dispute the fact that "Jesus had reckoned with the near future of the kingdom of God which was limited to his generation".[17] "Theological" and "historical" approaches among the different scholars lead to considerable differences of interpretation and threaten to precipitate a methodological crisis in NT studies unless some unanimity is reached on the

[14] In *R.G.G.* V, col. 915.
[15] "Die Naherwartung in der Verkündigung Jesu" in *Zeit und Geschichte*, Presentation to R. Bultmann (Tübingen, 1964), pp. 31–46.
[16] *Heil als Geschichte* (Tübingen, 1965), especially pp. 180f.
[17] *Op. cit.*, p. 45.

point of hermeneutic principles. It appears to me that one cannot leap over the historical question about the teaching of Jesus among his contemporaries by considering only the significance of the kerygma for the hearers of today. Only after ascertaining the historical meaning of his words as we have them, should we go on to the further question as to the timeless revelation which is contained therein, according to the true import of the words of Jesus as they were expressed in a certain period of history.

In trying to ascertain the original form of the preaching of Jesus a difficulty immediately arises as to which of the logia are to be ascribed to Jesus himself and which of them represent but an elaboration or change, a formulation which can be ascribed to the particular circumstances of the early Church, though carried out in the spirit of Jesus, and which are totally new formulations interpreting an utterance of Jesus and adapting it to a further developed situation. In this approach, which attempts to distinguish layers of traditions, and in which certainty is hardly to be expected, one always has the possibility of denying the authenticity of the sayings of Jesus which refer to periods of time and are more strongly coloured by apocalyptic considerations and to ascribe a "re-apocalyptizing" of his gospel to the early Church — a thesis which is not to be taken lightly in view of the form of the "discourse on the end of time" (Mark 13 par.) as it has been handed down.[18] But we must admit, in deference to historical truth,

[18] E. Stauffer, in a contribution to the Dodd *Festschrift*, "Agnotos Christos. Joh 11. 24 und die Eschatologie des vierten Evangeliums", proposed the idea that it was only in the early Church that the preaching of Jesus was interpreted in an apocalyptic way and that the author of the fourth gospel presented the figure and message of Jesus more truly than did his predecessors. "The fourth Gospel, at least so it seems to me, is a protest of the last apostle against the misinterpretation and distortions of Jesus which were dominant in that epoch of apoca-

that according to everything which we are able to ascertain by historical-critical methods, in spite of the peculiarity of our sources, Jesus at least stood in the general stream of eschatological-apocalyptic expectation of the Judaism of his time, even though his preaching diverges from the general apocalyptic view.[19] There is scarcely any other way of acheiving clarity on this point, however, except by examining the utterances of Jesus as they have been presented in the gospels, one at a time, from every side and according to all available methods, to discover how far they represent his original thought or how much they have been coloured or newly formulated by early Christian interpretation.

4. The solution to individual problems and passages has been advanced considerably. The parables of the kingdom, of which the "parable of growth" was mentioned in the foregoing pages (pp. 143–59), are being subjected to new approaches in order

lyptic enthusiasm": see *The Background of the New Testament and its Eschatology* (Cambridge, 1966), pp. 281–99, here p. 286. In his paperback, *Die Botschaft Jesu damals und heute* (1959), he speaks often of the "re-Judaizing" which took place after Jesus. A similar tendency, to ascribe the apocalyptic attitude (as the birth-place of theology) first to the early Church, is noticeable in the latest work of E. Käsemann (see Bibliography), though it is more carefully formulated by him. As against this, the majority of exegetes, however, hold fast to the opinion that Jesus himself had given his teaching an eschatological cast, though the early Christian circles have given certain features greater prominence and introduced more pronounced apocalyptic traits. Cf. esp. W. G. Kümmel in *N.T.St.* 5 (1958/59), pp. 113–26; also R. Schnackenburg, "Kirche und Parusie", in *Gott in Welt*, I, *Festgabe* for K. Rahner (Freiburg i. Br., 1964), pp. 551–78, more precisely 569 seq.

[19] A. Stobel, *Die apokalyptische Sendung Jesu* (Rothenburg, 1962), pictures Jesus in a one-sided way as an "apocalyptic". Cf. for a contrary view A. Vögtle, *Das öffentliche Wirken Jesu auf dem Hintergrund der*

to throw more light upon their significance. E. Jüngel is to be mentioned in this connection with his book *Paulus und Jesus*.[20] Attacking the hermeneutical approach of E. Lohmeyer und E. Fuchs, Jüngel considers the parables as "speech events", i.e. he believes they are not so much instructions upon the kingdom of God as verbal events which actualize the kingship of God, a "special manner of its coming" (p. 139). The *basileia* is articulated in the parable *as* parable" (p. 135). But this is not an entirely new idea; I wrote in connection with the parable of the sower: "And so in this parable Jesus is 'teaching something concerning the reign of God which is actually *taking place*" (p. 151). Jüngel, however, does not only see the "event" in connection with the other works of Jesus which together reveal the breaking-in of the kingship of God, but he sees it even more in the actual telling of the parable itself. The parable "gathers" the people together who hear it, "and thus leads those who are gathered together to the point which it contains, which is then to become *the point of its own existence*" (p. 136). This characteristic of the "existential interpretation" (deriving from his teacher E. Fuchs) is quite clear: the parables are seen as direct existential addresses to men. But even this is no new discovery. Whoever considers the "critical" function of the parables, as it is indicated in the transitional passage in Mark 4:11 seq., will not

Qumranbewegung (Freiburg i. Br., 1958); K. Schubert in the introduction to the collection *Der historische Jesus und der Christus unseres Glaubens* (Vienna, 1962): "Jesus belongs in the larger frame-work of the movement comprised by those who were awaiting the kingdom of God. But he showed himself clearly to be so different from the apocalyptic movement that it could not have been something made up by the early Christian community" (p. 9).

[20] E. Jüngel, *Paulus und Jesus* (Tübingen, 1964); the parables are presented under the title "Jesus und die Gottesherrschaft" in the extensive section covered by pp. 87–197.

be tempted to overlook its power to rouse the hearer to a personal decision, to faith or disbelief — not only the hearer of that time, but also of the present.[21] Jüngel proceeds ever further in developing his basic "existential" interpretation: "If the kingship of God is dealt with in the parables, then human existence has its point in the *extra nos* of the kingship of God" (p. 137). But here one must ask what he understands by the "kingship of God".

Jüngel then proceeds to give a concrete and stimulating interpretation of the parables themselves. He does not try to approach them from the position in which Jesus found himself, the correction of false ideas of the rule of God and the answering of objections, as is done in part by C. H. Dodd and J. Jeremias (cf. his criticism, pp. 107–20). He treats them solely as positive kerygmatic addresses. For him it is of no significance that Jesus tried to still the doubts of his opponents with the parable of the mustard seed or that he wished to bolster them up against the "depressing experience of the moment" (as I wrote on p. 156 above, though it was in reference to the "growth" parables in general). Instead of this, according to Jüngel, the parable of the mustard seed is meant to gather men together who are called for the Basileia so that those who are called for the kingship of God might then belong to the beginning of that surpassing end (pp. 153 seq.). This same "gathering" tendency is found by him in the parable of the fish-net which makes us more aware of the present gathering which precedes the future division, while the parable of the weeds is perhaps only modelled upon it only with special emphasis upon the coming judgement with its separation

[21] On Mk 4:11 seq. cf. the work of J. Gnilka, *Die Verstockung Israels, Isaias 6:9–10 in der Theologie der Synoptiker* (Munich, 1961). The direct existential demands which characterize the parables is also brought out by J. Blank, "Marginalien zur Gleichnisauslegung", in *Bibel und Leben* 6 (1965), pp. 50–60.

(pp. 145–8). On the whole the interpretations of Jüngel deserve attention because of their positive kerygmatic tendency, but it must be added that too little attention is paid by him to the situation in which Jesus preached and acted. With Jesus proselytizing and corrective motives could have been mixed, for Mark already referred to the simultaneous "revealing" and "concealing" character of the parables and explained it by reference to the ultimate wishes and activities of God which he alone knew. And so against Jüngel's attempt we must again pose the hermeneutical question about the relation between the historical, i.e. the kerygmatic and existential interpretation.

On the Catholic side H. Kahlefeld offers a valuable explanation of the parables designed for a broader circle of readers.[22] He observes well the various levels of the gospel in the life of Jesus, in the early Church, and in the conception of the evangelists, and he also knows how to speak in a direct way to the readers of today. Such an attempt, proceeding as it does from the original sense of the parables in the mouth of Jesus, through the understanding of the early Church to the kerygmatic meaning for our own lives, appears to me to be the only legitimate procedure. In his concrete interpretation, Kahlefeld presents the "growth" parables in the narrower sense, namely the parable of the sower, the weeds, the mustard seed, and the leaven, under the idea of "the gospel and its power". They are situated in the beginning of the activity of Jesus (p. 23), as the work of proclaiming the gospel was in full course, but also after the first opposition and especially the law of inertia had made themselves felt (p. 22). So far so good; but Kahlefeld does not find in them (even on the level of the original preaching of Jesus) any reference to the rule and kingship of

[22] *Gleichnisse und Lehrstücke im Evangelium* I (2nd edition, Frankfurt, 1964); the first two chapters are especially relevant here (pp. 13–72).

God: it is only the power of the gospel preached by Christ which he sees. Thus he says about the parable of the mustard seed: "It does not have to be the kingdom of God itself which establishes itself and shows its vigour; it suffices for the sense of the introduction that the subject of the parable be something connected with it. The parable does not require us to seek after something which is at first small and insignificant and then finally grows into something great and powerful" (p. 26). But the gospel is precisely the gospel of the kingship of God and in its preaching it is this which shows its power; thus it can scarcely be correct to say that this parable treats only of the power of the word of God or of the gospel as its final realization. It is not only the gospel which develops from the most modest beginnings and finally grows full of power, but it is the rule of God which grows with it and in it. The very image of completion (bearing of fruit, harvest, tree, and leavened mass) evidently refers to the kingdom of glory itself.

5. The problem of the Son of Man is still hotly debated. The exhaustive study of H. E. Tödt showed that the "eschatological" logia were part of the oldest layer and recognizes Luke 12:8 seq. as well as other passages as the original words of Jesus, though in the sense that by the Son of Man Jesus only meant the eschatological figure of the "advocate" before the judgement seat of God.[23] Against the thesis of Vielhauer (cf. pp. 166 seq.) that the utterances about the Son of Man and about the kingship of God originally had nothing to do with each other, Tödt shows that both groups of utterances belong to the same collection, the same layer of tradition (Q) and that this early collator found no difficulty in putting them together (pp. 302 seq.). F. Hahn, in his

[23] *Der Menschensohn in der synoptischen Überlieferung* (Gütersloh, 1959), pp. 50–56; cf. the article of A. Vögtle in *B.Z., NF* 6 (1962), pp. 135–8.

work on NT Christology, refers us even further back to the apocalypses and though he recognized the different levels of usage, he finds certain relationships in content and disputes the assertion that "the reign of God" and "the Son of Man" may be put in such opposition.[24] Since then Vielbauer has answered these objections in a new study and has held to his position, which is also shared by other exegetes.[25] Thus the discussion is far from being concluded on this topic, and even among Catholics the meaning of many of the utterances about the Son of Man and the Parusia is being disputed.[26]

The basic question, however, whether Jesus considered his own person to have a significance for the coming of the *basileia*, whether he possessed a "messianic" self-consciousness (messianic in the general sense of being significant for salvation) goes even further into this special topic. The Catholic exegete N. Brox can even allow that though the "radical" thesis that Jesus had not claimed for himself any of the titles of honour ascribed to him in the gospels remains undecided, he can still hold, on the basis of the "indirect self-witness" of Jesus, that the significance of the person of Jesus for salvation, as it was made explicit by the early Church in it profession (by using just those messianic titles), is "an element in the genuine gospel of the kingdom of God". "In that Jesus proclaims the *basileia*, he speaks of his own person, of his having come, and of his fullness of power."[27] Thus, even

[24] Christologische Hoheitstitel (Göttingen, 1963), pp. 27 seq.

[25] P. Viehaurer, "Jesus und der Menschensohn" in *Z.Th. K.* 60 (1963), pp. 133–77; cf. also E. Haenchen, "Die Komposition von Mk VIII, 27 – IX, 11 und Par." in *N.T.* 6 (1963), pp. 81–109, more specifically 95 seq.

[26] Cf. the contribution of A. Feuillet and B. Rigaux in *La venue du Messie*, Rech. Bibl., VI (Louvain, 1962).

[27] N. Brox, "Das messianische Selbstverständnis des historischen

though not a few individual utterances may remain questionable, there is still no reason to depart from the conception adopted in the present work, namely that the gospel of Jesus cannot be separated from his person.

6. A special difficulty is encountered by the texts referring to "imminent end" which contain a reference to specific times, i.e. Mark 9:1 par.; 13:30 par. and Matt. 10:23 (cf. 203–13). Since we scarcely expect any unanimity among scholars as to how these passages are to be judged, we could have left this question as it stands, were it not for the considerable impetus given on the Catholic side by the work of A. Vögtle in which he undertook to deal with these problems. In a contribution to the Rahner *Festschrift*[28] which is well thought-out both exegetically and theologically, he raised the question whether these tests which are at variance with the teaching of Jesus about the coming end witnessed to in other places, though without an indication of time or term, are not really secondary formulations of the community, though based upon genuine utterances of Jesus (cf. p. 641). He refers quite rightly to a similar process which can be seen in the composition of the discourse on the end of time in Mark 13 (p. 644). In fact, the early Church evidently saw no difficulty in applying the gospel of Jesus in its reference to the imminent approach of the kingdom of God to its own situation and to represent it in a very concrete way, in a living hope, though always with the knowledge that Jesus had left the time and the hour open (cf. Mark 13:32). If one accepts this supposition based on the composition of Mark 13, then the exegetical observations and arguments of Vögtle are easy to follow: Mark

Jesus", in *Vom Messias zum Christus* (Vienna, 1964), pp. 165–201, here p. 191.

[28] "Exegetische Erwägungen über das Wissen und Selbstbewußtsein Jesu", in *Gott in Welt* I (Freiburg i. Br., 1964), pp. 608–67.

13:30 was thus an utterance of Jesus concerning the destruction of the temple (pp. 652 seq.), but it has been presented in a context which relates it to the Parousia. The circle of Christians responsible for the composition of Mark 13 were awaiting the Parousia soon after that event – but always with the definite reservation of v. 32, i.e. not with dogmatic certainty but only in living hope, just as Paul at first "expected" the Parousia to occur in his own lifetime.[29] Vögtle wishes to interpret Mark 9:1 as a variant tradition, as an *aktualisierende Umformung* of Mark 13:30, for sound reasons derived from a comparison of the texts (pp. 644–7). Though Matt. 10:23 is more difficult to explain in this way, it probably had its basis in Jesus' missionary instructions to his disciples (Matt. 10:14 par.) which were also thought to contain the counsel to flight. In conjunction with an active expectation of the Parousia a formulation such as that of Matt. 10:23 could well have arisen: "A word of assurance combining Jesus' utterance in Matt. 10:14 and the consoling promise of the coming of the Son of Man which had its origin entirely in Palestinian Christendom" (p. 650). In view of the great difficulties which I have indicated in my book, this solution of Vögtle deserves serious attention and is certainly tenable from a theological point of view.

7. The idea of the kingship of God in the gospels is still in need of further study in one direction: according to the conceptions which each of the evangelists had of it at the time of writing. The so-called method of redaction-history which is used to clarify such problems is being assiduously applied in order to arrive at a clearer idea of the theology of the individual synoptics.[30] In

[29] Cf. J. A. Sint, "Parusie-Erwartung und Parusie-Verzögerung im paulinischen Briefcorpus" in *Z.K.Th.* 86 (1964), pp. 47–79; also printed in *Vom Messias zum Christus* (see footnote 27), pp. 233–77.

[30] For orientation cf. R. Schnackenburg, *New Testament Theology Today* (London, 1963).

this book I have tried to point out at least some of the larger and more striking features of this subject, such as in the Lucan formula "to announce the reign of God" (p. 138), and for formulations used in Acts (pp. 261–70), and the significance of the reign of God for Matthew's concept of the Church (section 18, pp. 234–49). These and other examples were only preliminary sketches (which were considered to be misguided by some critics and not radical enough by others) which need to be followed up, more critically tested, and elaborated upon. At that time I did not have the benefit of W. Trilling's useful work on Matthew, which has since appeared in a new edition.[31] He treats of the relation of the reign of God, the reign of the Son of Man, and the Church in a separate chapter (pp. 143–63). Though there is no space here to go into a detailed discussion of the topic, I would like to mention one or two things. His observation is certainly sound when he says that for Matthew the reign of God had already become a "doctrinal concept" (*Lehrbegriff*, pp. 144–51). To this it may be added that the concept had a broad range of usage and comprised in fact a very complex general idea (p. 151). Trilling also thinks it probable (as I had indicated for 21:43, p. 241) that certain rabbinic elements were included in this idea (pp. 148, 152 seq.). We have no evidence of a simple equation with "Church", not even in 13:41 which speaks of the "reign of the Son of Man". With regard to this passage I would like to correct my passing remark on p. 168. The present "Basileia of the Son of Man" actually has a broader basis in Matthew, as Trilling shows (pp. 152 seq.); besides the passages mentioned by him I might refer especially to the concluding scene in Matt. 28:18 seq., according to which the risen Lord is given complete authority

[31] W. Trilling, *Das wahre Israel. Studien zur Theologie des Matthäus-Evangeliums* (Munich, 1964; the first edition was published in Leipzig in 1959).

"in heaven and upon earth", thus exercising already in the present age, in this world, a cosmic kingship.[32] Similarly, in 13:41 (cf. also v. 38: "the field is the world") we must interpret the "reign of the Son of Man" as the form of the present rule of God in the world" (Trilling, p. 153) which reaches beyond the Church which is to be found upon earth. This is all the more significant as Matthew is here and in certain other respects very close (though not identical) to the interpretation of Paul, for whom the idea of the reign of Christ is a present and very real exercise of the rule of God, as I have explained above (cf. sections 22 and 23). That the Church, the reign of Christ, and the reign of God stand in closest relation to one another, I have attempted to make clear in my work on the idea of the Church in the NT,[33] which I would like to consider as a complement and an elaboration of the material contained in the present book.

[32] Cf. A. Vögtle, "Das christologische und ekklesiologische Anliegen von Mt 28, 18–20", in *Studia Evangelica* II (Berlin, 1964), pp. 266–94.
[33] R. Schnackenburg, *The Church in the New Testament* (Freiburg–New York–London–Montreal, 1965).

BIBLIOGRAPHY

Alt, A., *Gedanken über das Königtum Jahwes,* Kleine Schriften zur Geschichte des Volkes Israel I, München 1953, 345–57.

Aulén, G., *Ein Buch von der Kirche,* Göttingen 1951.

Balley, J. W., "The Temporary Messianic Reign in the Literature of Early Judaism" in *J.B.L.* 53 (1934) 170–87.

Bartmann, B., *Das Reich Gottes in der Heiligen Schrift,* Münster/W. 1912.

Beasley-Murray, G. R., *Jesus and the Future.* An Examination of the Criticism of the Eschatological Discourse, Mark 13, with Special Reference to the Little Apocalypse Theory, London 1954.

– *A Commentary on Mark XIII,* London 1957.

Bietenhard, H., *Das Tausendjährige Reich,* Zürich [2]1955.

Bohlin, T., "Die Reich-Gottes-Idee im letzten halben Jahrhundert" in *Z.Th.K.* 10 (1929) 1–27.

Bonsirven, J., *Le judaïsme palestinien au temps de Jésus-Christ,* 2 vols., Paris 1934/35.

– *Textes rabbiniques des deux premiers siècles chrétiens,* Rome 1955.

– *Le Règne de Dieu,* Paris 1957.

Bornkamm, G., "Enderwartung und Kirche im Matthäusevangelium" in *The Background of the New Testament and its Eschatology* (publication in honour of C. H. Dodd), Cambridge 1956, 222–60.

– *Jesus von Nazareth,* Stuttgart 1956.

Bousset, W. – Greßmann, H., *Die Religion des Judentums im späthellenistischen Zeitalter,* Tübingen [3]1926.

Bright, J., *The Kingdom of God in Bible and Church,* New York 1953.
Buber, M., *Königtum Gottes,* Heidelberg [3]1956.
Bultmann, R., *Geschichte der synoptischen Tradition,* Göttingen [2]1931, with supplement 1958.
– "Reich Gottes und Menschensohn" in *Th.Rdsch.* NF 9 (1937) 1–35 (article on the book by R. Otto).
– *Jesus,* Tübingen 1951 (= 1926).
– *Theologie des Neuen Testaments,* Tübingen 1953.
Burrows, M., "Thy Kingdom Come" in *J.B.L.* 74 (1955) 1–8.
Buzy, D., *Les Paraboles,* Paris [16]1948.
Cadbury, H. J., "Acts and Eschatology" in *The Background of the New Testament and its Eschatology* (publication in honour of C. H. Dodd), Cambridge 1956, 300–21.
Cerfaux, L., *The Church in the Theology of St. Paul,* Paris [2]1948, Engl. transl. New York, Edinburgh 1959.
– "L'Église et le Règne de Dieu d'après s. Paul" in *Eph.Th.Lov.* 2 (1925) 181–98; printed in *Recueil L. Cerfaux* II, Gembloux 1954, 365–87.
Charles, R. H., *The Apocrypha and Pseudepigrapha of the Old Testament,* 2 vols., Oxford 1913.
Clavier, H., "L'accès au Royaume de Dieu" in *R.H.Ph.R.* 22 (1942) 1–29; 215–39; 23 (1943) 185–36.
Conzelmann, H., *Die Mitte der Zeit.* Studien zur Theologie des Lukas , Tübingen 1954.
– "Gegenwart und Zukunft in der synoptischen Tradition" in *Z.Th.K.* 54 (1957) 277–96.
Cullmann, O., *Christus und die Zeit.* Die urchristliche Zeit- und Geschichtsauffassung, Zürich 1946.
– *Königsherrschaft Christi und Kirche im Neuen Testament,* Zollikon-Zürich [2]1946.
– *Le retour du Christ,* Neuchâtel-Paris [3]1948.
– *Christologie des Neuen Testaments,* Tübingen 1957.
Dahl, N. A., *Das Volk Gottes.* Eine Untersuchung zum Kirchenbewußtsein des Urchristentums, Oslo 1941 (Lit.).
– "The Parables of Growth" in *St.Th.* 5 (1952) 132–66.
Dalman, G., *Die Worte Jesu* I, Leipzig [2]1930.
Davies, G. H., "The Clues of the Kingdom in the Bible". A Survey in *Interpretation* 14 (1960) 155–61.
Delling, G., *Das Zeitverständnis des Neuen Testaments,* Gütersloh 1940.

Dodd, C. H., *The Parables of the Kingdom,* London 1935.
– *The Apostolic Preaching and its Developments,* London [2]1944.
Duncan, G. S., *Jesus, Son of Man,* London 1948.
Dupont, J., *Les Béatitudes,* Bruges-Louvain 1954 ([2]I 1958).
Eichrodt, W., *Theologie des Alten Testamentes* I, Göttingen [5]1957.
– "Heilserfahrung und Zeitverständnis im Alten Testament" in *Th.Z.* 12 (1956) 103–25.
Eissfeldt, O., "Jahwe als König" in *Z.A.W.* 46 (1928) 81–105.
Fascher, E., "Gottes Königtum im Urchristentum" in *Numen* 4 (1957) 85–113.
Feine, P., *Theologie des Neuen Testaments,* Berlin [8]1951 68–88 (Lit.).
Filson, Floyd V., *Jesus Christ, the Risen Lord,* New-York-Nashville 1956.
Flew, R. N., *Jesus and His Church,* London [3]1943.
de Fraine, J., *L'aspect religieux de la royauté israélite,* Rome 1954.
Frick, R., *Die Geschichte des Reich-Gottes-Gedankens in der alten Kirche bis zu Origenes und Augustin,* Gießen 1928.
Fuller, R. H., *The Mission and Achievement of Jesus,* London 1954.
v. Gall, A. Frhr., Βασιλεία τοῦ θεοῦ. Eine religionsgeschichtliche Studie zur vorkirchlichen Eschatologie, Heidelberg 1926.
Gewieß, J., *Die urapostolische Heilsverkündigung nach der Apostelgeschichte,* Breslau 1939.
– "Die Begriffe πληροῦν und πλήρωμα im Kolosser- und Epheserbrief" in *Vom Wort des Lebens* (Festschrift for M. Meinertz), Münster/W. 1951, 128–41.
Glasson, T. F., *The Second Advent.* The Origin of the New Testament Doctrine, London [2]1947.
– *His Appearing and His Kingdom.* The Christian Hope in the Light of its History, London 1953.
Gloegle, G., *Reich Gottes und Kirche im Neuen Testament,* Gütersloh 1929.
Grant, R. M., "The Coming of the Kingdom" in *J.B.L.* 67 (1948) 297–303.
Grässer, E., *Das Problem der Parousieverzögerung in den synoptischen Evangelien und in der Apostelgeschichte,* Berlin 1957 (Lit.).
Gray, J., "The Hebrew Conception of the Kingship of God. Its Origin and Development" in *V. T.* 6 (1956) 268–85.
– "The Kingship of God in the Prophets and Psalms" in *Vetus Testamentum* 11 (1961) 1–29.
Greßmann, H., *Der Messias,* Göttingen 1929.

Grosche, R., "Reich Gottes und Kirche" in *Pilgernde Kirche,* Freiburg i. Br. 1938, 41–76.
Groß, H., *Weltherrschaft als religiöse Idee im Alten Testament,* Bonn 1953.
– *Die Idee des ewigen und allgemeinen Weltfriedens im alten Orient und im Alten Testament,* Trier 1956.
Grundmann, W., *Die Geschichte Jesu Christi,* Berlin 1957.
Guardini, R., *Der Herr.* Betrachtungen über die Person und das Leben Jesu Christi, Aschaffenburg [5]1948.
Guntermann, F., *Die Eschatologie des heiligen Paulus,* Münster/W. 1932.
Guy, H. A., *The New Testament Doctrine of the "Last Things",* Oxford 1948.
Heinisch, P., *Theologie des Alten Testamentes,* Bonn 1940.
Héring, J., *Le Royaume de Dieu et sa venue,* Paris 1937 (Lit.).
Holmström, F., *Das eschatologische Denken der Gegenwart,* Göttingen 1936.
Hooke, S. H., *The Kingdom of God in the Experience of Jesus,* London 1949.
Hunter, A. M., "Interpreting the parables" in *Interpretation* 14 (1960) 70–84, 167–85, 315–32, 440–54.
van Imschoot, P., "Reich Gottes" in *Bibellexikon,* edited by H. Haag, Einsiedeln-Zürich-Köln 1951/56, 1412–18.
– *Théologie de l'Ancien Testament I Dieu,* Tournai 1954.
Jeremias, J., *Die Abendmahlsworte Jesu,* Göttingen [3]1960.
– *Die Gleichnisse Jesu,* Göttingen [4]1956.
– *Jesu Verheißung für die Völker,* Stuttgart 1956.
Junker, H., "Die offenbarungsgeschichtliche Bedeutung der alttestamentlichen Botschaft vom Reiche Gottes" in *Tr.Th.Z.* 62 (1953) 65–79.
Körner, J., "Endgeschichtliche Parusieerwartung und Heilsgegenwart im Neuen Testament" in *Ev.Th.* 14 (1954) 177–92.
Kraus, H. J., *Die Königsherrschaft Gottes im Alten Testament,* Tübingen 1951.
– *Das Volk Gottes im Alten Testament,* Zürich 1957.
Kuhn, K. G., Art βασιλεία (rabbinic literature) in *Th.W.B.* I, 570–73.
Kümmel, W. G., *Kirchenbegriff und Geschichtsbewußtsein in der Urgemeinde und bei Jesus* (SB Ups 1), Uppsala 1943.
– *Verheißung und Erfüllung.* Untersuchungen zur eschatologischen Verkündigung Jesu, Zürich [2]1953 (Lit.).
– "Jesus und die Anfänge der Kirche" in *St.Th.* 7 (1953) 1–27.
Kuss, O., "Bemerkungen zum Fragenkreis: Jesus und die Kirche im Neuen Testament" in *Th.Q.* 135 (1955) 28–55.

Ladd, G. E., "The Kingdom of God in the Jewish Apocryphal Literature" in *Bibliotheca sacra* 109 (1952) 55ff.; 164ff.; 318ff.; 110 (1953) 32ff.
Lagrange, M. J., "Le Règne de Dieu dans l'Ancien Testament" in *R.B.* n. s. 5 (1908) 36–61.
– "Le Règne de Dieu dans le judaïsme" ibid. 350–66.
Lindeskog, G., "Gottesreich und Kirche im Neuen Testament" in *Ein Buch von der Kirche,* Göttingen 1951, 145–57.
Lohmeyer, E., *Das Urchristentum I. Johannes der Täufer,* Göttingen 1932.
– *Das Evangelium des Markus,* Göttingen 1937.
– *Das Evangelium des Matthäus,* edited W. Schmauch, Göttingen 1956.
Lohse, E., "Die Gottesherrschaft in den Gleichnissen Jesu" in *Ev.Th.* 18 (1958) 145–57.
Lundström, G., *Guds Rike i Jesu förkunnelse,* Lund 1947.
Maag, V., "Malkût Jhwe" *Vetus Testamentum* Suppl. VII (congress volume Oxford 1959) 129–53.
Manson, T. W., *The Teaching of Jesus,* Cambridge [2]1935.
– *The Sayings of Jesus,* London 1949.
Manson, W., *Bist du, der da kommen soll?* Zollikon-Zürich 1952.
Matter, H. M., *Nieuwere opvattingen omtrent het Koninkrijk Gods in Jezus' prediking naar de Synoptici* (diss.), Kampen 1942.
Meinertz, M., *Theologie des Neuen Testaments,* 2 vols., Bonn 1950, particularly I, 27–146.
Michaelis, W., *Täufer, Jesus, Urgemeinde.* Die Predigt vom Reiche Gottes vor und nach Pfingsten, Gütersloh 1928.
– *Reich Gottes und Geist Gottes nach dem Neuen Testament,* Basel n. d. (1931).
– *Versöhnung des Alls.* Die frohe Botschaft von der Gnade Gottes, Gümlingen/Bern 1950.
Minear, P. S., *Christian Hope and the Second Coming,* Philadelphia 1954.
Mollat, D., Art. "Judgement dans le Noveau Testament, Les Évangiles synoptiques" in *D.B.* Suppl. IV, Paris 1949, 1344–59.
Moore, G. F., *Judaism in the First Centuries of the Christian Era.* The Age of the Tannaim, 3 vols., Cambridge 1927/30 (reprint 1946/48).
Morgenthaler, R., *Kommendes Reich,* Zürich 1952.
Mowinckel, S., *He That Cometh,* Oxford 1956.
Mußner, F., *Christus das All und die Kirche.* Studien zur Theologie des Epheserbriefes, Trier 1955.
– "Die Bedeutung von Mk 1, 14f. für die Reichsgottes-Verkündigung Jesu" in *Tr.Th.Z.* 66 (1957) 257–75.

Noack, B., *Das Gottesreich bei Lukas.* Eine Studie zu Lc 17, 20–24 (SB Ups 10), Uppsala 1948.

Noth, M., Gott, König, Volk im Alten Testament" in *Z.Th.K.* 47 (1950) 157–91 printed also in *Gesammelte Studien zum Alten Testament,* München, 1957, 188–229.

Oepke, A., "Der Herrnspruch über die Kirche Mt 16, 17–19 in der neuesten Forschung" in *St.Th.* 2 (1948) 110–65.

– *Das neue Gottesvolk in Schrifttum, bildender Kunst und Weltgestaltung,* Gütersloh 1950.

– Art. παρουσία in *Th.W.B.* V, 863–8.

Otto, R., *Reich Gottes und Menschensohn.* Ein religionsgeschichtlicher Versuch, München ³1954 (= ²1940).

Percy, E., *Die Botschaft Jesu.* Eine traditionskritische und exegetische Untersuchung, Lund 1953.

Perels, O., "Kirche und Welt nach dem Epheser- und Kolosserbrief" in *Th. L. Z.* 76 (1951) 391–400.

v. Rad, G., Art. βασιλεία (Altes Testament) in *Th.W.B.* I, 563–9.

– *Theologie des Alten Testaments* I Die Theologie der geschichtlichen Überlieferungen Israels, München 1957.

Reuß, J., "Die Kirche als 'Leib Christi' und die Herkunft dieser Vorstellung bei dem Apostel Paulus" in *B. Z.* NF 2 (1958) 103–27.

Ridderbos, H., *De komst van het Koninkrijk.* Jezus' prediking volgens de Synoptische Evangelien, Kampen 1950.

Rießler, P., *Altjüdisches Schrifttum außerhalb der Bibel,* Augsburg 1928.

Ringgren, H., "König und Messias" in *Z.A.W.* 64 (1952) 120–55.

Rissi, M., *Zeit und Geschichte in der Offenbarung des Johannes,* Zürich 1952.

Roberts, H., *Jesus and the Kingdom of God,* London 1955.

Robinson, J. A. T., *Jesus and His Coming.* The Emergence of a Doctrine, London 1957.

Schildenberger, J., "Verheißung und Erfüllung" in *Bibl.* 24 (1943) 107–24; 205–30.

Schlier, H., *Der Brief an die Epheser.* Ein Kommentar, Düsseldorf 1957.

– "Über die Herrschaft Christi" in *G. u. L.* 30 (1957) 246–57.

Schlier, H. — Warnach, V., *Die Kirche im Epheserbrief,* Münster/W. 1949.

Schmauch, W. — Wolf, E., *Königsherrschaft Christi.* Der Christ im Staat (Theol. Existenz heute, NF 64), München 1958.

Schmid, J., *Das Evangelium nach Markus,* Regensburg ³1954 (particularly pp. 31–39).

– *Das Evangelium nach Lukas,* Regensburg [3]1955.
– *Das Evangelium nach Matthäus,* Regensburg [3]1956.
Schmidt, K. L., Art. βασιλεία (hellenistisches Judentum und Neues Testament) in *Th.W.B.* I, 573–95 (Lit.).
– "Royaume, Église, État et Peuple: relations et contrastes" in *R.H.Ph. R.* 18 (1938) 145–73.
Schnackenburg, R., *Die sittliche Botschaft des Neuen Testamentes,* Munich 1954, Engl. transl. in preparation.
Schürmann, H., *Der Paschamahlbericht Lk* 22 *(*7–14*)* 15–18, Münster/W. 1953 (= Schürmann I).
– *Der Einsetzungsbericht Lk* 22, 19–20, Münster/W. 1955 (= Schürmann II).
– *Jesu Abschiedsrede Lk* 22, 21–38, Münster/W. 1957 (= Schürmann III).
Schurr, V., "*Reich Gottes*" *in der Verkündigung*: *Paulus* 23 (1951) 16–32.
Schweitzer, A., *Geschichte der Leben-Jesu-Forschung,* Tübingen [6]1951 (=[2]1913).
– *Das Messianitäts- und Leidensgeheimnis.* Eine Skizze des Lebens Jesu, Tübingen [3]1956 (= 1901).
Schweizer, E., *Erniedrigung und Erhöhung bei Jesus und seinen Nachfolgern,* Zürich 1955.
Sharman, H.B., *Son of Man and Kingdom of God,* New York - London [2]1944.
Sjöberg, E., *Der Menschensohn im äthiopischen Henochbuch,* Lund 1946.
– *Der verborgene Menschensohn in den Evangelien,* Lund 1955.
Sommerlath, E., "Reich Gottes und Kirche" in *Z.sy.Th.* 16 (1939/40) 562–75.
Staehlin, E., *Die Verkündigung des Reiches Gottes in der Kirche Jesu Christi* I, Basle 1951.
Stanley, D. M., "Kingdom to Church" in *Th.St.* 16 (1955) 1–29.
Strege, M., *Das Reich Gottes als theologisches Problem im Lichte der Eschatologie und Mystik A. Schweitzers,* Stuttgart 1956.
Taylor, V., *Jesus and His Sacrifice.* A Study of the Passion-Sayings in the Gospels, London 1937.
– *The Gospel according to St. Mark,* London 1952.
– *The Life and Ministry of Jesus,* London 1955.
Testa, E., *Gesù pacificatore universale,* Assisi n. d. (1956).
Theissing, J., *Die Lehre Jesu von der ewigen Seligkeit,* Breslau 1940.
Theologisches Wörterbuch zum Neuen Testament, edited by G. Kittel, continued by G. Friedrich, Stuttgart 1933ff. (= *Th. W. B.*).
Trilling, *Das wahre Israel.* Studien zur Theologie des Matth.-Ev., Leipzig 1959.

Vielhauer, Ph., "Gottesreich und Menschensohn in der Verkündigung Jesu" in the Festschrift for G. Dehn, Neukirchen 1957, 51–79.
Vögtle, A., "Messiasbekenntnis und Petrusverheißung. Zur Komposition Mt 16, 13–23 par." in *B.Z.*NF 1 (1957) 252–72; 2 (1958) 85–103.
– Art. "Binden und Lösen" in *L.Th.K.* [2]II 480–2.
Volz, P., *Die Eschatologie der jüdischen Gemeinde im neutestamentlichen Zeitalter,* Tübingen [2]1934.
Walter, E., *Das Kommen des Herrn* II. Die eschatologische Situation nach den synoptischen Evangelien, Freiburg i. Br. 1947.
Walvoord, J. F., "A Review of Crucial Questions about the Kingdom of God" in *Bibliotheca sacra* 110 (1953) 1–10.
Warnach, V., *Die Kirche im Epheserbrief* (see under Schlier).
– "Kirche und Kosmos" in *Enkainia.* Gesammelte Arbeiten zum 800jährigen Weihegedächtnis der Abteikirche Maria Laach, edited by H. Emonds, Düsseldorf 1956, 170–205.
Weinel, H., *Biblische Theologie des Neuen Testamentes,* Tübingen [4]1928.
Weiß, J., *Die Predigt Jesu vom Reiche Gottes,* Göttingen [2]1900.
Wendland, H. D., *Die Eschatologie des Reiches Gottes bei Jesus,* Gütersloh 1931.
– *Geschichtsanschauung und Geschichtsbewußtsein im Neuen Testament,* Göttingen 1938.
Wernle, P., *Die Reichsgotteshoffnung in den ältesten christlichen Dokumenten und bei Jesus,* Tübingen-Leipzig 1903.
Westerink, H. J., *Het Koninkrijk Gods bij Paulus* (diss.), Hilversum 1937.
– "De Malkoeth Siamaim bij Mattheus" in *Arcana revelata* (Festschrift for F. W. Grosheide), Kampen 1951, 149–62.
Widengren, G., *Sakrales Königtum im Alten Testament und im Judentum,* Stuttgart 1955 (Lit.) .
Wikenhauser, A., *Die Kirche als der mystische Leib Christi nach dem Apostel Paulus,* Münster/W. [2]1940.
– "Die Belehrung der Apostel durch den Auferstandenen nach Apg 1, 3" in *Vom Wort des Lebens* (Festschrift for M. Meinertz), Münster/W. 1951, 105–13.
– *New Testament Introduction,* Engl. transl. New York, Edinburgh 1958.
Wilder, A. N., *Eschatology and Ethics in the Teaching of Jesus,* New York [2]1950.
Windisch, H., "Die Sprüche vom Eingehen in das Reich Gottes" in *Z.N.W.* 27 (1928) 163–92.
Zorell, F., *Novi Testamenti Lexicon graecum,* Paris [2]1931.

BIBLIOGRAPHY TO SUPPLEMENT

Aalen, S., "'Reign' and 'House' in the Kingdom of God in the Gospels" in *N.T.St.* 8 (1961/62) 215–40.

Bammel, E., "Erwägungen zur Eschatologie Jesu" in *Studia Evangelica* II (1964) 3–32.

Bartsch, H. W., "Zum Problem der Parusieverzögerung bei den Synoptikern" in *Ev.Th.* 19 (1959) 116–31.

Berkey, R. F., "Ἐγγίζειν, φθάνειν and Realized Eschatology" in *J.B.L.* 82 (1963) 177–87.

Bernhardt, K. H., *Das Problem der altorientalischen Königsideologie im Alten Testament*, Leiden 1961.

Blatter, T., *Macht und Herrschaft Gottes*, Freiburg, Switzerland 1962.

Brox, N., "Das messianische Selbstverständnis des historischen Jesus" in *Vom Messias zum Christus*, Vienna 1964, 165–201.

Conzelmann, H., "Reich Gottes im Neuen Testament" in *R.G.G.*³ V, 914–18.

Cullmann, O., *Heil als Geschichte*, Tübingen 1965, especially 167–214.

De Montcheuil, Y., *Das Reich Gottes und seine Forderungen*, Mainz 1961.

Doeve, J. W., "Parusieverzögerung" in *Niederl. Theol. Tijdschr.* 17 (1962/63) 32–38.

Feuillet, A., "Parousie" in *Dict. de la Bible*, suppl. VI (1960) 1331–1419.

– "Le triomphe du Fils de l'Homme d'après la déclaration du Christ aux Sanhédrites" in *La venue du Messie*, Rech. Bibl. VI (1962) 149–71.

Galling, K., "Reich Gottes im Judentum" in *R.G.G.*³ V, 912–14.

Gnilka, J., "'Parusieverzögerung' und Naherwartung in den synopti-

schen Evangelien und in der Apostelgeschichte" in *Catholica* 13 (1959) 277–90.
– *Die Verstockung Israels*, Munich 1961.
Goppelt, L., "Apokalyptik und Typologie bei Paulus" in *Th.L.Z.* 89 (1964) 321–44.
Gray, J., "The Kingship of God in the Prophets and Psalms" in *V.T.* 11 (1961) 1–29.
Hahn, F., *Christologische Hoheitstitel. Ihre Geschichte im frühen Christentum*, Göttingen 1963.
Hempel, J., "Königtum Gottes im Alten Testament" in *R.G.G.*³ III, 1706–9.
Hoffmann, P., "Reich Gottes" in *Handbuch theologischer Grundbegriffe* II, Munich 1963, 414–28.
Hopkins, M., *God's Kingdom in the Old Testament*, Winona/Minn. 1963.
Jüngel, E., *Jesus und Paulus*, Tübingen ²1964.
Kahlefeld, H., *Gleichnisse und Lehrstücke im Evangelium* I, Frankfurt a. M., ²1964; II, 1963.
Käsemann, E., "Die Anfänge christlicher Theologie" in *Z.Th.K.* 57 (1960) 62–85.
– "Zum Thema der urchristlichen Apokalyptik", *ibid.* 59 (1962) 257–84.
Kraus, H. J., *Psalmen* I, Neukirchen 1960, 197–205; II, 1960.
– *Gottesdienst in Israel*, Munich ²1962.
Kümmel, W. G., "Futurische und präsentische Eschatologie im ältesten Christentum" in *N.T.St.* 5 (1958/59) 113–26.
– "Die Naherwartung in der Verkündigung Jesu" in *Zeit und Geschichte*, Tübingen 1964, 31–46.
Ladd, G. E., "The Kingdom of God – Reign or Realm?" in *J.B.L.* 81 (1962) 230–8
– *Jesus and the Kingdom*, New York 1964.
"Le Christ Roi" in *Lumière et Vie* 57 (1962): various contributions.
Levie, J., "Le message de Jésus dans la pensée des apôtres" in *N.R.Th.* 93 (1961) 25–49.
Linnemann, E., *Gleichnisse Jesu*, Göttingen 1961.
Lundström, G., *The Kingdom of God in the Teaching of Jesus*, Edinburgh [1963.
Neuhäusler, E., *Anspruch und Antwort Gottes. Zur Lehre von den Weisungen innerhalb der synoptischen Jesusverkündigung*, Düsseldorf 1962.

Perrin, N., *The Kingdom of God in the Teaching of Jesus*, London 1963.
Ridderbos, H., *The Coming of the Kingdom*, Philadelphia 1962.
Rigaux, B., "La seconde venue de Jésus" in *La venue du Messie*, Rech. Bibl. VI (1962) 173–216.
Robinson, J. M., *New Quest of the Historical Jesus*, London 1959.
Rüstow, A., "᾿Εντὸς ὑμῶν ἐστιν" in *Z.N. W.* 51 (1960) 197–224.
Schäfer, R., "Das Reich Gottes bei A. Ritschl und Johannes Weiss" in *Z.Th.K.* 61 (1964) 68–88.
Schmid, H., "Jahwe und die Kulttradition von Jerusalem" in *Z.A. W.* 67 (1955) 168–97. [80 (1961).
Schmidt, W., *Königtum Gottes in Ugarit und Israel*, *Z.A. W.* supplement
Schnackenburg, R., *The Church in the New Testament*, Freiburg i. Br., London, New York, Montreal 1965.
– "Kirche und Parusie" in *Gott in Welt* I, Freiburg i. Br. 1964, 551–78.
Schreiner, J., *Sion-Jerusalem, Jahwes Königssitz*, Munich 1963.
Schubert, K., "Die Entwicklung der eschatologischen Naherwartung im Frühjudentum" in *Vom Messias zum Christentum*, Vienna 1964, 1–54.
Schürmann, H., "Zur Traditions- und Redaktionsgeschichte von Mt 10, 23" in *B.Z.* NF 3 (1959) 82–88.
– "Eschatologie und Liebesdienst in der Verkündigung Jesu" in *Kaufet die Zeit aus*, Paderborn 1959, 39–71.
– "Das hermeneutische Hauptproblem der Verkündigung Jesu" in *Gott in Welt* I Freiburg i. Br. 1964, 579–607.
Sint, J. A., "Parusie-Erwartung und Parusie-Verzögerung im paulinischen Briefcorpus" in *Z.K.Th.* 86 (1964) 47–79.
Smith, C. W. F., "The Mixed Status of the Church im Matthew's Gospel" in *J.B.L.* 82 (1963) 149–86.
Staelin, E., *Die Verkündigung des Reiches Gottes in der Kirche Jesu Christi*, 5 vols., Basle 1951–59.
Stauffer, E., *Die Botschaft Jesu damals und heute*, Bern, Munich 1959.
Stelzenberger, J., "Reich Gottes bei den deutschen Moraltheologen 1800–1850" in *Moraltheologie und Bible* (1964) 70–98.
Strecker, G., *Der Weg der Gerechtigkeit. Untersuchungen zur Theologie des Matthäus*, Göttingen 1962.
Strobel, A., *Untersuchungen zum eschatologischen Verzögerungsproblem*, Leiden 1961.
– *Die apokalyptische Sendung Jesu*, Rothenburg o. d. Tauber 1962.

Tödt, H. E., *Der Menschensohn in der synoptischen Überlieferung*, Gütersloh 1959.

Trilling, W., "Zur Überlieferungsgeschichte des Gleichnisses vom Hochzeitsmahl Mt 22, 1–14" in *B.Z.* NF 4 (1960) 251–65.

– *Das wahre Israel. Studien zu Theologie des Matthäus-Evangeliums*, Munich 1964.

Van der Walt, T., *Die Koninkrijk van God-Nabijl*, Kampen 1962.

Vielhauer, P., "Jesus und der Menschensohn" in *Z.Th.K.* 60 (1963) 133–77.

Vögtle, A., "Das christologische und ekklesiologische Anliegen von Mt 28, 18–20" in *Studia Evangelica* II, Berlin 1964, 266–94.

– "Exegetische Erwägungen über das Wissen und Selbstbewußtsein Jesu" in *Gott in Welt* I, Freiburg i. Br. 1964, 608–67.

Walther, C., *Typen des Reich-Gottes-Verständnisses. Studien zur Eschatologie und Ethik im 19. Jahrhundert*, Munich 1961.

Wolf, E., ed., *Unter der Herrschaft Christi*, Beiträge zur Evangelischen Theologie 32, Munich 1962.

TEXTUAL INDEX

Old Testament

New Testament

16: 1–8 143, 198

EARLY CHRISTIAN WRITINGS:

SUBJECT INDEX